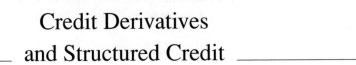

# Credit Derivatives
# and Structured Credit

For other titles in the Wiley Finance Series
please see www.wiley.com/finance

# Credit Derivatives
# and Structured Credit

## A Guide for Investors

### Richard Bruyère
with
### Rama Cont, Régis Copinot, Loïc Fery,
### Christophe Jaeck and Thomas Spitz

*Translated by Gabrielle Smart*

John Wiley & Sons, Ltd

Copyright © 2006      John Wiley & Sons Ltd, The Atrium, Southern Gate, Chichester,
West Sussex PO19 8SQ, England

Telephone    (+44) 1243 779777

Email (for orders and customer service enquiries): cs-books@wiley.co.uk
Visit our Home Page on www.wiley.com

*Other Wiley Editorial Offices*

John Wiley & Sons Inc., 111 River Street, Hoboken, NJ 07030, USA

Jossey-Bass, 989 Market Street, San Francisco, CA 94103-1741, USA

Wiley-VCH Verlag GmbH, Boschstr. 12, D-69469 Weinheim, Germany

John Wiley & Sons Australia Ltd, 42 McDougall Street, Milton, Queensland 4064, Australia

John Wiley & Sons (Asia) Pte Ltd, 2 Clementi Loop #02-01, Jin Xing Distripark, Singapore 129809

John Wiley & Sons Canada Ltd, 22 Worcester Road, Etobicoke, Ontario, Canada M9W 1L1

Wiley also publishes its books in a variety of electronic formats. Some content that appears
in print may not be available in electronic books.

*Library of Congress Cataloging-in-Publication Data*

Bruyère, Richard.
    Credit derivatives / Richard Bruyère with Rama Cont ... et al.
        p.   cm.
    Includes bibliographical references.
    ISBN 13 978-0-470-01879-8
    ISBN 10 0-470-01879-8
    1. Credit derivatives.   I. Cont, Rama.   II. Title.
HG6024.A3B778 2006
332.63'2—dc22

                                        2005026944

*British Library Cataloging in Publication Data*

A catalogue record for this book is available from the British Library

ISBN 13 978-0-470-01879-8 (HB)
ISBN 10 0-470-01879-8 (HB)

Typeset in 10/12pt Times by TechBooks, New Delhi, India
Printed and bound in Great Britain by Antony Rowe Ltd, Chippenham, Wiltshire
This book is printed on acid-free paper responsibly manufactured from sustainable forestry
in which at least two trees are planted for each one used for paper production.

# Contents

**Foreword**                                                                                      ix

**Introduction**                                                                                   xi

**1  Credit Risk and the Emergence of Credit Derivatives**                                          1
  1.1  Credit Risk                                                              1
      1.1.1  Definition and Typology of Credit Risk          3
      1.1.2  Characteristics of Credit Risk                  4
      1.1.3  The Importance of Credit Risk in Capital Markets 8
  1.2  Assessment and Measurements of Credit Risk                                11
      1.2.1  Bank Capital Adequacy Standards (Basel I)        11
      1.2.2  Credit Risk Analyzed by Rating Agencies          14
      1.2.3  Credit Risk Measured in the Financial Markets: Credit Spread   20
  1.3  Traditional Methods of Credit Risk Management and the Emergence of
      Credit Derivatives                                             24
      1.3.1  Traditional Methods for Managing Credit Risk (Issuer Risk)   25
      1.3.2  Counterparty Risk Management in Derivatives Markets   27
      1.3.3  Emergence and Advantages of Credit Derivatives   29

**2  Typology of Credit Derivatives and their Main Applications**                                   35
  2.1  Credit Default Swaps                                                      35
      2.1.1  Description of Credit Default Swaps               36
      2.1.2  Comparison Between the CDS Market and the Cash Market: Basis   45
      2.1.3  Main Variations on CDSs                          49
  2.2  Other Credit Derivatives                                                  55
      2.2.1  Credit Spread Derivatives                        55
      2.2.2  Synthetic Replication Products                   61
  2.3  Main applications of Credit Derivatives                                    66
      2.3.1  Applications for Institutional Investors and Other Capital
            Market players                             66
      2.3.2  Credit Derivative Applications in Bank Management   70
      2.3.3  Credit Derivative Applications for Corporates      74

**3   Second-Generation Credit Derivatives**                                         **81**
   3.1   Basket Credit Default Swaps                                                  81
         3.1.1   First-to-Default Credit Swaps                                        82
         3.1.2   Concrete Example                                                     87
         3.1.3   Extension of the First-to-Default Principle: $i$ to $j$-to-Default
                 Products                                                             89
   3.2   Hybrid Products                                                             90
         3.2.1   Capital-Guaranteed/Protected Products                               90
         3.2.2   Other Hybrid Products                                               92
         3.2.3   Concrete Example of a Transaction                                    93
   3.3   Credit Indices                                                              94
         3.3.1   Introduction to Credit Indices                                      94
         3.3.2   Credit Index Mechanism, Pricing and Construction                     96
         3.3.3   iTraxx Indices: a True Innovation to Benefit Investors              101

**4   Collateralized Debt Obligations**                                             **105**
   4.1   Cash-Flow CDOs (Arbitrage CBOs and CLOs)                                    107
         4.1.1   Origin of Arbitrage CBOs/CLOs                                        107
         4.1.2   Description of a CDO Structure                                       109
         4.1.3   Overview of the CBO/CLO Market and Recent Developments              113
   4.2   Balance Sheet-Driven CDOs                                                   114
         4.2.1   Securitization of Bank Loans                                         114
         4.2.2   The Impact of Credit Derivatives: Synthetic CLOs                     115
         4.2.3   Balance Sheet-Driven CDOs and Regulatory Arbitrage                   119
   4.3   Arbitrage-Driven Synthetic CDOs                                             124
         4.3.1   The First Arbitrage-Driven Synthetic CDOs                            124
         4.3.2   Actively Managed Arbitrage-Driven Synthetic CDOs                     128
         4.3.3   On-Demand CDOs (Correlation Products)                                133

**5   The Credit Derivatives and Structured Credit Products Market**                **149**
   5.1   Overview of the Market                                                      150
         5.1.1   Main Stages in the Development of the Credit Derivatives Market      151
         5.1.2   Size, Growth and Structure of the Credit Derivatives Market          152
         5.1.3   Size, Growth and Structure of the CDO Market                         159
   5.2   Main Players                                                                160
         5.2.1   Banks                                                                161
         5.2.2   Insurance, Reinsurance Companies and Financial Guarantors            163
         5.2.3   Hedge Funds and Traditional Asset Managers                           165
         5.2.4   Corporates                                                           167
   5.3   At the Heart of the Market: The Investment Banks                            168
         5.3.1   Position of the Investment Banks in the Credit Derivatives Market    168
         5.3.2   Position of the Investment Banks in the CDO Market                   170
         5.3.3   Functions and Organization of Investment Banks                       172

**6   Pricing Models for Credit Derivatives**                                       **175**
   6.1   Structural Models                                                           176
         6.1.1   The Black–Scholes Option Pricing Model                               176

6.1.2    Merton's Structural Model of Default Risk (1976)                    178
6.1.3    Limitations and Extensions of the Merton Model (1976)             180
6.1.4    Pricing and Hedging Credit Derivatives in Structural Models      183
6.2    Reduced-Form Models                                                     184
6.2.1    Hazard Rate and Credit Spreads                                     184
6.2.2    Pricing and Hedging of Credit Derivatives in Reduced-Form Models  187
6.2.3    Accounting for the Volatility of Credit Spreads                    188
6.2.4    Accounting for Interest Rate Risk                                  189
6.3    Pricing Models for Multi-Name Credit Derivatives                       189
6.3.1    Correlation, Dependence and Copulas                               190
6.3.2    The Gaussian Copula Model                                          191
6.3.3    Multi-Asset Structural Models                                      195
6.3.4    Dependent Defaults in Reduced-Form Models                         195
6.4    Discussion                                                             196
6.4.1    Comparing Structural and Reduced-Form Modeling Approaches        196
6.4.2    Complex Models, Sparse Data Sets                                   197
6.4.3    Stand-alone Pricing Versus Marginal Pricing                       198

7    **The Impact of the Development in Credit Derivatives**                  **199**
7.1    The Impact of the Growth in Credit Derivatives on Banking Institutions  200
7.1.1    Far-Reaching Changes in the Capital Markets                        200
7.1.2    An Economic Approach to Credit Risk Management                     204
7.1.3    Overview of the Banks of the Twenty-First Century: the Effect of
         Credit Derivatives on Banks' Strategy, Organization and Culture    217
7.2    Credit Derivatives and Financial Regulations                          223
7.2.1    Credit Derivatives and the New Basel II Regulations                223
7.2.2    Credit Derivatives and the Instability of the Financial System     234
7.2.3    A More Rounded Picture                                             237
7.3    Credit Derivatives: A Financial Revolution?                           241
7.3.1    Introduction to Particle Finance Theory                           242
7.3.2    Implications of 'Particle Finance Theory' for the Capital Markets 243
7.3.3    An Innovation that Heralds Others                                 247

**Conclusion**                                                                **251**

**References**                                                                **255**

**Further Reading**                                                           **259**

**Index**                                                                     **263**

# Foreword

As Chief Executive Officer of SG Corporate & Investment banking, I have had the pleasure of meeting some of the authors of this book. These people were all on the team that launched the credit derivatives business line at SG at the start of their careers (Richard Bruyère, Loïc Fery and Thomas Spitz) and some are still managing this activity at the bank (Régis Copinot and Christophe Jaeck). Having collaborated with them on a number of occasions, I have been able to appreciate fully their skills as marketers, financial engineers or traders, as well as their commitment to credit derivatives and structured credit products.

More than ten years after its creation, the credit derivatives market is no longer in its infancy. Indisputably, this market has allowed a better distribution of credit risk between players in the capital markets: banks, insurance companies, institutional investors and even hedge funds. Thus, I believe that credit derivatives contribute to a reduction in systemic risk for the financial markets and banking systems, because with CDOs, CDS and TRS, credit risk is spread over a greater number of market players. These instruments also increase market liquidity, are conducive to more active risk management, and help optimize the allocation of capital on the scale of the global economy.

The authors mention among others a remarkable feature: the huge number of defaults between 2001 and 2003 did not lead to defaults in the financial sector, contrary to what occurred in the previous phase in the early 1990s. Although this cannot be explained solely by the existence and increasing use of credit derivatives, I believe they have helped to improve the long-term stability of the financial system by strengthening banking institutions' risk profile, previously traditionally the weak link.

Although some may have expressed concern about the dangers of credit derivatives for the banking system, to my knowledge, these instruments do not pose a greater threat than equity derivatives or interest rate derivatives, for which Société Générale was one of the pioneers some 20 years ago. As is the case for other derivatives, these instruments may not always have been used properly, whether because of misguided or involuntary overstepping of limits, thereby entailing losses for institutions unfamiliar with derivatives, with inadequate risk management processes, or poor knowledge of these products. However, this operational risk falls steeply in mature markets as the number of specialist players (front and back-office, risk control management, senior management, corporate lawyers, financial services authorities, rating agencies, etc.) increases. Moreover, the trend is further strengthened as market participants rely on increasingly technical know-how, a better understanding of mathematical and financial models and a wider range of adequate tools (legal standards, market rules, capital adequacy regulations, etc.).

Readers will also find detailed information regarding developments in the credit derivatives market, notably with the new Basel 2 capital adequacy standards. In this new environment, banks may be less inclined to carry out investment-grade credit securitization transactions on their balance sheets, as was the case in past years, but instead be encouraged to dispose of lesser quality assets (leveraged loans, SME loans, etc.). The book addresses these issues with examples that are both very precise and similar to the transactions carried out daily by our specialized teams – some being actual descriptions of in-house cases.

We have little doubt that students, academics, capital market observers and participants, risk managers and senior managers of financial institutions will view this book as a standard reference work that will help them to update their technical knowledge and practices, understand the structure of some CDOs or reflect on the use of credit derivatives by financial institutions within a new European accounting and regulatory framework.

At Société Générale we are greatly honored to contribute to the circulation of such cutting-edge financial culture to the greatest possible number of people. We hope you enjoy the book!

**Jean-Pierre Mustier**
Chief Executive Officer
SG Corporate and Investment Banking
Société Générale Group

# Introduction

The past three decades in the capital markets have been characterized by the explosive growth of derivatives (futures, options, swaps, etc.). These are financial instruments the value of which depends on the fluctuations of an underlying asset, be it a corporate stock, an interest rate, a currency rate, an economic or financial index, or the price of another financial derivative.

Derivatives were designed to provide capital market players with efficient financial risk management tools (financial risk is traditionally measured by the price volatility of financial assets). The main advantage of derivatives is to enable the unbundling and individual management of the risks contained in a single financial asset. Let us take for example an American institutional investor looking to take a long position (i.e. buy) in a corporate bond issued in euros by a French company (say, France Telecom). This investor will bear at least three types of financial risk:

1. An interest rate risk depending on the bond coupon format, either fixed rate (i.e. paying a fixed percentage of par every year) or floating rate (variable coupon paying a spread over a market reference rate such as Euribor).
2. A currency risk as the performance of the investor will be measured in US dollars and the bond generates euro-denominated cash flows over time.
3. A credit risk related to the bond issuer, France Telecom, which, in the event of business problems or liquidity crisis, may not be in a position to pay the annual coupons or repay the principal on the bond at maturity.

Credit derivatives, a term that was coined for the first time at the 1992 International Swaps and Derivatives Association (ISDA) annual conference, are a new breed of financial instruments designed to manage credit risk. It is this focus on credit risk that differentiates them from other financial derivatives and makes them a groundbreaking innovation. In other words, a credit derivative may be defined as an over-the-counter[1] bilateral financial contract between two counterparties, the cash flows of which are linked to the credit risk of one or several underlying (or reference) entities.

Credit risk comprises the default risk of the reference obligor to the contract (i.e. the failure to pay under existing financial debt contracts, or bankruptcy) but also the risk that the obligor's creditworthiness may depreciate, such deterioration leading to an increase in the risk premium (credit spread) required by banks and investors in the capital markets and a corresponding drop

---

[1] As opposed to financial derivatives listed on an exchange.

in the market value of the obligor's outstanding debt instruments. In theory, credit derivatives could be structured on any asset incorporating credit risk.

The objective of *Credit Derivatives and Structured Credit* is to provide a detailed coverage of the credit derivatives market. It also attempts to relate the recent surging growth in these products to the fundamental, long-term changes in banks' business models and in the capital markets. This book is designed for students in business schools and financial courses, academics and professionals working in investment and asset management, banking, corporate treasury and the capital markets.

We have chosen to use a pedagogical approach, relying as often as possible on the authors' first-hand academic and professional experience in the field of credit derivatives to give practical examples. As a result, some areas of the book, such as those devoted to pricing models or structuring techniques, may seem superficial or incomplete to the experienced professional. We would suggest that they refer to the textbooks and articles listed in the References and Further Reading for additional information on these specific topics.

Chapter 1 deals with risk management in the financial markets and focuses on the imperative of credit risk management, particularly crucial in the banking world. A detailed definition of credit risk is provided, together with a review of the various methods for assessing and measuring this risk. We also discuss the traditional methods for managing credit risk and the emergence of credit derivatives to remedy their shortcomings.

A detailed typology of these new instruments is provided in Chapter 2. We focus on first-generation single name instruments (including credit default swaps and variations, credit spread options and total return swaps) and explain their mechanism through real examples of transactions. This second chapter is concluded by an overview of the main applications of credit derivatives for capital market players (institutional investors, hedge funds and asset managers, banks' trading desks, etc.), bank credit portfolio managers and corporates.

Following this detailed presentation of first-generation credit derivatives, Chapters 3 and 4 focus on the latest developments and structured variations of these products. Chapter 3 presents second-generation instruments (basket default swaps, hybrid structures, index products) created using the building blocks of the market described in Chapter 2. Chapter 4 reviews the rise of credit risk transfer products combining securitization techniques and credit derivative technology. So-called collateralized debt obligations (CDOs) are used to arbitrage credit markets or to optimize banks' balance sheet and capital management. These instruments saw the highest growth in the credit derivatives market and have been the key to its developments. In addition, CDOs enabled the implementation of 'regulatory capital arbitrage' strategies, which then caused the regulatory authorities to define new capital adequacy standards for banks (Basel II Capital Accord).

Chapter 5 provides an overview of the market for credit derivatives and structured credit products. We make a quantitative analysis of the various market segments, and also look at the major trends in the market and the players involved. Furthermore, we examine the specific role of investment banks, which through their market-making and trading activities, and structuring and financial engineering skills, act as a catalyst for the development of this market.

The thorny issue of modeling, pricing and risk managing credit derivatives is dealt with in Chapter 6. In this area, we have chosen a simple, 'plain English' and pedagogical approach without overwhelming the reader with too many financial mathematics and equations. Our aim is to present the main categories of models, the key assumptions and inputs required, and highlight their limitations.

The last chapter takes the reader through the many implications of the development of credit derivatives. These products are instrumental in the ongoing transformation of the banking business, from strategic, organizational and cultural standpoints. In addition, they have been one of the key drivers behind the changes in the capital adequacy rules for banks and the forthcoming implementation of the Basel II Accord. We try to restore balance in the heated debate about the contribution of credit derivatives, decried by some as 'financial weapons of mass destruction', to the instability of the global financial system.

Finally, we examine the emergence of these new instruments in the framework of the overall evolution of the capital markets and the rise of risk management as a discipline.

# 1
# Credit Risk and the Emergence
# of Credit Derivatives

Walter Wriston, the former Chief Executive Officer of the American bank Citibank, held that 'bankers are in the business of managing risk, pure and simple, that is the business of banking.'[1] Banks are distinct from other enterprises in that they seek risk,[2] which is the source of their profits and the basis of their business. However, these risks, deliberately taken, must be managed. In this respect, the 1990s emerged as a key period in financial practice, characterized by:

- Deregulation and growing internationalization of banking and financial activities.
- Considerable advances in information and communication technologies.
- Important conceptual advances resulting in better risk modeling (e.g. the *value-at-risk* concept for market risks).
- The phenomenal growth in derivatives (on organized and over-the-counter markets), now clearly the preferred instruments for managing financial risk.
- The widespread wish to optimize capital management,[3] the very essence of economic warfare, especially in the banking industry.

In this context, an examination of why credit derivatives have emerged is tantamount to considering credit risk as the main risk run by banking institutions. Indeed, it was the ever-more urgent necessity to manage credit risk that led to the development of the first credit derivatives, not least insofar as the traditional methods for managing credit risk were found to be unsatisfactory and sometimes ineffective.

In this first chapter we will give a definition of credit risk. Then we shall describe the particular context in which this risk is apprehended (including capital adequacy regulations applying to banking institutions, and the methods for analyzing and measuring this risk). Finally, we shall explain the context in which credit derivatives have been created, their nature, and their purpose. They provide financial market players with a new, relatively simple and direct, means of managing credit risk.

## 1.1 CREDIT RISK

In September 2003, the annual survey of the Center for the Study of Financial Innovation (CSFI), 'Banana Skins 2003, a CSFI Survey of the Risks Facing Banks,' baldly stated that 'credit derivatives top poll of risks facing banks.' Complex products and credit risk were cited as the main risks for the banking community in 2003, by the 231 financial professionals

---

[1] Quoted in Freeman (1993).
[2] In financial matters, risk may be defined overall as result volatility. In statistical terms, this is expressed by the standard deviation of these results around their mean.
[3] See Chapter 7.

2     Credit Derivatives and Structured Credit

**Table 1.1**    CSFI poll results (1996–2005)

| 1996 | 1998 | 2000 | 2002 | 2003 |
|---|---|---|---|---|
| 1. Poor management | 1. Poor risk management | 1. Equity market crash | 1. Credit risk | 1. Complex financial instruments |
| 2. Bad lending | 2. Y2K | 2. E-commerce | 2. Macro economy | 2. Credit risk |
| 3. Derivatives | 3. Poor strategy | 3. Asset quality | 3. Equity markets | 3. Macro economy |
| 4. Rogue trader | 4. EMU turbulence | 4. Grasp of new technology | 4. Complex financial instruments | 4. Insurance |
| 5. Excessive competition | 5. Regulation | 5. High dependence on technology | 5. Business continuation | 5. Business continuation |

[a] Shading refers to those risks that are directly related to credit risk or credit derivatives/structured credit products (e.g. bad lending, asset quality, complex instruments, etc.).
*Source:* Reproduced by permission of CSFI.

surveyed by the think-tank.[4] It was the first time that complex financial instruments were quoted as the number one risk in the annual ranking since its creation in 1995. It should also be noted that credit risk in the wider sense (in its various forms) was consistently quoted in this survey as among the major risks between 1996 and 2003, as evinced by Table 1.1.

Naturally, this result should be seen in the light of the overall deterioration of the economic climate over 2000–2002. Oliver Wyman and Company, the consultancy, thus noted that the amount of outstanding debt in default had reached $130 bn worldwide in 2002, as against $110 bn in 2001 and $60 bn in 2000. This 2002 figure tops the historic 1992 record, an estimated $113 bn credit losses for the banking system worldwide.[5]

Furthermore, the many bankruptcies and scandals linked to dangerous loan policies underline the fact that credit risk is the greatest one run by banking institutions. In the last 20 years alone, for example, there have been the debt crises in developing countries in the early 1980s; then the débâcle of the savings and loans banks in the United States between 1984 and 1991,[6] too deeply mired in the junk bond market designed to finance highly leveraged hostile takeovers; or again, the banking crises in the United Kingdom, Norway, Sweden and France, among others, from 1990–1995.

Banks also have to face other types of risk: market risks, of course (volatility in financial asset prices, linked to interest and exchange rate movements, and share and commodity prices), liquidity risks (market demand and supply for this or that instrument), funding risks (capacity to meet financing needs), operating risks (inadequate control systems), legal risks (validity of derivatives contracts in particular), etc. Because of their role in the economic system (selecting borrowers, centralizing information, monitoring risk) and their balance sheet structure (asset/liability management and portfolio diversification strategies are not enough to eliminate risk), it is truly credit risk that must be seen as the most important one for banks.

In this section we shall endeavor to define credit risk, show its characteristics, and measure its effect on capital markets.

---

[4] The panel includes professionals from banks, regulatory authorities, bank clients (institutional investors), and observers and analysts of the capital markets.
[5] See Chassany (2002).
[6] The losses in the wake of this crisis were calculated as 4% of US GDP (Goldstein and Turner, 1996).

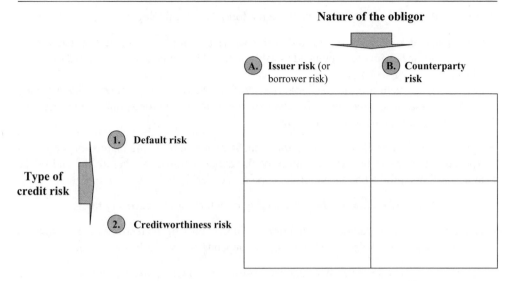

**Figure 1.1**   Typology of credit risk

### 1.1.1   Definition and Typology of Credit Risk

Credit risk may be defined overall as the risk of loss arising from nonpayment of installments due by a debtor to a creditor under a contract. The model in Figure 1.1 offers a typology of credit risk.

Two main types of credit risk may be distinguished:

1. Default risk, which corresponds to the debtor's incapacity or refusal to meet his contractual financial undertakings towards his creditor, whether by payment of the interest or the principal of the loan contracted. Moody's Investors Service gives the following definition of default: 'Any failure or delay in paying the principal and/or the interest.'[7] In this case, creditors are likely to suffer a loss if they cannot recover the total amount due to them under the contract.[8]
2. Creditworthiness risk, which is defined as the risk that the perceived creditworthiness of the borrower or the counterparty might deteriorate, without default being a certainty. In practice, deteriorated creditworthiness in financial markets leads to an increase in the risk premium, also called credit spread[9] of the borrower. Moreover, where this borrower has a credit rating from a rating agency, it might be downgraded.[10] The risks of creditworthiness deterioration and default may be correlated insofar as creditworthiness deterioration may be the precursor of default.[11]

---

[7] De Bodard *et al.* (1994).

[8] Be it a 'financial' (bond, credit line, etc.) or a commercial debt.

[9] Credit spread corresponds to the gap between the yield demanded of a risky borrower by the market, and the risk-free rate. The latter may be defined as the yield from sovereign debt issued by governments (the United States, Germany, the United Kingdom, France, etc.) in their own currency. Credit spread is intended to reflect the borrower's credit risk as perceived by the market, and the value of the market's debt instruments is in reverse relation to the changes in this credit spread. For more on credit spread see Section 1.2.3.

[10] See Section 1.2.2 for rating agencies.

[11] Except in the case of a sudden default such as that of Baring Brothers.

As regards the 'type' of debtor, we shall use the following terminology:

(a) We shall speak of issuer (or borrower) risk where the credit risk (default or deteriorated creditworthiness) involves a funded ('cash') financial instrument such as a bond or a bank loan.
(b) However, we shall use the terminology specific to the derivatives markets (counterparty risk) for cases where the credit risk concerns the counterparty for an unfunded instrument such as a swap, an option or a guarantee.

Simply put, credit risk is assessed by the amount of the debt or the claims on the debtor ('exposure') multiplied by the probability of the debtor defaulting[12] before the end of the contract, with the product adjusted for the hope of recovering from assets after default:

$$\text{Credit risk} = \text{exposure} \times \text{probability of default} \times (1 - \text{recovery rate})$$

One last component of credit risk is therefore the uncertainty of the recovery rate possible on the claim after default. This second-ranking risk depends on several factors, not least:

- For borrower risk, the seniority of the debt instrument on which the creditor is exposed (in other words, its priority ranking in cash flows where the borrower is put into liquidation).
- The existence of collateral to guarantee the creditor's position.
- The nature of the debtor (recovery rates varying depending on the debtor's size, country of origin, sector of activity, etc.).

We shall return to the notion of recovery rates in Section 1.2.2.

### 1.1.2   Characteristics of Credit Risk

Credit risk has three main characteristics:

1. It is a 'systemic' risk, in other words, it is influenced by the general economic climate and is therefore highly cyclical.
2. It is a 'specific' risk, in that it changes depending on specific events affecting the borrowers (credit risk is then said to have an 'idiosyncratic' component).
3. Contrary to other market risks, it has an asymmetric profitability structure.

### *1.1.2.1   A Systemic Risk*

Credit risk is strongly dependent on economic cycles: it tends to increase during depression and decrease during expansion. The cyclical nature of credit risk is illustrated by Figures 1.2 and 1.3, which show the business default rate in the world between 1987 and 2002, and in the United States since 1980.

It should be noted that in the years 2001–2002, the number of bankruptcies soared due to the sharp downturn in the economy, and that the amounts of defaults increased. Thus Moody's Investors Service noted that within the ranks of the rated issuers it handles, the amount of

---

[12] Case (2) of materialized risk due to creditworthiness deterioration is expressed theoretically by a higher probability of borrower or counterparty default.

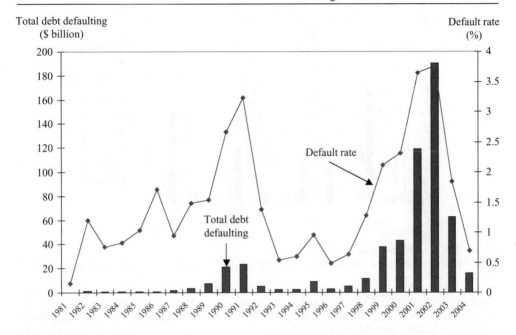

**Figure 1.2**   Bankruptcies in the world
*Note:* Borrowers rated by Standard & Poor's.
*Sources: The Economist*, Standard & Poor's, Commission Bancaire, authors' analysis.

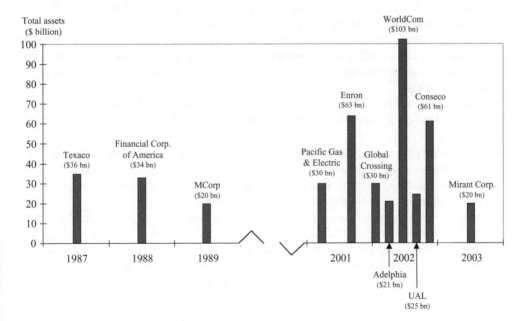

**Figure 1.3**   Largest bankruptcies in the USA (total asset value in excess of $20 bn)
*Source:* BankruptcyData.com. Reproduced by permission of New Generation Research, Inc.

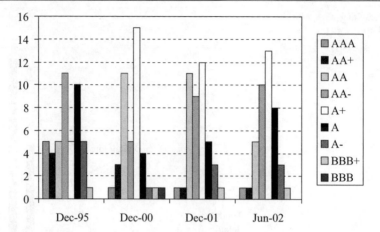

**Figure 1.4**   Top 50 European banks – rating trends
*Note*: Excluding German Landesbanken. AAA-rated banks have the best credit standing (see Section 1.2.2).
*Source:* Standard & Poor's. Graph titled "Top 50 European Banks – Rating Trends (excl. Landesbanks)" published in Bondholders Versus Shareholders – The Pressure of Managing Conflicted Expectations and the Implications for Ratings, Walter Pompliano, 2002, reproduced with permission of Standard & Poor's, a division of the McGraw-Hill companies, Inc.

defaults for the year 2002 (€43 bn) was greater than the total amount of defaults between 1985 and 2001 (€22 bn).[13] Furthermore, eight of the greatest bankruptcies in United States history took place between 2001 and 2003, as indicated by Figure 1.3.

This figure also illustrates the systemic nature of credit risk: four of the seven greatest bankruptcies of 2001–2002 were of companies in the telecommunications sector. This is not only dependent on overall macro-economic conditions, but also on the state of health in the telecom sector itself.

Naturally, this cyclical aspect has a direct impact on the health of banking institutions, as Figure 1.4 shows. It also has considerable impact on:

- The funding of the economy and growth, which shows pro-cyclical tendencies. In other words, banks are ready to fund the economy when everything is running smoothly, but they withdraw from the market when the first signs of cyclical downturn appear, and this behavior contributes to the creation of a 'credit crunch' (see Figure 1.5).[14]
- Financial instability, which appears to be inherent to a globalized, liberalized financial system which is itself characterized, among other things, by the absence of adjustment via prices. Too great an offer of credit does not lead to lowering prices or profits, but on the contrary, contributes to them increasing (credit growth sustains activity and increases the price of assets, thus favoring the perceived soundness of borrowers, and so on).[15]

---

[13] See *L'Agefi* (2003).
[14] Further analysis available in the 2002 annual report of the BIS and Chavagneux (2002).
[15] See the 2001 annual report of the BIS and Wolf (2001).

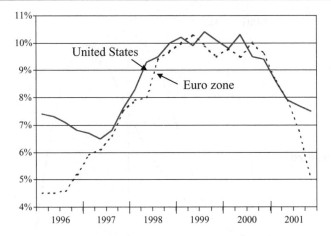

**Figure 1.5**  Credit cycles: annual variations of internal credit to the private sector (%)
*Source*: Bank of International Settlements.

### 1.1.2.2   A Specific Risk

The second characteristic of credit risk is its specific nature, that is to say, the fact that the credit risk linked to a borrower or counterparty is directly influenced by its characteristics: size,[16] corporate strategy, events affecting it, changes in its direct economic environment, etc. One example of this is the resounding bankruptcy of the Asian merchant bank Peregrine Securities in November 1997, which typifies the materialization of a 'specific' credit risk. It was obliged to close down after the Indonesian company Steady Safe had defaulted on a US$235 m bridge loan. It amounted to a quarter of the bank's capital![17]

### 1.1.2.3   A Risk with Asymmetrical Profitability Profile

One last characteristic of credit risk is its peculiar profitability structure. It is different from other market risks (share prices, interest rates, etc.) in that it is closely linked to the individual performance and capital structure of the borrower.

When the pattern of their associated profitability rates is examined, it becomes clear that market and credit risks differ:

• The structure of profitability linked to market risk is symmetrical and may, in statistical terms, be close to normal 'bell curve' patterns.
• On the contrary, profitability linked to credit risk is asymmetrical and shows a 'fat tail' structure.

The differences between profitability structures linked to market or credit risks are shown in Figure 1.6.

---

[16] In France, the chances of a company surviving are closely linked to its size. While the average liquidation rate is 88.8% for bankrupt companies overall, it is only 38.8% for companies with a turnover of more than €7.62 m. (*Source:* Deloitte & Touche Corporate Finance; see Fouquet, 2001.)

[17] Guyot (1998). Peregrine offered Thai and Indonesian companies high-yield bond issues in dollars, which it then placed with Korean and Japanese investors. Peregrine guaranteed its clients' issues and advanced the corresponding cash in the form of bridge loans. When the Indonesian rupee lost almost 75% of its value against the dollar between September and December 1997, PT Steady Safe was never able to pay back the bridge loans.

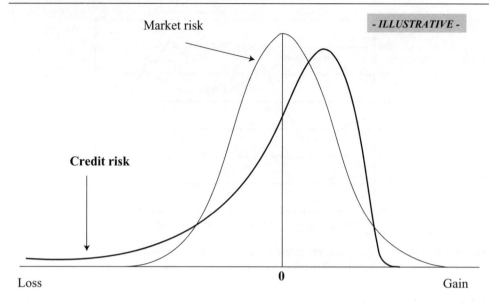

**Figure 1.6**    Profitability structure of credit and market risks

The profitability curve for credit risk can be interpreted thus: the creditor has a strong probability of making a relatively modest profit on the interest of the debt, and a small chance of losing a large part of the initial outlay (when the credit risk materializes). This observation has far-reaching implications for credit risk modeling techniques and for models of credit derivative pricing.[18]

### 1.1.3   The Importance of Credit Risk in Capital Markets

Credit risk is most certainly the largest class of risk in the world, if we keep the definition of credit markets as being those for bonds and banking debt, counterparty risk exposures arising from derivatives transactions, and credit risk arising from commercial activity. All commercial transactions incorporate a credit element, unless they are 100% paid for in cash immediately.

Leaving aside the special category of trade receivables and examining only financial instruments, it is possible to link the various derivatives to the underlying class of instrument. Thus, the spectrum of financial risk in Figure 1.7 shows that exposure to credit risk can come in different shapes, depending on the underlying asset.

Derivatives were traditionally developed at the two ends of the spectrum, in other words, in the equity and interest rate markets (based on domestic government debt issues) via organized markets such as Euronext, Liffe, Deutsche Börse–Eurex, Chicago Mercantile Exchange, Chicago Board of Trade, etc. As regards OTC derivatives, that is, those negotiated directly between operators not using an organized, regulated market, credit derivatives were the market segment with the strongest growth since 1999, although they represent under 2% of total outstanding contracts in notional amount according to BIS statistics.

---

[18] See Chapter 6.

| Financial risk | Financial instruments | Main risk | Derivatives |
|---|---|---|---|

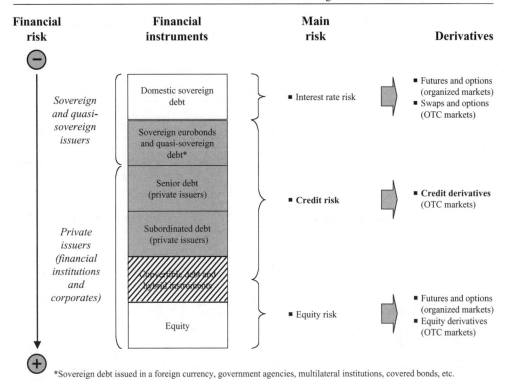

*Sovereign debt issued in a foreign currency, government agencies, multilateral institutions, covered bonds, etc.

**Figure 1.7**   The spectrum of financial risk and derivatives

Moreover, it should be noted that once they are linked to the vast range of underlying financial instruments, credit derivatives have a considerable scope of action. In recent years, the relative proportion of debt instruments for funding financial institutions and corporates has risen considerably in financial markets against that of shares. This is due more particularly to the excess offer of liquidity in credit markets, historically low interest rates, and lower equity volumes (see Figure 1.8).

The latter trend is due among others to a sharp fall in initial public offerings (IPOs), especially since the Internet bubble burst in 2000–2001, a relatively active takeover market (mergers and acquisitions) up to 2001, and vast share buyback plans set in train by companies to increase the return on their capital.

While the omnipresence of credit risk is a crucial issue for economic agents in the commercial and financing markets, it is also present in the derivatives markets. Traders in these markets are also exposed to credit risk, most often referred to as counterparty risk. We shall return to this in a special paragraph because it is measured and managed differently from that for the classic credit markets (cash) presented in the foregoing. It goes without saying that credit derivatives may also be used for management of counterparty risk in the derivatives markets.

Counterparty risk is practically non-existent on organized derivatives markets, as will be shown below;[19] however, it remains present in OTC markets. Here, credit risk assessment

---

[19] See Section 1.3.

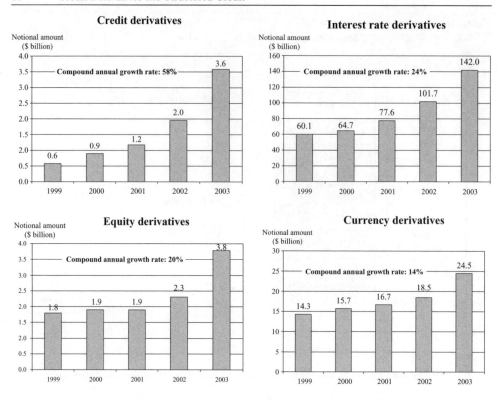

**Figure 1.8**   Size and growth of OTC derivatives markets (notional amounts)
*Sources:* Bank of International Settlements, BBA, authors' analysis.

follows a different logic from that applied in the classic credit markets, especially as regards measurement of exposure.

- On a classic financial instrument, credit risk exposure is equal to the creditor's obligation on the debtor (the amount used – outstanding – by the borrower on his credit line) to which accrued interest is added.
- On derivatives, exposure to credit risk depends on the mark-to-market. This is not equal to the notional amount of the transaction, but corresponds to the cost of replacing the contract in the market conditions prevailing at the time of the assessment.[20]

The example in Table 1.2 shows the off-balance-sheet market structure of JP Morgan Chase, one of the world's largest traders in the derivatives markets.

At end 2003, the replacement value of the contracts (that is, the counterparty risk the bank was exposed to) was only 0.25% of the total notional value of the contracts it had concluded, as against 0.32% at end 2002 and 0.33% at end 2001.

Credit risk is the main risk banking institutions are exposed to, both in their traditional loan activities and in their role as intermediaries in the financial markets. Let us see now the various

---

[20] Capital adequacy regulations of banking institutions determine the 'credit risk equivalent' on a derivatives position by adding to this mark-to-market value an amount corresponding to the notional of the contract multiplied by an add-on, which represents the potential risk of drift of the mark-to-market, depending on the evolution of the various market parameters.

**Table 1.2**   Derivatives exposure of JP Morgan Chase

| USD billion | Notional amounts | | | Counterparty risks | | |
|---|---|---|---|---|---|---|
| Class of risk | 2003 | 2002 | 2001 | 2003 | 2002 | 2001 |
| Interest rate | 31 252 | 23 591 | 19 085 | 60 | 55 | 41 |
| Foreign exchange | 1 582 | 1 505 | 1 636 | 10 | 7 | 10 |
| Equity | 328 | 307 | 284 | 9 | 13 | 12 |
| Credit | 578 | 366 | 262 | 3 | 6 | 3 |
| Commodities | 24 | 36 | 36 | 2 | 2 | 5 |
| Total | 33 764 | 25 805 | 21 303 | 84 | 83 | 71 |

*Source:* JP Morgan Chase annual reports (2003, 2002 and 2001).

approaches enabling this risk to be assessed, and then what traditional instruments can be used to manage it.

## 1.2   ASSESSMENT AND MEASUREMENTS OF CREDIT RISK

There are three main ways to assess credit risk:

- The regulatory standards applying to banking institutions in this field.
- The analysis performed by rating agencies, the traditional function of which is to measure the credit risk associated with a bond issue.
- The assessment of credit risk in capital markets via the issuer's credit spread.

These approaches are presented below.

### 1.2.1   Bank Capital Adequacy Standards (Basel I)

Because credit risk and the role of banking institutions are so important for the financial system, strict rules have been drawn up by the international banking supervisory authorities.[21] The first regulations on bank credit activity were made by the Basel Committee [22] in 1988, under the aegis of the BIS, and then spread to other countries via the appropriate supervisory authorities.

#### 1.2.1.1   The Context

Banking activities have always been regulated. This is due to the particular role played by financial institutions in the economy. There are two main reasons for the need to control banking activities:

1. Systemic risk, that is, the risk that the failure of one bank might cause others to fail by contagion due to the close links between them, not least the settlement system, and thus threaten the stability of the entire financial system.

---

[21] Only the measures pertaining to credit risk regulation in commercial banks are presented here. For more detailed information on the various capital adequacy regulations, see, for example, Bessis (1995), especially chapter 3.

[22] The Basel Committee membership includes the central bank representatives from 13 countries: Belgium, Canada, France, Germany, Italy, Japan, Luxembourg, the Netherlands, Spain, Sweden and Switzerland, the United Kingdom, the United States.

2. Insurance of bank deposits by the public authorities, which therefore means they will closely scrutinize banking activities. Bank deposits are inherently volatile and runs on banks where customers suddenly doubt the safety of their deposit could jeopardize the financial system.

The logic on which the 1988 international regulations were based was that banks' capital should be adequate for the risks they run, not least credit risk. The supervisory authorities in each country wished to come to an agreement, under the aegis of the BIS, to avoid diverging national regulations and create a 'level playing field' for all banks. The first proposals for capital adequacy were made by the Bank of England and the main American regulators,[23] along the lines of the preliminary work of the Basel Committee.

### 1.2.1.2   The Basel I Regulations

On 15 July 1988, the Basel Committee published the International Convergence of Capital Measurement and Capital Standards. This agreement, called the 'Basel I' Accord, the principles of which were to be applied by all banks in the countries party to the agreement before 1 January 1993, concerns only credit risk. It had two goals:

1. Strengthen the soundness and stability of the international banking system by encouraging international banks to raise their capital amount.
2. Establish a uniform regulatory framework (applicable to all the banking institutions of the countries signing the agreement) for the purpose of reducing an existing source of competitive inequality among international banks, previously caused by heterogeneous national regulations.

The main measures provided by the agreement are as follows:

• Each asset held by a bank is classified in one of the four categories defined by the regulations. Each category carries a corresponding risk weight of 0%, 20%, 50% or 100%,[24] which is applied to the amount of assets held in the category in order to determine the amount of the bank's risk-weighted assets (RWA).
• Bank capital is divided into core capital (basic equity) or tier 1, and supplementary capital or tier 2. The core capital is mainly capital in the accounting sense (shareholders' paid-up capital and common stock, disclosed reserves), while the supplementary capital mainly consists of hybrid debt capital and subordinated term debt. The target standard ratio of capital to risk-weighted assets must be at least 8%, whilst core capital must be equal to at least 4% of the bank's risk-weighted assets.[25]
• The bank's off-balance-sheet activities are taken into account in these ratios by converting exposure into a 'credit risk equivalent' by using a 'credit conversion factor' (CCF).
• Finally, the regulations provide for restrictions in respect of large risks. These are defined as positions higher than 10% of bank capital, and declaration thereof to the supervisory

---

[23] The Federal Reserve (Fed), which supervises bank holdings, the Federal Deposit Insurance Corporation (FDIC), which regulates the other banks, and the Office of the Comptroller of the Currency (OCC), which is responsible for supervising US banks.

[24] The main categories of risk weightings are the following: exposure to sovereign OECD member borrowers is weighted 0%, that to OECD banking institutions and local authorities 20%, mortgages are weighted 50%, and all the other debts (of which all corporate debt) are weighted the maximum 100%.

[25] Since 1966, the European Union has allowed a third type of capital (tier 3). This is a subordinated debt instrument with a minimum maturity of two years. This category of capital can be set against activities related only to the bank's trading book and not its banking book.

authorities is compulsory. Positions over 25% of the bank's capital are forbidden. Furthermore, the total amount of large risk must not exceed 800% of capital.

- The European Capital Adequacy Directive (CAD), published on 15 March 1993 and applying to banks and brokerage houses acting in the European Union, repeats most of the Basel Committee proposals set forth in 1988 and subsequently.

### 1.2.1.3    Criticism of the Basel I Regulations

The Basel Committee regulations have often been criticized. One particular criticism is that the static, arbitrary weightings of assets do not properly reflect the credit risks run by banking institutions and cause discrepancy between bank return on capital in the economic context, once it has been adjusted for risk (RAROC), and bank return on capital in the regulatory context. The most frequently expressed criticisms are that:

- The Basel I constraint is too high for large companies and too low for small businesses, on average more likely to default.
- By applying a single weighting for all types of credit, many unsophisticated banks have confused capital adequacy and loan pricing, whatever the counterparty's credit quality. Nothing could have been further from the initial intentions of the Basel Committee. Similarly, because many financial institutions have not developed internal rating systems, they are tempted to lend only to the highest-risk borrowers, since the capital allocation is similar to that required for a loan with a better-quality counterparty and the yield is higher.
- The difference in arbitrary weightings of sovereign borrowers, banks and private companies is not satisfactory. Let us take, for example, a three-year bond issued by Novartis, a borrower rated Aaa/AAA by Moody's Investors Service and Standard & Poor's. A bank investor must weight this asset 100% if it is held on his balance sheet. Its allocation in regulatory capital will be higher than that on a ten-year bond issued by an A-rated OECD bank (thus of poorer quality), weighted 20%. Yet the probability of default of the latter within ten years is far greater than that of Novartis within three years.
- The Basel I regulation does not take account of the term structure of the credit risk, because the treatment is uniform whatever the maturity.
- The rule of weighting by type of underlying asset does not take account of the effects of over-concentration. The capital to be set against a risk is directly proportional to the amount of exposure to this risk. This means that the marginal regulatory cost of a new operation is constant, while financial theory shows that the marginal economic cost is an increasing function of the size of the commitment.
- Finally, under Basel I regulations it is impossible either to take account of the overall risk of a loan portfolio (since the correlations between the various components of a portfolio may significantly modify the institution's overall risk profile), or to net exposures if the bank is both creditor and debtor of a counterparty.

This Basel I Accord has been amended several times since its implementation. The biggest change was the introduction of a separation between the trading book and the banking book[26] by the European Capital Adequacy Directive (CAD) of 1996, applied worldwide by the Basel

---

[26] Generally, assets, financial instruments and debt securities held for the purpose of short-term sale (within six months) or to take advantage of short-term price movements, can be handled in the trading book. It is imperative that assets in the trading book be valued marked-to-market. All assets not eligible to go into the trading book automatically go into the banking book.

Committee for Banking Supervision. This Directive created new rules for the allocation of capital for market risks.[27] Thus, treatment of credit exposures eligible for the trading book is more favorable in terms of capital requirement than that in force for those in the banking book: the weightings applied for the former are lower than those for the latter (the treatment methods for which remain those of the Basel I rules).

The many criticisms leveled at the 1988 agreement and the changes in regulations (not least the use of internal models for calculating the capital requirements for market risks) have led the supervisory authorities to review their approach. Other important factors have contributed to this evolution, more especially the emergence of credit derivatives, which have enabled:

- More sophisticated credit management by financial institutions, exposing the limits of the 1988 agreement.
- More commonly used practices of 'regulatory arbitrage.'[28]

These efforts resulted in the publication of a Revised Framework of the International Convergence of Capital Measurements and Capital Standards in 2001–2004, also known as the Basel II Accord. After many negotiations and adjustments between banking institutions, national supervisory authorities and the Basel Committee, this Accord should be implemented, by various methods, by the banks in the main countries by 2007. We shall return to the Basel II agreements, and their 'symbiotic' relationships with credit derivatives, in Chapter 7.

### 1.2.2   Credit Risk Analyzed by Rating Agencies

The second characteristic of credit risk is that, in addition to the ongoing scrutiny of the banking supervisory authorities, it has given rise to a dedicated system of analysis and measurement that has taken on growing significance over the past ten years: that of the rating agencies.

#### 1.2.2.1   Presentation of Rating Agencies

Rating agencies arose in the American market at the beginning of the 20th century, with the creation of the first agency, Moody's Investors Service, by John Moody in 1909.[29] Their initial purpose was to serve as intermediary between the issuers in the emerging, rapidly growing bond market in the USA, and investors, by supplying the latter with an independent assessment of the creditworthiness of the issues.

In economic theory, the role of rating agencies is clearly established. Acting as intermediaries, they enable the information asymmetry between issuers and investors during a bond issue to be reduced, by providing an independent assessment of the issue. Thus the rating agencies enable investors to build up portfolios more cheaply than if they themselves had had to collect the information needed to make a full assessment of the issuers' creditworthiness.

The three largest rating agencies in the world are Moody's Investors Service, Standard & Poor's and Fitch Ratings. Between them they share 95% of the world financial rating market. They are present in all the largest financial centers in the world and hold the highly coveted

[27] Interest and exchange rate risks, settlement–delivery risks, and large risks.
[28] Regulatory arbitrage, a practice where banking institutions reduce their level of regulatory capital while maintaining an equivalent economic ('real') risk, was one of the main factors for growth in the credit derivatives market in the late 1990s, not least the more sophisticated ones such as collateralized debt obligations (CDOs – see Chapter 4).
[29] This was soon followed by Fitch Investors Service in 1922, and by Standard & Poor's Corp. (S&P) in 1923. The other main rating agencies were created from the 1970s on, some having since disappeared due to mergers: Thomson Bankwatch (1974), Japan Bond Research Institute (1975), IBCA (1978), Duff & Phelps (1980).

Nationally Recognized Statistical Ratings Organizations (NRSRO) stamp of approval from the American regulatory authorities (Securities and Exchange Commission, SEC). By a series of mergers and acquisitions,[30] the three 'majors' have now gained a virtual oligopoly over the world rating market, with the exception of insurance and reinsurance companies where the specialized American agency A.M. Best & Co. holds a strong position.

Even though the American market is relatively mature, activity in the past few years has been spurred by the phenomenal growth in the European ratings market in the wake of the unification of the bond market in continental Europe when the euro was introduced at the end of 1999. Moody's rates over 4000 companies worldwide, of which almost 50% are outside the United States, as against 700 and 100 respectively in the early 1950s (and 3000 and 200 in 1920!).

Moreover, while initially, most of their income came from corporate bond issues, the rating agencies have found attractive growth opportunities in new structured transactions (securitizations, CDOs). Thus, Paul Mazataud, head of structured financing at Moody's, points out 'There is often a confusion between the agencies' activities and just corporate ratings. Some 40% of our income comes from rating of securitization operations'.[31] We shall return to this fundamental change in the role of the rating agencies in the bond market, which, from simple assessment of a borrower's capacity (corporate or sovereign) to meet his undertakings, has evolved into the assessment of the performance of ever-more complex structured products.

### 1.2.2.2   Assessment of Credit Risk

The traditional approach of the rating agencies to assessment of credit risk is to give a rating summing up their opinion of a borrower's creditworthiness and his capacity to meet his undertakings. Therefore, a rating expresses their opinion both of the probability of default and the loss severity were that default to occur.

The rating is made after a process of fundamental analysis combining quantitative (such as study of financial statements) and qualitative methodologies (strategic analyses, interviews with the issuing company's management, etc.). Moody's defines ratings thus: they are 'opinions of future relative creditworthiness, derived by fundamental credit analysis and expressed through the familiar Aaa to C symbol system. Fundamental credit analysis incorporates an evaluation of franchise value, financial statement analysis and management quality. It seeks to predict the credit performance of bonds, other financial instruments, or firms across a range of plausible economic scenarios, some of which will include credit stress. Credit ratings provide simple, objective and consistent measurements of creditworthiness.'

All credit rating agencies use a scale of ratings, usually symbolized by letters, measuring the risk of default and potential losses arising from the default. The scales used by the main agencies are shown in Figure 1.9.

There are generally two rating levels:

- Investment grade for the best issues (from AAA/Aaa to BBB/Baa3).
- Speculative grade (from BB+/Ba1 to default, D).

---

[30] Fitch Ratings thus merged with IBCA and then took over Duff & Phelps and Thomson Bankwatch, to form a third body capable of rivaling Moody's and S&P. In 2002, Moody's took over KMV Corp.

[31] Quoted by Raulot (2003a).

| | | S&P | Moody's | Fitch | Interpretation |
|---|---|---|---|---|---|
| | **Investment Grade** | AAA | Aaa | AAA | Highest quality, minimal credit risk |
| | | AA+ | Aa1 | AA+ | |
| | | AA | Aa2 | AA | High quality, subject to very low credit risk |
| | | AA- | Aa3 | AA- | |
| | | A+ | A1 | A+ | Upper medium grade, subject to low credit risk |
| | | A | A2 | A | |
| | | A- | A3 | A- | |
| | | BBB+ | Baa1 | BBB+ | Medium grade, subject to moderate credit risk and may possess speculative characteristics |
| | | BBB | Baa2 | BBB | |
| | | BBB- | Baa3 | BBB- | |
| | **Speculative Grade** | BB+ | Ba1 | BB+ | Include speculative elements and subject to substantial credit risk |
| | | BB | Ba2 | BB | |
| | | BB- | Ba3 | BB- | |
| | | B+ | B1 | B+ | Speculative obligations, subject to high credit risk |
| | | B | B2 | B | |
| | | B- | B3 | B- | |
| | | CCC+ | Caa | CCC | Obligations of poor standing, subject to very high credit risk |
| | | CCC | | CC | |
| | | CCC- | | | |
| | | C | Ca | C | Highly speculative, likely to default |
| | | D | C | DDD, DD, D | Obligations in default |

*(Left vertical axis label: Deteriorating credit quality ↓)*

**Figure 1.9**    S&P, Moody's and Fitch rating scales

This categorization is also clearly shown in the statistics published by the rating agencies on default rates and cumulative default rates (Tables 1.3 and 1.4).

Moreover, the rating agencies are precious sources of information for credit market practitioners as regards post-default recovery rates.[32]

The recovery rate depends directly on the seniority of the underlying debt, as shown in Figure 1.10.

As a rule, the recovery rate is higher for bank loans than for bonds, since the former are often collateralized[33] and rank *pari passu*[34] with the issuer's senior bond debt. This explains why, where there is an equal risk of default (due to cross-default provisions for the various classes of instruments), bank debts often have a better rating than bonds issued by the same borrower. Furthermore, it should be noted that the level of the recovery rate on a debt also depends on the borrower's sector of activity (in this regard, see the results of the Altman and Kishore survey, published in 1996). Finally, one last characteristic of recovery rates is their variability over time. Table 1.5. shows measurements of the historical volatility of recovery rates.

One final indicator of credit risk that is provided by rating agencies is transition matrices. These enable calculation of the probability of a borrower keeping his rating over a given period, moving up to a better rating, or being downgraded from the initial rating. As for the probabilities of default and recovery rates, these data are aggregated from historical series (see Tables 1.6 and 1.7).

---

[32] Recovery rates are most often estimated by the price at which the post-default debt is traded in the secondary market. In practice, this value may be determined by a survey of the various market-makers for the debt in question. In an efficient market, this price should equal the net present value of all future cash flows generated by the distressed security.

[33] The nature of this collateral influences the hope of recovery of a defaulted bank loan. The survey by Carty *et al.* (1998) shows that lenders holding collateral in the form of the borrower's short-term assets (cash flow, client receivables, inventory) recovered 90% of their commitment on average, as compared to 85% for claims secured by long-term assets (lands, buildings, plant) and 74% for those secured by stakes in subsidiaries' equity capital.

[34] Of equal rank in the case of default and asset liquidation.

**Table 1.3**   Cumulative default rates by rating categories on corporate bonds and loans 1983 to 2001 (%)

| Rating | Time horizon | | | | | |
|---|---|---|---|---|---|---|
| | Y1 | Y2 | Y3 | Y4 | Y5 | Y6 |
| Aaa | 0.00 | 0.00 | 0.00 | 0.07 | 0.22 | 0.31 |
| Aa1 | 0.00 | 0.00 | 0.00 | 0.23 | 0.23 | 0.38 |
| Aa2 | 0.00 | 0.00 | 0.06 | 0.19 | 0.42 | 0.51 |
| Aa3 | 0.05 | 0.09 | 0.16 | 0.24 | 0.34 | 0.46 |
| A1 | 0.00 | 0.02 | 0.27 | 0.43 | 0.54 | 0.67 |
| A2 | 0.04 | 0.10 | 0.28 | 0.57 | 0.77 | 0.98 |
| A3 | 0.00 | 0.11 | 0.21 | 0.29 | 0.42 | 0.64 |
| Baa1 | 0.12 | 0.40 | 0.69 | 1.10 | 1.52 | 1.81 |
| Baa2 | 0.09 | 0.39 | 0.76 | 1.46 | 2.18 | 2.98 |
| Baa3 | 0.37 | 0.88 | 1.51 | 2.47 | 3.26 | 4.40 |
| Ba1 | 0.62 | 2.03 | 3.68 | 5.83 | 7.67 | 9.51 |
| Ba2 | 0.62 | 2.43 | 4.75 | 7.33 | 9.55 | 11.27 |
| Ba3 | 2.43 | 6.81 | 11.95 | 16.64 | 21.04 | 25.46 |
| B1 | 3.47 | 9.81 | 15.99 | 21.64 | 27.26 | 32.49 |
| B2 | 7.18 | 15.65 | 22.96 | 28.87 | 33.57 | 36.80 |
| B3 | 12.45 | 21.81 | 29.63 | 35.80 | 41.13 | 45.05 |
| Caa–C | 21.61 | 34.23 | 44.04 | 52.18 | 57.44 | 62.52 |
| *Investment grade* | **0.06** | **0.20** | **0.40** | **0.69** | **0.96** | **1.25** |
| *Speculative grade* | **3.99** | **9.07** | **13.96** | **18.33** | **22.23** | **25.64** |
| Total | 1.34 | 3.02 | 4.62 | 6.04 | 7.24 | 8.27 |

*Source:* Moody's Investors Service. ©Moody's investors Service, Inc. and/or its affiliates. Reprinted with permission. All Rights Reserved.

**Table 1.4**   Cumulative average default rates 1981 to 2004 (%)

| Rating | Time horizon | | | | | | | | | |
|---|---|---|---|---|---|---|---|---|---|---|
| | Y1 | Y2 | Y3 | Y4 | Y5 | Y6 | Y7 | Y8 | Y9 | Y10 |
| AAA | 0.00 | 0.00 | 0.03 | 0.06 | 0.10 | 0.17 | 0.24 | 0.36 | 0.41 | 0.45 |
| AA | 0.01 | 0.04 | 0.09 | 0.19 | 0.30 | 0.41 | 0.54 | 0.64 | 0.74 | 0.85 |
| A | 0.04 | 0.13 | 0.24 | 0.40 | 0.61 | 0.84 | 1.11 | 1.34 | 1.63 | 1.94 |
| BBB | 0.29 | 0.81 | 1.40 | 2.19 | 2.99 | 3.73 | 4.34 | 4.95 | 5.50 | 6.10 |
| BB | 1.20 | 3.58 | 6.39 | 8.97 | 11.25 | 13.47 | 15.25 | 16.75 | 18.16 | 19.20 |
| B | 5.71 | 12.49 | 18.09 | 22.37 | 25.40 | 27.77 | 29.76 | 31.32 | 32.54 | 33.75 |
| CCC/C | 28.83 | 37.97 | 43.52 | 47.44 | 50.85 | 52.13 | 53.39 | 54.05 | 55.56 | 56.45 |
| *Investment grade* | **0.11** | **0.31** | **0.55** | **0.86** | **1.20** | **1.53** | **1.84** | **2.13** | **2.41** | **2.71** |
| *Speculative grade* | **4.91** | **9.76** | **14.05** | **17.52** | **20.22** | **22.46** | **24.32** | **25.80** | **27.13** | **28.25** |
| All rated | 1.64 | 3.29 | 4.78 | 6.04 | 7.08 | 7.97 | 8.71 | 9.34 | 9.92 | 10.45 |

*Source:* Standard & Poor's Global Fixed Income Research; Standard & Poor's CreditPro® 7.0. Table entitled 'Cumulative Average Default Rates 1981–2004' published in Annual Global Corporate Default Study: Corporate Defaults Poised to Rise in 2005, Global Fixed Income Research, Dianne Vazza, 2005, reproduced with permission of Standard & Poor's, a division of the McGraw-Hill Companies, Inc.

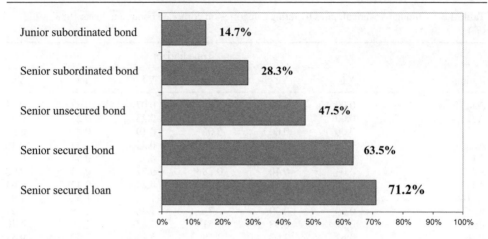

**Figure 1.10**   Recovery rates
*Source:* Moody's Investors Service. © Moody's Investors Services, Inc. and/or its affiliates. Reprinted with permission.
All Rights Reserved.

**Table 1.5**   Historical volatility of default and recovery rates

| | Historical volatility of default rates by categories of rating (%) | | Historical volatility of recovery rates by type of debt (%) | |
|---|---|---|---|---|
| | 1 year | 10 years | | 1977–1997 |
| Aaa | 0.00 | 0.00 | Senior secured loan (1989–1996) | 21.57 |
| Aa | 0.10 | 0.90 | Senior secured bond | 23.87 |
| A | 0.10 | 0.70 | Senior unsecured bond | 25.81 |
| Baa | 0.30 | 1.80 | Senior subordinated bond | 23.35 |
| Ba | 1.40 | 3.40 | Subordinated bond | 22.05 |
| B | 4.80 | 5.60 | Junior subordinated bond | 14.31 |

*Source:* Moody's Investors Service. © Moody's Investors Service, Inc. and/or its affiliates. Reprinted with permission.
All Rights Reserved.

**Table 1.6**   One-year rating transition (%)

| Initial rating | Final rating | | | | | | | |
|---|---|---|---|---|---|---|---|---|
| | Aaa | Aa | A | Baa | Ba | B | Caa | Default |
| Aaa | 93.40 | 5.94 | 0.64 | 0.00 | 0.02 | 0.00 | 0.00 | 0.00 |
| Aa | 1.61 | 90.55 | 7.46 | 0.26 | 0.09 | 0.01 | 0.00 | 0.02 |
| A | 0.07 | 2.28 | 92.44 | 4.63 | 0.45 | 0.12 | 0.01 | 0.00 |
| Baa | 0.05 | 0.26 | 5.51 | 88.48 | 4.76 | 0.71 | 0.08 | 0.15 |
| Ba | 0.02 | 0.05 | 0.42 | 5.16 | 86.91 | 5.91 | 0.24 | 1.29 |
| B | 0.00 | 0.04 | 0.13 | 0.54 | 6.35 | 84.22 | 1.91 | 6.81 |
| Caa | 0.00 | 0.00 | 0.00 | 0.62 | 2.05 | 4.08 | 69.20 | 24.06 |

*Source:* Moody's Investors Service. © Moody's Investors Service, Inc. and/or its affiliates. Reprinted with permission.
All Rights Reserved.

**Table 1.7**     Global average one-year transition rates 1981 to 2004 (%)

| Initial rating | Final rating | | | | | | | | |
|---|---|---|---|---|---|---|---|---|---|
| | AAA | AA | A | BBB | BB | B | CCC/C | D | N.R. |
| AAA | 87.44 | 7.37 | 0.46 | 0.09 | 0.06 | 0.00 | 0.00 | 0.00 | 4.59 |
| AA | 0.60 | 86.65 | 7.78 | 0.58 | 0.06 | 0.11 | 0.02 | 0.01 | 4.21 |
| A | 0.05 | 2.05 | 86.98 | 5.50 | 0.43 | 0.16 | 0.03 | 0.04 | 4.79 |
| BBB | 0.02 | 0.21 | 3.85 | 84.13 | 4.39 | 0.77 | 0.19 | 0.29 | 6.14 |
| BB | 0.04 | 0.08 | 0.33 | 5.27 | 75.73 | 7.36 | 0.94 | 1.20 | 9.06 |
| B | 0.00 | 0.07 | 0.20 | 0.28 | 5.21 | 72.95 | 4.23 | 5.71 | 11.36 |
| CCC/C | 0.08 | 0.00 | 0.31 | 0.39 | 1.31 | 9.74 | 46.83 | 28.83 | 12.52 |

*Source*: Standard & Poor's Global Fixed Income Research; Standard & Poor's CreditPro® 7.0. Table entitled 'Global Average One-Year Transitions Rates 1981–2004' published in Annual Global Corporate Default Study: Corporate Defaults Poised to Rise in 2005, Global Fixed Income Research, Dianne Viazza, 2005, reproduced with permission of Standard & Poor's, a division of The McGraw-Hill Companies, Inc.

Other private companies, such as DRI McGraw-Hill, offer products similar to those of the rating agencies, or credit scoring methodologies (such as the Z-score devised by Professor Edward I. Altman to predict the risk of corporate bankruptcy). The latter technique regresses a parameter representing the company default on a selection of variables (mostly accounting ones) to determine the most significant (historically) in terms of default prediction.

### 1.2.2.3   Limitations of Statistics and Criticism of Rating Agencies

The statistics supplied by the rating agencies (default probabilities and recovery rates) have some limitations:

- The rating agencies only partly cover reference assets, since they almost always use only bonds. Moody's rated bank debts for the first time in 1995, but the borrowers covered by these analyses were very often already active in the bond markets.
- Most of the statistics are only available for relatively large American borrowers. Therefore the corresponding default probabilities for international borrowers can only be deduced by analogy, since only their default statistics over the past five or ten years are available.
- It is unsatisfactory to base estimates of default probabilities solely on the borrower's rating since each credit risk is uniquely linked to the borrower (the idiosyncratic component).
- Another difficulty with default and recovery rate statistics as supplied by the rating agencies is their versatility over time. They are strongly dependent on the market environment (interest rate levels, economic recession or expansion, etc.). It may therefore be dangerous to apply a default rate valid in the past to a situation in the present. This problem of extrapolation is all the more acute as the agency ratings are based essentially on *a posteriori* accounting measurements.

Rating agencies have faced a mounting barrage of criticism in recent years due to their increasing importance in the financial markets and the significant rise in bankruptcies. The main target of criticism is their incapacity to anticipate sudden failures. It is accepted that the rating agencies were not capable of predicting the Asian crisis in 1997 or the resounding crashes of companies such as Enron, rated BBB a mere three weeks before it went into administration, unlike the financial markets, which measure a borrower's credit risk by credit spread (see later).

It is this that led to the development of prospective models for calculating a borrower's default probability (e.g. KMV,[35] acquired by Moody's in 2002) using market data (spreads or share prices). These methods are more and more frequently used by the rating agencies.

Finally, since the rating agencies will be called upon to play an ever-more important role in the coming years with the implementation of the Basel II rules (under which capital requirements will depend directly on borrowers' ratings), the banking supervisory authorities are today seeking to promote competition in, and diversity of, information sources. Thus, in March 2003, the Canadian firm Dominion Bond Rating Service was recognized as an NRSRO, an event that may be the first nail in the coffin of the oligopoly currently formed by the three leading agencies in the market. We shall return to the role of the rating agencies in relation to the new capital adequacy rules in Chapter 7.

### 1.2.3   Credit Risk Measured in the Financial Markets: Credit Spread

The credit markets operate by reference to two essential parameters:

1. Borrower rating, as we have seen, which enables investors to rank creditworthiness, and thus to deduce a risk premium by reference to the conditions in which bond issues of the same rating are traded.
2. The credit spread, which can in theory be defined as the market unit that compensates investors for the credit risk (default) inherent in any debt instrument not issued by a sovereign borrower in its own currency (deemed to be risk-free).

Although these two indicators are theoretically considered to be close, in practice they differ frequently, due to a number of factors:

1. Rating agencies are incapable of adjusting their estimations in real time, as and when events peculiar to each borrower occur. The survey by Wakeman (1990) shows that rating changes, whether upgrades or downgrades, only reflect information that has been assimilated long before into the price of the security in the market. See also Larrain et al. (1997) on this subject.
2. The nature of credit spreads, which is also distorted by exogenous factors and does not provide a 'pure' measurement of credit risk, as illustrated below.

#### 1.2.3.1   A First Approach to Credit Spread

As a first approach, credit spread can be defined as the compensation (the risk premium) expected by an investor. It depends on two parameters:

- The borrower's probability of default ($q$).
- The loss severity in the event of default ($1 - R$), where $R$ represents the recovery rate.

A simple case enabling credit spread to be apprehended is that of a one-year credit-sensitive zero-coupon bond with principal $P$. Two scenarios can be envisaged:[36]

1. The borrower defaults and the value of the position V at maturity is written

$$V = P - P(1 - R) = PR$$

---

[35] See Chapter 6.
[36] In the following example, for the sake of simplicity, the discounting of cash flows at the risk-free rate has been omitted.

2. The borrower does not default and pays back the principal ($P$) at maturity: $V = P$.

It is possible to express the mean value of position $Vm$ as:

$$Vm = q[P - P(1 - R)] + (1 - q)P$$

In a perfect world, the credit spread $S$ is supposed to compensate the investor for his risk of loss (denoted $X$). In this case, the loss may be expressed in two ways:

- $X = P - Vm$;
- $X = SP$.

It is possible to deduce from these simple relationships the following brief equation:

$$S = q(1 - R)$$

This equation enables us to confirm our intuition as to the nature of spread:

- It increases with the probability of default.
- It evolves in inverse proportion to the recovery rate (which means that for the same issuer, for instance, the credit spread of a subordinated debt will be higher than that for a senior debt).

### 1.2.3.2 Measurement of the Credit Spread on the Financial Markets: Asset Swaps

Before the arrival of credit derivatives in the financial markets, credit spreads could be measured either against the risk-free rates (that is, the yield-to-maturity on a sovereign issue) or against the swap or Euribor rates (that is, the rates at which the main banks obtain finance). These two measurements reflect the segmentation of the credit market. The former is the classic reference for fixed rate bond issues and institutional investors, but it includes a risk premium remunerating the interest rate risk, in addition to the spread.[37] On the other hand, spread against swap (risk premium on the interbank market) is the reference measurement for banking institutions, which are the main players in the credit markets. It has thus achieved reference status over time. In this context, the credit market has endeavored to separate credit risk from interest rate risk by using a special instrument: the asset swap.

An asset swap may be defined as the combination of a classic interest rate swap and a bond bought in the secondary market and then brought up to par.[38] The difference with a simple rate swap is that an asset swap is structured and offered to investors in the form of a package. The commonest asset swaps are a repackaging of a fixed-rate bond with an interest rate swap into a synthetic floating rate instrument, the value of which depends only on the credit spread and thus is insulated from interest rate fluctuations.

Similarly, it is also possible to change a security with floating interest rate into a synthetic fixed-rate security using an interest rate swap. Figure 1.11 shows the construction principles for an asset swap.

The huge growth in the asset swap market from 1994–95 onwards was a response to the penury in floating rate credit in the financial markets. Given the historically low interest rate level, borrowers were borrowing at fixed rates. These bonds were then bought up by secondary market intermediaries, who combined them with an interest rate swap or possibly a currency

[37] The difference between the swap rate and the risk-free rate is called the Ted spread.
[38] A currency swap may also be built into the structure where necessary.

Acquisition of fixed-rate bond in the secondary market
at time *t* for a value of 105

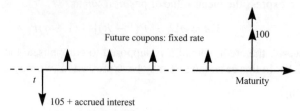

+   Interest rate swap (and possibly currency swap)

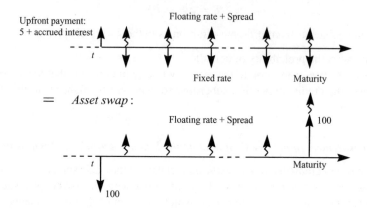

**Figure 1.11**    Assest swap structuring

swap, and sold them on to investors who funded themselves on a floating rate basis (Libor or Euribor). The result was a synthetic debt instrument with characteristics meeting the investors' requirements (immunization against interest rate risk).

While the asset swap market was previously preferred for observing a borrower's credit risk and its evolution, it has in the past five years been supplanted by the growing derivatives market, which offers 'pure' spreads not influenced by the exogenous factors found in cash instruments, as discussed later.

### 1.2.3.3   Nature of Credit Spread

As we have seen, spread is a measurement of credit risk. Although it integrates the borrower's real risk of defaulting (default probability and loss severity in the event of default) and the risk premium[39] demanded by investors (the latter are not risk-neutral and their aversion must be compensated for, all the more as a considerable proportion of risk for private issuers, especially corporates, is systemic and cannot therefore be diversified),[40] it cannot be considered as a 'pure' measurement. Altman's work (1989) on the performance of high-yield debt, for example, shows

---

[39] The Bank for International Settlements reviews the notion of risk premium in its 73rd Annual Report (p. 107) and holds it to be the explanation of why market spreads are significantly higher than theoretical spreads based on default probabilities.

[40] It could even be argued that the growing integration of the capital markets (see Chapter 7) has a direct impact on the risk premium level in credit markets, which increases at the same rate as volatility on the stock markets.

that the excessive yield on risky corporate securities as compared to US Treasury bonds cannot be entirely justified by those securities' default histories. Credit spread is generally influenced by other components, such as:

- The overall supply–demand balance in the credit markets.
- The liquidity of the security.
- The regulations applying to the security.
- Its characteristics (coupon rate, optional clauses, step-up coupons, etc.).

We maintain that, first, the supply–demand balance in credit markets and, therefore, the overall liquidity available to economic agents is a decisive parameter that influences risk assessment. Thus, as the Bank for International Settlements pointed out in its commentary on international banking and financial activity in 1998, 'The abundance of liquidity worldwide and the associated competitive pressures seem to have delayed a reconsideration of credit risk by major lenders.' The pricing conditions in the credit market are also, therefore, dictated by the balance between supply and demand, with each player developing his own assessment of a borrower's credit risk, independently of any theoretical reference. This situation leads structurally to under-pricing of credit risk where there is surplus offer of funds, and vice versa.

The importance of the commercial relationship between banks and borrowers only increases the problem. The former are led to price supplementary credit too low to cover their fixed costs and return on capital, in order not to compromise the privileged relationship they have built up with their best clients. In exchange, the banks expect the latter to come to them for other operations, such as cash management, custody, asset management, new issues, mergers and acquisitions advisory, interest rate and foreign exchange risk management, etc.

Another significant example is the impact of the structured credit product markets on the spread levels of the cash bond markets. The tightening of spreads in 2003 was thus probably due to the arrangers' need to cover exposures in structured products: in this type of transaction, intermediary investment banks are structurally long protection. Although they delta manage these long positions,[41] they are nonetheless led to buy large amounts of credit risk in the markets, which may explain the bond squeeze in 2003 and the resulting spread reduction.[42]

Other factors may intervene in determining credit spreads. One influence is the liquidity of the debt securities considered. This is closely bound up with the size and placement of the issue. Investors usually give a premium to liquid issues that enable them to exit their positions easily. On the other hand, a bond issue placed almost entirely with private investors is more difficult to handle in the market, and is traded at a higher credit spread. Several econometric works in this field have shown the pertinence of this analysis,[43] especially that of Houweling et al. (2002). These have sought to compare the liquidity premium of two bond portfolios issued by firms on the basis of four criteria for measuring liquidity: the size of the issue, its maturity, the number of available quotations, and their dispersion. This study resulted in the measurement of a premium for liquidity risk ranging from 0.2 to 47 basis points depending on the measurement criteria assessed.

A second factor determining credit spreads is the regulations on debt for investors, not least that for commercial banks applying the Basel I risk weightings in force since 1988. As recalled in Table 1.8, OECD sovereign borrowers weighted at 0% are likely to be better received by

---

[41] See section 4.3
[42] See Raulot (2003b).
[43] See Lubochinsky (2002).

**Table 1.8**   Credit spread by rating categories and types of issuers (January 1998)

| Basis points | Sovereign | Banks | Corporates |
|---|---|---|---|
| AAA | −2 | +2 | +10 |
| AA | 0 | +5 | +15 |
| A | +5 | +12 | +22 |

*Note:* Average credit spreads in the five-year asset swap market.
*Sources:* ISDA (1998), Rabobank, authors' analysis.

banks than corporate borrowers weighted at 100%, inasfar as the banks need not allocate regulatory capital against their position.

The influence of banking regulations on credit spreads can also be illustrated by the following anecdote.[44] On 16 April 1998, the Bank for International Settlements announced a cut in the weighting of debt securities issued by investment banks, from 100% to 20%. The announcement contributed to a rapid tightening of the credit spreads on these securities, until the market operators realized that only the operational subsidiaries of the investment banks were concerned by this measure. However, most of these institutions borrow at holding level, and the holdings are still weighted 100% for investing banks. The latter therefore liquidated their positions and the credit spread returned to its initial level.

One last factor influencing spread levels, independent of credit risk, is the security's characteristics, especially the coupon size. It has been clearly established that this parameter directly influences the discount rate (and therefore the spread for risky bonds.[45]) Thus, the credit spread observable in debt markets does not necessarily reflect the fair value of the credit risk: its liquidity, its intrinsic characteristics and its regulatory treatment are also taken into account by investors.

The emergence of a credit derivatives market has remedied this situation by contributing to the creation of an efficient market in which 'pure' credit risks are exchanged. The following section deals with the conditions under which these new instruments for managing and negotiating credit risk emerged.

## 1.3   TRADITIONAL METHODS OF CREDIT RISK MANAGEMENT AND THE EMERGENCE OF CREDIT DERIVATIVES

During the 1980s and 1990s, the surging growth of the financial markets and more especially of the derivatives markets was accompanied by considerable efforts to measure and control the market risks run by financial institutions. These efforts were crowned in the mid-1990s by the Value-at-Risk (VaR) method,[46] which has since become the norm for assessing market risks. It has to be acknowledged that credit risk management was not as thoroughly researched prior to this time. It was with the emergence of credit derivatives in 1996–1997 that the scientific and financial communities finally began to immerse themselves in this new field of investigation (see, Chapter 6).

---

[44] See Manda and Gutscher (1998).

[45] Thus, a simple approach, where a credit spread is determined by the difference between the discount rate of a risky bond and a risk-free security of the same maturity, would be an approximation, since the two securities would not necessarily have the same duration, nor the same modified duration (sensitivity), depending on the size of the coupons.

[46] In particular, with the publication of the RiskMetrics method by JP Morgan in 1994.

The subject of this third section is to describe the traditional approaches and measures for credit risk management, be it for issuer or counterparty risk on the derivatives markets, the context in which credit derivatives appeared, and the advantages inherent to these new financial instruments.

### 1.3.1 Traditional Methods for Managing Credit Risk (Issuer Risk)

Traditionally, exposure to credit risk is managed *a priori* by banking institutions and other investors in the credit market. These use classic financial analysis methods and apply counter-party limits. Once the credit has been granted, if the borrower's creditworthiness deteriorates, there are usually only two solutions for the banks: fall back on provisions or settle the position by posting a loss, the latter solution having a definitive impact on their profit and loss statements, while the former may leave a hope that the borrower will return to better fortune.

Traditional credit risk management is based on three main principles.

#### 1.3.1.1  Micro Management of Credit Risk

A lender may protect himself from borrower default by structuring the transaction such as to limit his risk of loss, not least by controlling the loan terms and conditions:

- The pricing of the loan, which normally corresponds to the cost of funding it (Euribor[47] for a bank with a reasonable rating), the administrative cost of the transaction, and the risk premium (which depends on the borrower's creditworthiness) should cover the potential risk of loss on the transaction.
- Syndication, the most commonly-used method for reducing credit risk on large loans in the primary market.[48] It enables risk to be spread over all the banks in the syndicate that underwrite the risk.
- Debt seniority compared to the borrower's other loans, which offers more or less security in the event of default and liquidation of assets.
- Collateral, earmarking certain assets on which the bank will have priority in the event of borrower default and liquidation.
- Covenants (clauses in the loan contract) providing for early repayment of the loans by the borrower should he not be able to comply with them. These clauses are most often expressed in the form of minimum financial ratios to be achieved, such as interest cover (EBITDA[49] over interest charge), the leverage (net debt over equity capital), the operating margin, or the borrower's rating.
- The credit or rating triggers[50] and other trigger mechanisms enabling the lender to be protected in theory where the borrower's creditworthiness deteriorates. Several types of clause may be identified in this category:
  - Step-up coupons, which provide for automatic increase of the spread if the borrower is downgraded.

---

[47] Euro Inter-Bank Offered Rate: rate at which good quality banks re-finance in the inter-bank market.

[48] The first syndications took place on the American market in the early 1970s. See CGFS (2003).

[49] Earnings before Interest, Tax, Depreciation and Amortization.

[50] The first triggers were introduced into bond documentation in the United States following the crash in the high-yield bond market at the end of the 1980s. Investors turned away from risky borrowers (corporates) and preferred risk-free borrowers such as states and other supranational organizations. The result of this investment strategy was imbalance in supply and demand in the market for corporate bond issuers, which led to an additional risk premium that they were obliged to offer investors. The introduction of triggers in bond documentation was one way of returning to supply–demand equilibrium.

- Collateral clauses, which provide for pledging of certain assets to lenders where the borrower's rating falls.
- Immediate repayment of the debt: the borrower is supposed to repay the entire debt to the creditors as soon as his rating falls below a predetermined level (usually from investment to speculative grade).
- Margin calls (this clause is usually implemented in third-party contracts or in the case of a guarantee, where the guarantor's rating is not deemed sufficiently sound by its counter-parties).

These mechanisms of credit trigger or covenant may, however, have a down side, or lead to a vicious circle: if lenders demand immediate repayment of the debt, this may push the debtor into bankruptcy and thus jeopardize even further the likelihood of repayment. As Eric de Bodard, Managing Director of Moody's France, pointed out, 'The rating trigger is self-perpetuating. If there are too many automatic repayments due to rating triggers, the first deterioration can lead mechanically to several notches being lost in the rating.'[51] This was recently illustrated by the battle between Alstom and its creditors in spring 2004, where the latter criticized Alstom for not sticking to some key financial ratios in the wake of their rescue plan of summer 2003.

Another side effect of rating trigger clauses is to place rating agencies firmly at the helm, any downgrading decision resulting in the death of the borrower in the short or medium term.

### 1.3.1.2   Macro Management of Credit Risk

Most lenders define limits to obligations (authorizations) in terms of amount and term of the loan for each borrower individually, and also concentration limits for each category of internal rating, industrial sectors, or geographical regions. Credit risk is an idiosyncratic risk that must be diversified over several borrowers, industrial sector, and geographical regions. Such diversification does not reduce the 'systemic' component of credit risk, which is connected to the overall economic climate.

### 1.3.1.3   A Posteriori Credit Risk Management

Lenders have two solutions when the quality of the assets on their balance sheets deteriorates:

1. Create provisions.
2. Dispose of the assets on the secondary market, if it exists and provides sufficient liquidity. This is valid mostly for market instruments (bonds and similar).

Over the last few years, a secondary market for bank loans has developed. It offers increasing liquidity to banks. We shall return to this in Chapter 7.

Furthermore, banking institutions can use sub-participations in risk and cash flows, a contract under which the bank transfers the cash flows of an asset (and the associated credit risk) to another institution, while maintaining first rank in the commercial relationship. However, this market offers relatively little liquidity, due more especially to the complex legal aspects to be taken into consideration in these operations and the small number of investors for this type of product (other banks).

---

[51] Cited by Lachèvre (2002).

Firms use traditional instruments such as letters of credit, guarantees, and credit insurance policies, to protect themselves against potential default by a trading partner or breach of contract (performance bonds, surety bonds, etc.). Most of these instruments are insurance contracts (except letters of credit and guarantees delivered by banking institutions).

Moreover, for projects in foreign countries or export contracts, corporates use credit insurance contracts supplied by specialized insurance companies or governmental bodies.[52]

### 1.3.2    Counterparty Risk Management in Derivatives Markets

Derivatives are traded in either organized or OTC markets. We shall therefore distinguish between these.

#### 1.3.2.1    Organized Markets

In organized markets, counterparty risk is much reduced by the institutional arrangements between players:

- There is a clearinghouse centralizing all transactions and playing a systematic role as counterparty for each participant in the market.
- There is a daily mark-to-market on which margin calls are calculated. The positions of the counterparties are re-assessed daily and variations in these positions must be settled in cash or Treasury bonds.
- Traders deposit an initial margin, often small compared to the amount of the transaction, serving as collateral in the event of default.
- Position limits are imposed on individual brokers and on the institutional members of the clearinghouse.

#### 1.3.2.2    OTC Markets: Netting and Collateral Agreements

Counterparty risk in OTC derivatives markets has quickly become a major anxiety for traders with the explosion in the numbers and volume of transactions. The main banks working in this market have therefore sought to implement risk management mechanisms via their representative association, the International Swaps and Derivatives Association (ISDA).

From the early 1990s, netting and collateral agreements were set up between the main players. The bilateral netting arrangements enable players regularly trading on these markets to make algebraic sums of their long and short market positions (expressed in mark-to-market values) with the same counterparty, thus producing a lower net 'at risk' value. This practice has been made possible by the use by all market players of a standard legal document, the Master Agreement, drawn up by the ISDA. This covers a more-or-less wide range of products, depending on the bilateral negotiations between the two counterparties.

Once the at risk value has been determined between two counterparties, the debtor party may be called upon to provide collateral in the form of cash or securities (risk-free Treasury bonds) to the creditor party (a mechanism comparable to that of margin calls in the organized markets). Positions are re-assessed daily for standard instruments by the main players in the markets.

---

[52] Such as the Export–Import Bank in the United States, Coface in France, or Sace in Italy.

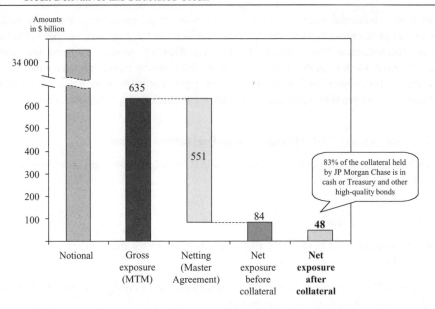

**Figure 1.12**   Derivative counterparty risk exposure: JP Morgan Chase (31 December 2003)
*Sources:* JP Morgan Chase, authors' analysis.

These netting and collateral mechanisms have contributed to drastic reduction of counterparty risk in the OTC derivatives markets. Figure 1.12 shows the figures for the exposure of JP Morgan Chase, the world leader in the derivatives markets, to counterparty risk in these markets at 31 December 2003.

In this example, it can be seen that the netting and collateral agreements contributed to cutting the counterparty risk by 92% (based on the gross amount of exposure). This corresponds in real terms to a mere 0.14% of the notional amounts handled by the bank.

### 1.3.2.3   Other Methods of Counterparty Risk Management in the OTC Markets

Other traditional methods for managing counterparty risk in the OTC markets are as follows:

- Position limits[53] with each counterparty are defined and managed on a portfolio basis (country or sector limits).
- Very often, participants in OTC swaps markets require the counterparty to pay an initial margin, deposited in an escrow fund, or to provide collateral, most often in the form of securities.
- The practice of re-couponing modifies the swap coupon periodically, to bring the market value of the swap back to zero. This arrangement implies a cash payment to the swap counterparty in-the-money, thus lowering the counterparty risk.
- Credit triggers have also gained popularity, not least for long-term transactions. These mechanisms offer protection by triggering early settlement of the swap by a cash payment where a credit event occurs (such as a rating downgrade).

---

[53] Banks usually fix two types of limit to hedge against credit risk, which is typically dynamic, on derivatives transactions. The first type is a limit beyond which a bank cannot undertake a new transaction with its client because it wishes to protect itself against any unfavorable change of value in its credit exposure to the counterparty. The second type is a higher limit beyond which the bank is involved in finding ways to decrease its passive exposure.

Counterparty rating in the OTC derivatives markets is of paramount importance. In this regard, some market players have been led to create specialized subsidiaries with triple-A ratings to do their transactions for them. These Derivative Product Companies (DPCs) are the strategic response of the main merchant banks not possessing an asset base and market capitalization comparable to those of the main commercial banks[54] when confronted with downgrading. DPCs have higher ratings than their parent companies due to their excellent capitalization and sophisticated risk management approaches. There are three classic types of DPCs: structured DPCs are distinct from the others in eliminating the market risk inherent in their activities by undertaking 'mirror' transactions with their parent or affiliated companies. The survey by Remolona *et al.* (1996) notes that although there are more and more of these specialized subsidiaries, they still only handle a marginal number of OTC derivatives transactions. Many of the main traders in the OTC markets (JP Morgan Chase, Citibank, Bank of America and the large European banks – Deutsche Bank, BNP Paribas, UBS, CSFB, etc.) do not use DPCs.

The credit risk management methods described above are relatively standard to all banks, lenders, and other investors in the credit markets. They have not been adequate to avert the disasters due to under-performing loan portfolios leading to excessive provisions. Fixing commitment limits does not enable a clear identification of the relationship between risk and expected profitability. Further, it is very probable that credit pricing does not properly compensate for the risk taken by banks due to the competition in the credit markets. This is a particularly clear tendency when there is surplus liquidity.

In addition to these factors, the most flagrant defect of the traditional credit risk management methods remains the impossibility to detach credit risk from the underlying asset, thus enabling it to be transferred to a third party.

### 1.3.3 Emergence and Advantages of Credit Derivatives

Generally speaking, a credit derivative is any derivative enabling the pricing and trading of the credit risk on an underlying asset, independently of the other market risks inherent to it. In this section, we shall return to the context in which credit derivatives were created, and then present their main characteristics. We shall explore their nature and *raison d'être*.

#### 1.3.3.1   Creation and Emergence of Credit Derivatives

The term credit derivative, used for the first time in 1992, referred to a new class of derivative the creation of which was intended to remedy the inadequacies of traditional methods and instruments used by banking institutions for managing credit risks.

**Reasons for the emergence of credit derivatives**

Among the various reasons for creating credit derivatives in the early 1990s are the following:

- The wish of financial intermediaries to protect themselves more effectively against credit risk.
- The observation that there was a growing discrepancy between increasingly sophisticated market (interest and exchange rate) risk management and credit risk management.[55]

---

[54] The commercial banks using such structures are those having been sharply downgraded, such as Crédit Lyonnais.

[55] Indeed, it is no accident that one of the early proponents of credit derivatives was the American bank Bankers Trust. It was a pioneer in the ordinary derivatives market in the 1980s, then in structured derivatives, while at the same time developing the most sophisticated internal risk management system in the world (RAROC, Risk-Adjusted Return on Capital). At the same time, Bankers Trust continued its historic activity as a commercial bank. The expertise in credit risk assessment gained during those years of active participation in the high-yield bond market also contributed to its analysis of credit derivatives.

- Banks' capital adequacy regulations, as defined by Basel I in 1988, which required financial intermediaries to gain better knowledge of the relationship between risk and profit, not least in terms of capital allocation, and much more dynamic asset/liability management.
- Exponential growth of OTC derivatives activities and the deep involvement of banks in these markets, which quickly led to overstepping the limits of counterparty authorization. This was one of the deciding factors leading financial institutions to seek solutions and generate new credit lines.
- Finally, for the most sophisticated financial intermediaries, which were responsible for structuring and offering such instruments, credit derivatives met the strategic need for innovation and use of new opportunities to generate higher profits than the by then traditional, so-called plain vanilla, derivatives, the intermediation and trading margins of which rapidly eroded under the pressure of the many new entrants in the market.

## Products pre-figuring credit derivatives

The principle of credit risk derivatives was not entirely new. Products for similar purposes did exist in the financial markets (e.g. bank guarantees). One of the first forms of credit derivative could be seen in bonds with put options, which gave the investor the right to sell the security back to the issuer at certain dates or during a precise period for a predetermined price, thus enabling him to limit his credit risk exposure. The price of the option was included in the bond characteristics, in the form of a reduced premium or coupon. The exercise of this option could depend on certain parameters.

These securities became popular in the late 1980s, when bond investors were seeking hedges against certain events (hostile takeovers, LBOs, etc.) likely to deteriorate an issuer's creditworthiness significantly. The 1980s also saw the development of other debt products integrating similar hedging mechanisms:[56]

- Floating rate rating-sensitive notes: the coupon rate was reset on a quarterly basis and adjusted depending on the reference rate (usually the Libor). On this occasion, the spread paid by the borrower increased according to a predetermined scale, if his rating deteriorated.
- Spread-adjusted notes: the spread over the reference rate was re-determined at each interest payment date via a Dutch auction.[57]
- Spread-protected debt securities: investors had a put option to sell the securities back to the issuer after two years at a price equal to the net present value of the cash flows remaining to be paid, discounted at the risk-free rate plus a spread fixed in advance.

Finally, since 1971, options on default risk have been offered in the American municipal bonds market by the American Municipal Bond Association Corp (AMBAC) in the form of bond insurance.[58]

Thus, even though the foregoing instruments that already exist in the debt markets comply with the principle of, and have the same goals as, credit derivatives, they still do not offer the advantages of credit derivatives, not least, their capacity to unbundle the credit risk component and deal with it separately.

---

[56] See Finnerty (1993).
[57] Dutch auctions in the bond markets use the average bid to serve investors' orders.
[58] However, these products are limited to this market.

**Birth of credit derivatives**

The first credit derivatives were designed by Wall Street investment banks for their own needs. They were facing growing counterparty risks on their swaps portfolios, due to the explosive growth of the OTC derivatives market. To reduce their risks, these financial intermediaries were led to repackage and transfer these credit risks.

The first transactions in credit derivatives were arranged in late 1991: Bankers Trust issued structured notes referenced to the default risk of a basket of several names of Japanese banks, placed with Japanese investors. These notes enabled the bank to hedge its exposure to the credit risk of the banks underlying the product, to which it had sold Nikkei-linked bonds mostly in-the-money. That same year, Bankers Trust also arranged the first total return swap with Mellon Bank, enabling the latter to advance a new loan to one of its biggest clients, while transferring the associated credit risk to Bankers Trust. As of 1992, structured notes and off-balance-sheet products on credit risk, in the form of swaps and options, began to be offered by the other large American banks. At that time, the transactions had mostly a defensive object, the main purpose being to generate new credit lines. Investors were offered a considerably enhanced yield compared to those available in the market for similar credit qualities, a usual feature of placements of particularly innovative structures.

In retrospect, it is clear that the credit derivatives market was first driven by supply and by the higher yields offered to investors on these new products. Demand for higher yielding instruments was high in an environment of falling interest rates and tightening credit spreads on loans, euro-credits, etc. The supply of products rapidly became diversified, covering the entire range of derivatives, including swaps, options, and structured notes.

After this brief outline of how credit derivatives came to be created, we shall show their main common characteristics, those making them a unique financial product.

### 1.3.3.2 Nature of Credit Derivatives

Some of the characteristics of credit derivatives resemble those of other derivatives in certain aspects, while at the same time differentiating them substantially in others.

**OTC derivatives**

Credit derivatives belong to the category of tailor-made derivatives such as forwards, options, swaps, or structured products, that are traded on the OTC market. As for the other types of derivative, the principle of hedging via credit derivatives means taking a position on the derivatives market such that any loss on the underlying asset in the cash market can be compensated for by a gain in the derivatives position.

**A new class of products**

Some market observers postulate that credit derivatives are a new class of product distinct from traditional derivatives.[59] This is because ordinary derivatives, unlike credit derivatives, can be unbundled into building blocks. It is always possible, for instance, to analyze an interest rate swap as a portfolio of forward rate agreements (FRAs) or futures. On the contrary, a credit default swap is a building block in itself. Thus, a bank debt or a bond can be seen as a

---

[59] See Parsley (1996)

**Table 1.9**   Equity and credit compared

|  | Equity | Credit |
|---|---|---|
| Characteristics | Homogeneous | Heterogeneous |
| Maturity | Perpetual | Between 30 days and perpetuity |
| Classes | Usually between one and three | Numerous, depending on seniority, rating and covenants |
| Investors | Individuals and institutional investors | Mainly institutional investors: banks, insurance companies and asset managers |
| Issuers | Firms | Firms (including financial institutions), local authorities, governments, supranational organizations |
| Markets | Transparent and organized | Mainly over-the-counter markets |

combination of a risk-free instrument with duration, and a swap on the issuer's default risk. Under the terms and conditions of such contracts, the holder of a risky bond receives a risk premium to compensate him for a possible loss should the borrower default.

Thus, although it is possible to create interest rate swaps *ex nihilo* in a market they do not exist in, by analyzing rate differentials and using risk-free instruments, there is no theory allowing construction of a derivative hedging the credit risk of a nonrated counterparty in a market, without listed debt securities traded publicly.

This is why it is possible to view credit derivatives as a new class of products in themselves. We shall return to this in Chapter 7.

### A unique underlying risk: credit

The value of a credit derivative instrument is a function of the price of a credit-sensitive underlying (or reference) asset. These reference assets usually include bonds, loans, and asset swaps, which strongly differ from traditional underlying assets of other derivative contracts, such as equity, as illustrated in Table 1.9.

#### 1.3.3.3   Advantages of Credit Derivatives

Like all financial innovations, credit derivatives meet a basic need for traders in the financial markets, which is to be capable of identifying credit risk, trading it easily via simple market instruments, and hedging it.

### Unbundling of market and credit risks

The innovation introduced by credit derivatives is that credit risk can be separated from the other risk components of an asset (usually referred to as market risks), and can be transferred to other market players. Unbundling of the credit risk is usually possible whatever the underlying asset. Thus, credit derivatives enable credit risk to be managed and hedged separately from the other types of risk associated with the underlying asset.[60]

---

[60] To some extent, interest rate fluctuations can cause the creditworthiness of the asset underlying a credit derivative to deteriorate, by impairing the debtor's profitability, for example. It is therefore possible to say that immunization is never perfect.

## Trading credit risk

In the early days of this market, Citibank promoted credit derivatives with the following slogan: 'Instead of selling the asset, sell the risk associated with the asset.'[61] The second *raison d'être* of credit derivatives, directly linked to the first, is therefore that it can unbundle the credit risk of a debt instrument and transfer it to a third party. As Ron Tanemura, former joint head of credit derivatives at Deutsche Bank, points out: 'credit derivatives are a new application of the risk-transference property of derivatives.'[62] Credit derivatives enable the credit risk to be transferred without abandoning the ownership of the asset; for banks, they enable credit risk to be dissociated from the funding risk.

## Hedging of credit risk

Each debtor is unique and has credit risk characteristics that cannot easily be compared to those of other borrowers. Moreover, as previously underlined, debt securities are very heterogeneous, depending on their maturity and seniority, and on the associated covenants. Rating of debt securities has proved to be inadequate to homogenize this risk, as evinced by the varying spreads observed in the market for a class of assets with the same rating. This is why it is not possible to hedge the credit risk of a given borrower by means of a market index, since there is very low correlation between a counterparty's default risk and that represented by a basket of underlying obligors, even if they are in similar sectors of activity. Therefore the best way of hedging credit risk is to use instruments directly linked to the borrower. This is the role played by credit derivatives.

Credit derivatives came about because banks needed a simple market instrument to help them manage credit risk dynamically. These new products have common general features, as we have shown. We shall identify the different types of credit derivatives in the next chapter, and also show how they work and how they are applied.

---

[61] Nisbet (1995).
[62] Van Duyn (1995).

# 2
# Typology of Credit Derivatives and their Main Applications

Credit derivatives may be classified into three main families, depending on their mechanisms and purposes:

1. Credit default derivatives. These are without doubt the products considered the most innovative, since they enable trading and hedging strategies that did not exist in the financial markets before their creation. They protect their users against the occurrence of one (or several) credit event(s), generally defined in the contract as the failure to pay of the reference entity.
2. Credit spread derivatives. These instruments enable investors to take a position on the future level of the credit spread between two debt securities, independently of the absolute interest rate levels. The value of these products depends on the evolution of the credit spread on the reference securities, but, contrary to the case of credit default derivatives, it is not explicitly linked to the occurrence of certain predetermined credit events.
3. Products enabling synthetic replication of the performance of an underlying asset. This type of derivative, which was developed previously on other underlying assets (especially equity), enables investors to replicate the economic performance of an exposure to a credit risk synthetically without being obliged to buy the reference instrument. In exchange, the party synthetically selling his exposure hedges against the credit risk of the underlying asset.

The first category of products has experienced undeniable growth in recent years, especially credit default swaps. These are today the building blocks of the credit derivatives market, so much so that observers frequently tend to liken credit derivatives to them. On the other hand, the two other product types have remained relatively unknown and are generally offered to customers to enable them to solve very specific problems.

We have therefore chosen to devote most of this chapter to credit default swaps. We shall now attempt to describe their characteristics and main variations. Our second section will be devoted to the other types of credit derivative, such as credit spread products and synthetic replication products. Finally, the third section of this chapter will describe the main applications of credit derivatives.

## 2.1   CREDIT DEFAULT SWAPS

The particularity of credit default derivatives, of which the credit default swap (CDS) is the classic example, is that their payout is linked to the occurrence or non-occurrence of a credit event. We shall start this section by describing CDSs, and then compare them to cash credit products (bonds). We shall conclude with some examples of how these products are used.

### 2.1.1  Description of Credit Default Swaps

CDSs allow the credit risk of a reference entity underlying a contract (a corporate risk, a sovereign risk, etc.) to be transferred from one party to another synthetically, that is without selling the reference asset. These contracts enable the protection buyer (or risk seller) to hedge against the occurrence of determined events such as bankruptcy or default of the reference entity, likely to cause losses, by transferring the risk to the protection seller (or risk buyer).[1]

#### 2.1.1.1  Standard Mechanism of a CDS

A CDS may be defined as a bilateral financial contract leading one of the counterparties (the buyer of protection against the risk of default, or fixed rate payer) to pay a periodical (quarterly) fee (premium) – typically expressed in basis points of the total notional amount of the transaction – and the other counterparty (the seller of protection against the risk of default, or floating rate payer) to hold himself ready to make a contingent payment upon occurrence of a default (or any other predetermined credit event defined under the contract) of a third-party entity serving as reference to the contract (reference entity). The mechanism of a standard CDS is shown in Figure 2.1.

At inception of the transaction, no payment is required between the parties. The protection buyer has transferred to the protection seller the credit risk associated with the contract reference entity, for the term of the contract (typically, five years). The protection seller is at risk on the reference entity (if a credit event occurs during the transaction and the contract is triggered) and on the protection buyer (to the extent that the premium payments are scheduled over the duration of the contract). The protection buyer, on the other hand, has diluted his risk: it would require both the protection seller and the reference entity to default for him to be at risk.

Like a classic interest rate swap, a CDS may be divided up into a fixed and a floating leg:

- The fixed leg of the swap ($\times$ basis points per annum multiplied by the notional amount of the transaction) paid by the protection buyer (fixed rate payer) remunerates the protection seller's risk taking. Payments are made until the term of the contract but are stopped after the contract is exercised due to the occurrence of a credit event. Classically, premium payments are made every three months and calculated on an Actual/360 basis. Thus, for a CDS with a notional amount of 10 million euros traded at 50 basis points, the protection buyer will pay every three months:

$$10\,000\,000 \times 0.5\% \times (\text{number of days in the period})/360$$

  Where the three-monthly period counts 91 days, the amount the protection buyer will have to pay will be 12 639 euros.
- The floating leg is activated only where a credit event occurs during the contract life and the contract is exercised. The related payment under the floating leg should compensate the protection buyer for the loss suffered following the occurrence of a credit event. There are several methods of CDS settlement, which are presented below.

---

[1] We shall see later that in reality these contracts also allow a buyer to take a position on credit quality (including taking short positions, that is speculating on a drop in creditworthiness) yet not hedge the exposure. Furthermore, the compensation received by the protection buyer under the contract does not necessarily reflect exactly the loss he may have suffered as a result of a credit event (this being the critical difference between a credit derivative and an insurance contract, the payout of which exactly mirrors the loss suffered by the protection buyer or insured party).

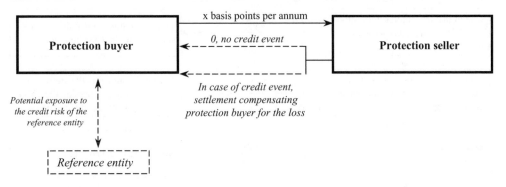

**Figure 2.1**   Mechanism of a credit default swap

Where a contract is triggered, premiums are no longer paid by the protection buyer, except for the last coupon, which is calculated on the period running from the previous premium payment to the date the contract is exercised.

### 2.1.1.2   Main Characteristics of a CDS Contract

Going beyond the features common to all derivatives contracts (trade and effective date, maturity,[2] premium, premium payment schedule, etc.), CDS contracts are particular in the conditions under which the contract is triggered. All these aspects are defined in the ISDA Definitions.[3] These detail the documentation and the legal definitions of the various terms used in a standard CDS contract. It should be noted that these Definitions were originally presented as a sort of menu on the basis of which the market gradually converged towards a standard contract: thus, five credit events are suggested in the Definitions, but only three are really used in standard European contracts, for instance.

**The reference entity**

As already mentioned, this item details the true nature of the entity on which the transaction counterparties swap the credit risk:

- Trade name for a corporate credit (e.g. France Telecom SA, Ford Motor Credit Company, etc.).
- Name of the country or the body issuing the sovereign debt guaranteed by the state for a sovereign credit (e.g. Republic of Italy, Bank of Greece, etc.).

This item, which at first view seems obvious, must be carefully handled by market traders. This is because multinational companies are usually made up of a large number of subsidiaries, and the name of the entity in the contract must correspond exactly to that on which the counterparties wish to exchange credit risk. It sometimes happens that a credit event concerns one group subsidiary without affecting the parent company, or vice versa.

---

[2] Called 'Scheduled Termination Date' in a CDS contract.
[3] 2003 Credit Derivatives Definitions (ISDA, 2003).

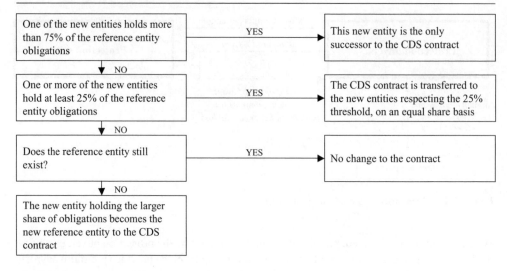

**Figure 2.2**    Process to be followed in case of merger or spin-off of the reference entity

*The case of Armstrong World Industries*

In 2000, Armstrong World Industries defaulted on its debt although its parent company, Armstrong Holdings, did not. At that time, some market participants had traded both these companies without differentiating between them, thinking they had hedged their positions back-to-back. Some contracts had even been referenced simply on 'Armstrong.' This example underlines the care that must be taken in choosing the reference entity. Indeed, it is worth noting that most large banks today use the services of a specialized lawyer in validating and monitoring reference entities, and that an external service provider (Mark-it Partners) offers market traders a database[4] updating information on reference entities.

*The notion of 'successor'*

Another problem raised by the notion of reference entity is what happens to the contract in the case of a merger, split or spin-off of the reference firm in the contract. Market players have been obliged to come to an agreement as to how to deal with this. Figure 2.2 shows their procedure.

**Obligations category**

This part of the contract precisely defines the type of debt or obligation to which the credit event occurs. The ISDA Definitions offer a range of options:

- Payment (i.e. any present or future payment by the reference entity).
- Borrowed money (the financial debt contracted by the reference entity).
- Bond or loan (bond debt or bank loan taken out by the reference entity).
- Other: bond only, loan only, reference obligation only.

---

[4] Reference Entity Database (RED).

The American and European markets use the standard borrowed money definition for obligations. Two remarks may be made about this clause:

1. The credit event must occur on a financial debt of the reference entity for the contract to be exercised by the protection buyer. This has important consequences, not least for corporates seeking to hedge against the risk of nonpayment of a trade receivable by means of a CDS. Trade receivables are not in the category of financial debts and so a company hedging against this type of risk using a 'standard' CDS would in fact not be protected against the risk of failure to pay (except in the event of a large default in which the reference entity fails on its financial debt simultaneously). This is one of the main obstacles to the massive entry of corporates in the credit derivatives market to manage their receivables.

2. In the early days of the market (1996–1997), CDSs were mostly based on a single reference obligation. Market traders quickly moved away from this model because the purpose of the credit derivatives market is not to make synthetic replications of existing risks on the underlying bond or bank loan markets, but rather to provide uniform handling of the credit risk, of whatever type, associated with a borrower (reference entity). In this way, the players in this market also managed to avoid the traps of the cash markets (liquidity constraints, issue size, or even absence of negotiable debt,[5] etc.). It is this evolution that has enabled the derivatives credit markets to become the preferred place for observing and trading credit risk (the notional amounts exchanged in this market are, indeed, often considerably higher than the amount of outstanding debt issued by the underlying credits).

## Credit events

This item in the contract enables the nature of the events giving rise to exercise of the CDS contract to be detailed. Existing credit events are:

- Bankruptcy of the reference entity, that is, any administrative document, declaration, action, or decision confirming that the reference entity can no longer fulfil its obligations (for example placing it in Chapter 11 administration in the United States).
- Failure to pay means, after giving effect to any applicable grace period, the failure by the reference entity to make, when due, any payments equal to or exceeding the payment requirement[6] (if any) under any obligations.
- Restructuring; the main causes of debt restructuring are acknowledged as being:
  - Decrease in the rates or amounts of interest due by the reference borrower.
  - Reduction of the nominal amount due.
  - Extension of the repayment installments.
  - Change in the subordination ranking of an obligation.
  - Change of currency (for a nonstandard one).
  Restructuring applies if and only if the following conditions are met:
  - The amount of the restructured debt is over $10 m or its equivalent in the currency concerned.
  - The changes were not anticipated when the issue was made (example of a debt issued with a step-up coupon, which then would not qualify as a restructuring event).

---

[5] For instance, Finnish mobile phone manufacturer Nokia has never issued bonds in the capital markets, yet the CDS indexed on Nokia's credit risk is traded daily in the derivatives market.

[6] Usually set at one million dollars (or its equivalent in other currencies).

- The occurrence of any of the above events is directly or indirectly due to deterioration in the creditworthiness of the reference entity.
- Obligation acceleration or obligation default: this credit event is virtually no longer used in the market.
- Repudiation or moratorium on the debt, a credit event that only concerns sovereign risks and can only trigger the contract if such an event is followed by a restructuring or failure to pay within a certain time frame.

While the first of these events concerns the reference entity (where it is a corporate), the others concern the category of obligations to which the event occurs. Thus, in the unlikely event that the counterparties have chosen only bond in the obligation type, for instance, a failure to pay would only trigger the contract if it happened under a bond security.

### Conditions to payment

Once a credit event has occurred, the contract will be triggered when the protection buyer or seller has served notice of the credit event upon the counterparty (Credit Event Notice), and delivered a Notice of Publicly Available Information, generally two paper or electronic news articles from reliable sources ('Standard Public Sources'), relating the occurrence of the event.[7]

### Methods of settling the contract (settlement terms)

Once the contract is exercised, the settlement procedure must be organized. Several options are possible.

#### Physical settlement

This is the most commonly used settlement method by market players. The protection buyer delivers a portfolio of the reference entity's obligations (usually bonds or loans) to the seller, in exchange for which the protection seller pays the buyer an amount equal to the notional amount of the transaction. This settlement method means that the protection buyer sells discounted debt instruments (because of the occurrence of the credit event) at par value. It is therefore critical to identify at inception of the contract which instruments (deliverable obligations) the protection buyer will be able to deliver to the seller should a credit event occur.

#### Reference obligation

There is often confusion between the reference obligation and deliverable obligations. In a standard contract, the protection buyer is not necessarily obliged to deliver the reference obligation. The only purpose of the reference obligation is to determine the seniority of the obligations the protection buyer can deliver to the seller should the contract be exercised. The protection buyer may in fact deliver obligations of at least equal seniority to that of the reference obligation.

---

[7] In the early days of the market, contracts involved a 'materiality test,' which was the measurement of the widening of the reference asset credit spread above a materiality threshold specified beforehand (e.g. 150 basis points over Euribor). This materiality test is now no longer used, due to the fact that the market has moved away from trading CDSs on a specific reference asset towards trading the generic credit risk of the reference entity ('Borrowed Money').

*Deliverable obligations*

Here, too, the ISDA Definitions offer several options, such as bonds, loans, etc. In the European market it is standard for the (bond or loan) category to be used, which means that the protection buyer can deliver any bond security or any bank debt to the seller. This rule comprises a number of restrictions.[8] The most important of these is that the residual maturity of the obligations delivered must not exceed 30 years, they must be in a G7 currency or Swiss francs, the buyer can only deliver bank loans if they are assignable (freely or with the borrower's consent), and can only deliver obligations if their seniority is at least equal to that of the reference obligation. This possibility for the protection buyer to choose the security(ies) he wishes to deliver actually gives him a cheapest-to-deliver option: it is likely that upon settlement of the contract, the buyer will seek to source the cheapest debt in the market (i.e. the most discounted) to deliver to the protection seller, in order to maximize the gain on the CDS.

---

*The Railtrack case*

This was a classic case in 2001. It became famous because of the disagreement between Nomura and Credit Suisse First Boston (CSFB). In the course of its standard trading activity on convertible bonds, Nomura had bought CDSs on Railtrack from CSFB. When Railtrack was placed in administration in October 2001, CSFB, contrary to the other investment banks, deemed that the CDS contract excluded convertible bonds from deliverable obligations.[9] As a result of this dispute, Nomura was obliged to sell its convertible bonds and buy more expensive fixed rate bonds, which cost the bank £1.2 m. The case went before the High Court of Justice in London and the judge held in favor of Nomura, confirming the opinion given by the ISDA at the time of the Railtrack credit event.

---

*Cash settlement*

An alternative settlement method enables delivery of obligations to be avoided. In this case, at settlement, the protection seller pays the buyer an amount equal to the par (100%) less the post-default value of the reference obligation. This value is determined by obtaining firm (or indicative) bid quotations in the secondary market for the reference obligation from a sample of market makers.

This type of settlement is practically no longer used in the market. The price discovery procedure is sometimes cumbersome and above all, this type of settlement is not equivalent to physical settlement since there is no cheapest-to-deliver option. It is therefore less advantageous for the protection buyer. Nevertheless, many investors do not wish (or, for regulatory reasons, for example, cannot) contract a CDS with physical settlement.[10] The solution that has gradually been adopted is to set up a cash settlement procedure on a portfolio of obligations that replicates the characteristics of a physical settlement.

---

[8] These are called deliverable obligation characteristics, which must be checked by the deliverable obligations.

[9] The argument was that these bonds were in reality contingent securities. There is traditionally an 'orphan and widow' clause converting bonds into shares when the embedded equity option is strongly in-the-money.

[10] Especially when deliverable obligations include loans. Many institutional investors are prevented by the regulations from holding loans on their balance sheet and have limited capacity to lead on the recovery procedure, as opposed to banks.

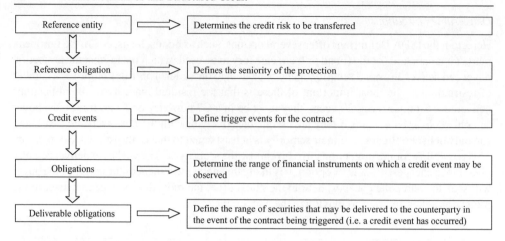

**Figure 2.3**   Structure of a CDS contract

*A special cash settlement: fixed payout*

In this type of contract, the amount the seller pays where a credit event occurs is predetermined (e.g. 50% of par).[11] Settlement of these contracts is thus very fast. Furthermore, they can be very attractive for investors wishing to take a position on the risk of an entity defaulting but not on the recovery rate of the obligations in default. However, these contracts remain relatively illiquid for the moment. In certain aspects, they resemble a new variation on CDSs, equity default swaps (EDSs), which we will return to in Section 3.2.

CDSs have many characteristics. In the early days of the market, the absence of standard contracts clearly hampered its development and liquidity, since the main market makers were led to take legal 'basis risks' to hedge their positions with contracts that did not all have the same legal characteristics. It was therefore crucial for the main players to come to a rapid agreement on a market standard. This evolution came after long and intense negotiations in the ISDA and also after several credit events that repeatedly raised new problems that needed to be sorted out. Figure 2.3 synthesizes the key items in a standard CDS contact.

### 2.1.1.3   Main Legal Evolutions and Creation of a Market Standard

In this paragraph we shall deal with the creation of the ISDA Definitions and the development of market standards.

**Birth of the ISDA Definitions: from absence of legal framework in the early 1990s to the debate on the definition of restructuring**

The creation of the Definitions and the standardization of CDS contracts played an important role in developing these products. It was only in 1999 that the ISDA published the first

---

[11] A particular form of fixed payout CDS is the 'digital' CDS, for which the level of recovery is arbitrarily fixed at zero should a credit event occur.

Definitions[12] adopted by the market as a whole. They came in the wake of the first massive wave of CDS contracts triggering in 1998, during the moratorium on sovereign Russian debt. The problems that arose at that time due to poor understanding of the contracts used (often over ten pages and differing from one counterparty to the next) highlighted the necessity to set up a uniform legal framework accepted by all market players. The publication of the ISDA Definitions in 1999[13] enabled the market to grow more swiftly with contracts limited to three or four pages, in which all the main terms were pre-defined.

The relatively high number of credit events occurring between 1999 and 2003 (Railtrack, Enron, Worldcom, Conseco, Pacific Gas & Electric, and Argentina, to name only the most well known) enabled the soundness of these contracts to be tested in practice. Some of the Definitions that might have given rise to confusion were also clarified.

Thus, it should be noted that while the definitions of bankruptcy or failure to pay were not subject to argument, the notion of restructuring was, and the main market players argued over it for a long time. More particularly, they criticized the fact that the original definition placed banks in a more advantageous situation than the other market players. In theory, it made it possible for a bank to buy protection on a company in trouble to which it had granted a bilateral loan, and then to offer to restructure this loan at better terms for the bank. It would then make money by benefiting from the re-negotiated loan at better conditions, and also by being able to trigger the protection it had bought.

To avoid this, the current definition of restructuring provides that the contract can only be triggered if the restructured loan is granted by three unconnected institutions and if a minimum of two-thirds of the creditors agree to the restructuring. This rule *de facto* excludes bilateral loans and is called the 'multiple holder obligation.'

---

*The Conseco case*

In August 2000, Conseco, a US-based company specialized in consumer credit, was taken over by the finance magnate Gary Wendt. This buy-out caused the restructuring of part of its debt (some $3 bn). CDS contracts referenced on the company were therefore triggered. This classic case has not only shown that there is a contingent cheapest-to-deliver obligation option embedded in CDS contracts, but has also highlighted the enviable position of the banking institutions party to the debt re-negotiation. Most of Conseco's bank debt was restructured during this transaction but it was also protected by a higher coupon, a new guarantee, and better safeguards for creditors. In no case could this bank debt be valued as cheaply as certain bond securities with residual maturity of over 20 years, trading at a considerably discounted price due to their low coupons. Naturally, these assets were the first to be delivered when the CDSs were settled, thus highlighting the favorable position of creditors when they control the negotiating process and have an influence on a credit event.

---

As a result of these events, the 2003 Credit Derivatives Definitions were published and are currently used by the market for credit derivatives transactions.

---

[12] In reality an initial document was proposed to market players in 1998, but the lack of liquidity in the inter-bank market hampered implementation of the Definitions.

[13] 1999 Credit Derivatives Definitions (ISDA, 1999).

**Restructuring/modified restructuring/modified modified restructuring**

However, while the foregoing Definitions provide the most polished version, it should be noted that the market has not adopted a uniform standard for all the underlying assets traded. Thus, the contract will be adapted depending on whether the reference entity is an American or European corporate or an Asian sovereign. While some differences can be explained naturally (thus, the notion of bankruptcy does not apply to a sovereign borrower and therefore this credit event does not appear in a contract dealing with a sovereign risk), others are due to banks' incapacity to come to an agreement on a single standard. The main point on which they disagree is (still) the definition of the restructuring credit event. We have already noted the heated discussions that this issue has caused in the credit derivatives market community.

Today, there are still two main uses of restructuring, depending on the underlying asset. If the latter is an American credit, the market trades it in modified restructuring (Mod R). However, if the reference entity is a European or Asian credit, the market uses modified modified restructuring (Mod Mod R).

In respect of North American reference entities, the modified restructuring standard prevents the buyer from delivering a deliverable obligation that has a final maturity date later than the earlier of:

- 30 months following the date of the relevant restructuring.
- The latest final maturity date of any bond or loan of the relevant reference entity in respect of which a restructuring credit event has occurred.[14]

This limit on the permitted maturity date of deliverable obligations provides some protection to sellers against the cheapest-to-deliver option embedded in the physical settlement procedure.

In respect of a European reference entity, however, where the contract is triggered by the CDS buyer, the modified modified restructuring standard prevents the buyer from delivering a deliverable obligation that has a final maturity date later than the later of:

- The scheduled termination date.
- 60 months following the date of the relevant restructuring (in the case of restructured bonds or loans) or 30 months following the date of the relevant restructuring (in the case of all other deliverable obligations).

Again, this rule provides some protection to sellers against the cheapest-to-deliver option, but the protection is less than that provided by Mod R.

Mod Mod R was developed by European participants in an attempt to bring together what had become a bifurcated market, following the adoption of Mod R by most North American participants. However, despite these efforts, the credit derivatives market remains bifurcated at this stage, no worldwide consensus having emerged from this debate. It should be noted, nevertheless, that these different standards do not give rise to 'basis risk' of legal documentation in the CDS portfolios, since they apply to different underlying assets (North American as opposed to European and Asian credits). It can also be observed that in the case of American high-yield credits, the standard deals with only two credit events: bankruptcy and failure to pay.

The future of restructuring as a credit event should largely depend on the importance the Basel Committee continues to give it in the framework of the new capital adequacy ratio. Hitherto, the regulatory authorities imposed the restructuring credit event in contracts so that

---

[14] In any event, the final maturity date of any deliverable obligation cannot be later than the date falling 30 months following the scheduled termination date.

**Table 2.1** Main market standards for CDS contracts

| | European corporates | US corporates | Emerging markets (Latin America, Eastem Europe) |
|---|---|---|---|
| Credit events | Bankruptcy Failure to pay Modified modified restructuring | Bankruptcy Failure to pay Modified restructuring | Failure to pay Repudiation/moratorium Obligation acceleration Restructuring |
| Obligation category | Borrowed money | Borrowed money | Bond |
| Obligation characteristics | None | None | Not domestic currency Not domestic law Not domestic issuance Not subordinated |
| Physical settlement period | 30 Business days | Section 8.6 of the 2003 ISDA Definitions capped at 30 business days | Section 8.6 of the 2003 ISDA Definitions |
| Deliverable obligation | Bond or loan | Bond or loan | Bond |
| Deliverable obligation Characteristics | Standard specified currencies Not subordinated Assignable loan Consent required loan Transferable Not contingent Not bearer Maximum maturity: 30 years | Standard specified currencies Not subordinated Assignable loan Consent required loan Transferable Not contingent Not bearer Maximum maturity: 30 years | Standard specified currencies Not domestic law Not domestic issuance Not subordinated Not contingent Not bearer Transferable |

the protection buyer could benefit from lower capital charges. With the new ratio, the regulatory capital relief should be limited to 60% of the underlying amount where there is no restructuring clause. This stringent requirement should ensure that this credit event remains in use, especially for contracts between banks seeking to optimize their regulatory capital base.

## Main market standards

As seen earlier, a market standard gradually developed from the existing Definitions, subject to the foregoing remarks on the restructuring clause. To be precise, it should be noted that the standard depends on the credit risk traded in the contract (corporate or sovereign).

Table 2.1 shows the main differences between a CDS contract on an underlying European corporate, an investment grade US corporate, and an emerging market sovereign risk.

### 2.1.2 Comparison Between the CDS Market and the Cash Market: Basis

The credit derivatives market enables a bond risk to be replicated synthetically, and so it seems relevant to compare the two markets to pinpoint the main differences. The main indicator between these two markets is the 'basis,' that is the difference between the CDS premium paid by the protection buyer and the spread of an asset swap.[15]

---

[15] See Section 1.2.3.2.

In theory, the absence of arbitrage opportunity in capital markets should bring the two indicators relatively close to each other. In other words, the basis should equal zero. In practice, many divergences may be observed between asset swap spreads and CDS premiums. These are due to both structural and cyclical factors.

### 2.1.2.1 Structural Factors

There are five structural reasons for the divergences between CDS premiums and asset swap spreads.

### Indexation to credit events

A CDS contract is exercised when a credit event occurs. The European standard cites three types of credit event: bankruptcy, failure to pay, and restructuring. These credit events may be observed on all underlying borrowed money.

The risk taken by the protection seller is therefore greater than that for the holder of a bond of the same maturity, since a credit event may not affect the particular security but would nevertheless trigger the contract. This tends to widen the basis (that is, it widens the difference between the CDS premium and the asset swap spread, for the same reference borrower).

### The cheapest-to-deliver option

When a credit event is observed, it is up to the protection buyer to determine the portfolio of deliverable obligations he envisages delivering to the protection seller. The buyer will probably seek to source and deliver the cheapest debt available in the market: this is the cheapest-to-deliver option.

In the event of a default, the protection seller will receive the cheapest deliverable obligations (i.e. the lowest priced) and it is therefore required that this option be paid for by the protection buyer in the form of a higher premium. This phenomenon therefore also tends to widen the basis.

### Cost of repos

While protection can be bought and sold in the CDS market quite easily, that is, taking a short position[16] or along one on a credit, in the bond market it is very difficult or even impossible to sell a security short beyond certain deadlines (usually a few weeks). When it is possible, taking a short position in the cash market actually means borrowing the security to sell it through a repurchase agreement (or 'repo') and therefore paying a 'repo' cost.

Because of these problems and the costs involved in taking short positions in the cash market, market players tend to prefer the derivatives market so that they can take short positions on a borrower's creditworthiness. This strategy for buying protection rather than selling a security short also contributes to widening of the base.

---

[16] In other words, taking the view that the reference entity's creditworthiness will deteriorate.

**An off-balance-sheet product**

One of the main differences between an asset swap and a CDS is that the latter is an off-balance-sheet product. It thus does not generate financing costs and does not affect the balance sheet of the institutions dealing in it. This characteristic makes it particularly attractive for investors, the funding cost of which exceeds Euribor.

---

*Example*

Let us take a bank XYZ rated A, procuring finance at an average Euribor +25 basis points over five years, which wishes to invest in the credit risk of firm S. It can either buy a five-year bond, swap the interest rate risk and receive Euribor +60 basis points, or sell a CDS with an annual premium of 50 basis points. In the first case, the bank would need to set up a carry strategy offering it 35 basis points of net margin (asset swap spread minus funding cost). In the second case, it would receive 50 basis points because there are no financing costs involved.

---

This phenomenon tends to reduce the spreads on the CDS market, all the more so as most players in the market obtain finance above Euribor.

**A tailor-made product**

One of the main advantages of CDSs for investors is their flexibility. In the bond market, paper buyers are constrained by the nature of the available stubs and their liquidity (which may sometimes be low). On the contrary, with CDSs, it is easy to take a long or short position on the maturity and size desired, since the product is completely synthetic and does not depend on the existence or the liquidity of a bond stub. Furthermore, with a CDS, the maximum loss possible for the protection seller is limited to the notional amount of the contract (corrected by the effective recovery rate) while in the bond market, the latter ultimately depends on the level of interest rates.

These characteristics also tend to shrink the credit spreads in the CDS market.

*2.1.2.2 Cyclical Reasons*

Several cyclical factors influence the evolution of the basis. The most important of these are presented below.

**The synthetic securitization market**

As we shall see in Chapters 4 and 5, the last few years have been marked by the phenomenal growth in the synthetic securitization market. Contrary to more traditional securitization in which the collateral used is composed of bonds or bank loans, synthetic transactions are based on collateral made up of CDSs. Thus, when a bank launches a new synthetic securitization transaction, it is directly led to buy large amounts of protection (investors usually being risk takers). These purchases must be covered by the resale of CDSs in the market.

The large volumes of synthetic securitizations thus led to significant shrinking of CDS margins in 2002 and 2003.

## The convertible bond market

A new issue of convertible bonds generally causes CDS spreads to widen. This is because a large number of players in the convertible bond market (especially hedge funds) are buying these new issues to arbitrage the embedded equity volatility available through the conversion option. These players buy securities at each new issue and cover their credit risk by buying protection via CDSs.

## Taking short positions on credit spreads

As described earlier, it is difficult to sell a bond short in the cash market. Thus, if an investor seeks to gamble on an issuer's deteriorated creditworthiness, he will naturally prefer to use the derivatives market to buy protection. This strategy is all the more worthwhile for low credit spreads or excellent ratings, for which the potential for improvement is poor.

These positions generally result in CDS spreads widening compared to the bond market.

### 2.1.2.3   Relationship Between Creditworthiness and Basis Level

Figures 2.4 and 2.5 illustrate the relationships between creditworthiness (measured by the reference entity's credit rating or by the bond spread) and the basis.

Figure 2.4 shows the relationship between a borrower's rating and the basis between the spreads in force on its bond debt and CDS. For highly rated borrowers, it is relatively cheap

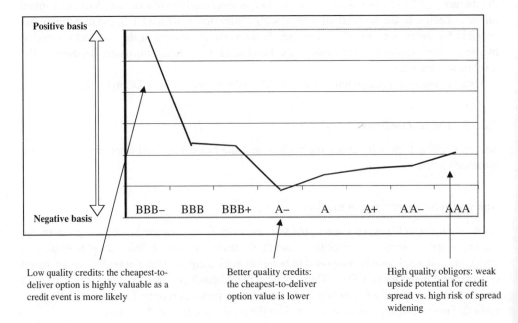

**Figure 2.4**   Relationship between rating and basis

**Credit spread vs. basis (in bp)**

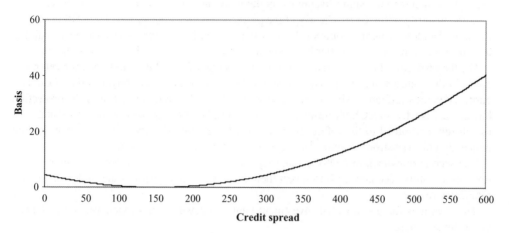

**Figure 2.5** Relationship between credit spreads and basis

to buy protection and the potential for deteriorated creditworthiness is high, thus justifying a generally positive basis. For the worst-rated firms, i.e. those with a high credit risk, the effects of the cheapest-to-deliver option and indexation of the CDS to several credit events dominate, and cause substantial widening of the basis.

Figure 2.5 shows the same effects in terms of credit spread.

### 2.1.3 Main Variations on CDSs

While CDSs are far and away the most commonly used credit derivatives, financial engineers have been led to create variations to widen the potential user base for these products, or to enable new applications. While not going into second-generation credit derivatives, which will be dealt with in the next chapters and can be distinguished by the fact that they use the building block that is the CDS, this section will present three variations of the standard CDS:

- The credit-linked note (CLN), or bond linked to the risk of default; this is the 'funded' variation of the CDS.
- The constant maturity default swap (CMDS), the creation of which has been inspired by instruments used in the interest rate derivatives market, among others.
- The equity default swap, the recent launching of which (in early 2004) was designed to create ever-closer links between the credit and equity markets.

#### 2.1.3.1  The Credit-Linked Note

This corresponds to a CDS embedded into a bond. Contrary to the CDS, it requires the risk taker (the protection seller) to fund its position in the credit risk.

#### Reasons for the creation of CLNs

Like all derivatives, CDSs generate a counterparty risk for both parties to the contract. Thus, the protection seller is at risk on the protection buyer in respect of the premium paid by the latter (which, in a standard contract, is in installments). The theoretical amount of the risk he bears corresponds to the sum (discounted at the risky rate) of all the premiums to be received until the maturity of the CDS. Clearly, if the protection buyer stops paying the CDS premium, the seller can terminate the contract (his risk then becoming a hedging risk on his remaining long position, supposing the seller has hedged his initial contract back-to-back in the market).

For the protection buyer the risk is different: it is one of correlation between the reference entity in the contract and the protection seller. The risk borne by the buyer is that these two entities default simultaneously. Here, the seller would not be able to indemnify the protection buyer. That is why, in a CDS transaction, it is essential that the protection seller's risk not be too closely correlated to the reference entity (the buyer should then avoid any shareholding connection or over-strong commercial dependence between the two entities, etc.).

The second drawback of CDSs is that they are off-balance-sheet products, yet many institutional investors seek above all to invest their cash, or are not able to trade in derivatives for regulatory reasons.

These various factors have led investment banks to develop the funded version of CDSs: credit-linked notes.

### Mechanism of a CLN

A CLN is the synthetic replication of a bond in the CDS market. Like an ordinary bond, a CLN can be described as a promise to make regular payments of interest (coupons) and repayment of the principal at maturity. The special feature of the CLN is that it links repayment of the principal and payment of interest to the performance of a reference credit.

A bank wishing to buy protection against the credit risk of entity XYZ issues a CLN, the repayment of which is indexed to the performance of credit XYZ. There are two possibilities. In the absence of a credit event on XYZ (corresponding to the standard credit events of a CDS contract), the bank pays the interest on the CLN until maturity and repays 100% of the principal at maturity. However, if a credit event does occur before the CLN maturity, it is terminated early (i.e. repaid in advance), and coupon payments stop at the early termination date. The method of advance repayment is the same as for settlement of a CDS: the investor receives a portfolio of obligations issued by XYZ (CLN physical settlement) or receives an amount representing the market value of the securities in default (CLN cash settlement).

Figure 2.6 shows the mechanism of a CLN.

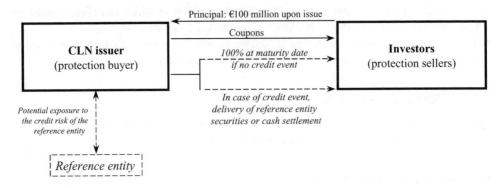

**Figure 2.6**  Mechanism of a credit-linked note

Mostly, credit-linked notes are issued either by banks via their euro-medium term notes program (or EMTNs), or by specialized issuing entities, bankruptcy-remote special-purpose vehicles (SPVs), usually located offshore.

- In the first case, it is important to note that investors are taking a double credit risk, that of the reference entity in the CLN and that of the issuing bank. In the event the latter defaults, the investors would find themselves ranked among the ordinary creditors, under the provisions of the EMTN prospectus, and could suffer loss even if the reference entity in the note did not default. In this case, the spread of the CLN should theoretically take account of this twofold risk and offer a coupon equal to the sum of the CDS premium of the underlying reference entity and the funding spread of the issuing bank above Euribor (in the absence of correlation between them).
- In the second case, the cash generated by the CLN issue is mostly invested in high-quality securities (usually rated AAA/Aaa), pledged to the investors in the SPV and thus avoiding a twofold credit risk to a large extent.

Contrary to a CDS, in which the protection buyer takes the risk of simultaneous default of the protection seller and the reference entity, in a CLN the protection buyer (the CLN issuer) bears no counterparty risk. He receives liquidity at the start of the transaction and only repays it if there is no credit event: a CLN is the equivalent of a fully collateralized CDS.

### Advantages and drawbacks of CLNs

The main advantage of CLNs is that they give investors an alternative to the traditional bond market and offer tailored investment opportunities. As for CDSs, investors can choose the maturity, the currency, and the underlying credit risk for their investment. Unlike CDSs, the CLN is in the form of a bond and therefore has those legal characteristics. It is therefore a means for investors without the right to trade off-balance-sheet products to invest in the credit derivatives/structured credit market.

These arrangements enable bond investors to diversify the risk profile of their portfolio, for instance by achieving exposure to names the securities of which are not available for direct purchase in the market. Furthermore, these structured notes are always less expensive and liquid than the securities of the underlying issuers, where they exist. Investors using such paper are seeking yield enhancement and so it is all the more worth their while to seek issuers with a positive basis since it enables them to structure papers with higher yields than those available in the cash market. On the other hand, the drawback of the CLN is that it is less liquid than a CDS or a bond. In general, issues are limited to some tens of millions of dollars and are directed at a small number of purchasers, and, as a result, there is no real secondary market in them. Thus, an investor seeking to exit a CLN position is likely to have no choice but to ask the bank having issued the note what it would pay to buy it back, thus exposing itself to a potentially unattractive bid–offer spread.

### 2.1.3.2   Constant Maturity Default Swaps

CMDSs are hybrids midway between CDSs and constant maturity swaps, a relatively popular form of interest rate swaps.

**Reasons for the creation of CMDSs**

The first CMDS transactions were carried out by Goldman Sachs in 1997. The rationale was to apply the techniques successfully developed in the interest rate derivatives market (CMSs) to the credit market.

CMSs were developed from the American mortgage-backed securities (MBS) derivatives market. A CMS works like a classic rate swap except that one of the legs references a swap rate other than the Libor or the Euribor and is reset at regular intervals to follow the fluctuations in the interest rate markets. These instruments allow investors to take positions on the forward interest rate curve and its volatility. They are relatively sought after in Europe by institutional investors, especially insurance companies, to implement effective asset/liability management strategies.

**Mechanism of CMDSs**

Most of the terms and conditions of a CMDS are identical to those of a standard CDS. Thus, CMDS credit events, triggering conditions, and settlement processes are similar to those of standard CDSs. However, the former differs in that the contract premium level is reset periodically in reference to the evolution of the CDS premium of the reference entity on a specified maturity (typically five years). Thus, a CMDS contract also includes a reference constant maturity, a percentage factor,[17] and a reset frequency.

The initial CMDS premium is set by multiplying the CDS premium on the reference maturity by the percentage factor. Then, at each date the CMDS rate is reset (generally every three months), the CDS rate on the reference maturity is observed, and the CMDS premium is recalculated by multiplying this rate by the percentage factor.

Example. Let us suppose that a CMDS is priced 80% to 90% (pricing is generally on the basis of the value of the percentage factor), with a reference constant maturity equal to five years and a quarterly reset frequency. At the same date the underlying five-year CDS is quoted at 100 basis points per annum. If the buyer purchases protection in the form of a 90% CMDS, the first rate will be fixed at 90 basis points (90% × 100 basis points). The CMDS rate will then be reset on a quarterly basis, as in Table 2.2.

**Table 2.2**   CDS and CMDS compared premiums

| Reset date | Five-year CDS premium at reset date (in basis points) | CMDS premium for the following quarter (in basis points) |
|---|---|---|
| 20 March 2005 | 100.0 | 90.0 |
| 20 June 2005 | 95.0 | 85.5 |
| 20 September 2005 | 80.0 | 72.0 |
| 20 December 2005 | 130.0 | 117.0 |
| 20 March 2006 | 100.0 | 90.0 |

---

[17] Also called participation rate.

**Table 2.3**   Main strategies using CMDSs

|                              | Strategy 1           | Strategy 2                                      | Strategy 3            | Strategy 4                                    |
| ---------------------------- | -------------------- | ----------------------------------------------- | --------------------- | --------------------------------------------- |
| CMDS                         | Sell                 | Buy                                             | Buy                   | Sell                                          |
| CDS                          | —                    | Sell                                            | —                     | Buy                                           |
| Exposure to default risk     | Yes, long position   | No                                              | Yes, short position   | No                                            |
| Exposure to credit spread risk | No                 | Short position: gain when spreads tighten       | No                    | Long position: gain when spreads widen        |

In a classic CDS, the premium is initially determined at inception of the transaction, and remains stable over the term of the CDS, whatever the changes in the underlying creditworthiness. Thus, a CMDS packaged with a classic CDS[18] enables the credit spread risk to be unbundled from the default risk (or that of a credit event), since the investors are exposed to one of the two, depending on their positions in the swaps, but not to both as in a classic CDS when protection is sold.

**Advantages and drawbacks of CMDSs**

Transactions on CMDSs are particularly attractive in an environment of low credit spreads, as was the case at end 2003–early 2004. The main transactions allowed investors to gamble on the widening of the credit spreads, without being protected against the risk of the reference entity defaulting. It was thus a cheaper means for investors to take a short position on the credit risk (without being protected against default) and thus gamble on the creditworthiness deterioration.

The main strategies using CMDSs are shown in Table 2.3.

In addition to their transactions on a single reference entity, investment banks offering this type of product have applied them to reference credit portfolios. Goldman Sachs thus arranged a CMDS transaction on an underlying portfolio of 72 reference credits in March 2004. This is the largest known transaction to date.[19]

For investors, the main drawback of CMDSs is their absence of liquidity, since they are relatively recent and are far from achieving the transaction volumes of 'vanilla' CDSs. Furthermore, dealing with this kind of product requires a sound understanding of the concepts of slope and forwards, and their volatility. As one Goldman Sachs trader noted, 'I expect this business to pick up but, despite the appeal of the product, I would urge investors to be careful. They need to understand the slope and volatility risks embedded in any CMS trade.'[20]

### 2.1.3.3   Equity Default Swaps

EDSs are a new hybrid product, halfway between credit and equity derivatives, launched by JP Morgan Chase in May 2003.

---

[18] This is then called a CMSS (constant maturity spread swap). See strategies 2 and 4 below.

[19] See de Teran (2004). In this particular instance, Goldman Sachs made use of its experience on the American MBS markets.

[20] Cited by de Teran (2004).

**Reasons for the creation of EDSs**

There are three main reasons for the creation of these new products:

1. First, the widespread narrowing of credit spreads as of 2003. The absence of high spreads made the CDS market less attractive for investors but also for the arrangers of structured products (not least synthetic CDOs),[21] which need yield to create high performance and attractive structures for investors, while maintaining high levels of profitability for themselves.
2. Second, the wish of arrangers to widen the range of risks available for credit investors. There are far more listed companies in the stock markets than are actively traded in the CDS or Eurobond markets.
3. Third, the increasing interpenetration between the various financial markets, in particular between the equity and credit derivatives markets. This increased overlapping can be seen, for example, in the implementation of convertible arbitrage via hedge funds, or in the equity–credit arbitrage strategies based on Robert Merton's firm value model and its adaptations.[22] More and more players in the market are trading in both of these segments, and need a product able to bridge the gap between them.

**Mechanism of EDSs**

An EDS functions like a CDS, but with reference to the stock market rather than the credit market. More correctly, the underlying risk of an EDS is that of the fluctuation in a share price or a basket of shares.

As with a CDS, an EDS buyer pays a premium to his counterparty in exchange for the undertaking that he will receive an amount in compensation should an event occur. In the particular case of an EDS, these two aspects differ fundamentally from those of the CDS inasmuch as:

• The event leading the EDS seller to compensate the buyer is a fall in the price of the underlying share(s) of the EDS beyond a predetermined threshold. Traditionally, that threshold is 30% of the value of the share(s) at the conclusion of the transaction.
• The amount paid by the seller to the buyer in compensation for the aforesaid event is a fixed payout, typically 50% of the notional amount of the transaction.
• These two items may in theory be fixed independently by the parties to the contract, even if market practice is largely based on the 30% and 50% levels, respectively.

**Advantages and drawbacks of EDSs**

The first advantage of an EDS (and indeed, why it was created) is to provide an instrument with a higher yield than a CDS inasfar as the seller must be remunerated for taking on equity volatility, which is considerably greater than mere default volatility. Thus, in mid-February 2004, a five-year CDS on Suez risk was traded at 52 basis points per annum, while the corresponding EDS offered 105 basis points. Thus, an EDS looks more like an out-of-the money put, with a strike set at 30% of the share price at inception of the transaction, than a CDS.

---

[21] Collateralized debt obligations, see Chapter 4 for a detailed discussion of these products.
[22] See Chapter 5 for the former and Chapter 6 for the latter (presentation of structural or firm value models).

The second advantage of EDSs compared to CDSs is that they simplify the mechanism of these products considerably, not least the more arguable sides of CDSs. Thus, with an EDS, the event triggering settlement of the swap is very easily identifiable and cannot be contested: all it needs is for the share or reference basket price to fall below the threshold. Similarly, the swap settlement procedure is simplified because it works like a fixed payout cash settlement. Even if this aspect is not revolutionary in itself, it enables uncertainty as about the recovery rate to be dispelled in the event of default.

A third advantage of EDSs is that they give access to a wider range of underlying risks than the credit market. This is valuable for structured products referencing risk portfolios, since it is possible to bundle CDSs and EDSs, thus offering investors not only more diversified portfolios (including underlying names not usually traded in the credit markets) but also higher yields.

Finally, these instruments are likely to provide new hedging means to credit portfolio managers, not least in banks. Thus, it has been shown that the liquidity of the CDS market had tended to drop sharply for reference borrowers on the brink of default, such as Alstom in 2002.[23] Risk managers may be tempted to hedge risk by using EDSs, which benefit from the virtually permanent liquidity of the underlying equity markets. This trend is also bolstered by the growing use of so-called 'structural' credit risk valuation models, which link default risk with the evolution of the share price of the reference entity.

Midway between CDSs and out-of-the-money equity puts, EDSs do not have major drawbacks, as long as they are mastered: they show greater volatility than CDSs. In this respect, they have contributed no fundamental innovation to the derivatives market, unlike CDSs, but have rather introduced attractive marketing packaging for hybrid instruments, above all of service to the arrangers of structured products.

## 2.2   OTHER CREDIT DERIVATIVES

This section presents the two other types of credit derivative:

- Credit spread products (forwards and above all, options).
- Synthetic replication products (total rate of return swaps).

These products are much less used than CDSs and do not offer the same liquidity. We shall nevertheless present them because they belong to the credit derivatives family, in the same way as default risk instruments.

### 2.2.1   Credit Spread Derivatives

Credit spread derivatives enable investors to take positions on the future credit spread between two securities (usually a risky and non-risky security, or the spread of the former compared to the swap rate). They are products based on the changes in remuneration of credit risk, the value of which does not explicitly depend on the occurrence of a predetermined credit event. Credit spread derivatives mostly take two forms: forwards and options, the latter being a little commoner than the former.

---

[23] See Batchelor (2004).

## 2.2.1.1   Credit Spread Forwards

Forwards are the simplest derivatives. The most basic credit derivative is no more or less than a forward on a bond. To protect himself against deterioration of the borrower's creditworthiness, the investor merely has to sell the bond as a forward. If the value has depreciated over the term of the contract, the symmetrical gain on the forward market enables the loss in the cash market to be offset. However, this strategy does not enable the credit risk to be unbundled from the other market risks (especially the interest rate risk), and so more appropriate instruments, credit spread forwards, can be used.

### Mechanism of credit spread forwards

Credit spread forwards are mathematically simpler than swaps or options, but paradoxically, they were not the first to appear. As with derivatives on interest rates, it was swaps and options that came first, with forwards appearing as of 1995.

The mechanism of these products is similar to that of forward rate agreements (FRAs). The buyer of a credit spread forward undertakes to acquire a bond at a certain spread above a reference rate (usually Euribor). The seller of the forward undertakes to sell the underlying credit at the strike spread. At settlement date, a payment takes place between the counterparties based on the difference between the initially agreed spread and that observed at maturity. Thus, at maturity of the forward contract, the buyer undertakes to pay the seller the following amount:

(forward strike spread – actual spread at maturity) × duration × notional amount

As for forward rate agreements, gains (losses) in the forward market compensate for the losses (gains) in the cash market. In the event of the default of the issuer of the reference security during the term of the contract, the transaction is settled. It is the buyer of the forward that bears the default risk.

Similarly, it is possible to replicate forwards using CDSs. In this case, the parties to the contract do not take a position on the evolution of the credit spread of a particular security, but on that of a reference entity. It is possible to structure these products by entering two CDSs of different maturity, or more simply by setting up a CDS with a 'forward' start. For example, an investor wishing to buy protection on an issuer for three years starting in a year's time will enter into a three-year forward CDS in a year's time.

Credit spread derivatives can also be structured in the form of options.

## 2.2.1.2   Credit Spread Options

Options, like forwards, enable a position to be taken on a future credit spread, but contrary to the latter, they offer the investor an asymmetrical risk profile.

Options can be applied to credit as they are to any other underlying asset, among which are equity, bonds or interest rates: the investor buys or sells the right to buy (call option) or the right to sell (put option) a credit at a determined spread (strike) at a precise date (European option) or at any time before maturity (American option). Thus, exercise of a put option on a credit spread is made possible by the depreciation of the reference credit, and that of a call option is made possible by the appreciation of the underlying credit.

As for forwards, options are most frequently used to hedge or take a position on the credit spread between a risky security and a non-risky reference security.

Most of the time, credit spread options are structured on asset swaps, that is, the bundling of a fixed-rate bond with an interest rate swap, enabling a synthetic floating-rate note to be created, the value of which depends solely on the creditworthiness of the issuer.

### Mechanism of credit spread options

In Figure 2.7, strike $K$ is equal to 100 basis points. If, at maturity, the spread on the reference asset is equal to $S = 200$ basis points, then the credit spread put option is in-the-money and can be exercised.

Upon exercise, the buyer of the put option delivers the reference asset to the seller (at market price $P_M$) against payment of the price of the same security, recalculated using the strike spread ($K$), thus a price $P_K$, higher than $P_M$ at the date of exercise. The put option seller pays $P_K$ and receives a security that is worth $P_M$. To exercise a call option, the mechanism is similar. Cash settlement can also be decided between the counterparties to the option.

In practice, a call option buyer records a gain if the spread on the reference security is within the strike, while a put option buyer profits from an increase in the spread beyond it. Symmetrically, a call option seller makes money on the premium and is not at risk as long as the spread does not fall below the strike; while a put option seller makes money as long as the spread remains below the strike.

The premium owed by the option buyer is usually paid upfront at inception of the transaction. It may be paid in installments but in this case, for American options, it must be decided whether the premium payments continue until the initially agreed maturity of the option, or whether they will stop upon exercise.

As for all options, these products are plays on the volatility of the underlying risk, here credit spread. There are several variations on these options, which are briefly outlined below.

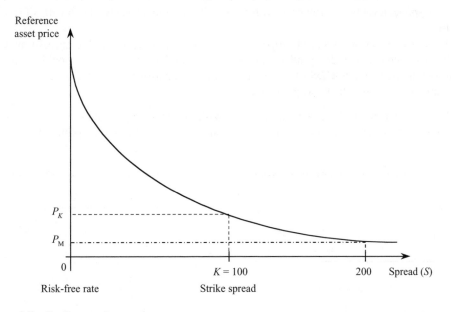

**Figure 2.7**    Credit spread put option

## 2.2.1.3  Variations

Many types of more sophisticated options ('exotic options') than those presented above have been developed by investment banks to provide an optimum response to investors' demands. Although the area of exotic options on credit spread is still largely undeveloped, we shall describe below a few structures already used in the market.

### Options on CDSs or default swaptions

There are two types of CDS options, those known as payer options, giving the right to buy protection, and so-called receiver options, giving the right to sell protection; each of these can be bought or sold. The value of these products is that they enable positions to be taken on credit spread volatilities.

*Payer options*

These become exercisable when the underlying CDS spread widens. Buying an option like this reveals a pessimistic view of the underlying credit: the investor pays the premium for the option and gambles on deterioration of the credit. At maturity, he can then, if the spreads have widened, buy protection at the level defined in the option (strike), below that of the market (so the option is in-the-money). On the other hand, selling an option like this shows optimism with regard to the credit since in this case, the seller sells a counterparty the right to buy protection at a predefined level. Figure 2.8 shows the payoffs of payer options.

*Receiver options*

Receiver options become exercisable when the underlying CDS spread narrows. They give the right to sell protection at a predetermined premium level. The option buyer will thus exercise it if the spread level has narrowed to within the strike. Figure 2.9 shows the payoffs of receiver options.

In general, CDS options are European, that is, they are only exercisable once, at maturity. The most frequently traded products are short-term options, three to six months' maturity, indexed on the five-year CDS (the most liquid underlying asset).

Common uses of default swaptions include:

- Yield enhancement strategies – an investor wishing to take a position on a credit risk at a higher spread level than the current market spread may sell a payer option. He will thus

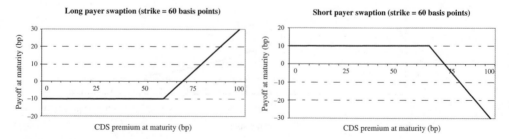

**Figure 2.8**  Payer default swaptions

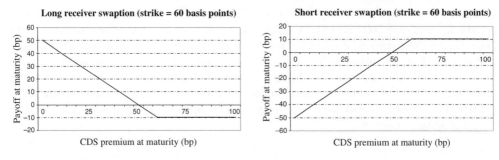

**Figure 2.9**   Receiver default swaptions

receive the option premium while taking the risk that it might be exercised at the spread level he has chosen.

- Taking a leveraged position on credit risk – an investor anticipating the deterioration in the underlying credit risk in the near future may decide to buy a payer call option. Thus, in exchange for the premium, the investor will be able to monetize profit by exercising the option in the event the underlying credit risk deteriorates.
- Taking a position on spread volatility – like all options, default swaptions are above all volatility products. For example, an investor may take a long position on a straddle by buying a payer swaption and a receiver swaption with the same strike. He will then benefit from a rise in volatility but will have to pay the premiums on both options. See Figure 2.10.

In theory, all the strategies used in the equity option market can be replicated on CDS options. However, the relatively low liquidity of these products (associated with that of CDSs compared to equity, entailing relatively high bid–offer costs) and the absence of choice in terms of maturity (mainly three and six months) limit their growth. In this regard, it is worth noting that most of the swaptions currenly traded use credit indices such as iTraxx[24] as underlying assets, since these offer a substantially narrower bid–offer spread.

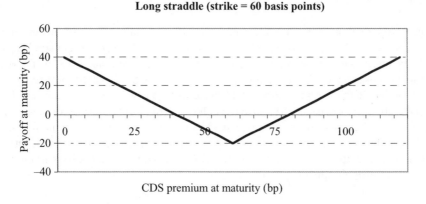

**Figure 2.10**   Payoff of a CDS straddle

---

[24] These are presented in Section 3.3.

A recent report by Fitch Ratings[25] shows that the default swaption market has approximately doubled in size over 2004. It confirms that the lion's share of this market goes to index credit options, which accounted for about $2 bn of trades (in notional amount) for the median dealer surveyed by Fitch as against $400 m for single-name contracts. Index options also seem to be growing faster than CDS options. The vast majority of trading action in 2004 was in North America, and more than three-quarters of underlying risks were rated investment grade. Only 10% of the contracts traded had a term longer than six months. Hedge funds were the main users of default swaptions.

### Default-and-out barrier options

Classic barrier options are activated or deactivated if the underlying asset reaches a predetermined level upon either rising or falling.

A default-and-out credit spread option is deactivated not when the underlying spread reaches a predetermined level but upon the occurrence of a credit event. This structure is used for put options where the investors selling the option only wish to gamble on the risk of the credit spread deteriorating, but do not, on the other hand, wish to take the risk of the reference entity defaulting. For the purchaser of the put, however, the option is deactivated where a credit event occurs, and he therefore runs the risk of finding himself long of a paper in default, while a standard credit spread put option, probably in-the-money in the case of a default, would have allowed him to get rid of the underlying paper (although he would have had to pay a higher premium).

### Binary or digital options

This type of option offers a fixed payoff profile if it expires in-the-money at maturity, whatever the relative level of the underlying asset spread compared to the strike.

### Credit spread caps

As for interest rates, corporates may buy a cap to fix upfront a maximum credit spread on their future borrowings.

Except for options on CDSs, the different variations on credit spread options are relatively rare in this market. At the end of May 2004, investment bank Dresdner Kleinwort Wasserstein (DKW) launched a new type of spread option, credit spread warrants (CSWs). These enable investors to subscribe to a liquid option (like all warrants, CSWs benefit from active market-making) giving them the right at maturity to subscribe to a new bond for a determined amount and spread. In this case, each CSW gave the holder the right to convert his option at maturity into a bond at a face value of 1000 euros issued by Casino Guichard Perrachon SA at an issue spread of 85 basis points over the mid-swap rate. By issuing these spread warrants, which could be traded relatively easily by investors, DKW hoped to avoid the trap of low liquidity common in traditional spread options.

As for default derivatives, the various credit spread derivatives described above can be re-bundled into structured notes linked to a credit spread.

---

[25] See Batterman and Merritt (2005).

## 2.2.2 Synthetic Replication Products

The products presented below enable investors to replicate the economic performance of an exposure to a credit risk synthetically without having to buy the reference instrument. Some observers consider that these products do not belong to the credit derivatives family as they can be used in various markets, not least the equity markets. Nevertheless, they are included here because they have been used in credit derivative structures.

The main instrument in this sub-category is the total rate of return swap or total return swap.

### 2.2.2.1 Total Rate of Return Swaps

These products enable investors to synthetically reproduce exposure to a reference asset incorporating a credit risk (debt or bond), a basket of credits or an index.

### Mechanism of total return swaps

This type of swap transfers all the economic benefits of an underlying financial asset (all cash flows associated with the reference credit: interest coupons or payments, including commissions, and variations in asset value) for a determined period. The payment corresponding to the variation in value (appreciation or depreciation) of the asset is made either at maturity of the swap or at regular intervals (such as when coupons are paid). Thus the protection seller (who receives the total return) acquires all the economic attributes of the asset without owning it. In exchange, he pays the protection buyer (who pays the total return) a periodic coupon (generally at a variable rate, Libor more or less a spread), which funds the protection buyer's position in the reference asset. The standard structure of these transactions is shown in Figure 2.11.

In the case of physical settlement at swap maturity, the protection buyer transfers the reference asset in the transaction to his counterparty and receives in exchange the value thereof as determined initially (when the contract was concluded).

### Cash flow structure

When the transaction is concluded, the counterparties define the reference asset and agree on an initial value ($P_0$). During the term of the swap, the protection seller receives all the cash

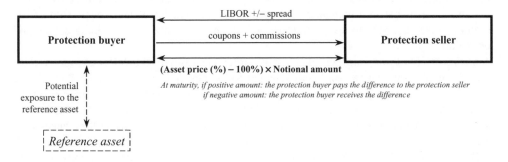

**Figure 2.11** Total return swap

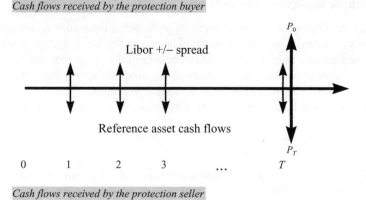

**Figure 2.12**   Cash flow structure of a total return swap

flows generated by the reference asset and in exchange, pays the agreed coupon (Libor +/− spread). At maturity, possibly at regular intervals, the reference asset is valued again ($P_T$). If the reference asset appreciates, the protection seller receives $P_T - P_0$; he pays $P_0 - P_T$ to the protection buyer if the reverse occurs. The method for re-evaluating the reference asset is flexible but generally it is a survey of the major market-makers in the underlying name, as is the case for a CDS cash settlement. See Figure 2.12.

The counterparty taking the risk on the economic performance of the reference asset also bears the risk of the issuer defaulting on this asset during the term of the swap. In the event of default, two solutions may be envisaged:

• The transaction may be terminated early and the settlement process (physical or cash) is then similar to that described for simple CDSs.
• Alternatively, the swap continues until the initial maturity date, but cash flow payments are re-adjusted on the basis of the discounted value of the reference asset (in order to reduce counterparty risk).

Total return swaps are therefore very similar to repurchase agreements, or repos, in which a market intermediary assigns a security to a counterparty and undertakes to buy it back for a predetermined amount, at a future date. The main difference between these two types of transaction is that in a total return swap, there is no transfer of legal ownership of the reference asset, contrary to a repo transaction, which effectively includes an asset sale and repurchase.

A reverse TROR swap is when a bank sells a reference asset to an investor and the investor pays the total return on the asset in exchange for a regular Libor-based cash flow. These strategies are commonly used by banks when their funding conditions deteriorate and they wish to avoid negative carry on their assets, or when they have the opportunity to arbitrage tax or accounting regulations, to transform an on-balance-sheet position into an off-balance-sheet one.

There are a number of variations to total return swaps, which we shall quickly describe below.

### 2.2.2.2    Variations on Total Return Swaps

There are three main variations on total return swaps.

**Capped/floored total return swaps**

This type of swap limits the potential gain of the protection seller on the reference asset to a predetermined level. In exchange, the funding spread paid is smaller. The system of floored total return swaps is symmetrical.

**Fixed payout total return swaps**

These are designed to avoid a conflict that might arise from the valuation process of the reference securities in the event of default. These contracts predetermine the amount to be paid by the protection seller in this case.

**Asset switch swaps**

In this type of structure, the protection seller pays the return on a second reference asset instead of the Libor +/− spread coupon paid in standard total return swaps.

Like other types of credit derivative, total return swaps can be incorporated into structured notes.

### 2.2.2.3    Example of a Transaction: the Wal-Mart Synthetic Bond

In early September 1996, JP Morgan Securities structured and issued a synthetic bond referenced on the Wal-Mart senior unsecured debt[26] in the amount of $594 m. Even if this transaction took place in the early days of the credit derivatives market, it is a typical example of arrangements based on synthetic replication products. It was elected Deal of the Year – Derivatives by the American magazine *Institutional Investor* in January 1997, such was its innovative nature when it was issued.

**Motives for the transaction**

JP Morgan's reasons for arranging this structured note were not revealed in public. Two explanations were put forward:

1. Wal-Mart was in the process of restructuring its balance sheet and perhaps wished to get rid of several layers of subordinated debt. This was not confirmed.
2. More probably, JP Morgan Securities might have been approached by several financial institutions wishing to reduce their credit exposure to Wal-Mart. They would have held this risk in the form either of mortgages or lease guarantees. These are amortizable and offer higher interest rates than those on Wal-Mart's conventional debt in the market,[27] thus enabling the transaction to be attractively structured for fixed income investors.

---

[26] Senior unsecured debt ranks first in repayment order in the event of default and liquidation of the borrower's assets, while not being secured by any particular asset of the borrower.
[27] This debt is exclusively in bullet form, that is, redeemable once and for all at maturity and offering a lower coupon, since the debt is entirely drawn over the period.

## Structure of the transaction

JP Morgan's clients sold the bank their securities and guarantees to get rid of their credit risk on Wal-Mart. The assets were held in the form of collateral in a special purpose vehicle (SPV). In parallel, JP Morgan entered into a total return swap with the SPV: the latter transferred to its counterparty (JP Morgan) the interest payments and performance of the collateral, that is to say, their appreciation or depreciation over the term of the transaction. In exchange, JP Morgan remunerated the SPV via an annual coupon fixed at 65 basis points over the yield of US T-bonds over a comparable term, ten years.

The SPV issued a ten-year note linked to Wal-Mart's default risk with a principal of \$594 m, paying an annual coupon equal to the remuneration of the SPV, i.e. Treasuries plus 65 basis points. This bond was amortized over the years, its average life being 5.8 years. The mechanism of this note was standard and the investors would only get back the principal if no credit event occurred on Wal-Mart. The principal, \$594 m, was transferred from the SPV to the JP Morgan clients who thus 'assigned' their credit risk.

The payments to the SPV were doubly guaranteed. The first guarantee came from JP Morgan. In the event of Morgan defaulting, the SPV could fall back on the second guarantee provided by an insurer specialized in this type of complex financial arrangement, AIG Financial Products, a subsidiary of the American insurer AIG (rated AAA at the time). The securities placed in the SPV as collateral did not bear prepayment risk and their nature was of little interest to the investors assessing the risk/profitability profile of the transaction. The investors only ran one risk: that of Wal-Mart defaulting on the reference securities, that is to say, its senior unsecured debt.

The structure of this transaction is shown in Figure 2.13.

The settlement of the structure was standard: if there was no default, investors would recoup 100% of their capital. In the event of default or credit event, a materiality clause was inserted into the documentation, so that the structure could not be terminated early for no good reason. The materiality threshold corresponded to a credit spread of 150 basis points between the Wal-Mart bonds serving as reference and the corresponding Libor (and not Treasury bond yields) over the three months following declaration of the credit event.

Once the default had been materially observed, the note would be paid back in anticipation. The investors would be paid the residual value of the securities following the default. This value was determined by checking with the five largest market-makers in the Wal-Mart debt every fortnight for three months[28] (cash settlement). The investors also had the option to leave the structure quickly in the event of default, the residual value then being determined by another check with the same market-makers immediately after the default. If no satisfactory value could be fixed for the debt, the price discovery mechanism would be postponed 18 months, after a significant incubation period.

## Advantages for the investors

The note was placed successfully. The investors were exclusively institutional, either drawn by the generous return promised by the structure, or seeking Wal-Mart risk. Fixed income funds were the main investors involved, as were insurance companies and banks.

The coupon paid at 65 basis points over the T-bond rate was deemed generous for an AA-rated credit risk (rating of the Wal-Mart senior unsecured debt). JP Morgan's assessments

---

[28] The settlement value was set at the average bid.

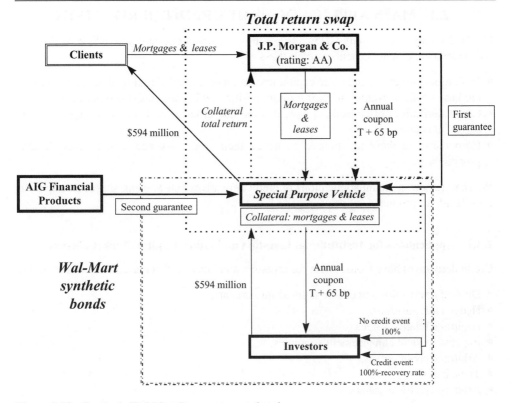

**Figure 2.13**   Synthetic Wal-Mart Stores corporate bond

showed that a bullet bond of similar quality yielded Treasuries +35 basis points, while an amortizable paper of equivalent quality brought in about Treasuries +40 basis points. Wal-Mart's debt, by comparison, was priced 40 to 45 basis points over Treasuries. It was possible to fix a higher coupon because the securities placed in the SVP as collateral offered a higher yield than the Wal-Mart debt available on the market, and also because the investors had to be remunerated for the risk[29] they took buying a structured product over-the-counter rather than a standard bond. In the secondary market, the spread narrowed from 65 to 60 basis points over Treasuries following the issue.

The market in credit spread derivatives, like that in synthetic replication, has historically lagged behind the CDS market. The latter offers the advantage of homogeneous characteristics that are not found for credit spread options, nor for total return swaps, and thus contributes to the establishment of a liquid market.

In Section 2.3, we present the main applications of credit derivatives.

---

[29] The risk taken by the investors using this structure was essentially one of liquidity (the secondary market for structured notes is not very well developed, although it is likely that JP Morgan, as an arranger, could envisage being a market-maker in these securities, or at least provide indicative prices to enable investors to mark-to-market their positions). Counterparty risk is virtually eliminated from the structure due to the double guarantee: it would require default of both JP Morgan as first guarantee and AIG Financial Products as second guarantee for investors to be exposed to this risk.

## 2.3    MAIN APPLICATIONS OF CREDIT DERIVATIVES

Credit derivatives, especially CDSs, are a simple means of exchanging credit risk. As such, they offer a great many benefits to their users:

- Institutional investors and other capital market players (banks' trading desks, hedge funds, etc.) use credit derivatives in their trading, position taking and investment strategies.
- Credit derivatives offer banks a new, flexible and efficient tool for managing credit and capital allocation.
- Corporates use these instruments to hedge their credit risk and manage their funding programs.

We shall review the main applications of credit derivatives below, using simple examples for each family of products.

### 2.3.1    Applications for Institutional Investors and Other Capital Market players

Credit derivatives have various uses for investors and other market players. Many are used to:

- Diversify portfolios and enable tailored investments.
- Hedge cash positions.
- Arbitrage relative values.
- Implement yield enhancement strategies.
- Arbitrage credit curves.
- Trade basis.
- Arbitrage recovery rates.

#### 2.3.1.1    Portfolio Diversification and Tailored Investment Strategies

In accordance with modern financial theory, credit derivatives enable fixed income portfolios of superior quality to be built up, because they foster:

- Diversification of the credit portfolio.
- Management of concentration and correlation risks by continuous adjustments at lower transaction cost.
- Short selling of debt instruments without going to the cash market (i.e. going long a CDS).
- Repackaging a credit risk or generating a new exposure to credit risk, by creating synthetic debt instruments.

One of the main constraints of the bond market is its low liquidity, and the lack of diversity in available risk. Thus, most bond issues are made by telecommunications or automobile companies, which require large amounts of working capital. Conversely, few securities are issued by retailers, for instance, which are structurally cash flow positive. Furthermore, most issues are five to ten-year bonds. For an investor seeking to constitute a diversified portfolio, the bond market is thus quite limited. There is also a currency problem for an investor seeking to invest in euros in an American company that has only borrowed in dollars.

One of the great advantages of credit derivatives is that synthetic debt can be built on any underlying issuer, with the characteristics required by investors in terms of maturity, currency, and coupon type, and thus meet their demand for diversification.

## Examples

Nokia, the Finnish telecommunications company, has never issued bonds. However, Nokia's risk trades in the CDS market (the five-year CDS was worth 28 basis points per annum at 1 March 2004) and can be offered to an investor.

Similarly, an investor wishing to take a ten-year risk on French retail leader Auchan in dollars cannot use the bond market, because Auchan has never issued bonds in dollars and the longest maturity available is 2008. In the credit derivatives market, however, a ten-year CDS in dollars was being traded at 40 basis points per annum at 1 March 2004.

Some institutional investors are limited in their investment choices by national regulations; they can only invest funds in assets of specific quality,[30] are only allowed to hold them for a short period, or are obliged to invest a certain percentage of their portfolios in assets issued in their national markets. These regulations are contrary to the financial theory of efficient borders. Credit derivatives reduce these constraints by offering investors synthetic exposures on securities that they cannot buy.

## Examples

According to his letter of engagement, a fund manager is not allowed to invest in high-yield debt. He can, however, contract a total return swap, which will synthetically replicate possession of the asset in question for a periodic fixed coupon over a predetermined period.

An investor wishes to take a short-term position on a name, which has only issued ten-year bonds. One solution would be for this investor to buy a one-year put option on this bond, enabling him to define upfront the conditions under which he can close out his position. However, the cost of the option could cancel out the economic benefit. An alternative solution would be to ask a bank to issue a credit-linked note on the issuer's credit risk, synthetically replicating the performance of the underlying bond over the one-year period envisaged.

### 2.3.1.2  Hedging Cash Positions

Bondholders have portfolios the value of which depends on the fluctuations in credit spread. They can protect themselves from these fluctuations or take positions on spread volatility by buying or selling options.

In another context, an investor might identify a bond likely to deteriorate. The most direct solution would be to sell this position in the cash market. However, several constraints inherent to this market might prevent him from doing so:

- The secondary market in this asset might be non-liquid and the selling price all the lower.
- The market conditions (interest or exchange rates) might be unfavorable.
- The mark-to-market on the security might be negative, and to sell the asset would mean materializing the loss. Conversely, if the mark-to-market were strongly positive, selling the asset would entail a potential high tax liability.

For all these reasons, to take a position in derivatives by buying protection via a CDS could be much more profitable for the portfolio manager.

---

[30] In the United States, the bond portfolios of insurance companies and pension funds must be composed of a minimum 90% of debt rated BBB or higher (investment grade).

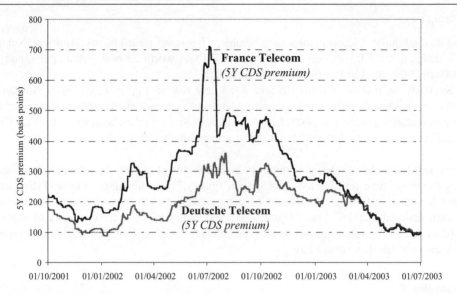

**Figure 2.14**   Relative value arbitrage

### 2.3.1.3   Relative Value Arbitrage

An investor wishing to gamble on the relative value of two credits, that is, wishing to take a long position on one credit and a short position on another to play on the convergence of the credit spreads in the medium term, will prefer CDSs to cash instruments. This is because it is not easy to find two securities from two separate issuers having exactly the same maturity. The CDS market offers the necessary flexibility.

Figure 2.14 shows this type of strategy on France Telecom (FT) and Deutsche Telekom (DT) risks. This example shows the evolution of spreads of the two foregoing issuers. In 2002, the five-year CDS for each issuer diverged by over 100 basis points, not least because France Telecom was more indebted.

However, an investor confident in the convergence of the two telecom operators' spreads at maturity could have sold protection on France Telecom and bought protection on Deutsche Telekom and then closed out his position a few months later, after the spreads converged. This type of strategy is very complicated to implement in the bond markets, because of the difficulty in running a short position on a security for several months.

### 2.3.1.4   Yield Enhancement Strategies

Credit derivatives can be used by institutional investors to pursue a yield enhancement strategy. One straightforward way of doing this is to combine spread options with bond positions.

**Examples**

Let us assume an investor has acquired a security with a spread of 10 basis points over Euribor. He expects the underlying credit to appreciate and looks to sell out at Euribor flat. The investor may materialize this anticipation as of today by selling a counterparty a call option on the underlying asset swap with a strike spread of Euribor flat. He will thus collect the premium on the option and increase the yield on the position.

The reverse strategy can be adopted where the investor wishes to enter a security but it is currently too expensive: it may be trading, say, at Euribor $+15$ basis points, while the investor would be prepared to invest at Euribor $+20$. One solution might be to sell a put option on this underlying asset swap at a strike spread of Euribor $+20$ basis points, thus improving the overall performance of the trade via the put premium.

Other strategies have been structured by investment banks, for example packages of callable asset swaps. For these, the bank sells an asset swap to an investor, and then buys from its counterparty a European call option on the package at par. The investor significantly increases the yield on his position by collecting the call premium but waives his right to benefit from narrowing of the underlying spread beyond the strike.

One strategy offering even higher yield for an investor is to sell a European put option to the bank on the asset swap. This option gives the bank the right to deliver the same underlying asset swap to the investor, in one year for example, for the same nominal amount. Here, for the bank, the operation boils down to acquiring from the fund manager a synthetic credit line on the borrower underlying the asset swap, and for this reason, the bank is prepared to pay a fairly high premium.

### 2.3.1.5   Credit Curve Arbitrage

CDSs also allow forward positions to be taken on a borrower's credit curve by trading opposing CDSs of different maturities to gamble, for example, on the steepness or flatness of the credit curve. Every strategy commonly used by interest rate market players comes into play here. It may also be used for credits where creditworthiness has deteriorated and the credit curve has reversed.

### Example

Let us suppose an investor wishes to take a position on a deteriorating credit XYZ. Suppose, for instance, that the five-year CDS is worth 350 basis points and the one-year CDS is at 500 basis points, thus showing a risk of short-term default. The investor can decide to sell the one-year protection to fund the purchase of five-year protection.

If he thinks the risk of default is likely in the medium or long term, sale of the one-year protection will enable him partly to fund the purchase of forward protection. On the contrary, if he anticipates default in the near future, but that the creditworthiness of the underlying asset will improve in future, he will take the opposite position.

### 2.3.1.6   Basis Trading

The basis is the difference between a CDS spread and that on an asset swap of the same reference entity. Sometimes, this basis is negative, thus enabling the investor to buy a bond, asset swap it, and a CDS of the same maturity and still make a positive carry. Generally, the net spread is seldom more than 10 to 15 basis points at best, and this strategy mostly attracts investors with low funding costs.

Another advantage of these operations is that it enables a negative position to be taken on a credit while financing it through the positive carry. Where a credit deteriorates, the CDS spread should widen more than that of the asset and the investor will gain by selling his position. If the credit does not deteriorate the investor continues to gain from carry.

### 2.3.1.7   Recovery Rate Arbitrage

As seen earlier, it is possible to trade CDSs on senior or subordinated debt. The default probability $(P)$ of these two types of contract is the same, since both are exercised when a credit event occurs on the financial debt of the reference entity.

The difference is in the range of deliverable obligations. In the first case, the protection buyer can deliver senior securities, in the second subordinated ones. Thus, the difference between a senior and a subordinated CDS spread results from the relative appreciation of recovery rates, depending on debt seniority.

At the first order, as seen in Chapter 1, the relationship between the spread $(S)$, the recovery rate $(R)$ and the default probability $(P)$ is as follows: $S = P(1 - R)$. In this framework, the theoretical relationship between senior spread $(S_{sen})$ and subordinated spread $(S_{sub})$ is as follows:

$$S_{sub} = (1 - R_{sub})/(1 - R_{sen}) \times S_{sen}$$

Supposing the subordinate spread trades at a level double that of the senior spread. If the recovery rate of the senior debt is 60%, that means the anticipated subordinated recovery rate will be 20%. An investor disagreeing with the market-implied recovery rates could buy senior protection and sell subordinated protection, or the reverse. However, it should be noted that liquidity on subordinated CDSs can be found mainly in the banking and insurance sectors.

Like all derivatives, credit derivatives offer many trading strategies and positions for players in the financial markets. Moreover, they are widely used by banks for managing their risk and their capital, due to their structural exposure to credit risk.

## 2.3.2   Credit Derivative Applications in Bank Management

Credit derivatives are a simple means for exchanging credit risk. As such, they offer a new, flexible and efficient management tool to banks, which are the most exposed to this risk. For a bank, buying a CDS on a borrower's default risk does not necessarily mean that it expects it to default in the near future. It is more a means of dynamically managing their credit commitments and lines at macro (sector and geographical exposures) and micro (risks on individual borrowers) levels.

### 2.3.2.1   Macro Management of Credit Risk

Most commercial banks' loan portfolios are geographically or sector biased in terms of credit risk exposure. Many financial institutions are specialized in certain sectors, to develop expertise in evaluating credit risk linked to the specificities of the industry in question and thus gain an edge against their competitors. Similarly, banks tend to be over-concentrated in names in their own countries. It is easier for an Italian bank to lend to an Italian firm, but it might possibly be more rational, for instance, for the risk associated with this new loan to be underwritten by an American bank, because its exposure to Italian credit risk will be low.

Being confidential over-the-counter instruments, credit derivatives enable bank portfolios to be diversified without jeopardizing commercial relationships. All banks have to do is, for instance, swap a European loan portfolio for an Asian loan portfolio over a specific period, by means of total return swaps. Alternatively, buying a CDS may also provide adequate protection.

Thus, credit derivatives enable banks to resolve the 'credit paradox,' which consists of being over-exposed to sectors in which they hold a comparative advantage in terms of transaction origination.

On the borderline between macro and micro management of credit risk, credit derivatives enable banks to dissociate the constraints arising from authorization limits imposed by their risk departments on their counterparties and countries, provided the latter accept that a credit derivative protection equates to an increased credit line.

**Example**

A bank wishes to develop its activities with a South African prospect but has exceeded its credit line for South African sovereign risk. It will therefore buy a CDS on South Africa and may continue its commercial activity in this country within the limits of the amount corresponding to the notional amount of the contract. This transaction is valid as long as, first, the CDS seller is not a South African institution or bank with a default risk closely correlated to that of South Africa, and second, that the bank's risk management department recognizes the validity of the hedge.

## 2.3.2.2   Micro Management of Credit Risk

Credit derivatives offer protection against the risk of individual debtors defaulting.

**Example**

A regional bank has what it deems over-exposure to a local client. It can find another bank (foreign, for instance, which will be unlikely to be exposed to correlated risks), and offer to sell it all or part of this exposure (via a CDS).

By granting a loan, while at the same time transferring the asset's credit risk to a counterparty, banks are able to dissociate credit risk from the financial risks inherent to their activity. The downside of such strategy is increased exposure to the counterparty in the swap. To avoid this, they can structure the transaction not in the form of an off-balance-sheet derivative contract but as a credit-linked note, which will be sold to the counterparty for cash.

By getting rid of the credit risk on a particular name, banks are able to actively manage the term and amount of individual authorizations.

**Example**

A bank has recurrent business with a client, ABC, but its seven-year credit lines are all fully used. However, it does have five-year lines. The solution is to conclude a two-year default swap in five years' time. This forward swap costs money, and the yield on the transaction will be less, but it means the bank can make the client an offer.

Similar examples can be given to show how individual credit lines can be managed. Banks can thus hedge credit risks on illiquid assets, market derivatives or other highly profitable products, underwrite bigger tranches when a new syndicated loan is arranged, or extend bridge loans to fund acquisitions.

Another application of credit derivatives is that they enable banks to overcome the issue of under-priced marginal risk on large clients.

**Example**

A client wishes to raise money via a bank loan. He goes to his reference lenders and expects very good terms. At the rate he is asking, the bank is 'losing money': i.e. it is not able to secure a return in excess of its cost of capital. However, it cannot refuse to lend the money for fear of losing the privileged relationship built up with the client. Banks wishing to pursue this relationship could argue that the ancillary products sold to the client would compensate for the low margin on the loan, and that therefore it is a valid transaction. Further, it is always easier for a bank to advance funds to a debtor that is already known (with the guidelines drawn and trust established) than to undertake a full credit analysis and due diligence for a potential new client.

However, the amount of marginal risk accepted by the bank is not taken into account in this case. To advance an additional loan at rates lower than or equivalent to those on the previous, ongoing loans, does not remunerate the bank enough to compensate for the additional marginal risk it takes on the client's signature. The theoretical credit spread needed to remunerate a bank more and more exposed to the same risk grows exponentially with the relative size of the exposure in the portfolio.

A CDS may resolve this problem. Although the spread does not increase with the amount being lent, the actual net exposure to the client is maintained at the previous level and the overall risk run by the bank is correctly managed.

In addition to credit risk management, credit derivatives can be used by banks for regulatory capital requirements optimization.

### 2.3.2.3  Banks' Management of Regulatory Capital

A credit derivatives transaction enables banks to free up regulatory capital and thus improve their return on equity, because the credit risk has been transferred from a corporate-type counterparty to a 'financial institution'-type counterparty.[31]

Use of CDSs enables two financial institutions to increase their return on capital, as shown below.

**Example**

A good quality bank lends $10 m for one year to an A-rated corporate counterparty, at Euribor +25 basis points. It obtains finance at Euribor less 10 basis points. Its net margin on the loan is 35 basis points, i.e. $35 000 per year. The risk weighting for corporate counterparties is 100%.

---

[31] It should be noted that pursuant to the Basel I Accords of 1988, loans to corporates are weighted 100% while those to an OECD financial institution are weighted only 20%. The type of transaction presented above is likely to become obsolete under the Basel II Accords (see Chapter 7).

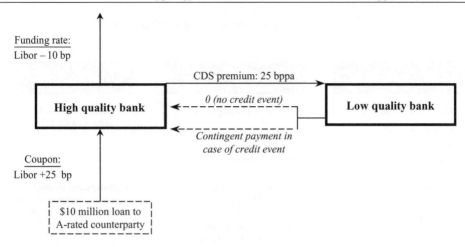

**Figure 2.15**   Funding conditions and regulatory capital arbitrage using CDSs

The bank must therefore set 8% of its regulatory capital aside to cover the risk of default. Thus its return on regulatory capital for this transaction is:

$$\$35\,000/\$800\,000 = 4.375\%$$

An OECD bank of lesser quality lends an identical amount to the same borrower. It obtains finance at Euribor +10 basis points, thus generating profit of 15 basis points on the transaction. Its return on regulatory capital will be:

$$\$15\,000/\$800\,000 = 1.875\%$$

The use of a CDS between the two banks enables these ratios to be increased substantially. See Figure 2.15.

For the good quality bank, the net margin is reduced to 10 basis points per year, but the capital requirements are also drastically cut since it is exposed to the default risk of another OECD bank (20% weighting). The new return on capital is therefore:

$$\$10\,000/\$200\,000 = 5.0\%$$

The lesser quality bank keeps the credit risk exposure to the corporate borrower. However, it improves its margin on the transaction to 25 basis points, profiting from the comparative advantage of the good quality bank in the finance markets:

$$\$25\,000/\$800\,000 = 3.125\%$$

This transaction is based solely on funding and regulatory arbitrages, and it goes without saying that the economic capital level required for each bank is not necessarily reduced by it. We will return to these issues later.

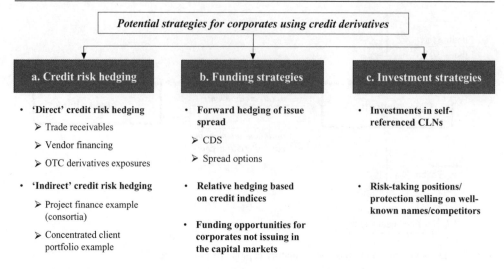

**Figure 2.16**    Potential applications of credit derivatives for corporates

Furthermore, use of credit derivatives may avoid the economic cost of provisions for the bank, if it hedges the credits it deems to be potentially under-performing in time.

One final category of market players can benefit from the use of credit derivatives: corporates.

### 2.3.3   Credit Derivative Applications for Corporates

Corporates are the third category of potential users of credit derivatives. The purpose of this sub-section is to present the various potential applications of credit derivatives used by this population.

First, it should be noted that even if many credit derivatives uses may attract firms, very few of them have actually used them, for reasons that will become clear. However, there is no doubt that if the credit derivatives market were used by this category of users, it would be particularly beneficial to the investment banks, constantly in search of means of growth beyond the market for institutional investors. This explains their aggressive marketing ploys over 2003–2004, all the more so as the appeal of the institutional investor segment is waning, given its increasing sophistication and the growing competition in this market. Only a successful move into the corporate segment would ensure a growth profile in the credit derivatives market comparable to that in the interest rate derivatives market. Moreover, the strong growth in the synthetic securitization market has led to dissymmetry between the numbers of protection buyers and sellers, most traditional investors being risk-takers by nature. The use of credit derivatives by corporates [especially in strategies (a) and (b) presented is Figure 2.16] could enable the overall balance between supply and demand for credit risk to be restored.

Three strategies based on credit derivatives can be envisaged by corporates, as shown in Figure 2.16.

### 2.3.3.1   Hedging of Credit Risk

Provided some conditions are met, corporates can use credit derivatives, especially CDSs, to hedge their credit risk.

## Potential fields of application: direct exposure to credit risk

Several fields of application of credit derivatives can be envisaged by corporates to hedge credit risk, not least credit risk borne directly.

### Hedging commercial risk generated by business operations

Any commercial transaction not immediately settled in cash can entail potential credit risk. For corporates, the problem of exposure to the credit risk of their main customers may then arise. For example, aircraft manufacturers such as Boeing or Airbus may be exposed to the risk of the airline companies defaulting during the lapse of time between the order and delivery and payment of the aircraft.

### Hedging financial risks arising from vendor financing

Large equipment manufacturers are often required to pre-finance their clients' purchases in sectors like infrastructure, telecommunications, aeronautics, energy, rolling stock, etc. These portfolios are characterized by their high degree of concentration and are often of average or even poor quality. Furthermore, contrary to banks, firms do not allocate capital to cover these potential risks and do not implement a risk management portfolio approach. Several now famous examples show how large firms have managed this risk in less than optimum fashion: Nokia and Lucent (Telsim risk), Alstom (Renaissance), Alcatel in Canada, etc.

### Hedging sovereign risks

To finance industrial projects abroad or export or trade transactions, especially in emerging markets, corporates generally use national export agencies (e.g. the Export–Import Bank in the USA) that provide insurance policies against political risk (up to 95% of project outstanding for the French Coface, for instance). The amount of residual exposure can be covered with a CDS on the sovereign debt of the country in question. One of the main limits of these hedging strategies is that they are generally far more expensive than the insurance premiums required by the national export agencies, which are backed by states.

### Hedging exposure on derivatives

Some firms are major players in the OTC interest rate and currency derivatives markets or the commodities markets. If they have not set up netting and collateralization contracts with their main counterparties (mostly banks), they are potentially at risk on these transactions, depending on the mark-to-market on their positions. Credit derivatives can be used in this case to reduce exposure (even if the main difficulty is to anticipate the evolution of these mark-to-market values) or generate additional credit lines so as to trade with certain counterparties.

## Other potential fields of application: indirect exposure to credit risk

In addition to these direct exposures to credit risk, some firms are also indirectly exposed. As for interest rate and currency risks, they must realize that exposure to a credit risk is not necessarily linked to the existence of a credit position on a counterparty or a client. The following are two examples of this.

*Consortium of sponsors in a project finance transaction*

When structuring large projects, industrial sponsors are regularly led to form consortia and invest in project vehicles (SPVs). Concessionaires usually require joint and several liability clauses between sponsors in the event of non-performance by one of them. Mechanisms to manage this risk are provided between sponsors, but they often do not work if any of them defaults. Buying protection on co-sponsors may be one way of reducing the risk of over-concentration to regular partners in project finance consortia.

*Corporates with a portfolio of very concentrated key accounts*

For some corporates, two or three key accounts may represent up to 50% of operating profit. Above and beyond possible exposure to trade receivables, the disappearance of a large account will have considerable impact on earnings. In both these cases, the use of credit derivatives could be envisaged to hedge against the risk of default of a partner, or else to diversify the credit risk portfolio. However, use of these strategies requires firms to adopt a sophisticated approach to their exposure to credit risk, as they do for interest or currency risks.

### Advantages and drawbacks of credit derivatives for corporates

Firms do not immediately turn to credit derivatives in these cases, because there are all sorts of competing instruments (bank guarantees and letters of credit, ABCP,[32] credit insurance, factoring, surety and performance bonds, etc.), which enable them to manage their client accounts. As experienced by other market players, the value of credit derivatives, especially CDSs, lies in their characteristics as capital market instruments and characteristics: they are liquid, with prices permanently available in the market, and they enable dynamic hedging adjustment as and when a position evolves.

However, several drawbacks can be identified for corporates using credit derivatives:

- They perform well for 'large' exposures to a few counterparties listed in the market, but this is a small universe compared to all the clients with whom a firm contracts and the credit exposure it is called upon to manage.
- The maturity of these instruments is often longer than the exposure (for example trade receivables at 90–120 days). Using credit derivatives therefore supposes that the exposure is fairly 'permanent'.
- It may be difficult to find attractive prices for small hedging amounts (one million euros and under).
- As we have seen, credit events in the CDS market are specific to the banking market ('borrowed money'). Therefore, simple failure to pay on a trade receivable would not be hedged by these contracts.
- There is a secondary risk in the event of default: discrepancy between the hedge amount under a CDS (par less the value of the defaulted deliverable obligations) and the real loss

---

[32] Asset-backed commercial paper (short-term securitization of corporate trade receivables).

incurred by the firm. Credit derivatives do not operate on the indemnification principle of insurance contracts. Therefore, it is necessary to judge the amount of protection to be bought carefully.

- Another risk in using these instruments is that of 'notification'. One requirement for triggering the CDS contract, as we have seen, is that public information sources relate the occurrence of the credit event. This is seldom the case for a simple failure to pay on a trade receivable.
- Finally, the many alternative instruments traditionally fulfilling the role played by credit derivatives (credit insurance, factoring, bank guarantees and letters of credit, export insurance contracts, etc.) generally offer more attractive pricing levels for corporate users.[33]
- For all these reasons, credit derivatives remain relatively ill-adapted to the needs of companies to hedge their credit risks. The rare firms having ventured into this field (Siemens Financial Services for the Siemens Group) have indeed been led to set aside the ISDA standards and replace them by tailor-made hedges.[34]

A second, more promising, field of application for corporates is the use of credit derivatives in funding strategies.

### 2.3.3.2  Funding Strategies

One strategy that is increasingly being examined by firms regularly issuing in the bond markets is to use credit derivatives to fix in advance the spread at which the firm can issue securities in future.

Theoretically this can be achieved in several ways:

- Buying a CDS on the firm's own risk on the maturity of the issue, which will enable mark-to-market hedging in the event of an unfavorable spread evolution (if the firm has to issue in future at a higher spread level, then the corresponding loss would be compensated for by improved mark-to-market on the short position on the CDS).
- Buying a put option on the spread of the future issue with the bank underwriting the issue (a perfect hedge except for counterparty risk, but potentially expensive depending on spread volatility, and rarely offered by underwriting banks).
- Sell the underwriting bank spread calls, which will enable an immediate premium to be collected but will not, however, dispel uncertainty as to issue timing.

One of the main reasons which has hitherto limited growth of these pre-hedging strategies for issues is the amounts at stake. Where a normal CDS transaction is concluded for amounts from 5 to 10 million euros (perhaps rising to 30 or even 50 million in a few rare cases), issuers seeking to cover their issue spreads are more interested in amounts from 500 million to several billion. In this case, to ask a bank to subscribe this amount in CDSs would actually mean it taking the total risk arising from the envisaged issue, a thing very few banks are capable of or willing to do. In any case, the bank would then need to hedge this exposure and would have to go to the market for protection, thus contributing to widening the issue's spread. Ultimately, the transaction could then produce a result contrary to that initially wished.

---

[33] There is a strong disparity between the pricing of credit risk in the credit derivatives market and that of credit insurance for instance. This disparity is one of the reasons for insurance companies' appetite for risk-taking in the form of credit derivatives, since this market remunerates them more than their traditional activities for a risk that is *a priori* comparable. We shall return to this later.

[34] See Thind (2003).

Rather than adopt an idiosyncratic cover strategy for its issue spread, a corporate can also choose to adopt a hedge using a credit index such as iTraxx.[35] This strategy can be appropriate if the treasurer considers that a future discrepancy in the issue spread will above all be due to across-the-board widening of spreads and not negative appreciation by the market specific to his company. The advantage of these strategies is to offer generally more liquid and less expensive hedging.

Finally, the recent innovation, credit spread warrants (CSWs)[36] may well, if they develop, provide issuers with a new tool for managing their funding programs.

### 2.3.3.3 Investment Strategies

A third generic use of credit derivatives by corporates is in their cash investment strategies.

One strategy that is often presented but rarely used for the moment,[37] due to the legal uncertainties involved, is for a corporate to take a long position on its own credit risk. Should the corporate have surplus cash, it can invest in a tailor-made CLN referencing its own credit risk. The fact that it carries out this transaction in the form of a CLN immunizes the protection buyer, generally a bank, against counterparty risk.

The advantages for the corporate are:

- Higher returns: rather than make a deposit remunerated at Euribor $-X$ basis points with its bank, it can underwrite a CLN issued by that same bank which should in theory increase the interest rate paid on its cash by the spread of the CDS.
- No additional risk: because it has subscribed a CLN, the corporate remains a creditor of the intermediary bank in the event of that bank's default, just as for a deposit.
- This strategy is the 'synthetic' equivalent of a debt withdrawal transaction (should the issued debt be illiquid and costly to buy back).

Naturally, economically speaking, a transaction like this can only be structured for a minimum size and tenor (which requires the corporate to have available cash and no immediate need for it as the funds will not be available before maturity, as for all structured products).

Furthermore, this type of strategy was recently criticized by the rating agencies. It was used, among others, by the Italian group Parmalat, which had invested €290 m in self-referenced CLNs.[38] In a report dated January 2004, rating agency Fitch wrote that 'investment in self-referenced CLNs raises legitimate concerns, and it could be argued the risks outweigh any short-term benefits,'[39] not least by accelerating liquidity problems in firms at the very moment they are most in need of it (because it can be assumed that a borrower nearing bankruptcy will tend to liquidate its investments to improve its solvency, a strategy that cannot be implemented for a CLN referenced on its own credit risk).

A second investment strategy that can be envisaged for corporates would be, for instance, to sell protection on their direct competitors via a CDS. The rationale of such a strategy would

---

[35] See Section 3.3 for a discussion of these products.
[36] See Section 2.2.1.3.
[37] This strategy was, for instance, set up by United Business Media (UBM) with the American bank Bear Stearns (see Thind, 2003).
[38] Source: Bloomberg.
[39] See Merritt et al. (2004).

be that a firm would thus be naturally hedged in this type of transaction:

• If the competitor is in difficulty, or even nearing bankruptcy, the loss on the CDS would be covered 'naturally' by the potentially increased market share likely to accrue to the CDS seller.
• Conversely, if the competitor continued to do well, the first corporate would gain on the protection it sold.

However, although this seems an attractive idea in theory, it would require precise calibration of the amount and maturity of the protection that might be sold, not to mention the fact that such activity, of essentially speculative nature, is rarely the 'core business' of corporate treasurers.

There are three main families of credit derivatives. Default risk derivatives enable hedging against the occurrence of determined credit events. These are the first credit derivatives to have appeared and to date, are the most commonly used in the first generation. Recent new variations (CMDS, EDS) are likely to reinforce this trend in default products, which today are the only ones to offer market players true liquidity and price transparency. The two other families of credit derivatives (spread and synthetic replication products) are much less used and remain relatively confidential.

Finally, this chapter has enabled us to make a quick overview of all the main uses of credit derivatives. Their field of application is potentially vast, but they are above all capital market instruments, even though banks have used them a great deal to manage their credit portfolios and regulatory capital base before moving on to more sophisticated solutions (second generation and synthetic securitization products). Finally, corporates might well begin to make considerable use of these instruments, although they might encounter a number of difficulties in using them, as we have explained.

Now that the mechanisms and main practical applications of first-generation credit derivatives have been presented, we can go on to discuss the evolution of the structured forms of these products in the next two chapters.

# 3
# Second-Generation Credit Derivatives

The market in credit derivatives has benefited from the increased sophistication of financial techniques, not least in equity and interest rate derivatives. Thus, using the existing building blocks in the credit market, especially CDSs, the investment banks have been quick to find the theoretical resources and engineering skills needed for designing more complex structured products that met investors' every need.

The purpose of this chapter is to present these 'more complex' products that we call 'second-generation or structured credit derivatives'. We shall divide them into three main categories.

1. Basket credit default swaps or correlation products.[1] With the standardization and growing liquidity of the first-generation credit derivatives market, new opportunities to use them, not least as investment products, have opened up. One of the main changes in the credit derivatives market has been the development of products indexed on credit risk baskets. These enable investors to take a leveraged exposure on an underlying basket of reference entities: these are basket credit default swaps.
2. Hybrid products. The second change in the credit derivatives market is its growing inter-penetration with the other derivatives markets. Thus, hybrid products have been developed that enable investors to take highly leveraged positions by playing on several strategies simultaneously. These instruments range from the simplest (capital-guaranteed CLNs) to more complex ones requiring structuring, pricing and hedging skills in several markets for contingent credit/rate or credit/equity products.
3. Credit indices. The third category of credit derivatives was invented in 2001. These are instruments referenced on credit indices and no longer on single credit risks or baskets of risks. This type of derivative enables the investors to replicate the performance of a credit index synthetically and/or take positions relating to it.

We shall now go over these three second-generation product categories and give a few practical illustrations of transactions, to show the advantages of using them.

## 3.1 BASKET CREDIT DEFAULT SWAPS

In this section, we shall present the main second-generation credit derivatives: instruments indexed on a basket of credit risks. They are a popular variation on simple CDSs. They give the investor (the protection seller) much more flexibility inasfar as they are swaps on several reference credits, thus enabling the contract buyer to offer exposure to a credit portfolio tailored to meet the investor's requirements. Most baskets contain five names, and can go up to 15 or

---

[1] Although they are structured correlation products, collateralized debt obligations (CDOs) and other synthetic securitization products have been treated in a special chapter (Chapter 4) because of their importance, and their various uses and specific analysis tools.

even 20 reference credits.[2] They can be a mix of sovereign and private borrowers, of greater or lesser creditworthiness, from varied industrial and geographical sectors.

We shall begin by the commonest instrument in this category, the first-to-default credit swap, of which we shall describe the mechanism and management principles. We shall then present a concrete example, and will examine variations on this product.

### 3.1.1  First-to-Default Credit Swaps

These were developed in 1993 by several Wall Street investment banks and offered to American commercial banks in early 1994. Their use became more widespread in all markets towards the end of the 1990s, especially in Asia and emerging countries. The main advantage of this type of product for investors is the leverage achieved on yield compared to the risks taken.

#### 3.1.1.1  Product Structure

The structure of first-to-default swaps, referenced on a basket of credit risks, is similar to that of simple CDSs as presented in Chapter 2. Payment of the variable leg of the swap is triggered by the first reference entity in the basket to undergo a credit event. Therefore, the protection seller only pays for the first default in the basket. This first credit event terminates the contract early and the protection seller is no longer at risk on the other credits in the basket.[3] The buyer of the first-to-default swap therefore keeps the credit risk on the second default, the third, etc., and, obviously, does not know which name will undergo a credit event first. This structure supposes dynamic management of the underlying credit positions (which are typically delta-managed by the product arrangers).

Figure 3.1 shows the classic structure of a first-to-default CDS. Like a vanilla (single-name) CDS, where there is a credit event, the first-to-default CDS will be settled by the standard method, in accordance with the various possibilities offered by the ISDA Definitions (physical or cash settlement), and this settlement will of course be for the reference entity in the basket having undergone the credit event that triggered the swap.

#### 3.1.1.2  Variation: the Credit-Linked Note on a Basket of Credits

As we saw earlier, any default swap can theoretically be packaged into a structured note (CLN), thus offering investors a cash instrument. As for first-generation CDSs, investment banks structure CLNs referenced on baskets of obligors. These instruments offer investors an enhanced yield compared to that on equivalent securities in the market or a synthetic single-name structure.

As for a basket default swap, investors are exposed to the first default occurring on the reference entities, in which case the note is repaid early. In the case of a physical settlement,

---

[2] Beyond 15 names, baskets are usually treated by a statistical approach like those used for securitization transactions.

[3] A swap like this could be structured so as to require the protection seller to pay as and when the defaults occur to the credits in the basket. However, it would be no different than a portfolio of simple CDSs on each name and would cancel the economic benefit (leverage) of the basket structure. This is because the condition of contract termination upon occurrence of the first default enables advantage to be taken of the default correlations among the underlying names in the basket.

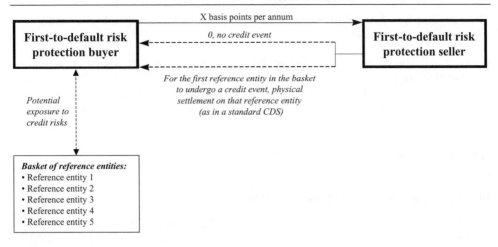

**Figure 3.1**    First-to-default credit swap

the investors receive a nominal amount of the securities in the reference entity in default equal to the principal amount of the CLN issued.

### 3.1.1.3   Initial Analysis of a First-to-Default Swap

The main question arising from first-to-default swaps is how to price them. How can the spread (or premium) be determined so as to compensate the protection seller in these structures adequately? First of all, the boundaries of this premium can be defined: it must be greater than the highest premium on the individual CDSs on each reference name, while at the same time being lower than the sum of these individual premiums. Thus, the protection buyer is ready to pay a higher premium on the product, because the statistical probability of a credit event occurring on the basket is higher than on each individual name. However, he pays a premium, not to protect himself against all the names but only against the first credit in the basket to undergo a credit event. As a result, the first-to-default swap premium must be lower than the sum of the individual premiums on the CDSs:

$$\text{Max (individual CDS premiums)} \leq \text{first-to-default swap premium}$$
$$\leq \sum \text{(individual CDS premiums)}$$

As for standard CDSs, the level of this premium logically depends on the probability $P_{FtD}$ of the first credit defaulting and therefore on the following parameters:

- The number of underlying reference entities in the basket (the more reference credits there are, the greater $P_{FtD}$).
- The maturity ($P_{FtD}$ increases with maturity).
- The average creditworthiness of the reference entities and their individual default probabilities ($P_{FtD}$ is in reverse proportion to the creditworthiness of the reference entities, and therefore increases with spreads).
- The average recovery rate expected on the reference entities in the basket, should a credit event occur. Assuming a fixed spread, $P_{FtD}$ increases when the recovery rate rises.

There are two essential parameters in addition to these basic ones that must be considered when pricing these products:

- The default correlation between the credits underlying the product ($P_{FtD}$ increases where correlation decreases).
- The homogeneity of the reference credit risks and therefore of the underlying spreads (the leverage on the first-to-default premium is optimized when the underlying spread distribution is homogeneous).

We shall now examine these two parameters in detail.

### Introduction to the notion of default correlation

Default correlation is one of the key parameters enabling the first-to-default swap premium to be determined, inasfar as it enables assessment of the protection buyer's risk of undergoing several credit events on the underlying basket (since the protection buyer is only covered for the first of these events). The greater the correlation rate, the higher the probability of having either no default or multiple defaults.

To understand the effect of default correlation on the first-to-default swap premium, let us examine the two following situations, concerning an underlying basket with five reference entities:

- If the default risks of all the credits in the underlying basket are perfectly correlated (theoretical assumption of a parent company and four subsidiaries with cross-default provisions), there will be only two possibilities: either all the credits default, or none do. In this case, the default probability on the first-to-default is equivalent to the highest default probability in the underlying basket, i.e. that of the credit with the highest spread (assuming market efficiency and identical recovery rates for all the reference entities). In this configuration, the first-to-default swap premium should be equal to the spread of the riskiest credit.
- If the correlation between the default risks of all the credits in the basket is nil, then the first-to-default swap premium should be equal to the upper boundary, that is, the sum of the spreads of the underlying credits. This second result can be arrived at by reasoning that there is no arbitrage opportunity between buying protection via the first-to-default swap, and hedging by five long positions in individual CDSs referencing the credits underlying the basket. Should a credit event occur on one of the reference entities, the two situations are equivalent, because, since the default correlation is nil, this default has no impact on the default probability (and therefore the spread) of the other reference credits in the basket. The position can therefore be unwound at no extra cost (subject to the bid–offer spread). Failing an arbitrage opportunity, if the default correlation is nil, the level of the first-to-default swap premium should be equal to the sum of the spreads (in this demonstration, we assume that the term structure of the credit spreads of the reference credits is flat over the maturity of the basket).

The effect of the default correlation on a first-to-default swap premium is described in diagram form in Figure 3.2. Default correlation is a measurement of the systemic risk in the market:

- It does not change the individual default probability of the reference credits in the basket.
- On the other hand, it enables measurement of multiple default risks.

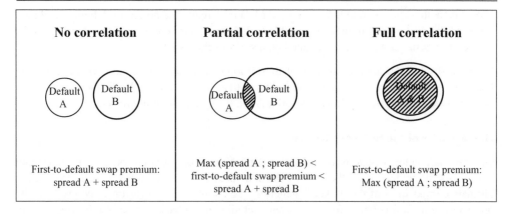

| No correlation | Partial correlation | Full correlation |
|---|---|---|
| First-to-default swap premium: spread A + spread B | Max (spread A ; spread B) < first-to-default swap premium < spread A + spread B | First-to-default swap premium: Max (spread A ; spread B) |

**Figure 3.2**   Intuitive approach of default correlation and impact on the first-to-default CDS premium

## Practical 'determination' of default correlation

Default correlation is not a tradable asset, and thus it cannot be deduced from market data. In practice, several approaches are possible:[4]

- There are historical statistical studies but they are incomplete and contain only a relatively small number of data. These are mostly historical default correlation noted in certain sectors, or again, the volatility of average default rates. The rating agencies also supply useful data in this field, such as rating migration data.[5]
- The second way of assessing the correlations between credits by means of historical data is to examine the fluctuations in the price of bonds and CDSs. It is agreed that changes in the creditworthiness of a borrower immediately affect asset prices in efficient markets. Therefore, it should be possible to extract the level of the credit spreads from market prices and compute a correlation coefficient. The limitations of this approach are the nature of credit spreads (do they only reflect default risk?)[6] and the relative scarcity of high-quality public databases providing historical credit spread information.
- The rating agencies were obliged to formulate their own approaches to correlation when analyzing structured products, not least collateralized debt obligations (CDOs). This is the case of Moody's, for instance, the methodology of which is based on the notion of diversity score, a relatively conservative measurement of default correlation.[7]
- Finally, mathematical models also enable the notion of correlation to be apprehended. It is the case, for instance, of the firm value model (Merton):[8] the default occurs when the value of the total assets of the firm (which follows a stochastic diffusion process) falls below a threshold amount representing the value of the debt. A relationship can thus be established between the default correlation and the correlation in asset value. As the latter cannot be observed in the market, the equity returns correlation is used as a substitute. The advantage

---

[4] Excluding the use of a constant correlation rate.
[5] See Section 1.2.2.
[6] See the discussion on the nature of credit spread in Chapter 1.
[7] This approach boils down to allocating credits in the underlying pool to a number of uncorrelated industry sectors. In other words, the diversity score represents the number of uncorrelated assets equivalent to the initial pool of correlated credits. This methodology is primarily used for the analysis of CDOs.
[8] See Chapter 6.

of this method (used, among others, by KMV) is to make the notion of default correlation more 'observable' and to make it possible to deduce it from market data (stock prices of the reference entities, when they are listed on a stock exchange).

We shall discuss the appropriateness of these models and approaches to correlation risk in Chapter 6 of this book. It is the latter solution that is used mostly by financial engineers, because there are substantial histories and it is relatively simple to implement.

### Homogeneity of the reference basket

One last parameter to take into account in determining the premium on the first-to-default swap is the homogeneity of the credit risks and spreads in the reference basket. Even if the ultimate composition of the basket is generally the choice of the investor in the product (the protection seller), it is better for the reference credits in the basket to be of relatively similar creditworthiness (similar ratings and identical seniority), to arrive at maximum leverage on the premium paid to the investor.

Figure 3.3 presents a pricing simulation on two baskets of five reference credits, both with an average spread of 100 basis points. Thus, the greater the homogeneity of the credit spreads in the basket, the greater the leverage on the first-to-default premium (calculated as a percentage of the widest spread in the underlying basket).

This reasoning can be taken further by imagining an underlying basket with four assets, the credit spreads of which are respectively 1000, 1, 1 and 1 basis points. In this case, it is easy to understand that their heterogeneity will give no leverage on the final spread served by the basket. It will be 1000 basis points (that is, 100% of the highest spread). This is because the added value of the marginal addition of the other credits in the basket is virtually nil,

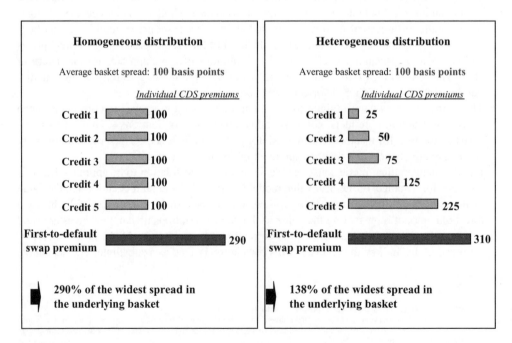

**Figure 3.3**  Homogeneity of underlying credit spreads and impact on the first-to-default CDS premium

because the probability of first-to-default in these cumulated credits (with an individual spread of 1 basis point) is not significant in comparison with that of the asset with a spread of 1000 basis points. The latter is far and away the likeliest to default first.

Even assuming nil correlation between the underlying assets in the basket, the premium would correspond to the sum of the spreads, i.e. 1003 basis points, that is, 100.3% of the widest spread in the basket. If the spreads are too heterogeneous, the first-to-default product will not attract risk-takers.

To conclude, factors affecting traditional CDS premiums have an impact on first-to-default prices, but two other factors are vital in assessing their value: first, default correlation, and second, the homogeneity of the underlying credit spreads. These are the factors that enable the creation of highly leveraged credit products sought by yield-hungry investors. This is why first-to-default products are described as correlation products.

Below is a concrete example of a first-to-default swap transaction. We shall follow it by describing extensions to these structures.

### 3.1.2   Concrete Example

#### 3.1.2.1   Description and Analysis of the Product Envisaged

Let us take the example of a diversified basket referenced on five investment-grade credit risks: Dow Chemical, Merrill Lynch, Reuters, SBC and Suez. The composition of the basket is given by Figure 3.4.

This underlying basket was created to offer considerable diversification, in terms both of sector and of rating. With a homogeneous correlation assumption of 30%, it offers a premium of 191 basis points, that is, 3.5 times the widest spread in the basket (Dow Chemical, 55 basis points).

A rapid simulation shows the effect of the correlation rate on the premium (in basis points). See Table 3.1. Similarly, it is possible to illustrate the effect of homogeneous underlying spreads on the final spread of the product. If Dow Chemical risk came to be traded on the CDS markets at a spread of 150 basis points instead of the 55 basis points used in the foregoing simulation, the first-to-default premium would rise from 191 basis points to 199, but the leverage for the

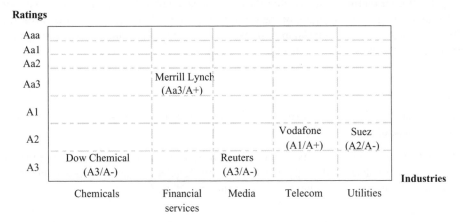

**Figure 3.4**   First-to-default swap example

**Table 3.1**    Correlation rate and first-to-default CDS premium

| Correlation rate | 30% | 40% | 50% | 60% | 70% |
|---|---|---|---|---|---|
| FtD CDS premium | 191 | 179 | 163 | 148 | 132 |

investor would fall steeply, from 374% (compared to the greatest spread in the underlying basket) to a mere 133%.

### 3.1.2.2   Advantages of the Product and Reasons for Investing

First-to-default swaps offer investors a tailor-made structured credit product (insofar as they have the possibility to choose the underlying basket), while at the same time benefiting from significant leverage compared to individual investments in the various credits in the product.

For the commercial banks that have invested heavily in these products, the main advantage is to be able to diversify their risk in the upper echelons of the ratings, while ensuring satisfactory returns. Medium and small commercial banks do not have sufficient financial surface to enter into contact and maintain a profitable relationship with large borrowers. They have no means of syndicating credit. Cross-selling opportunities are virtually non-existent when the bank's participation is perhaps 10 million dollars in a syndicated transaction worth a billion. Furthermore, these banks often have internal criteria for return on investment that are a minimum 50 to 60 basis points to cover their funding and administrative costs and remuneration of their shareholders. Returns like this can only be found in the market by going down the rating ladder, or targeting transaction niches like LBOs (leveraged buyouts) or HLTs (highly leveraged transactions), etc., that is, by managing a portfolio with a relatively risky profile. For all these reasons, first-to-default swaps are a relatively popular credit derivative for bank investors, since it enables them to increase the return on their investments without compromising on the intrinsic creditworthiness of the underlying names.

The arranger's motives are fairly clear: he must manage his portfolio of outstanding loans on the various names in the basket more actively, be able to free up credit lines with these large customers so as to develop other types of more profitable transactions (such as derivatives, for example), while being insured against an event that might occur to one of the names in the portfolio. Furthermore, structuring these products enables the arrangers to make money on the dynamic risk management of these products, as they do for any structured instrument. First-to-default swaps are delta-managed, like any derivative, since the arrangers dynamically replicate their positions with a portfolio of 'vanilla' (single-name) CDSs.

### 3.1.2.3   Limitations

Basket products are for the moment traded in a more restricted market compared to that for CDSs, because of:

• Capital adequacy requirements sometimes unfavorable to banks. The attraction of the leverage on these products is strongly dependent on the regulatory treatment applicable to these transactions (that the banks tend to analyze through ROE).[9]

---

[9] Return on equity, the ratio corresponding to the gross margin made on the product divided by the average amount of regulatory capital allocated to the transaction.

– In France, for instance, the Commission Bancaire requires the protection seller in a first-to-default swap to record risk-weighted assets equal to the sum of the risk-weighted assets of all the underlying names in the product. Needless to say, this approach singularly detracts from the charm of these transactions for credit institutions. However, the risk weighting can be capped at 200% of the notional amount where the position can be analyzed as equivalent to a BBB-rated risk at least, on the basis of an analysis of default rates compared to the historical data of the rating agencies. Selling protection on a first-to-default swap referenced on five corporate credit risks would therefore require regulatory capital of at least 16% of the notional amount of the transaction, up to a maximum 40% ($5 \times 100\% \times 8\% = 40\%$).

– In Italy, on the other hand, only the riskiest name in the basket is subject to the ratio, which thus reduces the associated regulatory capital requirements (in the foregoing example: $1 \times 100\% \times 8\% = 8\%$).

• The technical incapacity of most investors to analyze the correlation risks in a basket.
• The non-existence of a secondary market (except for a bid that can be obtained from the arranger of the structured product).

### 3.1.3   Extension of the First-to-Default Principle: $i$ to $j$-to-Default Products

In theory, it is possible to extend the principles of first-to-default products and structure more complex instruments with a different risk profile. Thus, some sophisticated market players are ready to sell credit protections against the risk of a second default in the basket (or even a third, for baskets including five names). The mechanism of these products is intrinsically the same as for classic CDSs or first-to-default swaps: the protection buyer is at risk on the first credit event affecting one of the names in the reference basket, but is protected on the second (or third) credit event.

The difficulty with arranging these products is (again) pricing them. Although they have been little used in the past, they have become more and more popular with the growing sophistication of the players in the credit markets and their wish to diversify risk portfolios. Figure 3.5 shows a pricing simulation of an underlying basket of five credits and shows the yield profile of the various possibilities that can be envisaged (first-, second-, third-, fourth- and fifth-to-default).

It can be observed that for $i$-to-default products, with $i$ increasing, the spread (expressed as a percentage of the widest spread) increases when the correlation rate rises. As seen earlier, the greater the correlation rate, the more likely it is that there will be multiple defaults in the underlying basket. Of course, the sum of the spreads of the $i$-to-defaults is in theory equal to the sum of the spreads on the underlying credits in the basket at all times.

To conclude, it should be noted that if the principles used in these basket-type products are taken to their logical conclusion, they begin to resemble the mechanism of collateralized debt obligations (CDOs).[10] The main difference between these two types of instrument is that the basket product operates on the basis of a number of defaults, while the CDO offers exposure on a percentage of losses, calculated on the basis of the total amount of the transaction. Thus, selling first-to-default protection on a portfolio of 50 equally-weighted credits can be likened to a CDO equity tranche (the riskiest), representing the first percentage of loss on the same underlying portfolio (with a recovery rate assumption of 50%). Indeed, there are close links between these two market segments, with CDO arrangers sometimes led to use correlation

---

[10] See Chapter 4.

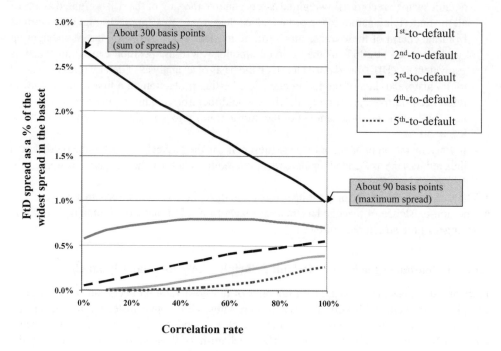

**Spreads of the first-, second-, third-, fourth- and fifth-to-default**

**Figure 3.5**   $i$ to $j$-to-default spreads and correlation rate

products of $i$ to $j$-to-default type to manage their correlation books. We shall return to the operating principles and management of CDOs in the next chapter.

We shall now examine the other categories of second-generation credit derivatives: hybrid products and credit indices.

## 3.2   HYBRID PRODUCTS

Hybrid products are the second category of second-generation credit derivatives. They are characterized by the fact that they are investment vehicles combining a credit performance and an additional performance derived from exposure to another asset class, such as interest rates (and/or exotic rate exposure), equity, inflation or commodities. These instruments typically enable an investor to adopt a multiple investment strategy (that is, covering several underlying markets) in a single investment structure.

Later in this section we shall present capital-guaranteed/protected credit products, which were the first variation on hybrid rate–credit products to be developed, and then an example of a structured hybrid product.

### 3.2.1   Capital-Guaranteed/Protected Products

Capital-guaranteed products are one of the simplest forms of hybrid product. A mixture of credit and interest rate-based products, they enable investors typically to take a risk on the

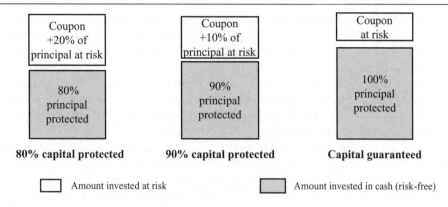

**80% capital protected**        **90% capital protected**        **Capital guaranteed**

☐ Amount invested at risk        ▨ Amount invested in cash (risk-free)

**Figure 3.6**    Capital-guaranteed/protected product structures

coupons and not the principal invested, like the guaranteed products that are available in other markets, such as the equity market.

The protection level varies depending on investors' expectations. It can be:

- Equal to 100% of the principal invested (it is then known as a capital guaranteed product).
- Under 100% (under-guaranteed capital product, or $X\%$-protected capital).
- Over 100%, which enables the investor to obtain a guaranteed minimum yield on the product.[11]

In a structured capital-guaranteed/protected credit product, the investor will recover at least the protected amount of the capital invested, whatever happens to the underlying credit risk. For instance, an investor who invests in a capital-guaranteed first-to-default basket will recover 100% of his initial outlay at maturity, even where a credit event occurs to any of the underlying credits in the basket.

Figure 3.6 shows some structures of capital-guaranteed/protected products. Since quite a substantial part of the capital is guaranteed at maturity, the only amount available for taking exposure on a risky product (the risk envelope) is represented by the interest payment on the principal, plus the potential amount of capital at risk, for under-guaranteed products. The higher the interest rates and the longer the term of the investment, the greater the potential amount of capital at risk (and thus the greater the leverage).

For investors, there are many advantages to this type of structure: they enable them to take exposures on risky names, because of the protection arising from the capital guarantee, and so they can diversify their portfolios into types of name that they could not aspire to directly. Since the principal is guaranteed at maturity (except, of course, if the bank sponsoring the transaction fails!)[12] these structures attract to the credit markets the more conservative investors, those who have specific asset/liability management targets (obligation to preserve the capital at maturity), or those subject to specific regulatory constraints.

---

[11] A guaranteed minimum yield is a formula that protects the investor better, but the financial return potential is lower. Conversely, under-guarantee entails risk-taking beyond the amount invested by the underwriter, but there is higher leverage. Thus, the choice of a formula depends on the maturity of the investment, each investor's strategy, and his risk aversion.

[12] When it provided the capital guarantee (capital protected notes are often issued by bank intermediaries using their own Euro-Medium Term Note issuance program).

Thus, these guaranteed capital structures were a huge success with German insurance companies as of mid-2002. They needed to repackage all their non-investment grade structured credit exposures to bring the ratings up to investment grade levels, following the publication of a BAFIN circular that changed the capital adequacy regulations in respect of the eligibility of structured credit products for the Deckungstock.[13] The transformation of these exposures into capital-guaranteed products was one of the means chosen by these investors for complying with the new regulations without having to sell these relatively non-liquid and often discounted assets (which would have entailed a write-off in their balance sheet).

Naturally, capital-guaranteed structures offer a lower yield than standard CLNs for which there is a risk of capital loss (subject to recovery rate in the event of default). This type of structured product is widely offered by many arrangers to institutional investors. It is probable that they are also suitable for retail investors (especially private banks), as is the case in the equity markets.

### 3.2.2   Other Hybrid Products

In addition to guaranteed capital products, which are relatively simple, other more complex structures enable exposures to credit risk to be combined with those to other underlying markets (rates, equity, commodities, etc.). This type of structure typically poses the problem of the contingency of the instrument where a credit event occurs.

To illustrate this problem, let us take the simple example of a fixed-rate credit-linked note. This can be built simply by a banking intermediary, buying protection, using a standard floating-rate CLN[14] and an interest rate swap. A structure like this theoretically requires an ability to manage a residual interest rate position, contingent upon the occurrence of a potential credit event. Should this happen, the CLN is repaid early and the structure is unwound. Then comes the question of the mark-to-market of the interest rate swap (which is probably not zero, since the credit event has occurred during the life of the transaction and not at maturity).

Where a hybrid interest rate–credit product cannot be structured, there are two possibilities for the bank intermediary:

- The mark-to-market risk can be transferred to the investor. If the bank takes a loss on the interest rate swap, the amount of mark-to-market would be deducted from the amount of the recovery rate upon settlement of the CLN.
- It can underwrite an interest rate swaption enabling it to cancel the swap at any time during the life of the transaction, and will pass the option premium payment on to the investor (deducted from the yield on the structure). The drawback of this is the cost of the protection, since the swaption price will be directly indexed to the full volatility of the underlying interest rates but not adjusted for the default risk (which *a priori* will be much smaller).

In both cases, the overall economics of the structure would be relatively unattractive for the final investor in the structured product (assuming that the bank intermediary, as it should, retains no unhedged risk).

The advantage of hybrid products therefore resides in the possibility to offer investors innovative, tailor-made investment vehicles, offering yields that meet their expectations. To

---

[13] Regulated reserves.

[14] Standard CLNs offer a variable rate coupon theoretically representing the funding costs of the arranger bank (indexed to a variable market rate such as Euribor), to which is added the spread of the underlying credit risk (that is, the CDS premium).

do this, the investment bank intermediaries are led to model the 'cost' of this contingency to default risk.

We shall conclude this section by studying a concrete example.

### 3.2.3 Concrete Example of a Transaction

We have chosen a so-called step-up range accrual CLN structure for our example.

#### 3.2.3.1 Analysis of the Product

Our example is a credit–interest rate type hybrid product associating a corridor (a relatively classic rate derivative) with a CDS. The buyer takes a reference credit risk as in the case of a classic CDS, but in addition, he agrees to receive the CDS premium only if the reference interest rate (e.g. the Euribor) moves within a predetermined range.

The main characteristics of the transaction are as follows.

| | |
|---|---|
| Issuer: | arranging bank or SPV (special purpose vehicle) |
| Currency: | euro or US$ |
| Maturity: | 5 years |
| Reference entity: | Republic of Turkey |
| Coupon: | (6-month Libor + 1000 basis points per annum) × $N/360$ with $N$ being the number of days during which the reference rate is within the following ranges: |
| | Year 1: 0 and 2.5% |
| | Year 2: 0 and 3.5% |
| | Year 3: 0 and 4.0% |
| | Year 4: 0 and 4.5% |
| | Year 5: 0 and 5.0% |

Figure 3.7 shows the principle governing this product, which combines credit risk with interest rate risk.

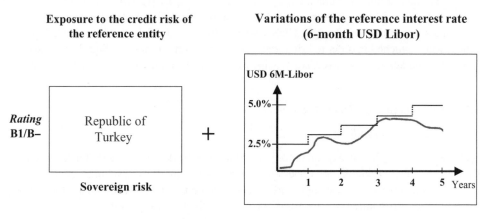

**Figure 3.7**  Step-up range accrual credit-linked note

*3.2.3.2   Advantages of the Product and Reasons for Investing*

This type of product is for qualified investors having anticipated trends in both the interest rate and credit markets, and seeking to materialize them in enhancing their yield. Let us, for instance, imagine an investor with an accurate opinion of the rate environment. He seeks to take advantage of this anticipation to maximize the yield on his CLN. In the foregoing example, this profit is substantial since a simple CLN (not hybrid) would give a coupon worth Libor +500. By combining exposure to both risks, our investor will be able to double his yield.

In terms of hedging, these instruments rely on a 'contingent' approach, since the bank arranging the product will bear the risk of a possible unwind of the exotic rate transaction (in this case, a corridor with step-up range), should a credit event occur on the reference entity – the Republic of Turkey – which is relatively risky (rated B1/B−).

These products require dynamic, delta-hedging strategies (since the notional amount of the rate product traded changes with the market value of the underlying credit. This strategy theoretically allows the arranging bank to have virtually no residual exotic (rate) exposure where the underlying credit is on the brink of defaulting (which is never the case in practice, since the bank always bears a 'jump-to-default' risk, that is, the probability that the credit event will occur any minute and the bank will therefore be led to unwind the remaining rate hedge with a negative mark-to-market). By definition, it is therefore almost impossible for the intermediary to hedge these products perfectly. However, they can theoretically integrate any structured rate instrument and any credit risk exposure. It would be possible, for instance, to combine this corridor with a first-to-default swap.

## 3.3   CREDIT INDICES

Credit indices are the third category of second-generation credit derivatives products. These instruments are linked to the evolution of an underlying credit index, and not to the credit risk of a single obligor (such as first-generation products) or basket of obligors (such as basket default swaps). This index is constructed to reflect the performance of the whole credit market or a segment of the latter (e.g. European investment-grade borrowers, American high-yield issuers, etc.).

Indices are not new to the credit world. Such instruments already existed in the stock market (the most famous indices include the Dow Jones, the S&P 500, the FTSE or the Eurostoxx) and had been developed for cash instruments (e.g. bond or loan indices). What is new, however, is the creation of indices based on the CDS market, which are the subject of this section. Credit indices were launched in order to bring transparency and further increase liquidity in the credit derivatives market and also to create new investment benchmarks for market participants.

### 3.3.1   Introduction to Credit Indices

*3.3.1.1   Cash Credit Indices*

Cash credit indices already existed before the creation of the derivatives-based index contracts. They are not easily tradable *per se* but are used as a benchmark by asset managers and other institutional investors to assess their performance. In the US fixed income market about two-thirds of all US corporate bond investors track one of the following indices:

- The Citi Big (which uses the higher of either Moody's or S&P's rating to determine if the bonds should be included in the index).

- The Merrill Lynch Master (which uses the weighted average rating of all Moody's, S&P and Fitch Ratings to determine eligibility of the bond).
- The Lehman Brothers Credit Index (which uses, as of 1st July 2005, the best two out of the three ratings to determine index inclusion).

The Lehman Brothers Credit Index is the most widely used index in the industry. Around 90% of institutional fixed-income investors who manage their portfolios against such credit indices use it as a benchmark.

In Europe, two cash indices are closely monitored by investors:

- The iBoxx Cash Index, which evaluates the spread of a basket of eligible investment-grade benchmark bonds.
- The Lehman Brothers European Cash Index.

Other specific indices were also created to provide a benchmark for other segments of the credit markets:

- The Citibank Loan Index, which measures the performance of US syndicated loans.
- The Lehman Brothers High Yield Index, which tracks the performance of US junk bonds.
- The Goldman Sachs/Loan Pricing Corporation Leveraged Loan Index.

### 3.3.1.2  Inefficiency of Cash Credit Indices

There are three main disadvantages using cash credit indices:

1. Their liquidity is rather poor and, as a result, credit spread movements are not necessarily directly related to a real change in creditworthiness in the underlying names.
2. They offer a relatively low diversification. Bond issuers are over-concentrated in terms of sectors, with the automotive and telecom sectors, for instance, being over-weight. At the same time, cash indices cannot capture the full breadth of credit risks as some industry sectors are clearly under-represented in the bond market (e.g. retail companies) and some borrowers restrict their activities to particular segments of the market (Nokia only borrows money via loans, British Airways only issues in the sterling market, etc.).
3. Last, bond issues are highly heterogeneous in terms of maturity, which prevents the creation of homogeneous indices.[15]

From 2002 onwards, the CDS market reached critical mass and offered a level of liquidity that enabled the investment banks to create credit derivatives-based indices, thus allowing them to bypass the inefficiency of cash credit indices.

### 3.3.1.3  CDS-Based Credit Indices

JP Morgan and Morgan Stanley were the first in the market to come up with new CDS-based credit indices in 2002:

- TRACERS by Morgan Stanley;
- JECI[16] by JP Morgan.

---

[15] Thirty-year corporate bonds have only been issued from 2003 onwards. Early 2005, Telecom Italia issued a 50-year bond, on the back of the success of the 50-year OAT launched by the Agence France Trésor. So far, it is the only corporate bond with a maturity greater than 2033 in the Eurobond market.

[16] JP Morgan European Credit Index-linked security.

That said, the market for derivatives-based indices really took off in 2003 with the emergence of two leading families of indices:

- TRAC-X (resulting from the merger between TRACERS and JECI);
- iBOXX, initially created by Deutsche Bank and ABN Amro during the summer of 2002 and joined in September 2003 by Citigroup and SG. This new family of indices gained popularity with investors through its fact-based independent selection process and process control (carried out by a third-party company independent from the index market-makers). These two features strongly differentiated iBOXX, which proved a better model than TRAC-X.

As a result, JP Morgan and Morgan Stanley gave away the control and management of the TRAC-X Indices to Dow Jones in November 2003, in an attempt to meet the independency requirements of final investors. In April 2004, end-users forced a convergence between the two index families, in order to promote greater liquidity and create a unique reference in the market. The two competing sides eventually decided to create a single set of indices and to merge TRAC-X with iBOXX: the iTraxx market standard was born. It is managed by an independent company, the International Index Company (ICC).[17]

### 3.3.2 Credit Index Mechanism, Pricing and Construction

#### 3.3.2.1 Credit Index Mechanisms

A credit index can be defined as the tradable premium of an over-the-counter CDS contract, providing protection on the credit risk of a static portfolio of reference entities, whose list makes up the index. The mechanism of a credit index is similar to that of a standard CDS.

On the launch day of the index, the premium is set for the life of the contract and can be approximately determined by the 'naive average'[18] of the constituents of the portfolio. As for a plain vanilla CDS, if a credit event occurs on one of the underlying entities in the index, a physical settlement takes place.

Thus, in a €125 m iTraxx Main Benchmark transaction, where one entity (say XYZ) out of the equally weighted 125 undergoes a credit event, counterparties to the transaction enter into a settlement for a notional amount of €1 m. Once settlement has taken place, the defaulted entity is taken out of the underlying list of reference entities. The transaction then continues on an adjusted notional amount of €124 m, referencing the 124 remaining entities, as shown in Figure 3.8.

The occurrence of credit events and the withdrawal of reference entities from the list underlying the credit index have a direct impact on the latter's premium. Figure 3.9 shows the impact of the Parmalat bankruptcy on the credit spread of the TRACX-100 Series 1.

#### 3.3.2.2 Credit Index Pricing: Market Price, Spreads Average and Theoretical Value

The price of a credit index can be constructed as the sum of its theoretical value and its skew:

$$\text{credit index price} = \text{theoretical value} + \text{skew}$$

---

[17] ICC is a joint venture of major fixed-income market players (ABN Amro, Barclays Capital, BNP Paribas, Deutsche Bank, Dresdner Kleinwort Wasserstein, HSBC, JP Morgan, Morgan Stanley and UBS) and Deutsche Börse (Germany's stock and derivatives exchange operator).

[18] Arithmetic average of the CDS premiums of all the reference entities in the index.

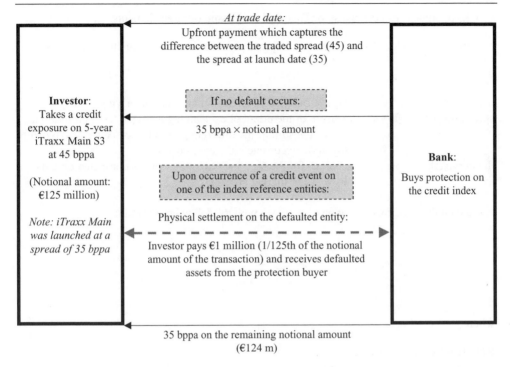

**Figure 3.8**   Mechanism of a credit index

**TRAC-X 100 Series 1**

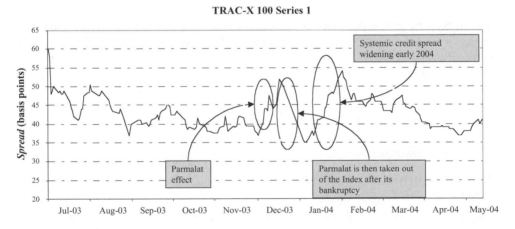

**Figure 3.9**   TRAC-X 100 Series 1 spread

The skew is a positive or negative number, which evaluates market expectations depending on supply and demand. When market participants are bearish on credit markets, they buy macro protection through credit indices as bid–offer spreads are much narrower on indices than on single-name contracts and liquidity is greater. This type of one-way flow would typically push the skew into positive territory. This was recently observed in May 2005 when correlation market players rushed to buy the index cover against systemic credit risk.

The theoretical value can also be analyzed as the sum of three elements:

theoretical value = naive average + spread dispersion factor + flat curve adj. factor

with

naive average:                  average of the CDS premium on each underlying name
spread dispersion factor:  measure of the effect of exchanging a unique fixed premium as
                                       against the sum of the different premiums as fixed rate payments
                                       stop upon occurrence of a credit event
flat curve adj. factor:       accounts for the fact that the index value is computed on a flat
                                       curve as per market convention

On launch date, the index coupon ($C_{IN}$) is set with the following formula:

$$C_{IN} = \frac{\sum\limits_{i=1}^{N} S_i \times RD_i}{\sum\limits_{i=1}^{N} RD_i}$$

where

$RD_i$: risky sensitivity of credit $i$
  $S_i$: credit spread reference entity $i$
  $N$: number of entities making up the index on an equally weighted basis

It is to be noticed that this value is not equal to the weighted average of the underlying reference spreads. Indeed, the riskier a credit is, the lower its risky sensitivity. This also leads to the following formula:

$$C_{IN} \leq \frac{\sum\limits_{i=1}^{N} S_i}{N}$$

### 3.3.2.3  Construction Rules

The ICC is responsible for constructing the indices, using a dealer liquidity poll. The typical process is described below.

**Step 1.** On the first day of a roll month (typically June and December), every index market-maker submits to ICC a list of names that:
  • are incorporated in Europe;
  • have the highest CDS trading volume over the previous six-month period.
  These names are then ranked according to trading volumes, in decreasing order.

**Step 2.** ICC removes from these samples the non-investment grade companies and those with Baa3/BBB− ratings and negative outlook from rating agencies. ICC then assigns each name to its relevant Dow Jones sector. These sectors are then mapped against the iTraxx sectors and each reference entity ranked by decreasing order within its iTraxx sector. The final list is chosen according to the required number of names per sector. Markit Partners' RED database is then used to define the reference obligation for every reference entity.

**Step 3.** Weights are rounded to 2 percentage decimal places. If the total weight of a sector is greater than 100%, the weight of the first component using alphabetical order is diminished by 0.01%. This is repeated with the following name in alphabetical order until the total weight decreases to 100%. If the total weight is less than 100.00%, a similar process is used, increasing single weights by 0.01% in alphabetical orders.

At each roll date three main indices are created:

### iTraxx Europe

This index replicates the European investment-grade credit market. The final portfolio comprises 125 reference entities and is constructed by selecting the highest ranking issuers by trading volume in each sector below.

- Autos: 10
- Consumers: 30 (15 cyclical and 15 non-cyclical)
- Energy: 20
- Industrials: 20
- TMT (telecom, media and technology): 20
- Financials: 25 (with separate senior and subordinated indices)

Each name is weighted equally in the overall and sub-indices. See Table 3.2.

### iTraxx Europe Hivol

From the iTraxx Europe portfolio, the 30 senior unsecured entities with the widest five-year credit default swap spreads are selected to form the Hivol index. The spreads are determined by Markit Partners (independent data collector and provider) from spreads submitted by the market-makers on a specific date. Each name is equally weighted. See Table 3.3.

Market makers typically make a 0.5 basis point bid–offer spread to clients in €50 m notional amount on the Hivol index.

### iTraxx Europe Crossover

A static equally weighted portfolio of 35 European crossover credits[19] make up the Crossover index. The reference entities in this index meet the following criteria:

- Ratings better than Baa3/BBB− with negative outlook.
- Non-financial entities.
- Minimum credit spread of twice the DJ iTraxx Europe non-financial spread and a maximum of 1250 basis points per annum or upfront 35% premium.
- More than €100 m of outstanding publicly traded debt.

See Table 3.4. Market-makers typically make a 3 basis points bid–offer spread to clients in €10 m notional amount on this index.

---

[19] Those rated Baa3/BBB− or with negative outlook, high-yield issuers and 'fallen angels' (i.e. issuers that were downgraded from investment to speculative grade).

**Table 3.2**   Reference portfolio – iTraxx Serie II

| Benchmark | Weight % | Benchmark | Weight % |
|---|---|---|---|
| 1 AB Volvo | 0.80 | 52 Electricidade de Portugal, S.A. | 0.80 |
| 2 Abbey National Plc | 0.80 | 53 Electricite de France | 0.80 |
| 3 ABN Amro Bank N.V. | 0.80 | 54 Endesa, S.A. | 0.80 |
| 4 Accor | 0.80 | 55 Enel S.P.A. | 0.80 |
| 5 Adecco SA | 0.80 | 56 Energie Baden-Wuerttemberg AG | 0.80 |
| 6 Aegon N.V. | 0.80 | 57 Finmeccanica SPA | 0.80 |
| 7 AKZO Nobel N.V. | 0.80 | 58 Fortum OYJ | 0.80 |
| 8 Allianz AG | 0.80 | 59 France Telecom | 0.80 |
| 9 Allied Domecq Plc | 0.80 | 60 Gallaher Group Plc | 0.80 |
| 10 Anglo American plc | 0.80 | 61 GKN Holdings Plc | 0.80 |
| 11 Arcelor Finance | 0.80 | 62 GUS Plc | 0.80 |
| 12 Assicurazioni Generali SPA | 0.80 | 63 Hannover Rueckversicherung AG | 0.80 |
| 13 Aventis | 0.80 | 64 Hanson Plc | 0.80 |
| 14 Aviva Plc | 0.80 | 65 Hellenic Telecommunications | 0.80 |
| 15 AXA | 0.80 | 66 Henkel KgaA | 0.80 |
| 16 BAA Plc | 0.80 | 67 Hilton Group Plc | 0.80 |
| 17 BAE Systems Plc | 0.80 | 68 HSBC Bank Plc | 0.80 |
| 18 Banca Intesa S.P.A. | 0.80 | 69 Iberdrola, SA | 0.80 |
| 19 Banca Monte dei Paschi di Siena SPA | 0.80 | 70 Imperial Chemical Industries Plc | 0.80 |
| 20 Banco Comercial Portugues, S.A. | 0.80 | 71 Imperial Tobacco Group Plc | 0.80 |
| 21 Banco Santander Central Hispano SA | 0.80 | 72 Investor AB | 0.80 |
| 22 Bank of Scotland | 0.80 | 73 J Sainsbury Plc | 0.80 |
| 23 Barclays Bank Plc | 0.80 | 74 Kingfisher Plc | 0.80 |
| 24 Bayer AG | 0.80 | 75 Koninklijke KPN N.V. | 0.80 |
| 25 Bayerische Hypo- und Vereinsbank AG | 0.80 | 76 Koninklijke Philips Electronics N.V | 0.80 |
| 26 Bayerische Motoren Werke AG | 0.80 | 77 Lafarge | 0.80 |
| 27 Bertelsmann AG | 0.80 | 78 Linde AG | 0.80 |
| 28 Boots Group Plc | 0.80 | 79 LVMH Moet Hennessy Louis Vuitton | 0.80 |
| 29 BP Plc. | 0.80 | 80 Marks and Spencer Plc | 0.80 |
| 30 British American Tobacco Plc | 0.80 | 81 Metro AG | 0.80 |
| 31 British Telecommunications Plc | 0.80 | 82 MMO2 Plc | 0.80 |
| 32 Cadbury Schweppes Plc | 0.80 | 83 Muenchener Rueck AG | 0.80 |
| 33 Capitalia S.P.A. | 0.80 | 84 National Grid Transco Plc | 0.80 |
| 34 Carrefour | 0.80 | 85 Nokia Oyj | 0.80 |
| 35 Casino Guichard-Perrachon | 0.80 | 86 Pearson Plc | 0.80 |
| 36 Commerzbank AG | 0.80 | 87 Peugeot SA | 0.80 |
| 37 Compagnie de Saint-Gobain | 0.80 | 88 Pinault-Printemps-Redoute | 0.80 |
| 38 Compagnie Financiere Michelin | 0.80 | 89 Reed Elsevier Plc | 0.80 |
| 39 Compass Group Plc | 0.80 | 90 Renault | 0.80 |
| 40 Continental AG | 0.80 | 91 Repsol YPF S.A. | 0.80 |
| 41 Credit Suisse Group | 0.80 | 92 Reuters Group Plc | 0.80 |
| 42 DaimlerChrysler AG | 0.80 | 93 Rolls-Royce Plc | 0.80 |
| 43 Deutsche Bank AG | 0.80 | 94 RWE AG | 0.80 |
| 44 Deutsche Lufthansa AG | 0.80 | 95 Safeway Ltd. | 0.80 |
| 45 Deutsche Telekom AG | 0.80 | 96 Scottish Power UK Plc | 0.80 |
| 46 Diageo Plc | 0.80 | 97 Siemens AG | 0.80 |
| 47 Dixons Group Plc | 0.80 | 98 Six Continents | 0.80 |
| 48 Dresdner Bank AG | 0.80 | 99 Sodexho Alliance | 0.80 |
| 49 E.on AG | 0.80 | 100 STMicroelectronics N.V. | 0.80 |
| 50 EADS N.V. | 0.80 | 101 Stora Enso Oyj | 0.80 |
| 51 Edison SPA | 0.80 | 102 Suez | 0.80 |

**Table 3.2**   *(Continued)*

| Benchmark | Weight % | Benchmark | Weight % |
|---|---|---|---|
| 103 Swiss Reinsurance Company | 0.80 | 115 United Utilities PLC | 0.80 |
| 104 Tate & Lyle Plc | 0.80 | 116 UPM-Kymmene Oyj | 0.80 |
| 105 TDC A/S | 0.80 | 117 Valeo | 0.80 |
| 106 Technip | 0.80 | 118 Vattenfall AB | 0.80 |
| 107 Telecom Italia SPA | 0.80 | 119 Veolia Environnement | 0.80 |
| 108 Telefonica, SA | 0.80 | 120 VNU N.V. | 0.80 |
| 109 TeliaSonera Aktiebolag | 0.80 | 121 Vodafone Group Plc | 0.80 |
| 110 Tesco Plc | 0.80 | 122 Volkswagen AG | 0.80 |
| 111 The Royal Bank of Scotland Plc | 0.80 | 123 Wolters Kluwer N.V. | 0.80 |
| 112 Thomson | 0.80 | 124 WPP Group Plc | 0.80 |
| 113 Unilever N.V. | 0.80 | 125 Zurich Insurance Company | 0.80 |
| 114 Union Fenosa, S.A. | 0.80 | | |

**Table 3.3**   Hivol reference portfolio – iTraxx Serie II

| High volatility | Weight % | High volatility | Weight % |
|---|---|---|---|
| 1 Accor | 3.34 | 16 Hilton Group Plc | 3.33 |
| 2 Arcelor Finance | 3.34 | 17 Imperial Chemical Industries Plc | 3.33 |
| 3 BAE Systems Plc | 3.34 | 18 Imperial Tobacco Group Plc | 3.33 |
| 4 Boots Group Plc | 3.34 | 19 J Sainsbury Plc | 3.33 |
| 5 British American Tobacco Plc | 3.34 | 20 Marks and Spencer Plc | 3.33 |
| 6 Casino Guichard-Perrachon | 3.34 | 21 Metro AG | 3.33 |
| 7 DaimlerChrysler AG | 3.34 | 22 MMO2 Plc | 3.33 |
| 8 Deutsche Lufthansa AG | 3.34 | 23 Pinault-Printemps-Redoute | 3.33 |
| 9 Deutsche Telekom AG | 3.34 | 24 Sodexho Alliance | 3.33 |
| 10 Dixons Group Plc | 3.34 | 25 Tate & Lyle Plc | 3.33 |
| 11 Finmeccanica SpA | 3.33 | 26 Telecom Italia SPA | 3.33 |
| 12 France Telecom | 3.33 | 27 UPM-Kymmene Oyj | 3.33 |
| 13 Gallaher Group Plc | 3.33 | 28 VNU N.V. | 3.33 |
| 14 GKN Holdings Plc | 3.33 | 29 Volkswagen AG | 3.33 |
| 15 HellenicTelecommunications | 3.33 | 30 WPP Group Plc | 3.33 |

### 3.3.3   iTraxx Indices: a True Innovation to Benefit Investors

According to a great many professionals, iTraxx indices are one of the most significant developments in the credit markets over the last few years. This effort has won the 2004 Innovation of the Year award of the International Financing Review as well as the Trading Initiative of the Year at the 2005 Risk Awards.

#### 3.3.3.1   *Advantages of the iTraxx Platform*

iTraxx indices are now highly liquid and standardized. The iTraxx platform brought together 27 market-makers and enabled market liquidity to be concentrated in a single index family. Typical bid–offer spreads are much lower than on the traditional CDS market (a mere 0.25

**Table 3.4**   Crossover – reference portfolio – iTraxx Serie II

| Crossover | Weight % | Crossover | Weight % |
|---|---|---|---|
| 1 ABB International Finance Ltd | 3.34 | 16 International Power Plc | 3.33 |
| 2 Alcatel | 3.34 | 17 Invensys Plc | 3.33 |
| 3 Alstom | 3.34 | 18 Kabel Deutschland GMbH | 3.33 |
| 4 BCP Caylux Holding Luxembourg SCA | 3.34 | 19 Koninklijke Ahold N.V. | 3.33 |
| 5 British Airways plc | 3.34 | 20 Metso Oyj | 3.33 |
| 6 Cable and Wireless plc | 3.34 | 21 M-real Oyj | 3.33 |
| 7 Cablecom Luxembourg SCA | 3.34 | 22 NTL Cable Plc | 3.33 |
| 8 Clariant AG | 3.34 | 23 ProSiebenSat.1 Media AG | 3.33 |
| 9 COLT Telecom Group plc | 3.34 | 24 Publicis Groupe SA | 3.33 |
| 10 Corus Group plc | 3.34 | 25 Rhodia | 3.33 |
| 11 Eircom Ltd | 3.33 | 26 Scandinavian Airlines System | 3.33 |
| 12 EMI Group plc | 3.33 | 27 Seat Pagine Gialle SpA | 3.33 |
| 13 FIAT SPA | 3.33 | 28 Sol Melia SA | 3.33 |
| 14 Havas | 3.33 | 29 Telefonaktiebolaget L M Ericsson | 3.33 |
| 15 HeidelbergCement AG | 3.33 | 30 TUI AG | 3.33 |

basis points spread on iTraxx Europe). In addition, it is not unusual for customers to trade up to €250 m in one single transaction, whereas the average transaction size for a CDS is in the €10–20 m range.

Transparency is definitely another advantage of the iTraxx products. The IIC is responsible for administering the iTraxx credit derivatives indices and the iBOXX bond indices. Its mission is to set the market standard and be the leading credit and bond index provider. As an independent index supplier, it is committed to an open and transparent market and to improving efficiency. As a result, iTraxx indices are fully replicable (the construction rules being transparent and known to all market participants), which is usually not the case for proprietary indices, i.e. those created, promoted and maintained by individual investment banks.

### 3.3.3.2   Main Application of iTraxx Indices

Dealing in iTraxx indices enables relatively efficient long and short position-taking in the credit markets. For instance, selling the iTraxx Europe index is a cheap and easy way to get access synthetically to a diversified credit portfolio and play the whole European credit sector, which would be burdensome through individual CDS or cash instruments. Indices are thus used to take quick macro bets on the direction of the credit markets.

Another favorite application of market players is macro hedging. Shorting the index (i.e. buying protection) can help rebalance the risk profile of cash investors who are inherently long credit risk.

Finally, iTraxx indices can also be used to build simple relative value trades. Hedge funds and banks' proprietary trading desks are frequent users of indices to take a position between the relative performance of a given name and that of its sector. Arbitrage transactions can also be set up efficiently with credit indices:

- Term structure trades can be engineered using the 5 to 10-year curves on a duration-weighted basis.

- Capital structure arbitrage plays are made by proprietary credit traders, who play short-term spread moves using credit to equity correlation or equity volatility indices. In the second quarter of 2005, when the structured credit market was affected by a massive drop in correlation and a massive sell-off of equity tranches of both iTraxx and bespoke portfolios, the credit markets were technically affected and spreads pushed wider. This led to a sharp increase of volumes in index transactions, as is typically the case in other mature markets such as the equity market.

### 3.3.3.3  Overview of iTraxx Index Market Players

The main users of iTraxx indices include:

- Credit protection buyers, such as loan portfolio managers, fixed-income cash investors, proprietary traders and hedge funds for relative value trades.
- Credit protection sellers, e.g. asset managers, single tranche products and other option investors.
- Market-makers, who stand in the middle and provide liquidity to customers by recycling the flows. They also use basket trading in order to hedge their positions and thus balance the credit index market.

In the fast-growing credit derivative market, CDSs constitute the main building block based on which investment banks and other intermediaries are able to structure second-generation instruments. These require new pricing, hedging and analysis techniques:

- Understanding default correlation embedded in basket default swaps.
- Modeling contingent risks to build hybrid instruments.
- Managing and analyzing credit risk from a macro or sector-based angle to play in the index market segment.

These new products, in turn, fuel market liquidity in first-generation products in a never-ending virtuous circle.

Beside this first family of second-generation instruments, which are primarily used by traditional credit investors, a new class of structured credit products has emerged over the past 10 years, which builds on securitization and credit derivatives techniques: collateralized debt obligations (CDOs). These products are reviewed in the next chapter.

# 4

# Collateralized Debt Obligations

Collateralized debt obligations, which we shall refer to hereafter by their acronym CDO, cover a large range of products and currently represent one of the most dynamic segments in the credit derivatives market.

One common denominator of these transactions was, until recently, the application of securitization techniques to assets sourced in the financial markets, such as bonds (collateralized bond obligations or CBOs), or from corporate or financial institutions' balance sheets, such as bank loans (collateralized loan obligations or CLOs). In this area, however, the development of credit derivatives has led to the emergence of a new type of products, synthetic CDOs,[1] the recent variations on which are more like the exotic credit derivatives described in the previous chapter than traditional securitization transactions.

The relative position of CDOs among securitization products is shown in Figure 4.1.

Although traditionally, the majority of CDO underlying assets were unitary credit risks (e.g. corporates), the range of products covered by CDOs has recently increased considerably, and now covers other securitization issues (CDOs of ABSs),[2] or even other CDOs (CDOs of CDOs or CDO-squared).

Several types of CDO can be identified depending on:

- The objective of the transaction (arbitrage or balance sheet management-driven).
- The risk transfer mechanism: acquisition of securities (cash CDOs) or use of derivatives (synthetic CDOs).
- The management strategy applied to the product (cash-flow CDOs or market value CDOs).

This typology of CDOs is presented in Figure 4.2. Not all types of transaction are possible (for instance, there are no synthetic market-value balance sheet-driven CDOs). Later in this chapter we shall concentrate on the commonest arrangement types.

First of all we shall examine the cash-flow CDO market, especially arbitrage CBOs/CLOs: securitizations of bonds or loans – historically the first type of CDOs. We shall then analyze the structures created by financial institutions to manage their balance sheets, their aim being to reduce their regulatory capital requirements and/or obtain long-term funding, and the implications of the increased use of credit derivatives in this type of arrangement (synthetic CLOs). We shall conclude the chapter by a detailed review of the latest generation of products, synthetic arbitrage CDOs.

---

[1] 'Synthetic' inasfar as the mechanism for transferring risk is synthetic, using a derivative. A 'CDO' because the underlying risk is the credit risk of the reference entity (i.e. the financial debt in the wider sense, 'borrowed money').

[2] Asset-backed securities (securities representing a securitization issue).

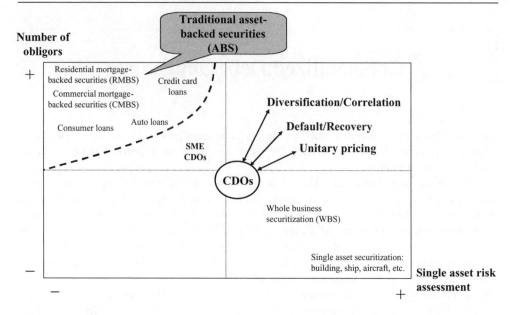

**Figure 4.1**    CDO position in the spectrum of asset-backed securities

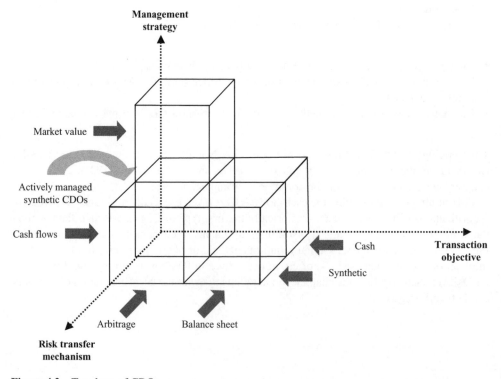

**Figure 4.2**    Typology of CDOs

# 4.1   CASH-FLOW CDOs (ARBITRAGE CBOs AND CLOs)

These were the first form of CDO. They were created to enable investors to benefit from credit spread arbitrages. They are cash arrangements, with no credit derivatives involved. They originated from the asset securitization market.

## 4.1.1   Origin of Arbitrage CBOs/CLOs

These transactions are based on securitization techniques. The latter enable financial institutions or corporates to issue tradable securities in the market, the repayment of which is backed by the cash flows or market value of specific assets. The first securitization transactions took place in the 1970s, when American federal agencies[3] securitized residential mortgage portfolios guaranteed by the American government. In the 1980s, securitization techniques were applied to an extended pool of assets, including: credit card debt, consumer loans (e.g. auto loans), commercial mortgages, student loans, corporate trade receivables, etc.

### 4.1.1.1   Mechanism of a Standard Securitization Transaction

The traditional mechanism of a securitization transaction is as follows: the assignor (the financial institution or firm, also called the sponsor of the securitization transaction) sells assets (usually held on its balance sheet but which may be purchased in the market) by means of a true sale[4] to a trust or bankruptcy-remote special purpose vehicle (SPV), an ad hoc structure created and managed by the sponsor. The sole purpose of the SPV is to hold the assets (the 'collateral') and issue securities backed by them in the capital markets (hence 'asset-backed securities' or ABS). The SPV effectively funds the purchase of the collateral through the issuance of ABSs. All the cash flows generated by the assets are collected by the sponsor, which then passes them on to the investors by means of the SPV (which is a transparent structure).

As the collateral is being repaid, the ABS are amortized. The SPV may also issue new securities corresponding to new assets (in the case of a revolving master trust). The SPV usually benefits from stand-by credit facilities, which, in the unforeseen event of a liquidity crisis, should enable it to refund the investors even if the quality of the underlying assets portfolio deteriorates. In addition, it may also benefit from credit enhancement, a form of financial insurance underwritten by highly rated specialized insurance companies (monoline insurers), enabling a high rating to be attained on the securities issued (AAA/Aaa).

Several factors impact the rating of an ABS issued by an SPV:

- The level of guarantee provided to the SPV by the sponsor and banks.
- The historical delinquency record on the collateral.
- The level of protection provided to the senior tranches by the subordinated tranches[5] and the over-collateralization[6] mechanism.

---

[3] The first was Ginnie Mae (Government National Mortgage Association) followed by the other agencies: Fannie Mac (Federal National Mortgage Association), Freddie Mac (Federal Home Loan Mortgage Corporation) or again, Sallie Mae (Students' Loan Marketing Association).

[4] This mechanism enables the risk of loss attached to the assets to be entirely transferred to the SPV.

[5] A standard securitization transaction can include three or four tranches with different ratings depending on their exposure to the credit risk of the collateral, should the trust be liquidated prematurely. The most exposed tranche is generally not rated and subscribed entirely by the program sponsor.

[6] This over-collateralization corresponds to the difference between the amount of assets assigned to the SPV and the amount of securities effectively issued to investors. Practically speaking, the securities issued by the SPV represent between 90% and 95% of the value of the collateral.

The advantages of securitization for financial institutions and corporates are:

- They allow them greater flexibility in balance sheet and liquidity management.
- They reduce their funding costs, in some cases.

The credit risk attached to the underlying assets is transferred to the investors through the securitization mechanism. A direct consequence of this risk transfer for banks is that it usually enables them to free up regulatory capital.

Securitization can also contribute to reducing asset funding costs. These programs are generally structured to reach high ratings (AAA or AA minimum) on the vast majority of the securities being issued (typically 90% or more), which thus automatically reduces the sponsor's funding costs as its rating may be lower (and insofar as the securitized assets are funded through debt). The total savings achieved by the sponsor in a securitization program also depend on the structuring costs (paid to investment banks and rating agencies) and potential credit enhancement costs.

With a few variations, the securitization technique is also applied to corporate credit risks to create CBO/CLO transactions.

### 4.1.1.2 Introduction to CBO/CLO Transactions

The collateralized bond obligation market was created in the United States in the mid-1980s, at the time of the boom in junk bonds (bonds rated as speculative grade, i.e. below Baa3/BBB−). It was this new type of security that provided the raw material for arranging CBOs. The aim was to exploit an arbitrage opportunity between the yield generated by a portfolio of junk bonds and that required by investors on the securitized debt, the great majority of which (80–90%) is rated investment grade due to the various credit enhancement mechanisms (tranching, diversification, over-collateralization, etc.) inherent in securitization techniques.

In CBO transactions, an ad hoc vehicle issues one or several classes of securities, the repayment of which depends directly on the performance of an underlying bond portfolio, which is acquired by the SPV at financial close.

These structures have also been rapidly extended to the market for leveraged loans, an asset relatively close to high-yield bonds. They were given the generic name of CLO (collateralized loan obligation). A leveraged loan may be deemed an alternative or complement to a junk bond. It is generally a more senior asset, with a higher recovery rate (due to collateralization by physical assets and a more senior position in the capital structure of the obligor), but offering a lower yield. Leveraged loans are also less liquid than bonds, being primarily harbored on bank balance sheets. Structuring CLOs has thus required slight adjustments compared to that of standard CBOs.

### 4.1.1.3 Reasons for the Development of CBO/CLO Transactions

The arrangers of the first transactions of this type sought to meet the specific needs of investors in certain types of asset (so-called investor-driven CBOs/CLOs). The issuance of such structured securities generally enabled the investors to obtain higher yields than those offered in the standard corporate bond market, for BBB-rated risks or more on the senior tranches, thus making them eligible for most investment portfolios. This strong rating could be obtained because of the high degree of diversity in the assets comprised in the portfolio (on average 40 to 60 bonds or loans) underlying the CBO/CLO. The senior tranches thus allowed a large number of institutional investors to take an indirect exposure in the high yield or leveraged loan markets (most of them being prevented from doing so directly by regulations that require that they invest only in investment-grade securities).

A second incentive to structuring CBOs/CLOs was that investors were seeking highly leveraged investment opportunities. They subscribed to the most subordinated tranche of the CBO/CLO structure (the 'equity' tranche).

CBOs/CLOs enable leveraged investments to be made at highly attractive conditions: the cost of the leverage is generally less than a bank credit line (the only alternative) and above all, requires no margin call. Bank loans usually provide for collateralization and forced sale mechanisms where the market value of the investments falls, whereas a CBO/CLO can be analyzed as a term financing (the senior creditors making a commitment for a long period, usually up to 10 or 12 years).

The collapse of the junk bond market in the United States in the early 1990s after the failure of Drexel Burnham Lambert put a temporary stop to the development of arbitrage CBO/CLO transactions. The virtues of these arrangements were rediscovered in 1994–1999 and their numbers again soared. CBOs thus became a major tool in high-yield financing, in both the primary and secondary markets (these vehicles may subscribe to new issues in the primary market or acquire securities in the secondary market to feed their underlying portfolios).

CLO transactions have continued to grow steadily, while the CBO market has begun to lose steam in recent years due to certain excesses, aggravated by a very adverse climate (strong increase in the rate of defaults in the early 2000s).

### 4.1.2   Description of a CDO Structure[7]

From a strictly accounting viewpoint, a CDO may be analyzed like any normal firm, on the basis of its balance sheet and income statement. The assets of a CDO comprise a portfolio of underlying credits, the purchase of which is funded (on the liability side of the balance sheet) by three categories of debt:

- So-called 'senior' debt, the less risky form of the CDO capital structure for investors.
- 'Mezzanine' debt, an intermediate risk category.
- Capital (the 'equity' tranche).

When the CDO is liquidated the senior creditors have priority over the mezzanine investors, who have priority over the equity holders. As in all firms, the amount of capital is an essential factor in determining the cost of funding of the senior and mezzanine tranches (via the level of subordination and leverage of the structure). See Figure 4.3.

The structure of a CDO income statement may also be analyzed. The revenues of a CDO are mainly composed of the coupons paid by the underlying credit portfolio. Annual deductions from this flow of income include:

- CDO administration costs and senior portfolio manager fees.
- Payment of interest to senior creditors.
- Payment of interest to mezzanine investors.
- Junior portfolio manager fees.

---

[7] In this sub-section, we shall use the term CDO to cover both CBOs and CLOs since the structuring mechanisms are essentially the same.

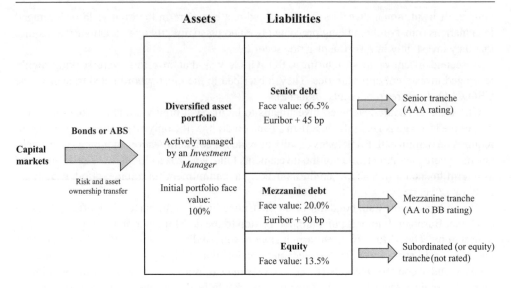

Figure 4.3   Overview of a standard CDO structure

The remaining amount is the CDO net income. This is then paid out to the shareholders (i.e. equity tranche holders) in the form of dividends.

This rule of sequential allocation of income is generally referred to as a cash-flow waterfall. At first sight, therefore, it is possible to model a CDO fairly simply, but it will be seen that the characteristics of these transactions may rapidly lead to more complex modeling requirements.

### 4.1.2.1  Default Risk

In a CDO, the main cause of uncertainty is the performance of the underlying portfolio, itself depending on the risk of the various credits defaulting. A default has a twofold consequence for a CDO structure:

- The amount of assets decreases (and therefore the amount of capital also decreases, the equivalent of a write-off in accounting terms).
- Future income streams decrease (since the coupon is no longer being paid on the asset in default) and so the dividend ultimately paid to the equity tranche investors falls in proportion.

### 4.1.2.2  Portfolio Management

The second cause of uncertainty is dynamic management of the portfolio. The CDO manager may trade on the underlying asset portfolio. These transactions may have the same impact as a default (fall in net worth or in portfolio income). Where there is a gain, the problem becomes more one of normal corporate operation. It can either be paid out in dividends (resulting in no benefit for senior creditors) or added into the CDO capital (the profit then being shared between shareholders and creditors via greater subordination level).

Portfolio management for the CDO is governed by a number of rules, generally laid down in close collaboration with the rating agencies. Compliance with these rules is a major factor in analyzing a CDO and assigning a rating to the senior debt. The manager must comply with a set of criteria, covering the quality of the credit portfolio, its sector diversity, its maturity profile, the maximum annual trading allowance, etc. The rules must enable the rating agencies to model the CDO performance using various scenarios, and then to allocate probabilities to these scenarios, so as to arrive at an estimate of the risk of loss incurred by the senior creditors.

Generally, the portfolio manager is able to modify the portfolio for a given period (five to seven years, the so-called reinvestment period), for the purpose of aligning the duration of the underlying portfolio with the CDO liabilities, or replacing securities, which have been repaid ahead of time, for instance. The portfolio manager does, however, have considerable leeway in his discretionary trading. This dynamic management has a significant impact on the CDO performance, and it is difficult to predict the manager's choices.

As a result, the manager's specific experience and track record in CDO management is important in gauging how a transaction will perform. Thus, recognized managers in the high-yield market (running mutual funds, for instance) were not able to do as well in the CDO market since the environment is markedly different in terms of management constraints, investment processes or trading goals (a traditional manager is often used to benchmark management, with the aim of outperforming a reference index, unlike in CDOs). While experience is a key aspect of a CDO manager's quality, other parameters are also used in judging them:

- Personnel quality, with some CDOs actually containing 'key people' clauses providing for replacement of CDO managers where these key figures are no longer present.
- Clear separation of manager and marketer functions.
- The number of credit analysts.
- The systems and controls set up (autonomy of the manager, nature of the decisional procedures, data collection and processing systems, etc.).
- Financial resources.

### 4.1.2.3   Cash-Flow Diversion Rules (O/C and I/C)[8]

As for bank loans, CDO transactions generally include specific contractual clauses linked to the firm's performance (covenants). Thus, for a traditional loan, the bank may demand repayment of the loan when certain requirements are not met, such as leverage ratios (net debt/capital) and interest cover ratios.

Similar requirements are built into CDOs: cover tests called over-collateralization (O/C) and interest cover (I/C) tests. The difference between CDOs and ordinary loans is that non-compliance with these tests does not lead to early repayment of the debt (which would translate into liquidation of the CDO pure and simple), but rather modification of the rule for distributing dividends. When there is a breach in cover tests, the remaining profit (or repayments of the principal on the portfolio) is no longer paid out to the shareholders or reinvested, but is used to repay the more senior investors (in sequence, depending on their ranking in the capital structure). If, after a certain period, these early repayments lead to renewed compliance with the cover tests, then the initial rules for distributing the dividends will be reinstated.

---

[8] O/C for over-collateralization and I/C for interest cover.

One of the direct consequences of this mechanism is that it enables equity investors to benefit from higher leverage. The mechanism of diverting dividends in a high-loss scenario enables the level of subordination to be reduced (and therefore the amount of the equity tranche) and thus mechanically increases the tranche's internal rate of return (IRR). However, the dividend flows become riskier, since they can be diverted if the cover tests are no longer checked.

One indirect consequence, of equal importance, is the effect of such a mechanism on the manager's behavior. Since the manager is usually the main equity tranche holder in the CDO, he might be inclined to 'secure' the first dividend flows rather than work towards the final repayment of the capital. In a highly leveraged structure, the net present value of the first dividends is often far greater than the net present value of the repayment of the principal at maturity.

The credit enhancement accruing to the senior debt holders in a CDO thus stems partly from the size of the equity tranche, and partly from the cash-flow diversion mechanisms. The second is more difficult to quantify for rating agencies, since it entails a new parameter, the spread of defaults over time. While the rating agencies have reliable data for their default and recovery rate probability calculations over a relatively long period (five to ten years), these data do not allow the most probable time distribution scenario to be ascertained. Thus, supposing all the defaults occur at the start of the period, the diversion mechanism will be activated very quickly and the amount redirected towards the senior investors will be all the greater.

### 4.1.2.4   Interest Rate Risk

To analyze this risk, CBOs must be distinguished from CLOs.

Although the portfolio underlying a CBO generally comprises fixed rate bonds (the commonest in the high-yield bond market), funding in the form of senior debt on the liability side is found at floating rates. Investors in these tranches (generally 80% of a CDO) are mainly banks or banking conduits (ABCPs,[9] SIVs[10]), which traditionally obtain finance on a Libor or Euribor basis. This structural difference thus entails significant interest rate risk, partly dealt with by macro (such as buying options on the scale of the portfolio) or micro (arrangement of an asset swap on each asset in the underlying portfolio) hedging strategies. As for the mezzanine tranches, they are generally issued in fixed rates, placed with fixed rate investors such as insurance companies or pension funds, thus enabling overall interest rate risk to be limited.

CLO-type structures do not entail this type of risk, since leveraged loans are floating rate assets, and assets and liabilities are thus matched.

### 4.1.2.5   Ramp-up and Reinvestment Risks

As seen earlier, the efficacy of the mechanism for diverting dividends is particularly sensitive to default distribution scenarios. Another significant risk parameter is the amount of interest diverted (average portfolio coupon), which corresponds to a market risk. When a CDO is launched, the underlying portfolio cannot immediately be constituted by the manager (essentially to avoid disturbing market liquidity). The portfolio is therefore built up over three to six

---

[9] Asset-backed commercial paper, a 'transformation' vehicle investing in term credit products and refinancing by issuing short-term securities in the capital markets (commercial paper) backed by these assets.

[10] Structured investment vehicles.

months (the ramp-up period). During that time, asset prices may go up and the initial average coupon target for the portfolio might not be attained. In this case, the senior investors would be offered a lower credit enhancement than expected.

Moreover, during the life of the transaction, the manager is regularly led to replace assets (due to prepayments or repayments) and therefore to reinvest part of the portfolio. The market conditions may change and here again, the average coupon level might not be attained. This risk is generally referred to as a reinvestment risk, and is generally limited, since the manager (and the other investors in the equity tranche) have a call option on the CDO, which enables them to terminate the structure early where market conditions are no longer favorable. In this case, at settlement, any potential appreciation of the portfolio would be paid out to the equity investors.

These various characteristics of CBO/CLO structures make them quite difficult to analyze. Highly specialized financial engineering and modeling skills are thus required to create them.

### 4.1.3   Overview of the CBO/CLO Market and Recent Developments

The development of CBOs on high-yield bonds has slowed considerably in recent years (2001–2004). The increased rate of default in the high-yield market over this period was a major factor in CBO underperformance, and investors also realized the behavioral risks inherent in these structures. The major traditional investors thus left this market. One example is American Express, which had to declare a significant amount in losses and provisions on its CBO investments and now no longer invests in them.

The development of CBOs in the mid-1990s enabled some issuers to have access to the capital markets (high yield), despite their financial situation. This appetite for risk is largely due to the strong demand from CBO managers wishing to load their vehicles. Thus, a kind of race for yield began between managers in the CBO segment, unlike in the leveraged loan market, in which the banks (who are still the major actors here) continued to act as a filter. This fundamental difference in market structure (depending on the degree of intermediation) may partly explain the relatively poor performance of CBOs compared to CLOs.

In Europe, the CBO market also went through a difficult period, due to poor anticipation of recovery rates (not least due to the implicit subordination in holding/operating subsidiary relationships).

There are other explanations for the relative underperformance of CBOs recently, such as the portfolio manager's behavior. There have been a certain number of transactions with no real implication of the manager, who did not even provide dynamic management, or for which arbitrage of the rating agencies' requirements was excessive (to ensure an almost guaranteed yield on the equity tranche).

These excesses have led investors to be more selective and to choose their managers more carefully: those having demonstrated poor results in previous transactions have been excluded from the market. Thus, only 47% of managers issuing a CDO in 2001 were able to conclude another transaction in 2002.

The combination of these cyclical (increased default rate, poor performance of existing transactions) and structural factors (fewer managers accepted by investors) has thus logically led to a slump in high-yield CBO transactions. Thus, in 2003, only 2% of the CDOs rated by Moody's in the United States were high-yield CBOs, as against 5% in 2002 and 24% in 2000! This fall was offset by a move by investors towards more stable asset classes. Thus, leveraged loan CLOs and ABS CDOs are now the two main types of cash-flow CDOs, with 25% and 32% of the market in 2003 respectively, according to Moody's.

The main innovations in the cash-flow CDO market recently have mostly concerned currency risk management within the structure. One example of this is the Duchess I CDO (arranged by CIBC, the Canadian bank), launched in the second quarter of 2001. This transaction was backed by a portfolio of underlying assets mostly composed of leveraged loans picked up on the European (in euros) and British (in sterling) markets, to diversify the pool. However, funding was in euros only. These multi-currency transactions cause complex hedging problems that must be handled in collaboration with the rating agencies. The banks have therefore developed macro hedging models for currency risk so that they can offer this type of transaction.

Other structural improvements have recently appeared to make CDOs more attractive for senior bondholders: incorporation of new hedging tests, taking account of assets bought under par, etc. Finally, observers have noted new classes of assets underlying cash-flow CDO transactions, like hedge funds[11] or equity participations in unlisted companies[12] (private equity), even if the CDO volumes on these assets are still marginal.

These recent developments illustrate the fact that the cash-flow CDO technology has become a more and more universal feature of financial engineering, applicable whatever the type of underlying asset. However, it has also been used for other purposes than creation of arbitrage and tailor-made investment instruments. This is particularly the case for balance sheet-driven CDOs, which will be the subject of the next section.

## 4.2  BALANCE SHEET-DRIVEN CDOs

Since the early 1990s, CBO/CLO structures have also been used regularly by banking institutions to manage their credit risk and regulatory capital requirements (these are known as balance sheet-driven CBOs/CLOs). This section first of all presents how these transactions originated (cash-flow CLOs). Then we shall review the effect the development of credit derivatives had on them, and then finish by analyzing an example of 'regulatory arbitrage', one of the prime motives behind the development of synthetic balance sheet-driven CDO transactions.

### 4.2.1  Securitization of Bank Loans

Securitization of bank loans by commercial banks is a relatively recent phenomenon, with securitization programs being developed initially on homogeneous assets for which historical default statistics can easily be compiled and are widely available, such as credit card loans, trade receivables, residential and commercial mortgage debt, etc.

However, the ever-more pressing need to optimize the use of capital and dynamically manage credit portfolios[13] has led banks to explore the possibility of using securitization techniques on their loan portfolios. These securitization transactions enable banking institutions to free up capital, under certain conditions, hitherto allocated to their loan portfolio.

The balance sheet CLOs market truly took off at the end of 1996 with the securitization of loans arranged by NatWest (since bought up by Royal Bank of Scotland) for five billion

---

[11] These are then known as collateralized fund obligations (CFOs). The main transactions were those sponsored by Man Glenwood (Man Glenwood Alternative Strategies I) with JP Morgan in July 2002, and Investcorp (Diversified Strategies CFO) with CSFB in March 2002.

[12] 'Princess' in 1999, arranged by Swiss Re, was the first high-profile transaction in that area.

[13] See Chapter 7.

dollars (ROSE[14] Funding I). The market swiftly reached critical mass in 1997–1998, with many transactions carried out by the leading credit institutions such as NationsBank ($4.3 bn), NatWest ($5 bn, ROSE Funding II), Credit Suisse ($7 bn in three transactions), ABN Amro ($4.4 bn) and several Japanese banks: Tokyo-Mitsubishi ($817 m), Industrial Bank of Japan ($1.9 bn in two transactions), Sakura Bank ($351 m), Sanwa Bank ($1.5 bn) and Sumitomo ($4.7 bn in two transactions)[15]. Over $50 bn in bank loans to large corporations were probably taken off bank balance sheets in this way, and transferred to investors over a period of two years.

These cash-flow balance sheet CLOs are all based on a similar securitization structure: the sponsor bank sells its loans to a vehicle, which issues securities to refinance itself. Alongside this transaction, the bank maintains its commercial relationship with its clients by remaining lender of record, and continues to service the underlying credit lines. Depending on the terms of the loan contracts, the bank may have had the obligation to inform clients of the debt transfer, others may have been asked to give their agreement. Thus, securitization mechanisms do not necessarily all manage to keep the bank's actions secret from customers, unlike credit derivatives. Furthermore, the true sale of the loans to the vehicle enables the bank to reduce the amount of regulatory capital tied up against the underlying portfolio effectively transferred to the SPV.

However, a major drawback of these securitization arrangements is their lack of flexibility. These structures provide for reloading of the vehicle with new loans[16] (Master Trust principle), but require prior agreement from the rating agencies. Moreover, the credit exposures hedged in these transactions are necessarily those linked to the bank loans sold to the vehicle. In this respect, structures based on synthetic transfer of credit risk offer many advantages.

From 1998 onwards it was, indeed, essentially synthetic transactions that developed (first in the United States, then in Europe after 1999). Cash-flow CLO-type transactions gradually disappeared.

### 4.2.2  The Impact of Credit Derivatives: Synthetic CLOs

By using credit derivatives, a CLO structure can benefit from all their inherent advantages in managing credit risk. Thus, synthetic transactions have allowed underlying portfolios to be dynamically managed, and have anticipated hedging of future obligations, as well as hedging of credit exposures on other assets than loans (such as bonds or positions on derivatives). In this respect, it is more appropriate to talk of CDOs than CLOs. A CDO-type transaction is said to be synthetic when the assets are not sold to the investors in the legal sense but where an equivalent economic result is obtained through the use of credit derivatives.

One innovative transaction in this field was the Glacier Finance CDO, launched in September 1997 by Swiss Bank Corporation (since bought up by UBS), in the amount of $1.7 bn. Its competitor Credit Suisse First Boston immediately followed suit with an offer of a similar arrangement, Triangle Funding, in October 1997, on an underlying portfolio worth $5 bn. These operations are on the borderline between traditional balance sheet CLOs and synthetic CDOs, inasfar as they use CLNs to ensure the transfer of credit risk between the bank and the

---

[14] Repeat Offering Securitization Entity.

[15] This list does not include the first transactions using credit derivatives: Swiss Bank Corp. (Glacier Finance), based on $1.7 bn of CLNs, and JP Morgan (BISTRO I), $9.7 bn in notional amount, to which we shall return later.

[16] This reloading option is simply the possibility to substitute assets in the first years should certain underlying assets disappear, in order to maintain the outstandings at the same level.

vehicle. These CLNs are subscribed by the vehicle, which refinances itself by a securities issue. Each CLN represents a credit exposure to an individual debtor, of whatever origin (loan, bond, swap, trade finance, etc.), and can be called back at par by the sponsor bank at each coupon payment date, where the exposure is nil, thus enabling dynamic portfolio management.

These structures are as effective as a real transfer (sale) in terms of management of the sponsor bank's regulatory capital. The reduction in regulatory capital is recognized inasfar as the bank receives cash from the SPV via the issuance of CLNs.[17] Furthermore, contrary to classic CLOs, the use of credit derivative techniques maintains the confidentiality of the exposures transferred.

On the other hand, this type of structure means that the rating cap of the sponsor bank cannot be avoided, since the ultimate payment of the notes depends on the sponsor bank not defaulting, as for any CLN. Moreover, the use of CLNs does not enable the credit risk transfer to be unbundled from the funding, the cash raised by the SPV being deposited on the bank's balance sheet. For highly rated banks, this means raising funds at an unattractive cost (because a securitization transaction requires a risk premium whereas a straightforward bond issue does not). Due to these drawbacks, balance sheet CDOs based on CLNs were never re-used, and were replaced by more efficient arrangements based on CDSs.

### 4.2.2.1   A Pioneering Transaction: JP Morgan's BISTRO

JP Morgan was one of the first banks to combine securitization techniques and credit derivatives on an industrial scale, using its BISTRO program (Broad Index Secured TRust Offering) launched in December 1997. The market had seen earlier transactions like Glacier Finance, but these were not as successful as those launched by JP Morgan, which truly created a new class of assets *per se* with BISTRO.

The principle of this new structure was as follows: the ceding bank, Morgan Guaranty Trust (MGT) and the issue vehicle contracted a five-year CDS referenced on a portfolio of existing and future exposures to 307 good-quality credits.[18] The notional amount of the swap was $9.7 bn. MGT paid a premium in installments to the vehicle, BISTRO, for the CDS.

The SPV issued two tranches of securities, senior and subordinated, for a nominal amount of $697 m, and invested the cash received in risk-free Treasury bonds, used as collateral for the structure and pledged in first rank to MGT, then to the senior investors, and finally to those in the subordinated notes. MGT kept one deeply subordinated tranche, a reserve account, funded up to $32 m over the five-year term of the transaction, by the excess spread paid by MGT to the SPV.

The use of a credit derivative introduced leverage into the structure. This was calculated jointly with the rating agencies so that the senior tranche (the principal of which was $460 m) issued by the SPV was sufficiently secured and obtained the maximum Aaa rating. The subordinated notes ($237 m) were rated Ba2 by Moody's. At maturity, the risk-free portfolio of securities was liquidated by the SPV. The cash was paid first to MGT to offset any losses on the portfolio of exposures over $32 m (i.e. the reserve account serving to offset possible losses). Beyond $269 m of losses on the underlying portfolio ($32 + $237), the investors in the

---

[17] SBC as well as CSFB did in fact benefit from a 'window of opportunity' offered by the Swiss authorities at the time, agreeing to regulatory capital offset against the loan portfolio.

[18] One of the particularities of this transaction is that JP Morgan published a list of the underlying obligors included in the reference portfolio of the CDS. That was not the case in the other CLO transactions.

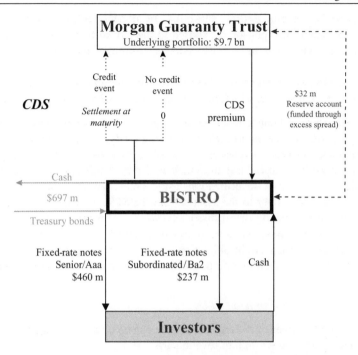

**Figure 4.4**    BISTRO

senior tranche lost capital, and the holders of subordinated notes would not be repaid.[19] Beyond $729 m of losses on the underlying portfolio, MGT would again be at risk (theoretically $9.7 bn less the $697 m placed with investors), and the SPV would not be able to repay any amount, either on the senior or the subordinated tranches of the notes issued. See Figure 4.4.

The drawback of the BISTRO arrangement was that it was less efficient than the cash-flow CLO arrangements as regards regulatory capital optimization: the recognized risk offset and corresponding amount of regulatory capital to be freed up was lower than the notional amount of the default swap.[20] However, paradoxically, it gave MGT a very efficient hedge by transferring to the investors the risk of loss on the underlying portfolio from the first dollar (not counting the $32 m reserve funded over time by the CDS premium), contrary to other CLO arrangements in which the protection of investors' principal is ensured by several subordinated tranches, the most junior of which is usually nonrated and retained by the sponsoring bank.[21] JP Morgan did actually repeat this structure in April 1998, issuing BISTRO II. This transaction covered a portfolio of 145 credit risk exposures for a total amount of $4.8 bn. It comprised a three-year senior tranche rated AAA for $200 m, one subordinated tranche rated Baa2 for $150 m and one

---

[19] It is worth noting that since the structure was settled only at maturity, the investors ran no risk on coupon payments.

[20] The hedge offered by the default swap was partly recognized by the Fed inasfar as it would have allowed MGT to retain only the higher regulatory capital charge between its long position (the credit exposure linked to the portfolio hedged by the transaction) and its short position (linked to the five-year CDS).

[21] This causes critics of classic CLO arrangements to remark that they are merely regulatory arbitrage transactions, since the ceding bank manages to reduce the amount of regulatory capital, but keeps the majority of the 'economic' credit risk by underwriting the most subordinated tranche of the CLO. Theoretically, if this reasoning is pursued, the banks should be led to securitize all the assets held on their balance sheets, the marginal risk of which corresponds to an amount of economic capital under 8% of assets, to maximize this regulatory arbitrage.

nonrated tranche for $60.5 m, entirely subscribed by JP Morgan (thus resembling traditional cash-flow CLOs where the sponsor is exposed to the risk of first loss via its investment in the equity tranche, which has to be fully deducted from capital under the capital adequacy regulations).

However, the BISTRO arrangement offered several crucial advantages, enabling it to impose itself as the reference model on which the balance sheet CDO market could build:

- It enabled investors to benefit from the leverage inherent in derivatives, contributing to increased yield without having to compromise on underlying creditworthiness.
- MGT did not need to forgo its funding conditions in the market by dissociating the transfer of credit risk from fund raising (whereas they are irremediably linked in cash-flow CLOs).
- Finally, whereas in ordinary securitizations using a real transfer mechanism, the credit risk transferred corresponds only to the asset sold to the SPV, the appeal of credit derivatives in a CDO structure is clearly that it dissociates the actual management of credit risk from the underlying asset. Thus, synthetic transactions enable the sponsoring banks to move from management of their credit obligations on a case-by-case basis (for each individual instrument) to an overall view of their portfolio and treatment of credit risk at obligor level.[22]

### 4.2.2.2 Key Elements of a Synthetic CLO

Even though a large number of different structures can be observed, it is possible to divide a classic synthetic CLO transaction into several parts.

- An SPV issues CLN-type bonds and uses the nominal amount of the CLNs to acquire assets as collateral, typically in the form of triple-A rated securities such as T-bonds (weighted 0% under the Basel I rules).
- The collateral will be sold in the market or bought back by the sponsor bank when the CLNs are redeemed.
- The sponsoring bank contracts a subordinated CDS with the SPV for a notional amount of about 9% to 15% of the total of the reference portfolio. Under the swap, the SPV will be required to pay the bank the amount of losses on defaulting assets, allocating the losses to the various bonds issued in sequential order (depending on their degree of seniority). This hedge is remunerated by the premium paid by the bank under the CDS.
- The interest on the CLN issue is funded by the coupons paid on the collateral securities and the CDS premium from the sponsor bank.
- The latter keeps the most subordinated tranche issued by the SPV (equity or first loss tranche), which usually represents between 1% and 3% of the total amount of the underlying portfolio.
- The sponsor bank contracts a second CDS, senior to that with the SPV, enabling it to hedge the residual losses (i.e. 85% to 91% of the portfolio). This second CDS is commonly known as a super senior swap.
- The reference portfolio on which the two CDSs are based comprises reference entities, each of which is allocated a protection amount.
- The reference portfolio is generally dynamic (that is, actively managed by the sponsor bank) and must correspond to the criteria of diversification, creditworthiness and eligibility laid down by the rating agencies. The reference portfolio is not usually divulged to the investors, only anonymous statistical data are given.

---

[22] We shall return to the implications of credit derivatives in bank portfolio management in Chapter 7.

**Table 4.1**   Main balance sheet-driven synthetic CDO transactions

| Transaction | Date | Amount (m) | Sponsor |
|---|---|---|---|
| Bistro Trust I 1997 | December 1997 | $9700 | JP Morgan |
| Bistro Trust II 1998 | April 1998 | $4800 | JP Morgan |
| C*Star 1991–1 | June 1999 | €4000 | Citibank |
| Blue Stripe 1999–1 | July 1999 | $5000 | Deutsche Bank |
| Scala | November 1999 | €4000 | BCI |
| C*Star 1991–2 | November 1999 | $4000 | Citibank |
| Sundial | May 2000 | €2537 | Rabobank |
| Cygnus Finance | June 2000 | €4300 | KBC |
| Olan II | June 2000 | €4000 | BNP Paribas |
| Blue Stripe 2000–1 | June 2000 | $3000 | Deutsche Bank |
| BAC Synthetic CLO 2000–1 | September 2000 | $10 000 | Bank of America |

The advantages of this type of transaction are their simplicity and confidentiality, as well as the fact that the risk is dissociated from the funding (which enables highly rated banks to avoid the higher funding costs of securitization). Secondly, as we have seen, synthetic transfer enables all types of credit exposure to be hedged, independently of any particular asset. Thus undrawn credit facilities (off-balance-sheet obligations) cannot be included in cash-flow CLOs; yet these obligations represent a considerable percentage of the credit risks run by banks and use up a large amount of regulatory capital. On the other hand, there is less opportunity to distribute these products to final investors, as underlined earlier, and the reduction of regulatory capital is not as efficient as in a cash CLO.[23] Moreover, the sponsoring bank must also take account of counterparty risk.

However, there is no doubt that the economic advantages and increased flexibility of these structures were the cause of the boom in synthetic transactions in 1999–2000, and they have now completely supplanted cash-flow CLO transactions.

### 4.2.2.3   Overview of the Synthetic Balance Sheet-Driven CDO Market

Table 4.1 provides an overview of the development of the market in synthetic balance sheet-driven CDOs. Most of the transactions began in 1999–2000.

The surge in synthetic balance sheet-driven CDO transactions gradually receded for several reasons, among which were the expectations of a change in the regulations with the implementation of Basel II. We shall return to the question of how long this type of instrument is likely to last under the Basel II provisions in Section 7.2. Meanwhile, the following paragraphs will enable us to analyze these transactions in the light of the current Basel I standards and thus highlight the notion of regulatory arbitrage.

### 4.2.3   Balance Sheet-Driven CDOs and Regulatory Arbitrage

The primary reason for sponsor banks issuing a balance sheet-driven CDO is to optimize their use of regulatory capital. It is therefore worthwhile to examine the current regulatory treatment of these transactions.

---

[23] In a cash CLO, the amount of freed-up regulatory capital will not, in any case, be 100%, since the sponsor bank generally subscribes to the most subordinated tranche in the structure, the amount of which is fully deducted from its capital base.

### 4.2.3.1    Brief Outline of the Regulatory Analysis of Synthetic CLO Transactions

One first thing about balance sheet-driven CDOs is the definition, determination and allocation of losses in the reference credit portfolio. The losses are defined on the basis of credit events in standard use in the credit derivatives market. Bankruptcy and failure to pay are events defined in all transactions. The inclusion of restructuring depends on the regulations in force in the country of the sponsor bank. The amount of losses is generally calculated by a cash settlement of the CDS, with the sponsor bank asking for market prices on the defaulting assets from various market dealers. The allocation of losses is sequential, as for any securitization transaction, with possible extra credit enhancement mechanisms (such as, for instance, a reserve account fed over time by the sponsor bank until the term of the transaction).

Regulatory treatment for this type of transaction varies with the country of origin of the sponsor institutions. The main differences occur in only a few details. The main one is the treatment of super senior tranches. Since November 1999, the Fed has authorized the banks it supervises to keep these tranches on their balance sheets without immobilizing capital. This flexibility enabled the American sponsor banks, especially JP Morgan, the most active among them, to carry out many transactions in more attractive economic conditions than for its main competitors (they saved almost 50% of the total transaction cost on hedging of the super senior tranches). On the other hand, some European supervisory authorities (like the French Commission Bancaire) showed themselves to be far more conservative than their American counterparts, not least in the treatment of transactions with a step-up call option (which provides for an increased premium after an anticipated redemption date if the CDO is not called by the sponsor bank) or in the interpretation of the credit enhancement mechanisms (reserve account for instance).

The new Basel II framework should foster convergence of the regulatory interpretations and thus reduce the competitive advantages structurally available to American banks in this market. The provisions in this area are much more precise and leave a relatively small margin for manoeuver to the national regulators. From current discussions, it looks as though the new regulations will enable better control of the efficacy of these transactions, particularly in terms of effective transfer of credit risk.

### 4.2.3.2    Economics of a Balance Sheet CDO and Regulatory Arbitrage

In order to explain why it is in banks' interest to use synthetic CDO transactions to optimize their use of capital under the current capital adequacy regulations, we shall present a fictitious transaction inspired directly from the securitizations implemented in 1999–2000.

**Main assumptions**

Let us imagine a banking institution with the following balance sheet structure:

|  | €(bn) | % |
|---|---|---|
| Total risk-weighted assets (RWA) | 164.0 | 100.0 |
| Tier II capital | 7.5 | 4.6 |
| Tier I capital | 10.7 | 6.5 |
| **Total capital** | **18.2** | **11.1** |

Like many banking institutions, it has surplus capital in respect of the minimum requirements of Basel I (8% of weighted assets).

In order to optimize its use of regulatory capital, this banking institution envisages synthetic securitization of a credit portfolio currently held on its balance sheet. This portfolio represents €3 bn in credit commitments, two-thirds being drawn. The weighted assets relating to this portfolio therefore represent €2.5 bn,[24] the total amount of regulatory capital allocated to this portfolio is €277.5 m and the amount of Tier I capital €162.5 m (on the basis of the ratios presented in the above table).

## Transaction structure

A synthetic securitization transaction is planned on this portfolio of underlying credits. It is divided into several risk tranches:

- The majority of the portfolio (90%) is rated AAA/Aaa and will be hedged via a super senior CDS with a 20% weighted counterparty (OECD bank).[25]
- The rest of the portfolio (10%) will be hedged through a subordinated CDS with an SPV, which in turn will issue CLNs to institutional investors. The cash thus generated will be invested in 0% weighted Treasury bonds pledged to the sponsor bank. This 10% tranche will in reality comprise four risk tranches, each rated differently.
- The credit risks corresponding to the three most senior tranches (AAA/Aaa, A2/A and BB/Ba2), representing 3% of the portfolio each, will be transferred to the investors.
- However, the first loss risk (the 1% representing the most subordinated, nonrated risk tranche of the portfolio) is retained by the sponsor bank.

Figure 4.5 shows the synthetic CDO transaction.

## Analysis of the transaction

The first stage in the analysis is to assess the savings enabled by the transaction in terms of regulatory capital. Secondly, this capital saving must be compared to the transaction cost for the sponsor bank.

The regulatory treatment of the various tranches is as follows:[26]

- The portion of the portfolio hedged under the super senior CDS draws a new risk weighting of 20% (that of the guarantor).
- The 9% corresponding to the CLNs issued by the SPV benefit from the risk weighting of the collateral, i.e. 0% for OECD government securities.
- Finally, as for all securitization transactions in which the sponsor bank retains the risk of first loss, the most subordinated 1% tranche must be deducted from the sponsor bank's capital base (i.e. an equivalent theoretical risk weighting of 1250% for a target capital ratio of 8%).

Figure 4.6 presents the structure and the savings in terms of capital and risk-weighted assets (RWA).

---

[24] $2/3 \times 3.0 \times 100\% + 1/3 \times 3.0 \times 50\% = 2.5$ bn.

[25] This bank can only play the role of intermediary, hedging in turn by a back-to-back transaction with another counterparty such as a monoline insurer or a reinsurer.

[26] Where the transaction criteria comply with the constraints laid down by the supervisory authorities.

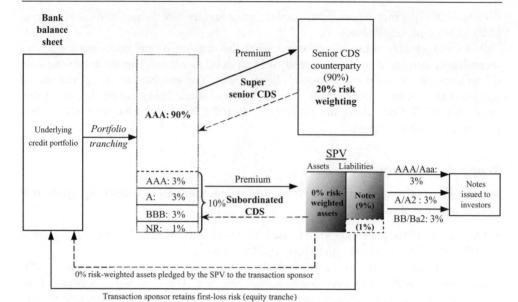

**Figure 4.5**   Synthetic CDO transaction

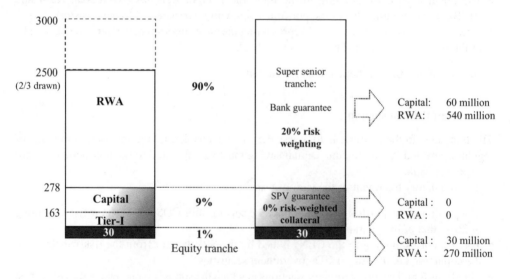

**Figure 4.6**   Transaction analysis and estimate of capital savings

The super senior tranche risk-weighted assets post-transaction amount to €540 m (3000 × 90% × 20%).[27] This tranche will now draw capital in the amount of €60 m (540 × 11.1%). The tranches covered by the CLN issue no longer attract any capital charge since they are collateralized by 0% weighted securities. Finally, the most subordinated tranche, which must

---

[27] Amount of portfolio multiplied by the share of the tranche in the structure (90%) multiplied by the guarantor's risk weighting (20%).

**Table 4.2**   Analysis of the synthetic CDO transaction cost structure

| Structure/tranche | % | Cost (bppa) |
|---|---|---|
| Super senior tranche | 90 | 10 |
| Subordinated tranches | 9 | |
|    AAA/Aaa | 3 | 40* |
|    A2/A | 3 | 110* |
|    BB/Ba2 | 3 | 350* |
| Unrated equity tranche | 1 | ** |
| **Average cost to the bank** | | **24** |
| Structuring fees | | 3 |
| **Total cost to the bank** | | **27** |

*Notes*: *Including negative carry. **Underwritten by the sponsor bank.

be deducted from the bank's capital base, is weighted 'one for one', thus representing 30 million in regulatory capital (i.e. 270 million in RWA).

This transaction thus enables the sponsor bank to save:

- 1.69 billion in risk-weighted assets (2.5 – 0.81); and
- 188 million in regulatory capital (278 – 90).

To what extent is an operation like this beneficial to the sponsor bank? To evaluate its worth, the second aspect of the transaction, i.e. the cost to the bank, must be considered. The hypotheses in terms of cost are shown in Table 4.2.[28] The overall cost of the transaction for the sponsor bank is therefore €8.1 m per year (3 billion × 27 basis points).

This annual expense should be compared with the savings made on capital multiplied by the target return on equity (ROE) for the bank (let us say, 15% before tax), which theoretically corresponds to the minimum rate of return to be generated on the capital freed up by the transaction:

$$188\,\text{million} \times 15\% = 28.2\,\text{million}$$

As long as the transaction costs are lower than this target amount, it should be worth the sponsor bank's while to undertake the transaction.[29] Theoretically, in this configuration, the total maximum cost that can be envisaged by the bank is 94 basis points.

This analysis of the worth of the transaction for the bank is based on a major assumption, the rate of reinvestment of the freed-up capital (15%). If in fact the available capital is recycled by the bank to grant low-yielding loans to corporate borrowers, then the overall savings generated by the transaction are not worth the while. For the bank to improve its ratios, its freed-up capital must be invested in activities with a higher ROE than the classic bank loan business for which the synthetic CDO was put in place.

Finally, we must conclude this example with the notion of 'regulatory arbitrage'. For this type of transaction, we refer to regulatory arbitrage inasfar as it is an arrangement enabling the sponsor bank to reduce its amount of regulatory capital (by 188 million in the foregoing

---

[28] The securities placed in collateral in the SPV are typically sovereign OECD bonds, trading at sub-Libor spreads. As a result, there is an additional cost for the sponsor bank (the '*negative carry*') to take account of, since the CLNs issued by the SPV pay Libor-based coupons.

[29] Another comparable analysis criterion is to calculate the 'reverse ROE' of the transaction by dividing its cost by the amount of capital freed up. As long as this ratio is lower than the bank's target ROE, it should be worth its while.

example) without reducing the level of (real) economic risk it runs on the underlying portfolio, inasfar as the sponsor bank keeps the risks of first loss (up to 30 million) on the portfolio. It is the development of these transactions that led the banking authorities to revise the rules governing securitization transactions, set forth in the Basel I Accords. In Chapter 7 we will review these new regulations and will return to this example and analyze it in the light of the new regulations provided for by Basel II.

Following the wave of balance sheet-driven synthetic CDOs in 1998–2001, investment banks have used these techniques to seize arbitrage opportunities, thus giving birth to a new class of products: arbitrage-driven synthetic CDOs. These have fuelled the development of the structured credit market since 2001–2002. These transactions will be examined in the last section of this chapter.

## 4.3   ARBITRAGE-DRIVEN SYNTHETIC CDOs

The market in arbitrage-driven synthetic CDOs was initially a natural extension of balance sheet transactions. As described earlier, these transactions use underlying assets (bank loans) originated from a commercial bank's balance sheet, the latter usually keeping the most sub-ordinated risk tranche in the transaction. The development of the CDS market, its growing liquidity and the emergence of sophisticated risk management techniques have facilitated the replication of these structures for arbitrage purposes, resulting in the emergence of a new product class: arbitrage-driven synthetic CDOs.

Although the first transaction of this kind took place in June 2000, these new instruments only really took off as of 2001, a period marked by an across-the-board widening of credit spreads (with the crisis in the telecommunications sector in the first half of the year and then 9–11, leading to an unprecedented wave of defaults, including Enron). While the initial structures were mere replications of balance sheet-driven synthetic CDOs (with real transfer of all the risk tranches linked to a CDS portfolio), the market soon moved to new structures:

- First, managed synthetic CDOs.
- Second, on-demand or bespoke single-tranche CDOs, the characteristics of which are to enable investors to select an underlying portfolio and the risk tranche desired (usually a mezzanine tranche). The residual position is then delta-managed by the investment bank structuring the product, thus avoiding having to distribute the entire capital structure of the CDO, contrary to the earlier transactions in this area.

### 4.3.1   The First Arbitrage-Driven Synthetic CDOs

The first arbitrage-driven synthetic CDOs (i.e. fulfilling the wish to earn a risk-free profit rather than ensure risk management or capital adequacy requirements optimization) replicated synthetic balance sheet-driven CDO structures.

#### 4.3.1.1   Typical Structure of the First Arbitrage-Driven Synthetic CDOs

As for synthetic balance sheet CDOs, the first arbitrage transactions were based on a complete back-to-back principle. The bank intermediaries assembled a portfolio of underlying credit risk, used the tranching techniques usually found in securitization transactions to create tranches with a risk profile corresponding to investor expectations. They then covered 100% of the underlying risk portfolio via purchase of protection in funded form (CLNs) or not (CDSs). It is thus via tranching techniques and their optimization that the bank intermediaries managed arbitrage between the average spread of the underlying portfolio and the hedging cost.

More precisely, the CDO structure typically included:

- Issue of mezzanine CLNs using an SPV.
- Direct purchase of super senior protection via a CDS.

The securities issued by the vehicle (CLNs) generally protected the arranging bank for its subordinated mezzanine exposure (typically between 3% and 10% of the portfolio losses) while the super senior counterparty was liable for losses beyond this exposure (in this example, beyond 10%).

Moreover, in the case of these first arrangements, the bank intermediary needed to place the first loss tranche (0% to 3% of losses) to hedge the portfolio completely (unlike the synthetic balance sheet CDOs for which this tranche was usually kept by the sponsor bank). The bank thus purchased complete protection on an underlying portfolio of individual CDSs, enabling it to sell on these protections in the CDS market to hedge the structured product and generate a premium that would be the source of the arbitrage. The assets used as references in these structures were not bank loans but generic credit exposures to reference entities, as in the case of a standard CDS ('borrowed money'). See Figure 4.7.

The majority of the transactions in 2001 and 2002 were structured on the basis of static underlying portfolios, thus without portfolio managers (unlike arbitrage CBOs). Because investors were generally familiar with the credit risks referenced in these transactions (large multinational companies), a manager did not seem required. The main advantages of this approach were the increased transparency of the transaction and its economic efficiency. This type of transaction in fact enables the active management cost to be avoided, as well as significant savings on structuring costs (legal, rating agency and auditor fees, etc.).

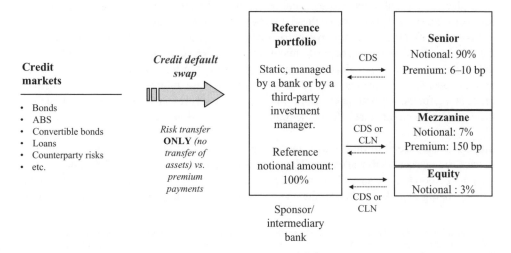

**Figure 4.7**  Typical structure of the first arbitrage-driven synthetic CDOs

### 4.3.1.2   Characteristics of the First Synthetic Arbitrage CDO Structures

The underlying credit portfolios were usually very homogeneous, composed of the most liquid credits in the CDS market, generally some hundred European or American names, usually investment grade. It is the relative homogeneity of the portfolios underlying these transactions that partly explains the underperformance of these products during the 2001–2002 wave of defaults, since all these CDOs referenced names such as Worldcom or Enron.

The first synthetic CDOs were generally bullet (a determined, identical maturity for all risk tranches), contrary to arbitrage CBOs, which amortize sequentially, and include early repayment options. This characteristic enables a wider range of investors to be targeted (investment in bullet securities is more attractive for asset/liability management purposes).

Other characteristics make these structures simpler and more attractive overall than traditional arbitrage CBOs:

- Easy interest rate and currency risk management (e.g. CDSs on American names can easily be sold in euros).
- No reinvestment risk since it is a static, bullet structure.
- Absence of manager behavioral risk (a manager might be tempted to maximize the excess spread to secure an attractive return on capital, to the detriment of senior bondholders, as discussed above).

Furthermore, from the arranger's point of view, the use of CDSs makes structuring more flexible than for cash instruments.

The economic cornerstone of these first synthetic arbitrage CDOs was the bank intermediaries' capacity to get rid of first loss risk, a prerequisite for hedging effectiveness, and therefore their ability to convince investors to underwrite the equity tranche. Consequently, the key success factor in this market was to have first-class fixed income distribution capabilities. It is not surprising that the big American houses and the world's fixed income leaders (Morgan Stanley, Lehman Brothers, Deutsche Bank, JP Morgan, CSFB, etc.) rapidly took over this market segment (unlike in the balance sheet CDO market, where the large commercial banks had a natural advantage because of their balance sheet sizes). Once the first loss tranche had been placed, the bank intermediary went on to subscribe the senior and mezzanine tranches for later sale, since distribution of these tranches of risks was relatively easy.

In order to offer the most attractive returns on the equity tranches and thus draw new investors, the investment banks rapidly began to maximize the arbitrage of the analysis methods used by the rating agencies. This mainly consisted of optimizing portfolio selection using the various criteria considered by the agencies (diversity score, average rating) to achieve an investment grade rating for the senior tranches while minimizing the level of subordination (which, roughly, meant selecting credits that offered the highest spread possible for a given rating class).[30]

This systematic trend towards optimization was like the windfall deal phenomenon observed in the CBO market, analyzed earlier. The widening of credit spreads in late 2000 and above all after 9-11, soon led to transactions in which the arranging banks could keep the equity tranche without being at risk. In this arrangement, the excess spread on the portfolio completely

---

[30] Thus, in 2002, it was estimated that the name most often found in arbitrage CDO reference portfolios was the American issuer Philip Morris. This appetite for Philip Morris risk can be explained by the fact that CDO arrangers sought to arbitrage between its BBB rating and the actual credit spread offered on Philip Morris CDSs: because of the potential risk of a lawsuit against the tobacco firm, it was simply the investment grade signature trading at the highest spread level in the CDS market!

**Table 4.3**   Repon 15 CDO capital structure

| Class | Amount (€ m) | Rating | % | Subordination | Spread* |
|-------|-------------|--------|---|---------------|---------|
| A | 4029.60 | Super senior | 92.00% | 8.00% | 10 |
| B | 148.92 | AAA | 3.40% | 4.60% | 40 |
| C | 35.04 | AA | 0.80% | 3.80% | 70 |
| D | 43.80 | BBB+ | 1.00% | 2.80% | 210 |
| E | 30.66 | BBB− | 0.70% | 2.10% | 375 |
| F | 30.66 | BB | 0.70% | 1.40% | 775 |
| G | 61.32 | *First loss* | 1.40% | — | |

*Note*: *In basis points per annum.
*Sources*: Creditflux, S&P, Bloomberg.

offsets the provision made by the bank for the retained risk, which means in effect that the bank intermediaries could buy the equity tranche of the CDO for free. The number of synthetic arbitrage CDOs literally exploded from then on, since all the intermediaries could join in as the placement of the first loss tranche became superfluous.

The following example will serve to illustrate this 'free equity tranche' pattern: we shall make a quick analysis of the Repon 15 CDO issued by Deutsche Bank in March 2001. This was a synthetic CDO on a five-year portfolio of 120 credits. Table 4.3 shows the capital structure of the CDO (tranching of the transaction).

On the basis of this information, we can calculate an average financing cost of 22 basis points. Let us suppose that the average premium on the underlying CDSs is 65 basis points. The excess spread on the portfolio is therefore 43 basis points, which, discounted over five years (with an assumed discount rate of 4), should generate an income of about 1.74% on the portfolio (0.43% × 4). This amount is more than the amount of the first loss tranche (1.4%) the arranger is exposed to if the tranche is retained on its books. This is the 'free equity tranche'. However, it should be noted that this income is not certain: should credit events occur in the portfolio, the excess spread will decrease. This risk can be hedged dynamically by buying short-term protection on the names with the widest spreads.

This mechanism enabled banks to step up the volume of transactions considerably, inasfar as placement of the first loss tranche was no longer needed for the structures to take off. A rapid explosion in these synthetic CDO transactions, referenced to static investment grade credit risk pools, was therefore observed. Most of them were large public transactions such as Morgan Stanley's Epoch/Spices, Deutsche Bank's Repon, and Bank of America's Helix programs. The transparency and simplicity of these structures attracted large numbers of investors, especially in Europe.

### 4.3.1.3   Financial Débâcles: the Reversal of the Synthetic Arbitrage CDO Market

Nine-eleven and the Enron bankruptcy nipped the development of this type of arrangement in the bud:

- First of all, some programs had disastrous performances (those referencing static portfolios mainly).
- Secondly, many investors recorded significant losses on their investments and withdrew from the market.

Thus, in the Repon 15 transaction mentioned earlier, five obligors in the reference portfolio underwent credit events (Enron, Genuity, Railtrack, Solutia and Teleglobe). The amount of losses thus exceeded 2.5%. Tranche C, initally rated AA by Standard & Poor's, is currently rated B, while tranche E, initially rated BBB−, is in default (rated D).

Many financial institutions have been hit by this market downturn. The reinsurer Scor, or European banking group Dexia, in particular, have recorded significant losses in their investments in this type of product.

### Examples

SCOR was a major player in the credit derivatives and synthetic CDO market until September 2001. The reinsurance company's strategy was to build up a portfolio of exposures to investment grade names in addition to its traditional business in credit guarantees. The Group's exposure to risks linked to credit derivatives totalled an overall portfolio of 669 names, virtually all the available risk in the CDS market. After the default rates increased and credit spreads widened in the wake of 9/11, SCOR's operating losses on its credit derivatives book reached €65 m in 2002 and €72 m in 2003.[31] In 2003 the amount of provisions was €110 m. On 1 December 2003, SCOR concluded an agreement with Goldman Sachs under which it withdrew completely from the credit derivatives market. The net cost in accounting terms for this, including a switch transaction in the fourth quarter of 2003, amounted to €45 m, given the provisions previously built up.

In early 2001, at the same time as it acquired the bank Artesia, the Dexia bank detected a fraudulent transaction on a CLN portfolio. Restructuring and hedging of this portfolio led to substantial charges and provisions. Thus, in 2000 and 2001, Dexia was obliged to declare the following costs:[32]

- €103.8 m in provisions on the CLN portfolio;
- €26.6 m in insurance costs on the CLN portfolio;
- €11.6 m in legal costs on the CLN portfolio.

The cascade of bankruptcies or restructuring in the wake of the Enron case (especially in the field of telecommunications and new technologies, with WorldCom, Teleglobe, AT&T Canada, Marconi or Genuity) moved the spotlight to the main drawbacks of these products. The static character of these transactions suddenly became a major drawback, as was the absence of a secondary market and the lack of pricing transparency. The synthetic CDO market thus logically evolved under the influence of new structures incorporating portfolio managers (actively managed arbitrage-driven synthetic CDOs).

### 4.3.2 Actively Managed Arbitrage-Driven Synthetic CDOs

The first dynamically managed transactions were directly inspired by balance sheet-driven CDOs. They were usually initiated by commercial banks' investment banking departments. The only difference was that the underlying asset in the transaction was not a bank loan but generic credit exposure embedded in CDSs.

---

[31] *Sources*: SCOR annual reports for 2002 and 2003.
[32] *Sources*: Dexia annual reports for 2001 and 2002.

**Table 4.4**   Main actively managed synthetic arbitrage CDOs

| Transaction | Date | Amount (m) | Manager |
|---|---|---|---|
| Robeco CSO III | December 2001 | €1000 | Robeco |
| Blue Chip Funding | December 2001 | €1000 | Dolmen Securities |
| Sutter CDO 2001–1 | December 2001 | $1000 | Wells Fargo |
| Port Royal Synthetic CDO | December 2001 | $1000 | Deerfield |
| GIA Synthetic CDO | January 2002 | $1000 | Global Investment Advisors |
| Jazz CDO I | February 2002 | €1500 | Axa IM |
| Robeco CDO IV | May 2002 | €1000 | Robeco |
| Cheyne Investment Grade CDO I | June 2002 | $4500 | Cheyne Capital |

### 4.3.2.1   The First Actively Managed Arbitrage-Driven Synthetic CDOs

Abbey National (Marylebone CBO I and II) in December 2000 and April 2001, comprising notional amounts of 500 million and 1 billion dollars, respectively, and UBS Principal Finance in August 2001 (Brooklands 2001–1, with 1 billion euros), were the first to launch synthetic structures in the market while retaining the first loss tranches and the possibility to manage the reference portfolio actively. In these structures, the possible substitutions in the portfolio did not, however, produce an impact in terms of capital structure for the investors, since the trading gains or losses were fully taken by the manager. This brings these transactions closer to synthetic CLO transactions while differentiating them from arbitrage CDO-type structures. However, this specificity could entail a risk of collusion, since the manager could be tempted to maximize the average portfolio spread to improve the yield on the first loss tranche to the detriment of the senior tranche investors.

The first actively managed transaction of any significance truly to replicate the mechanisms of arbitrage CDOs was no doubt Robeco CSO III, arranged by JP Morgan in December 2001 and managed by asset manager Robeco. It was immediately followed by a great many similar transactions. See Table 4.4.

The Jazz transactions, managed by Axa Investment Managers, and Cheyne Investment Grade CDO I (managed by Cheyne Capital) marked the evolution of these products, first because of their structural innovations (Jazz fully benefited from the management options made possible by synthetic technology) and also because of the volumes issued (the Cheyne Capital CDO is similar in size to the largest synthetic balance sheet-driven CLO transactions).

### 4.3.2.2   Analysis of Jazz CDO I

The Jazz CDO I transaction was arranged by Deutsche Bank for Axa Investment Managers (IM). The CDO structure was based on the creation of an SPV, the role of which was active management of a credit portfolio. The active management could involve:

- Trading of protections (sale and purchase, including short positions) with one or several counterparties in the CDS market.
- Taking long positions in bonds, since the vehicle was granted a credit line by Deutsche Bank.

**Table 4.5**   Jazz CDO I structure

| Class | Amount (€m) | Rating | % | Subordination |
|---|---|---|---|---|
|  | 1235 | Super senior | 82.06% | 17.94% |
| A | 78 | AAA | 5.18% | 12.76% |
| B | 78 | AA | 5.18% | 7.57% |
| C | 27 | A− | 1.82% | 5.75% |
| D | 27 | BBB | 1.82% | 3.99% |
| E | 60 | NR (first loss) | 3.99% | — |

The face amount of the reference portfolio was €1488 m. The SPV issued CLNs (classes A, B, C and D) in the amount of €270 m, 17.94% of the total amount issued (€1505 m).[33] See Table 4.5.

Contrary to a static deal or a synthetic CLO, the SPV was able to contract CDSs with various counterparties and buy bonds (in this sense, the transaction is a sort of hybrid between a cash and a synthetic CDO). Axa IM was able to substitute assets in the reference portfolio in the course of the transaction, on condition it complied with the management criteria laid down in agreement with the rating agencies. Axa IM was given considerable leeway in managing the portfolio over the first five years (the reinvestment period) and then would be able to carry out defensive trading deals during the final three years. Thus, despite the 20% annual limit set on discretionary trading, Axa IM could, in addition, replace credits the creditworthiness of which had improved or had become impaired. In the Jazz I transaction, Axa IM carried out trading operations in a volume equivalent to almost 100% of the portfolio value from February 2002 to December 2003.

Axa IM also had considerable flexibility as regards taking account of trading losses and gains on CDSs. A CDS could be replaced:

• Either upon unwinding a position, the net present value of the gain or loss thus being carried over into subordination or principal.
• Or by offsetting the position, i.e. taking a CDS position mirroring the exposure to be hedged, the premium differential therefore affecting the CDO interest account over time. The offset method enables the manager to speculate on the possible occurrence of default in the entity covered, in which case the loss will be merely the premium differential paid up to the default, thus considerably less than the net present value of the premium differential until maturity.

There are many investment strategies available to the manager:

• Long positions in CDSs (the majority of exposures).
• Long positions on bonds (funded by drawing under the credit line).
• Short positions in CDSs.
• Taking 'basis' positions, i.e. arbitraging between CDSs and traditional bonds (buying a bond and hedging it with a CDS, to capture a positive differential between the asset swap spread and the CDS premium adjusted for the funding cost).

The availability of a credit facility also enabled Axa IM to manage the recovery process more flexibly, since the defaulting assets delivered under a CDS contract could be kept in custody

---

[33] The difference between the amount issued and the portfolio amount represents all the initial costs of the transaction, deducted from the amount of the equity tranche.

by the CDO if the manager thought that the price of the assets was likely to improve later. This option reduced the risk of valuing assets at the worst time, and therefore that of not getting the best recovery rate. In the case of WorldCom, for instance, the defaulting bonds were valued at 11% at the time of the credit event, whereas their value rose to 30% a few months later.

The possibility of taking short credit positions by means of CDSs (buying protection via CDSs enabling quasi-arbitrage or speculation strategies) was very attractive for a manager, but nevertheless entailed additional risk for the structure: erosion of the average spread, and counterparty credit risk. The rating agencies do not currently value short position strategies, or at least, very little (Moody's idea being to grant a slight benefit in terms of diversity score).

This type of structure brings in a large number of players (the bank providing the credit facility, the asset custodian, the CDS counterparties, etc.) likely to lead to significant counterparty risks. This, however, is limited by the constraints imposed by the rating agencies:

- For the bank providing the credit line – rating trigger or making available the full amount of the credit facility.
- For the custodian of the SPV assets – rating trigger, substitution or guarantee.

The counterparty risks arising from CDS positions are controlled via rating triggers. The default of a CDS counterparty may have an effect on the premium payments, settlement of a protection or again, the mark-to-market value of the CDS.

In managed transactions, there is a possibility of channeling the excess spread to maintain balance between assets and liabilities. This margin can either be paid to the equity investors (therefore having no effect on the rated tranches) or retained within the structure (this will lead to creation of extra protection for the rated tranches and siphoning-off of this excess spread where the amount of losses exceeds a certain amount).

The Jazz structure provided a diversion mechanism similar to those used in cash-flow CBOs (over-collateralization tests). The excess spread is diverted to enable early repayment of the senior investors in order, which progressively reduces the leverage in the transaction. Since the largest senior tranche was the super senior swap, it could not be repaid directly. The interest payments were therefore channeled into a reserve account, mechanically triggering a fall in the notional amount of the super senior swap.

The cash-flow waterfall of the transaction may be analyzed as follows:

- Interest income (premiums of CDSs sold + Euribor rate on the collateral + coupons on the bonds acquired).
- Miscellaneous charges (trustee, rating agencies, etc.).
- Commitment fees and interest costs on the credit facility.
- Payment of the premiums on short CDS positions (short or offset).
- Senior CDO manager fee.
- Premium payments on interest rate and currency hedges.
- Premium payments on super senior swap.
- Class A interest.
- Class B interest.
- Class C interest.
- Class D interest.
- Junior CDO manager fee.
- Dividends to the equity investors (Class E).
- Incentive fee to the CDO manager.

**Table 4.6**  Evolution of the actively managed synthetic arbitrage CDO market

| Year | Number of transactions | Volume (€m) |
|------|------------------------|-------------|
| 2003 | 21 | 20 986 |
| 2002 | 19 | 20 769 |
| 2001 | 7  | 5 213 |

*Source*: CreditFlux. Reproduced by permission of CreditFlux.

### 4.3.2.3   Analysis of the Latest Developments

The Jazz I and Cheyne transactions characterized the emerging market in actively managed synthetic arbitrage CDOs. Initial growth in this market was not sustained, however (the issue volume in 2003 was barely more than that in 2002), mainly due to the market conditions and the development of 'on-demand' products managed by the investor or an external manager, as shown below. 2003 was a year marked by narrowing credit spreads, which thus made these products less attractive in terms of arbitrage (many transactions initially scheduled for 2003 were cancelled or postponed). See Table 4.6.

In terms of structure, few innovations have been made since Jazz I. Developments have mainly been in CDO distribution methods. Robeco has thus actively sought to develop distribution to retail and private banking investors in the Netherlands. Although the first Robeco transaction was sold to institutional investors, the following three were mainly sold to retail investors (for a total portfolio amount of €5.3 bn, each tranche sold representing a nominal amount of €804.6 m). The type of tranche sold is a combination of equity and mezzanine tranches, rated A2/A3 by Moody's, with a variable coupon (due to the percentage of equity sold). See Figure 4.8.

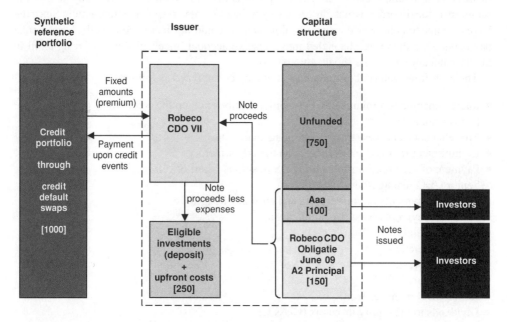

**Figure 4.8**  Robeco-sponsored actively managed synthetic arbitrage CDOs

Finally, in December 2003, Axa IM and JP Morgan launched Overture CDO on the same model as Jazz I, but in cooperation with a pool of banks selected per geographical zone: Wachovia for American investors, or IXIS for French ones. The goal was to make this CDO similar to the syndicated bond issue model, including the widest possible distribution to investors and a formal undertaking by the syndicate banks to provide active secondary market-making. Although the amount of the transaction – about €3 bn – was no surprise, the marketing effort and the number of investors approached marked a new advance in the actively managed synthetic CDO market. The Overture transaction thus considerably enhanced perception of these products by a large number of investors and contributed to making the actively managed synthetic arbitrage CDO market more transparent.

It is possible that the years to come will see these products coming back into favor, and the added value of professional managers recognized, in part to the detriment of static on-demand CDOs, which have been the main instruments offered in the market in 2002–2004.

### 4.3.3   On-Demand CDOs (Correlation Products)

The development of on-demand or bespoke single-tranche synthetic CDOs was fostered by the evolution of tranche hedging techniques, which had themselves benefited from design and method improvements: on the one hand, the emergence of the first correlation products (first-to-default basket swaps) and improved risk management models (for example, the introduction of the Copula models), and, on the other hand, economic imperatives such as intermediary arrangers' need to cover exposures that they had not been able to place with investors or again, the strong demand for on-demand products from institutional investors.

These hedging techniques (delta hedging) rapidly enabled banks to offer 'on-demand' products, by creating a synthetic CDO tranche without needing to issue the entire capital structure (the first loss and super senior tranches being, in this case, retained by the arranger and their risk managed dynamically). A typical example would be a mezzanine tranche with an attachment point at 3% and a detachment point at 6%, where the investor only takes the risk on 3% of the capital structure of the CDO for losses in excess of 3% but capped at 6%. This type of product is commonly described as bespoke single-tranche CDO and, in this, it is more like an option than a traditional CDO derived from traditional securitization techniques.

The appearance of these new pricing and risk management technologies enabled rapid growth in the volume of synthetic CDOs, since investors could define their type of structure and had more flexibility as regards maturity, currency, underlying portfolio, reference borrowers, attachment and detachment points (i.e. degree of subordination), size, coupon, etc. These products were in strong demand from senior credit (AA/AAA) investors, who found traditional structures alone unsatisfactory because they required placement of a large amount of subordinated tranches.

Furthermore, these new technologies led to the creation of many new products and strongly influenced the development of the CDO market. Separate structuring and trading teams were thus set up by most banks, with operating methods more like those used by the teams in the derivatives markets than those used in the traditional CDO market teams, usually attached to securitization teams. A specific investor typology also emerged, especially in Europe, as did an inter-bank correlation market.

### 4.3.3.1  Introduction to Delta Hedging

Delta hedging techniques are based on credit portfolio pricing methods. In these transactions, the arranging bank does not sell the total amount referenced, as in a traditional synthetic CDO, but only a fragment of the notional amount (delta), determined for each reference entity. This delta must then be readjusted dynamically depending on the changes in the credit spreads.

A synthetic CDO tranche can thus be modeled using the following parameters:

- Credit spreads and recovery rates for each reference entity.
- Default correlation between entities.
- Subordination and tranche size.
- Maturity.

It is possible, using these variables, to determine the theoretical price of a tranche. The goal of hedging techniques is to neutralize the price variations in the tranche that are linked to changes in the spread of the entities in the underlying portfolio. The delta of an entity is therefore defined as the CDS amount, which enables the effect of a change in this entity's spread on the price of the tranche to be offset.

While the delta concept seems at first view relatively straightforward, its behavior is much more delicate to interpret. An intuitive interpretative clue would be to imagine that all the reference entities in the CDO are ranked in decreasing spread order (i.e. the order in which the entities should theoretically default). The first entities (which should therefore default first) will most probably have an impact on the first loss tranche of the portfolio, and their delta is therefore large for the equity tranche. However, the last entities (with narrow spreads) should default last and their delta is therefore larger for the senior tranches. This reasoning enables delta behavior to be understood in the light of the individual spread changes for each type of tranche. Figure 4.9 displays the individual delta/spread relationship for each type of tranche (equity, mezzanine and senior).

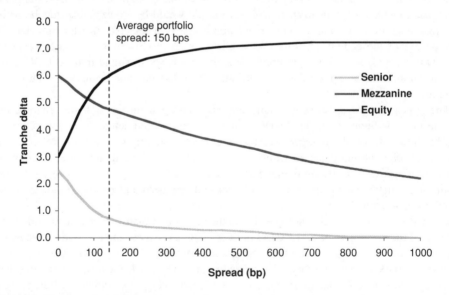

**Figure 4.9**   Deltas and underlying asset spreads

Deltas are also sensitive to product residual maturity, and this relationship can also be explained intuitively. When moving closer to maturity, the senior and mezzanine tranches grow progressively less risky compared to the equity tranche. This result explains why the deltas of an equity tranche increase over time, while those of the mezzanine and senior tranches gradually move towards zero.

This hedging mechanism, however, is not perfect, since it does not allow neutralization of the variations in the recovery rate or correlation rate assumptions. It merely allows hedging of first-order risks, that is credit spread variations. The other risks (recovery or correlation rate volatility, risk of sudden default) are only realized in the event of default, and so they have less impact.

For this reason, CDO arrangers are often encouraged to carry out transactions enabling them to neutralize or reduce these second-order risks, either by selling off existing positions to other banks or hedge funds, or by distributing different parts of the capital structure to investors.

### 4.3.3.2   Risk Management of On-Demand Arbitrage CDOs

In the next paragraph we will deal with the first-ranking risk (credit spread variation) and second-ranking risks (recovery rates, default jumps and correlation).

**The concept of gamma and dynamic hedging of spread risk**

Delta is determined using a marginal variation of spread. For more significant variations, a profit or loss will be made on the position depending on the convexity of the price formula for the tranche in relation to spread movements. In option language, this convexity is usually described as the gamma. A detailed study of the effects of spread movements on gamma would not be appropriate here, but we shall present some important effects below.

First of all, let us consider a senior tranche and suppose that all the spreads in the portfolio move uniformly. It is clear that the value of the protection on this senior tranche will appreciate, and in fact it should become more sensitive to defaults. Its delta will therefore increase. A senior tranche therefore has a positive gamma for parallel spread increases. The effect is reversed for equity tranches (negative gamma).

One important result is that spread volatility is profitable for senior protection buyers. This buyer is said to be 'gamma positive' (convexity buyer). The opposite is true of the junior protection buyer, who is said to be gamma negative (convexity seller). The mezzanine tranches are more complicated to analyze. Their behavior depends on the position of the tranche in the capital structure, compared to the average loss in the portfolio.

Now let us look at an uncorrelated spread movement (only one entity's spread varies). In a senior tranche, an individual spread increase means the entity considered will probably affect it less (if this reference entity becomes riskier than the other entities in the portfolio, it will affect the equity tranche first). Therefore its delta will fall for the senior tranche, making the individual gamma (iGamma) negative. However, the portfolio becomes riskier because of this individual spread widening, although the situation remains the same for the other entities. The price of protection will rise and the deltas of the other entities will rise too. This is generally referred to as a positive cross gamma. The behavior of the equity tranche will be exactly the opposite to that of the senior tranche.

The term nGamma refers to the convexity of a tranche to uniform spread movements, with half the spreads narrowing and the other half increasing in the same proportions.

Bank intermediaries must therefore dynamically hedge single-tranche CDOs to manage their convexity risks. This dynamic management has been made possible by the improved liquidity of the CDS market. First of all, gamma hedging requires the execution of very small CDS amounts, which is only possible if the bank has industrial-scale CDS trading facilities. Secondly, gamma hedging is expensive, due to the bid–offer spread in the CDS market. Thus, although spreads vary from day to day, gamma management is performed at less regular intervals to limit transaction costs and execute larger sized CDSs.

### Management of residual risks: recovery rates and jump-to-default

Pricing models rely on recovery rate assumptions, even though this variable cannot be observed in the market (except for entities nearing default, with very wide spreads, for which the recovery rate may be deduced from CDS up-front premiums or bond prices).[34]

The banks generally handle this risk by calibrating the recovery rate in their models with a bid–offer spread. Senior tranches, for example, have positive sensitivity to a fall in the recovery rate value, and so they are generally valued on a high assumption (for instance, 50%). The sensitivity of the junior tranches is the reverse and so the recovery rate assumption is lower (say, 30%). Thus, arrangers implicitly build reserves/provisions into their models to hedge this specific risk.

This exposure can also be neutralized by executing transactions involving other tranches in the capital structure, by executing first-to-default or structured transactions with fixed recovery rates. Furthermore, one recent phenomenon has been inter-bank recovery swaps,[35] enabling banks to exchange offsetting positions on certain entities.

As seen earlier, tranches show convexity properties that are magnified in the event of sudden default. This risk is generally designated as the 'P&L in the event of default'. It corresponds roughly to the difference between the loss observed on the delta and the gain arising on the tranche increase in value. The P&L in the event of default is negative for the senior tranches because, as seen earlier, an entity with narrow spread has a large delta. Where there is a sudden default, the bank is usually not able to reduce this delta and therefore the loss on the delta is higher than the gain arising on the improved tranche value. For junior tranches, this pattern is reversed and the P&L in the event of default is positive.

This can be explained in carry terms. For a senior tranche the initial delta amount is high compared to the size and risk of the tranche involved. Thus if a tranche is valued at 100 basis points per annum, the delta hedge can have an initial implicit carry of 700 basis points (corresponding to the sum of the spreads on the deltas compared to the tranche size). This positive carry enables the losses expected on the deltas to be absorbed if a credit event occurs, and the carry expectancy corresponds to the P&L expectancy in the event of default. Again, the relationship is reversed for a junior tranche, since the carry is negative (the bank pays more

---

[34] For entities nearing default, CDSs no longer trade in annual premiums but in upfront premiums, as for a classic insurance policy. This upfront premium is quoted in % of the notional amount of the contract, which enables the implicit value of the recovery rate expected by the market to be worked out. There is a similar effect in bonds: distressed securities are no longer traded in spread but in % of the par.

[35] Recovery swaps are a new variation on CDSs. These trade not on premiums but on implicit recovery rate levels (e.g. 35%/38%). These contracts do not provide for cash-flow payments, except in the event of default, in which case the protection buyer delivers a portfolio of discounted securities as for a CDS, while receiving an implicit percentage payment (38% in this case) multiplied by the notional amount of the transaction. The combination of a standard CDS with a recovery swap enables a fixed payout-type CDS to be replicated.

premium on the product than it receives on the deltas), but the P&L in the event of default is positive.

In this field also, it is possible for banks to neutralize their risk by topping up the capital structure or by using first-to-default swaps. It is also possible to hedge this risk by buying short-term maturity protection on the entities for which the overall P&L position in the event of default is negative.

The banks must also manage residual interest rate or currency risks, since the portfolios are usually composed of CDSs in various currencies and the CDO tranche may be offered in the form of fixed rate bonds.

These risks are generally known as hybrid risks, and they have relatively little influence.

## Correlation risk management

The pricing and risk management of single-tranche CDOs is also based on correlation assumptions. These parameters are the most important ones after credit spreads, not least for the very junior or very senior tranches. In fact, interpretation of the correlation effect is relatively intuitive for these tranches. Where the correlation rate is equal to 100%, there are no differences between the equity and super senior tranches: heightened correlation therefore benefits the junior tranches. Thus, purchase of an equity risk or senior protection leads to a long correlation position, while the reverse is short correlation. The mezzanine tranches may be neutral in correlation, i.e. the correlation parameter has no influence on the pricing of the tranche (this is known as the inflexion point).

Table 4.7 shows tranche pricings for various correlation levels. The average portfolio spread is 50 basis points, maturity is five years, and the model used is a standard Copula-type model.

The sensitivity of a tranche price to correlation rates is usually denoted by Rho (variation of the tranche price for a 1% variation in the correlation rate). The factors influencing this sensitivity include:

- Tranche position (long or short correlation).
- Tranche subordination and size.
- Average portfolio spread.
- Residual maturity.
- Current implied correlation rate.

The Rho variable is essential in analyzing a CDO tranche, because it helps to determine if a tranche is senior or junior, which, as we have seen, has considerable effect on the concepts of gamma, recovery rate risk and P&L in the event of default. See Table 4.8.

**Table 4.7**   Correlation rate and tranche spreads

| Spreads (%) | Correlation rate assumptions | | | | | |
|---|---|---|---|---|---|---|
| Tranche | 0% | 10% | 20% | 30% | 40% | 50% |
| 12–22% | 0.00% | 0.01% | 0.10% | 0.25% | 0.42% | 0.59% |
| 6–12% | 0.05% | 0.47% | 0.94% | 1.27% | 1.50% | 1.63% |
| 3–6% | 2.43% | 3.51% | 3.80% | 3.81% | 3.68% | 3.47% |
| 0–3% | 20.89% | 17.19% | 14.42% | 12.20% | 10.34% | 8.74% |
| 0–100% | 0.50% | 0.50% | 0.50% | 0.50% | 0.50% | 0.50% |

**Table 4.8**   Convexity and correlation risk

| Correlation position | Tranche type | P&L in the event of default | Convexity | | |
|---|---|---|---|---|---|
| | | | Gamma | iGamma | nGamma |
| Long correlation | Long equity/short senior | Positive | Long | Short | Short |
| Short correlation | Short equity/long senior | Negative | Short | Long | Long |

Since correlation is not an observable variable, the banks usually value tranches using a bid–offer spread method enabling an amount of reserves to be quantified. The bid–offer range enables, for instance, account to be taken of hedging management costs (transaction costs on gammas). However, as we have seen, some mezzanine tranches are not sensitive to the correlation hypothesis, which therefore does not allow a reserve policy to be defined. Arrangers are therefore led to treat reserves more subjectively (for example, setting aside an arbitrary percentage of the tranche value) to take account of transaction costs for the mezzanine tranches, which, indeed, are those for which the gamma is the most volatile. The sensitivity of these tranches to correlation may be positive or negative, depending on the level of the credit spreads or the residual maturity, while the correlation sensitivity of an equity tranche will always be positive and that of a super senior tranche always negative.

Furthermore, it soon became clear that risk management using a single correlation rate (that is to say, valuing all the tranches in the capital structure using a single hypothesis, for example 15%) did not reflect market reality (supply and demand), even for the non-mezzanine tranches. Thus, equity investors' return expectations could correspond to an implicit 15% correlation while the premium demanded by the super senior protection sellers would entail an implicit correlation rate of 40%.

Two new concepts have therefore been developed by a few leading banks, which have since spread to most dealers today.

- First, correlation is determined on the basis of a smile (or skew), which depends on the subordination of the tranche considered. In fact, this method is similar to that used in the options markets, not least for equity volatility, and enables market prices to be followed closely.
- Second, a different approach to mezzanine tranche pricing has emerged, also inspired from the equity volatility market. A mezzanine tranche can be considered as a 'put spread'[36] on portfolio losses (the attachment and detachment points of the mezzanine tranche being equivalent to the two strike prices of this option combination). Thus, the pricing of a mezzanine tranche ($x\%$ to $y\%$) can be deduced from the value of the portfolio (i.e. the losses from 0% to 100%) from which the value of the equity tranche (0% to $x\%$), and that of the super senior tranche ($y\%$ to 100%) are subtracted. Different correlation rates can thus be given to the attachment and detachment points $x$ and $y$. This approach by correlation pairs offers many advantages, because it enables the implicit correlations in the equity or super senior tranches to be observed and bid–offers to be introduced on the correlation smile, the value of which is not nil even for the mezzanine tranches that are correlation-neutral. Such an approach is commonly referred to as 'base correlation'.

---

[36] Combination of two put options on the same underlying asset, at two different strike prices.

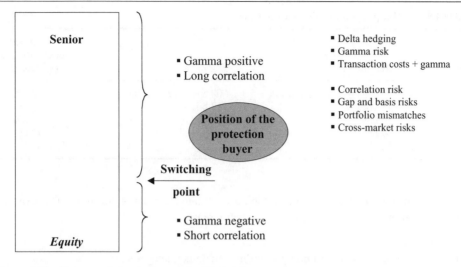

**Figure 4.10**    Framework for single-tranche CDO risk management

As we have seen, management of correlation products and synthetic CDO tranches leads to the management of a considerable number of residual risks. The goal of the correlation trader is to minimize the gamma and correlation risks, and to diversify these residual risks.

Figure 4.10 shows the framework for managing synthetic single-tranche CDO risks.

While most residual risks can be managed by bid–offer spread systems (correlation, recovery rates) and execution of transactions to neutralize these risks (for example, buying junior protection after having bought senior protection), the development of this activity today is curbed by the accumulation of correlation risks. Investors have mostly chosen senior tranches, which has led investment banks to accumulate long positions in correlation, that cannot be neutralized by their much more limited capacity to place junior tranches.

It is interesting to note the analogy with the equity derivatives business, especially as regards equity correlation products (e.g. best-of or worst-of types). This activity presents the same problems of correlation risk management and the commercial flows are such that the banks are very heavily exposed in one correlation direction, which is in fact the reverse position (short correlation) to that of exotic credit trading activities. Because these correlations (equity versus credit) are very different in nature, it is unlikely that these opposing exposures could neutralize each other.

However, over the past few years, the banks have benefited from new methods for managing their correlation books, with the development of the index market (TRAC-X and iBoxx,[37] now merged into iTraxx for the European market and CDX.NA for the US market). Tranches are now traded on the main indices in the inter-bank market. The main advantages of the index market are standardization of contracts, greater liquidity and transparency, and above all justification of the correlation parameters used for the pricing of non-index tranches. Table 4.9 shows a series of tranche prices on the five-year iTraxx index at 27 May 2005.

These recent developments have fostered the emergence of new players in the correlation market, such as hedge funds and other sophisticated investors. These have provided a substantial

---

[37] These instruments were described in the previous chapter.

**Table 4.9**   Market prices for credit index tranches

| Tranche | Bid price | Ask price | Implied base correlation (*mid-market*) |
|---|---|---|---|
| 0–3% | 500 bps + 32.00% upfront | 500 bps + 32.75% upfront | 13.1% |
| 3–6% | 111 bps | 117 bps | 25.6% |
| 6–9% | 36 bps | 40 bps | 34.5% |
| 9–12% | 19 bps | 23 bps | 42.0% |
| 12–22% | 13 bps | 16 bps | 57.5% |

outlet for bank intermediaries to offload their accumulated correlation positions. This exposure (long correlation) attracts hedge funds for several reasons:

- Positive carry.
- Convexity properties and trading possibilities in delta management.
- Low counterparty risk (since the position is delta-hedged, sensitivity to spread movements is negligible).

The correlation market has set its benchmarks and now enables risks to be recycled more effectively. Modeling techniques are converging towards standard models and methods (Gaussian copula, correlation smile and pricing with base correlation), and a relatively efficient inter-bank market has developed, enabling risk management to be optimized.

### 4.3.3.3   Latest Developments in the Single-Tranche CDO Market

While the first correlation products consisted of mezzanine tranches referencing investment grade static credit portfolios, the structures on offer very quickly became more sophisticated in terms of format and flexibility. In addition, new classes of assets were integrated into the delta-hedging technology (high yield, ABS, other CDO tranches, etc.). The banks also made considerable progress in risk modeling and management.

### New product developments: increased flexibility

Initially, investors wished to have the possibility to manage the reference portfolio dynamically, in reaction to criticism leveled at static products. This flexibility also enables liquidity issues to be addressed, since the investor can replace an individual credit risk without having to sell the product itself (which would be expensive in bid–offer terms).

The formulation of these products, known as 'self-managed' CDOs, developed progressively, with various initial structures being proposed by the bank intermediaries. Gradually, these converged towards a standard model in which the management mechanism was based on quantitative data supplied by the bank at regular intervals (delta, sensitivity, etc.) and the relevant CDS market prices (spreads of the entities exiting and entering the CDO). It should also be noted that most of these structures now have mechanisms for checking market prices, and the investor can use other market intermediaries than the arranging bank to determine CDS prices. Dynamic management entails gains or losses that can be allocated to the product subordination, the coupon or reserves (the three methods being ultimately the same in terms of economic consequences).

Quite naturally, these structures quickly took on board the notion of delegating portfolio management to a third party such as a fund manager, for instance. They were then known as externally managed single-tranche CDOs. The first transactions were engineered by JP Morgan and Deutsche Bank in 2002, on a bilateral basis, and both used DWS – Deutsche Asset Management as portfolio manager. There was then a slowdown in this type of transaction in the wake of the sharp narrowing of credit spreads (the average portfolio spread no longer enabled expensive third-party management fees to be paid). Managers' familiarization with these correlation products and the heightened competition that ensued contributed to a downward adjustment of management fees, and there was a gradual revival of this type of transaction in 2004: traditional managers such as Fortis Investments, Axa Investment Managers, IXIS Asset Management and specialized boutiques such as Cheyne Capital or Solent Capital are gradually becoming the major players in this market.

The growth of the managed single-tranche market was fueled by the issue of the Aria CDO in July 2004 – the first single-tranche CDO managed by Axa IM. Aria has been arranged the same way as Overture CDO; the arranger (JP Morgan) having also assembled a global syndicate of banks, each with strong distribution capabilities in a particular region. The single-tranche format provided potential investors with greater flexibility: 27 tranches were issued, with five and seven-year maturities, in different currencies such as euro, dollar, British pound, Swiss franc, yen, etc. The transaction was unusually large, with more than €1 bn of notes issued. By comparison, most mezzanine portfolio tranches are between €10 m and €100 m. In addition, the arranger has made a much stronger commitment to liquidity than was previously the case, including the provision of on-screen trading prices.

## New asset classes and CDO-squared

The combination of CDO and delta-hedging technologies requires a minimum liquidity on the underlying asset. Since the CDS market has progressively spread to high-yield and emerging markets bonds (with, for instance, the Deutsche Bank Repon 17 transaction launched in July 2001), it has been possible to integrate these assets quite naturally into correlation products. As a result, a significant number of high-yield and emerging market transactions took place in 2005, fueled by the development of tranches on the high-yield CDS index (CDX.NA.HY) and the emerging market CDS index (CDX.EM). The most successful format is currently the managed single tranche, with specialized managers such as Ares or TCW with respect to the high-yield portfolios, Bluebay or Ashmore with respect to emerging market collateral.

The assets eliciting the most interest from investors have been securitization issues (ABS, or asset-backed securities). However, the only segment of this market offering sufficient liquidity is the most senior tranches (rated AAA), for which the spread is relatively low (on average between 5 and 25 basis points over the swap rate). As a result, because the CDS market has not developed into this asset class yet, the only solution for banks wishing to offer single-tranche ABS CDOs is to buy the asset itself for the delta amount needed. This strategy implies that banks have the ability and balance sheet size to fund the purchase and warehouse the assets. This reduces the number of potential arrangers to those with the capacity to ensure the sourcing of the assets in adequate economic conditions.

It is worth noting that exploration of this asset class finally led to the development of a new pure credit product. The first delta-hedged transaction including ABSs was structured by BNP Paribas in November 2001 (CDO Master Investment 2, and the reference portfolio combined investment grade CDSs and AAA-rated ABSs). It was followed by the CDO Master Investment 3 transaction in February 2002, and by Aurum Investments in May 2002, which, this time, replaced the investment grade CDS-type exposures by AAA-rated CDO-type exposures. The reference portfolio therefore only comprised structured finance assets (ABS and CDO). The portion of the underlying portfolio comprising CDOs only contained single-tranche CDOs, which meant implicitly that the transaction could be delta-hedged (this is because a bucket of cash-flow CDOs would not have given the arranger sufficient liquidity to implement this type of hedging strategy).

The use of single-tranche CDOs enables the arranger to determine a delta on the final CDO (called the master) sold to the client, which can be multiplied by the delta of the underlying CDO tranches (called 'inner' tranches) to determine the final delta applicable for each of the reference entities in the inner tranches. This type of structure spread widely since 2003, with some banks offering transactions made up solely of single-tranche CDOs, called CDO-squared or CDOs of synthetic CDOs.

Figure 4.11 shows an example of a CDO-squared comprising ABSs and CDOs. The master portfolio comprises 50 ABS securities (70% of the portfolio) and four inner CDO tranches (30% of the master portfolio, each comprising 100 reference unities) for a total of 1 billion euros. The losses likely to arise in the master CDO will either arise from ABS or from the credits underlying an inner CDO where the subordination of that inner CDO (6% in the following example) is totally wiped out by a succession of credit events.

These products offer a different risk-return profile from that of an ordinary single tranche, because of the size of the underlying risks referenced in the transaction. The number of reference entities can be very large, depending on the overlap percentage accepted by the investors among the various CDO tranches (it is common to see transactions with over 300 different underlying entities).

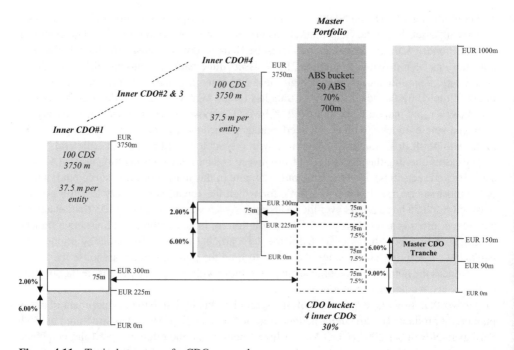

**Figure 4.11**   Typical structure of a CDO-squared

A first difference between CDO and CDO-squared $CDO^2$ structures is the double level of subordination. In order for the $CDO^2$ mezzanine tranche to be impacted, successive credit events need to have eroded one of the inner CDO subordinations (6% in Figure 4.11) and then eaten into the inner CDO tranche, in an amount sufficient to have also eroded the $CDO^2$ equity tranche. This feature gives greater initial protection to $CDO^2$ holders from idiosyncratic risk.

The second difference is the double leverage. Looking at notional leverage, this can be illustrated by the following example. Assume that, following the complete erosion of the 6% subordination (i.e. €225 m in the first inner CDO), we have a €37.5 m subsequent credit loss, which impacts the first inner (2%) tranche. This loss represents only 1/100th of the original reference notional amount of the inner CDO portfolio (€3750 m) but 50% of the inner tranche (€75 m is the size of the inner tranches in Figure 4.11), thus reflecting the levered position of the latter. This loss represents an even larger 41.7% (37.5/90) of the $CDO^2$ equity tranche, since any loss occurring on the inner CDOs will immediately impact it. This higher ratio is the proof of a higher level of leverage. Because of this higher leverage (and greater sensitivity to broad market movements), but similar protection from idiosyncratic defaults, the $CDO^2$ premium is also higher, making it attractive to many investors. Such investors need however to accept the market volatility that leverage brings.

The third important point is path dependence of credit events. Path dependence is irrelevant in any of the individual inner CDOs, as each subsequent default progressively reduces the subordination below the inner tranche. This is not the same with a $CDO^2$. If, in the example mentioned above, the first €225 m of losses had been equally split among three inner CDO portfolios and not just been present in one portfolio, the $CDO^2$ equity tranche would not have been affected, as each of the inner tranches provided €225 m of subordination protection. In a $CDO^2$, the distribution of credit events among the inner CDOs is almost as important as the number of those credit events. A last difference between the two structures is highlighted by the issue of credit overlap. A single CDO has many individual reference credits, each of which appears only once in the collateral. A typical $CDO^2$ portfolio, however, will often have the same credits featuring in several of the inner portfolios. Overlap introduces perfect correlation in the way two inner CDO tranches are affected by a single credit event, thereby exacerbating the impact of single-name defaults.

As for the single-tranche market, managed $CDO^2$ transactions have recently been structured (such as Voltaire, a CDO with ABSs and CDOs arranged by Société Générale and managed by Deutsche Asset Management) and represent a growing share of the structured credit products market. In these transactions, the manager of the master portfolio can dynamically manage each of the inner CDO tranches. Recent developments include the 'cross subordination' feature, whereby inner CDOs share all inner subordination: as long as there is subordination left in at least one inner CDO, it is used to offset 'potential losses' on inner CDOs whose subordination has been used up.

CDO-squared products have met with great success. From what was seen in 2004, it can be assumed that these represent nearly two-thirds of correlation products on offer in the market.

### Overview of the developments in the on-demand synthetic arbitrage CDO market

The development of correlation products, especially single-tranche CDOs, has strongly influenced trends in the CDO market. Pricing of the tranches in the first synthetic CDOs was based first on a historical approach (used by the rating agencies) and then on relative value, i.e. comparison with similarly rated ABS issues[38] (without really taking account of the market value of the reference portfolio or of an implied market correlation rate). This relationship has now reversed. The pricing of managed or balance sheet-driven transactions (whole capital structure) is now being based on model prices.

The development of single tranche-type products also led to greater transparency in the CDO market. There has been a genuine effort to teach and inform on the part of the bank intermediaries structuring these transactions; investors are provided with daily valuations for each correlation product, the bid offer-range has narrowed considerably, quantitative data such as deltas are regularly communicated, and so on. Thus, many investors have quantitative valuation tools similar to those used by the arrangers. The spread of these tools has indeed been encouraged by some of the leading banks in the market. JP Morgan, for instance, devotes considerable resources to the dissemination of quantitative information (academic research or popularization, valuation models, etc.). Morgan Stanley has notably contributed to the success of index tranches through its role as market-maker and has also contributed to implement a single-tranche pricer on Bloomberg.

### Development of the institutional customer base

While these innovations have enabled the CDO market to see investors like hedge funds arriving, they have also fostered the growth and stability in the institutional investor base (regional banks, insurers, asset managers, etc.). It could almost be said that the client base has been rationalized, in the sense that the investments now correspond to previously identified and justified needs. Prior to this, the very few investors were divided into relatively confused segments, which contributed to the opacity of the CDO market (see the examples of Dexia or Scor presented earlier). The first investors in this market very often withdrew due to significant financial losses, but were replaced by institutions with more rational investment policies, and with risk-redistribution capacities (via their retail networks, or via life-insurance contracts, etc.). They were encouraged by the greater transparency and the heightened liquidity of the products on offer.

AXA is a case in point. CDOs were used as early as 1999 in the overall asset allocation strategy of the Group's insurance companies, to improve the efficient frontier of its investment portfolio. The Group's strategy was to invest a very small amount (15% of the allocation in the asset class) in the subordinated tranche of a CDO and the remaining 85% in highly rated securities (AAA-rated ABSs, virtually risk-free assets). AXA's analysis was that this strategy offered a return expectancy slightly lower than that of the underlying asset class but, on the other hand, it offered better resilience, should credit events occur (in value-at-risk terms). This allocation strategy enabled diversification to new asset classes such as high-yield, leveraged loans, etc., with a risk–return profile adapted to the Group's overall constraints.

### Emergence of a retail clientele in Europe

While institutional demand has consistently developed and the market has been rationalized, retail clients represent a growing market segment (distribution in the retail networks or via the

---

[38] This approach led to the success of senior single tranches insofar as the spread was higher than that available on more traditional instruments with the same rating.

private banking branches). This strategy has been successfully pursued by asset managers such as Robeco in the Netherlands. However, it is still limited to certain geographical areas, the regulations in which are more favorable to distribution of credit derivative-based products to private investors (e.g. the Netherlands, Scandinavia, Switzerland). In July 2003, in Luxembourg, the first transaction in the form of a UCIT integrating credit derivatives took place. This was arranged by Fortis and offered only to Belgian clients (Fortis L Fix Credit Quality 1). The creation of this UCIT was made possible by the transposition of the European UCIT Directives into Luxembourg law. The UCIT III Directives apply in all EU member states since February 2004, and it is likely that this distribution format will quickly become widespread. The Directives considerably widen the range of financial assets in which funds with single authorization (the European passport) may invest (not least credit derivatives). They also lay down harmonized rules governing market access and the conditions for exercising as an asset manager (capital requirements, etc.).

These developments and the increased number of arrangers have led to decreasing margins for correlation products, partially offset by the considerable increase in the volume of transactions. In Europe, for instance, it has been estimated that over 30 institutions are now capable of offering correlation products and there are some 20 domestic players not capable of trading but that can ensure local distribution of these products such as Fortis Bank and Rabobank in Benelux, BBVA and SCH in Spain, etc. However, it is very likely that the number of bank intermediaries (involved in correlation product structuring and management) will fall significantly in the years to come, while the number of institutions offering distribution and issuing calls for tender will increase. This trend will resemble that observed in structured equity products and can be explained by the ever-increasing cost of exercising this business, be it in terms of trading, risk management, R&D, back- and middle-office infrastructure, etc.

*Huge growth in transaction volumes*

It is difficult to measure the current size of the synthetic CDO market exactly, mostly due to the huge number of single-tranche transactions, which are generally concluded on a bilateral basis, but we can roughly estimate that the volume of issuance for synthetic CDOs doubles year-on-year. We estimate the current market size to be in the area of €35 bn (in terms of notional amount of risk transferred),[39] the major shift being the fact that 60% of the market now comprises CDOs of ABS/CDOs or $CDO^2$. The majority of the transactions are still based on investment grade collateral. We expect even higher volumes in 2005, although with a more limited growth rate. Structured credit products being leveraged instruments, the equivalent notional of underlying risk would be in the €175 bn area, assuming an average leverage factor of 5 times, which is roughly the combined size of the investment grade corporate bond primary market in 2004.

It is difficult to grasp the significance of this volume as it stands. However, if a recent Fitch survey based on the analysis of 41 transactions is to be believed,[40] it can be seen that some credits are present in many CDOs. A reference entity like Ford Motors could, for instance,

---

[39] CDO market sizes are traditionally measured in terms of notional amounts of transactions. With the rise of bespoke CDOs and single-tranche trading, we believe that the most relevant measure should be the amount of risk effectively transferred to investors (in other words, the size of the mezzanine tranche). An alternative, and possibly better, measure would be to compute the amounts of delta-hedging traded by CDO arrangers (to also take into account the nature of risk transferred). However, the latter would require to make a number of assumptions for each transaction and is almost impossible to implement.

[40] Synthetic Index – Benchmarking Portfolio Performance (Fitch Ratings, June 2003).

be found in over half of CDO portfolios. Supposing the average number of entities in CDO portfolios is 100, this means that almost 875 million worth of protection was generated on Ford in 2004 by the arbitrage CDO market. Compared with Ford's outstanding debt volume, this does not indicate a significant impact on the Ford CDSs market. However, it is quite possible that an entity like Electrolux could be found in 20% of these CDOs, which would correspond to 350 million euros worth of protection. This figure should be compared to the amount of debt issued by Electrolux in the Eurobond market: €600 m.

Thus, in 2003 and 2004 it was feared that the credit derivatives market would be dislocated by the huge growth in volume of single-tranche transactions, which outgrew the CDS market's capacity to absorb them for certain risks. The phenomenon was all the more significant as demand from the traditional protection buyers slowed considerably (especially from bank credit portfolio managers, who deemed the spreads too wide, and hedge funds, which chose to materialize their profits on the short positions taken in 2002). Correlation products thus contributed strongly to the fall in spreads observed throughout 2003–2004.[41]

However, this supply/demand distortion was recently reduced by several factors:

• Some players are now taking short positions on tranches (thus not generating any deltas).
• Credit portfolio managers have replaced synthetic CLOs by standard CDSs, or have even bought single-tranche protection.
• The number of entities included in correlation products has grown considerably (there are now over 1000 different reference entities) and should increase further by the use of new instruments such as EDSs.[42].
• Many transactions now reference very diversified portfolios (a CDO-squared generally comprises over 300 reference entities).
• Many investors have sold products they bought in 2002 and 2003 (thus generating reverse delta flows).

The other significant lesson of 2004 has been the understanding that correlation is now a market in itself. As we have shown before, correlation is a key parameter in the pricing of structured credit products. Whereas it has been considered for a long time as a 'static' input, mostly driven by historical data and in-house assumptions, it is now implied from market prices observed on the tranched-index market. The significant volume of CDOs executed in 2004 from June to September has caused a dislocation of the tranched-index market, leading to a worsening of the correlation assumptions for senior CDO tranches (that constitute the vast majority of the trades structured). Credit spreads are not any longer the sole 'market' driver for the pricing of structured credit products, correlation also now being a major factor.

In May 2005, a sharp rise in the cost of equity tranche protection has sent the correlation trading strategy favored by hedge funds into deep negative territory, producing heavy losses for those that have been forced to unwind their positions. The price movements in correlation were driven by certain blow-outs in individual credit spreads, including Ford and General Motors,[43] that were de-correlated from the rest of the credit market, and hence badly hurt the return of the long equity/short mezzanine position (which is delta-neutral with respect to parallel spread variation, but not with respect to idiosyncratic spread widening). Losses for correlation

---

[41] See also Section 1.2.3.
[42] See Section 2.1.3.
[43] This was triggered by the downgrade by Standard & Poor's of Ford, General Motors and their finance subsidiaries to below investment grade, which both ranked among the largest borrowers in the corporate bond market (up to 3% of the investment grade bond market and 15% of the high-yield market following the downgrade) and were widely included in CDOs.

traders were further compounded by their rush to unwind their positions, which put downward pressures on the spread of mezzanine tranches.

This event highlights the fact that even though the correlation market seems to be a fairly liquid market, there are still dislocation risks and huge market imbalances. A majority of the sellers of mezzanine and senior protection in the correlation space are investors who can carry the risk on an accrual basis (institutional investors), thereby mitigating much of the mark-to-market risk. In a moderately negative credit environment, they are unlikely to be forced sellers. The concern is that those who have bought protection on the same tranches are generally mark-to-market investors (hedge funds, dealers), and may be forced to unwind this protection (as a hedge against something else that is falling in price) before its full hedging potential is realized.

As most of the arrangers fear such dislocation of the correlation market, there is consequently a growing effort from arrangers to structure products based on first loss instruments or to propose strategies based on short positions on mezzanine tranches, which would restore some balance in the correlation market. Hence, the growing number of capital-guaranteed products where the coupon is indexed on the first loss of a corporate portfolio and of institutional investors using tranched-index in order to hedge their corporate bond portfolio or existing CDO positions.

CDOs are one of the fastest growing segments of the credit derivatives market. This development has been constantly fed by changing structures, as seen above, and there appears to be no limit to the kinds of product the financial engineers can create with their fertile imaginations.

While the first arrangements applied the traditional securitization techniques to high-yield bond portfolios or bank loans, the market made a u-turn with credit derivatives, whether in balance sheet management or arbitrage of credit markets. Today most transactions take place in the latter compartment, which in many ways increasingly resembles an options market.

Finally, it should be noted that the structuring techniques specific to CDOs are now no longer limited to the credit markets. As mentioned earlier, cash-flow securitizations of new underlying assets such as hedge funds or private equity participations have been structured.

The latest developments show how bank intermediaries are trying to structure new products, such as collateralized equity obligations, which apply the synthetic arbitrage CDO technology we have described here, not just to a CDS portfolio, but to a basket of equity put options (inspired among others by EDSs). In this capacity, CDOs contribute to building links between the various compartments of the capital markets. This increasing financial integration is probably the most important result of the development in the credit derivatives and structured credit market, as we shall see in the last chapter of this book.

# 5

# The Credit Derivatives and Structured Credit Products Market

Since its emergence, the market in credit derivatives and structured credit products has grown exponentially and most observers agree that this growth should accelerate in the years to come. There are several reasons for this:

- First, the omnipresence of credit risk in the commercial and financial markets (cash and derivatives) means that these instruments offer ample opportunities, in theory greatly superior to interest rate, equity or currency derivatives, among others.
- Second, the emergence of second-generation products (such as 'exotic' credit derivatives and structured products) has over the past few years fuelled this market and fostered liquidity in the 'vanilla' segments.
- Finally, the recent development of arbitrage operations (particularly via CDOs) has greatly contributed to this steady growth.

Thus, some observers have no hesitation in drawing a parallel between the credit derivatives market and that of interest rate swaps and options. These, unheard of in the early 1980s, have recorded colossal growth since then. Outstanding notional amounts on OTC interest rate derivatives stood at $58 000 bn worldwide at end 1998 (in notional amount) according to the Bank of International Settlements. By the end of 2004 that figure was $187 340 bn! Indeed, the development of these two markets has been very similar: first came standard products (CDS in the former, rate swaps in the latter), then followed by a boom in structured and 'exotic' products, growth being further boosted by the ever-larger number of users spreading out from banks to other market players (institutional investors, corporates, etc.).

In comparison, the total notional amount outstanding in credit derivatives rose from $180 bn in 1997 to $3548 bn at the end of 2003, according to the British Bankers' Association (a 64% compound annual growth rate). It could reach up to $5021 bn by the end of 2004 and $8206 bn by the end of 2006! According to the Bank of International Settlements (BIS), the total notional amount of credit derivatives stood at $6400 bn at the end of 2004.

It can be deduced, on the basis of these estimations, that the credit derivatives market represented 2.6% of the total amount of OTC derivatives worldwide at end 2004. Figure 5.1 shows the structure of the world OTC derivatives market.

The main difficulty in assessing an exploding market like the credit derivatives one is the lack of data, and also the discrepancies between the various data sources.[1] The British Bankers' Association (BBA) published a series of biannual reports (1997/98, 1999/00, 2001/02, 2003/04), which have since the first edition been based on data supplied by market professionals. This approach guarantees a degree of methodological consistency and enables statistics to

---

[1] In addition to the British Bankers' Association and Fitch Ratings, on whose data this chapter is based, other organizations supply regular evaluations of the size and structure of this market: ISDA, *Risk Magazine*, the other rating agencies, the IMF and the OCC (for American commercial banks only) and other banking regulatory bodies.

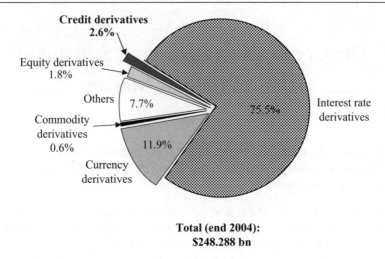

**Total (end 2004):**
**$248.288 bn**

**Figure 5.1**   Structure of the world market for OTC derivatives (end 2004)
*Sources*: Bank of International Settlements (2005), ISDA, JP Morgan, authors' analysis.

be compared. However, the reliability of the results in these surveys depends on the quality of the data supplied by the main participants, and their knowledge of the market.

Fitch Ratings has published two surveys (March 2003, updated in September 2003, and September 2004) of the global credit derivatives market, which provide for additional detailed information on its dynamics and the strategies of the various players involved.

## 5.1   OVERVIEW OF THE MARKET

The credit derivatives market, which emerged in 1991–1992, is a relatively recent one compared to the other derivatives markets (interest and exchange rate, equity, commodities), which date from the 1970s and 1980s, or even earlier. It developed relatively slowly, with most transactions occurring in Wall Street up to 1994–1995.

Today, most of the players in the financial markets agree that this market has reached critical mass. It was capable of notable resistance during the Asian crisis of late 1997, and rose above the 1998 credit crunch. In more recent years, the introduction of the single currency in Europe gave it vital impetus, as well as stimulating the credit market as a whole. 1999–2000 saw greater structuring of the credit derivatives market via standardized legal documentation and increased liquidity on corporate spreads in both Europe and the United States. Finally, the blows to the market in the second half of 2001 caused by a wave of large defaults had no significant impact on its growth, quite the contrary. Contract soundness was tested for real during the bankruptcies of end 2001 and through 2002 and 2003 (Enron, Worldcom, Parmalat, etc.).

As we saw, some specific situations over the last two years have led to a number of changes in contracts from a legal standpoint, but overall, they have proved the soundness of credit derivatives. As the BBA 2001/2002 report underlined: 'In a year fraught with major bankruptcies … credit derivatives have proven their effectiveness in buffering major shocks to the global financial system.'

One of the main blows to the credit derivatives market in the last few years was without a doubt the bankruptcy of Enron in 2001. This, the biggest ever recorded for a company at the time,[2] proved the undoubted maturity of the credit derivatives market.[3] Furthermore, a special feature of this bankruptcy was that Enron was also a major player in these products. As counterparty in the CDS market and many synthetic securitization transactions, the Enron default led some of its counterparties to incur mark-to-market losses. The whole process was settled satisfactorily.

We shall now describe the main stages of development in the credit derivatives market, and its current structure.

### 5.1.1  Main Stages in the Development of the Credit Derivatives Market

Although credit derivatives are relatively recent, various incarnations can be discerned.[4]

#### 5.1.1.1  A Defensive Product

It is because market operators confronted exponential growth in OTC derivatives transactions that credit derivatives were created and developed in the early 1990s. As we have seen, the intermediary merchant banks in this market could not be content with the traditional methods of managing credit risk. They were, moreover, hampered by modest capitalization and the need to mark their portfolios to the market every day. They therefore needed new tools for managing fairly nonliquid credit exposures. The banks therefore structured credit risk swaps to hedge against their clients' potential defaults, and were able to find counterparties through the lure of higher yields.

#### 5.1.1.2  A Bilateral Market

In the years 1994–1995, the credit derivatives market became a bilateral one in which the banks structuring these products began to talk to the potential investors, arranging products tailored to their needs as regards risk/reward profiles.

#### 5.1.1.3  A Booming Market

From 1996–1997, the credit derivatives market soon 'democratized', not least in the emerging sovereign risk segment. The most sophisticated traders began to manage their risk on the basis of a portfolio, in the same way as they managed an interest rate derivatives book (whereas previously, most transactions had been designed on a back-to-back basis). Third parties (the regulatory authorities,[5] rating agencies) began to take a closer look at the market.

The Asian crisis at the end of 1997 justified the increased importance of credit derivatives, which sometimes offered more liquidity than that of the underlying bond market. As one market observer noted at the time: 'The real price of Korean risk is in the credit market, not in the bond market.'[6]

---

[2] Before Worldcom filed for Chapter 11 in 2003 (see Chapter 1).
[3] This huge default caused losses to protection sellers on average of 80% of the notional value of the contracts since the recovery value of the assets after the default was estimated at about 20% in the bond market.
[4] See Smithson et al. (1996).
[5] The first banking regulations on credit derivatives date from August 1996 (Fed). The Fed was rapidly followed by the other regulatory bodies (the Bank of England in December 1996, revised in 1997, then the Commission Bancaire in France in June 1997, and then April 1998).
[6] Cited by Iskandar (1998).

*5.1.1.4  An Established Derivatives Market*

As of 1999–2000, the credit derivatives market underwent major structural changes, which enabled it to guarantee its future:

- Introduction of the euro in the capital markets at the end of 1999 and emergence of a true credit market at European level.
- Emergence of second-generation products ('exotic' credit derivatives and structured products), having a knock-on boost on liquidity in the 'vanilla' markets.
- Regulatory capital arbitrage transactions undertaken by many banks.

The amounts handled rose considerably, as did the number and diversity of players: commercial banks, insurance and reinsurance companies, other institutional investors (pension funds, asset managers, hedge funds, etc.). As a result, the market in credit derivatives, as we have seen, is now the reference market for assessing credit risk, be it for existing issuers or for future borrowers. The five-year Nokia CDS, for example, is today a liquid instrument used in many structured baskets, although no bond has yet been issued by this Finnish company. Liquidity on this instrument is due to the need to cover possible existing exposures related to bank loans, or to take an *ex ante* position on the future level of spreads of a possible bond issue.

The latest developments in the credit derivatives market indicate that it will soon resemble the other OTC derivatives markets. In this regard, three major challenges may be identified:

1. The question of extending the user base to new market segments and potential users (corporates or retail investors). A very small number of companies, for instance, use these instruments today, as seen earlier.[7] This seems essential if credit derivatives are to attain the degree of success met by interest rate derivatives, as the most optimistic market observers predict.
2. The completion of the industrialization process in transactions, which will entail:
   - The creation of independent databases fed by the main market-makers, listing the legal reference entities, offering valuation services, etc., as currently developed by such providers as Mark-it Partners.
   - The arrival of electronic trading via dedicated platforms, providing automated links between front- and back-offices (straight-through processing, STP), and improved operator productivity.
3. The increasing interpenetration between this market and the other segments of the capital markets. This is the result of growth in hybrid products and flourishing investment management strategies based on convertible bonds or capital structure arbitrage. This trend must continue to ensure that the credit derivatives market is firmly entrenched in the financial markets and that these instruments become indispensable tools in the arsenal of market operators.

### 5.1.2  Size, Growth and Structure of the Credit Derivatives Market

Several surveys on the evolving size of the credit derivatives market have been published. The most reliable of these is the biannual BBA survey. Other reliable data has been provided by Fitch, one of the three leading rating agencies, in their 2003 and 2004 surveys.

---

[7] See Section 2.2.3.

On the whole, these surveys have comparable results:

• Rather slow beginnings (for the foregoing reasons).
• Gigantic potential for applications ensuring the future development of this market.
• Players limited to the large international banks in the first years.
• Activity centered mostly on sovereign risk (1997) and then banking risk (1998), with corporate risk arriving more recently (2000 and onwards).

### 5.1.2.1  Size and Growth of the Credit Derivatives Market

An initial survey by the BBA was conducted in early October 1996 and published in the following November. Fifteen institutions in the London credit derivatives market were questioned on their estimation of the volume of notional outstanding in the London market only. The estimated size of the London market at that time was $20 bn, ranging from $15–$75 bn, some 50% of the world market.

This early estimation should be compared with the figures of the last survey published by the BBA in 2003–2004. The average size of the world market was estimated at $3548 bn at end 2003, not counting asset swaps. The BIS provided a figure of $6400 bn at end 2004, which translates into a compound annual growth rate of 106% between 1996 and 2004. In other words, the credit derivatives market size doubles year on year. See Figure 5.2.

Among factors that might hamper the growth of this market in the future are:

• The occurrence of large scandals/financial losses with these products and the potentially harmful reaction of the regulatory authorities (the Italian credit derivatives and structured credit products market, for example, was severely shaken by the Cirio, Parmalat and other

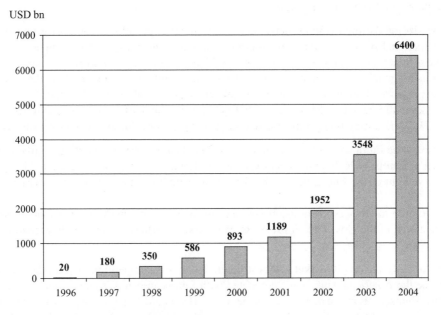

**Figure 5.2**   Growth of the global credit derivatives market
*Source*: British Bankers' Association, BBA Credit Derivatives Reports (1996–2004), Bank of International Settlements. Reproduced by permission of BBA.

crashes in 2003–2004, which led to more restrictive regulations on insurance companies' use of CDOs as a funding support for retail index-linked life insurance policies).
- Regulatory obstacles, which have still not been removed. As underlined by the BBA report in 2001–2002: 'Regulatory uncertainty, such as the outcome of Basel II, constitutes one of the major constraints to the growth of the credit derivatives market.'[8]
- The dislocation of the correlation market, as mentioned at the end of the previous chapter, which could put a halt to the growth in structured products and have a knock-on effect on the vanilla products used to hedge the former.
- The necessary creation of appropriate infrastructure and control systems designed to support trading and risk management activities.
- The capacity of market players to hire and train professionals suitably qualified for this market. They should ideally have solid experience in derivatives, know the credit markets and how to analyze financial statements, and thoroughly understand the legal risks associated with contracts.

### 5.1.2.2  Structure of the Credit Derivatives Market

In this sub-section we present the various conclusions of the market surveys as regards credit derivatives volumes per geographical zone, product type and maturity, and type of underlying risk.

**Market structure by geographical zone**

Although credit derivatives were initially created and structured by the Wall Street merchant banks, the main drive for growth since then has come from London. The comparative advantages of London as a financial market are:

- The size of the international debt market – London is the global capital for eurobonds, international syndicated loans, euro commercial paper and euro medium-term notes.
- The regulatory environment, provided by the Financial Services Authority, is acknowledged for its pragmatic approach, acceptance of innovation and policies favorable to the market.
- The presence of all the largest international banks and a pool of first-class talent.
- Unlike Wall Street, London has a highly liquid asset swap market, and undeniable expertise in OTC derivatives. It is the most active market in the world for this type of instrument.

Moreover, the European single currency in 1999 enabled the development of a unified credit market in Europe (which, paradoxically, benefited London, even though the United Kingdom has stayed out of the Eurozone), to the detriment of traditional domestic bond markets. See Figure 5.3.

According to BBA estimations, almost half of the world credit derivatives market is thus concentrated in the City. The North American market is different from the European one in several ways:

- Historically, the credit market is less structured with less competition in secondary trading.
- While the American banks have competed with European banks in their domestic market, only Deutsche Bank and, to a lesser degree, UBS, could today claim a worldwide role, including a strong position in the American market (the former profited from the takeover

---

[8] BBA Credit Derivatives Report 2001/2002.

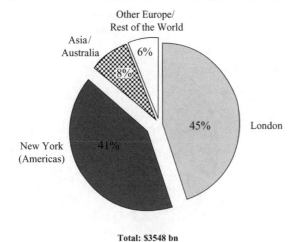

Other Europe/
Rest of the World

Asia/
Australia          6%

8%

45%     London

New York          41%
(Americas)

Total: $3548 bn

**Figure 5.3**   Geographical breakdown of the global credit derivatives market (end 2003)
*Source*: British Bankers' Association. Reproduced by permission of BBA.

of Bankers Trust in 1997, while the latter bought up Dillon Read and PaineWebber, two
well-established brokerage houses in Wall Street).
- The cash credit market still deals mostly on the basis of US Treasury bonds. It is therefore
  sealed off from the derivatives market, the finality of which is mainly to build structured
  credit products and provide hedging solutions to commercial banks. This is not true of
  Europe, where the cash and derivatives markets are strongly integrated.

In the other large financial markets, not least Japan, the credit derivatives market has grown
more slowly. However, it would appear that credit derivatives are slowly gaining ground even
though, as yet, there are no official data on the subject. CDOs and CDSs are the most commonly
traded instruments at this time. The main uses are to build products that will offer leverage to
investors penalized by an extremely unfavorable interest rate structure on the yen, and hedge
the credit risk inherent to certain popular instruments, such as convertible bonds. However,
the market is above all one in which protection is sold, and which does not necessarily reflect
borrower ratings nor allow efficient credit pricing. The dominant role of the state, which
intervenes to support the banks, has also biased the observed recovery value on defaulting
assets over the past few years.

The other two main markets are Hong Kong and Singapore. What characterizes these markets
since the creation of credit derivatives is above all the domestic nature of the credit risk traded
there. For several years, the most active investment banks have opted to distribute value-added
'exotic' products, with some success.

Finally, Sydney remains a very domestic-orientated market, focused mainly on local underlying assets. It offers an attractive complementary range of risks, which can be used to diversify
structured baskets.

### Market structure per product type

CDSs are the main credit derivative instrument (50% of transactions recorded). Conversely,
the growing proportion of CDOs and indices indicates that these second-generation products

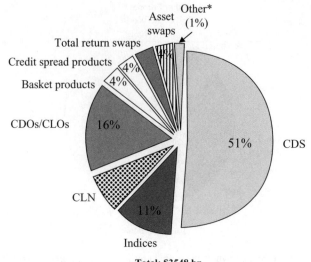

**Figure 5.4**   Breakdown of the global credit derivatives market by product types (end 2003)
*Notes:* * Equity credit-linked products. Shares do not add to 100% due to rounding error.
*Source*: British Bankers' Association. Reproduced by permission of BBA.

are gaining ground. According to the latest BBA survey, the market is divided up as shown in Figure 5.4.

The Fitch survey gives fairly similar results, using a different typology.

### Market structure according to maturity

The standard maturity of CDSs in the market is five years. This figure is reflected by the structure of the market according to transaction maturities, since the BBA reports that the maturity of more than three-quarters of credit derivatives transactions is between one and five years. This is confirmed by the BIS, which estimates that more than 70% of CDSs and 60% of multi-name products have a maturity shorter than five years at end 2004.

Most bank loans contain one five-year tranche, and most arbitrage CDOs are similar, thus channeling the market even further into a standard five-year maturity.

The 2003 Fitch survey confirms these results, its figures for transactions of between one and five years maturity being:

- 53% of European and Asian banks' transactions.
- 48% of North American banks' transactions.
- 58% of insurance and reinsurance companies' transactions.
- 43% of financial guarantors' transactions.[9]

Since the start of 2003, the market has been gradually moving towards the standardization of maturities, with quarterly contract scheduled termination dates (dated March 20, June 20,

---

[9] This market segment includes monoline insurance specialists in credit enhancement and financial guarantees, such as ACE Guaranty, AMBAC Assurance Corp, IXIS Financial Guaranty, Financial Security Assurance Inc. (a subsidiary of Dexia), MBIA Insurance Corp, MBNA Corp, or again XL Capital Assurance/XL Financial Assurance.

September 20 and December 20). The main purpose of this is to minimize the risk arising from maturity differentials on market-maker flow books.

Finally, the low percentage of transactions with maturities over 10 years should be noted: these represent less than 10% of total transactions in the BBA survey. According to Fitch, this percentage is higher for financial guarantors: 18%, showing how important they are to this market as long-term investors specialized in credit. Moreover, demand from bond investors for long-term securities and the redoubled wish of issuers to extend debt maturity, in order to secure attractive interest rates in a context of historically low long-term rates, have led to the creation of a liquid ten-year credit curve.

## Market structure per type of underlying risk

This may be analyzed by taking into account the ratings or the nature of underlying risks exchanged.

## Market structure per rating class

Although the BBA survey anticipated the likelihood of the market moving towards lower quality assets, this did not occur at the speed predicted. Investment-grade credits still represent the bulk of risks being exchanged in the credit derivatives market. According to Fitch, the breakdown of reference entities by rating class was as in Table 5.1.

**Table 5.1** Structure of the credit derivatives market per rating class

|  | 2003 | 2002 |
| --- | --- | --- |
| AAA | 17% | 22% |
| AA | 10% | 14% |
| A | 25% | 29% |
| BBB | 30% | 28% |
| Below investment grade | 18% | 8% |

Source: Fitch Ratings (2004 and 2003). Reproduced by permission of Fitch Ratings.

## Market structure per type of reference entity

Although the majority of assets on which credit derivatives were structured up to 1999 were sovereign assets, the largest percentage of identified classes today is corporate assets, a situation that has remained relatively stable since the 1999–2000 BBA survey. This phenomenon can no doubt be explained partly by the increase in synthetic securitization transactions and partly by the deterioration of credit risk in certain corporate sectors such as telecommunications. This led to (i) more pressing needs for hedging and active exposure management and (ii) a correlating increase in spreads, entailing the growing inclusion of these names in structured products.

The 2003–2004 BBA survey thus confirms the decline of sovereign assets as reference credits from 54% in 1996 to 35% in 1997, 20% in 1999, 15% in 2001 and a mere 11% in 2003. See Table 5.2.

This market structure is confirmed by the Fitch figures at the end of 2003:

• Corporates: 65%
• Financial institutions: 17%

- Sovereign: 6%
- Asset-backed securities: 5%
- Others: 7%

A new trend that should be noticed is the rise in asset-backed securities (ABS) underlying credit derivatives. This increase is due especially to the considerable rise in CDO-type structured products based on ABSs or CDOs as underlying assets. Thus, according to the Fitch survey, ABS-type underlying assets represented 18% of the credit derivative portfolios of financial guarantors in 2003, versus 4% for insurance portfolios and 1% for bank portfolios.

As regards the reference entities actually traded in the market, the Fitch survey went further and gave an overview of the most actively traded credits. This ranking showed the relative importance taken by corporate issuers in the market.

The eight main reference entities are corporate credits (in bold type in Table 5.3). Financial institutions were the second most traded risk class (shaded in Table 5.3). The other entities are sovereign issuers.

**Table 5.2**  Structure of the credit derivatives market per type of reference entity

|                        | BBA (2001/2002) | BBA (2003/2004) |
|------------------------|-----------------|-----------------|
| Sovereign credits      | 15%             | 11%             |
| Corporate credits      | 60%             | 64%             |
| Financial institutions | 22%             | 22%             |
| Others                 | 3%              | 3%              |

*Source:* BBA Credit Derivatives Reports. Reproduced by permission of BBA.

**Table 5.3**  Main reference entities in the global credit derivatives market (end 2003)

| Protection sold | Protection bought |
|-----------------|-------------------|
| **1. Ford Motor Company/FMCC** | **1. Ford Motor Company/FMCC** |
| **2. General Motors/GMAC** | **2. DaimlerChrysler** |
| **3. France Telecom** | **3. General Motors/GMAC** |
| **4. DaimlerChrysler** | **4. France Telecom** |
| **5. Deutsche Telekom** | **5. Deutsche Telekom** |
| **6. General Electric/GECC** | **6. General Electric/GECC** |
| **7. Altria Group** | **7. Telecom Italia** |
| **8. Telecom Italia** | **8. Verizon** |
| 9. Japan | **9. Altria Group** |
| 10. France | 10. Japan |
| 11. Italy | 11. Merrill Lynch |
| 12. Portugal | **12. Volkswagen** |
| 13. Fannie Mae | 13. Bayerische Hypo-und-Vereinsbank |
| **14. Verizon** | **14. Bayer** |
| 15. Allianz | 15. Brazil |
| 16. Merrill Lynch | **16. BT** |
| **17. Volkswagen** | 17. Citigroup |
| 18. AIG | 18. Credit Suisse First Boston |
| 19. Citigroup | 19. JP Morgan Chase |
| 20. Germany | 20. Lehman Brothers |

*Source:* Fitch Ratings (2004). Reproduced by permission of Fitch Ratings.

**Table 5.4**   Main credit events in 2003 and 2002

| 2003 | 2002 |
|------|------|
| 1. Parmalat | 1. Worldcom |
| 2. British Energy | 2. Enron |
| 3. Mirant | 3. Marconi |
| 4. Solutia | 4. Railtrack |
| 5. Air Canada | 5. Xerox |
| 6. HealthSouth | 6. Argentina |
| 7. Fleming Companies | 7. Teleglobe |
| 8. TXU | 8. Pacific Gas & Electric |
| 9. Northwestern Corp. | 9. Swissair |
| 10. Marconi | 10. AT&T Canada |

*Source:* Fitch Ratings (2004 and 2003). Reproduced by permission of Fitch Ratings.

Furthermore, the Fitch Ratings reports identified the main credit events. Table 5.4 shows their ranking per number of occurrences. Unsurprisingly, it shows the large defaults of the year 2002. The top three credit events accounted for 50% of total reported credit events in 2003, versus 32% in 2002, reflecting the improvement in the credit cycle.

### 5.1.3   Size, Growth and Structure of the CDO Market

This has been developed fully in Chapter 4, and so only the main lines of this experience will be mentioned here. CDO transactions form one of the most dynamic segments of the credit derivatives market. Figure 5.5 indicates the size of this market and its development.

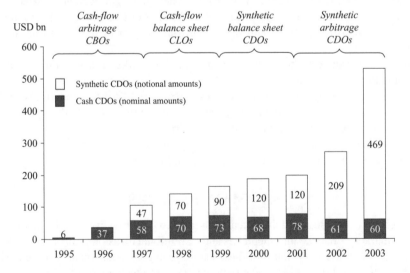

**Figure 5.5**   Size and growth of the global CDO market
*Sources*: Bank of America, Creditflux, Moody's, Standard & Poor's, International Financing Review, authors' analysis.

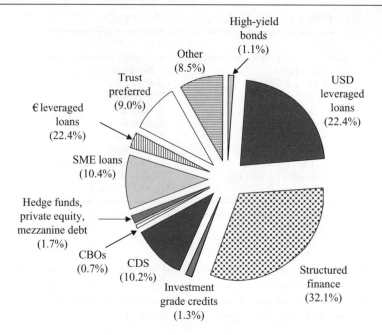

**Figure 5.6**   Structure of the global arbitrage CDO market by type of underlying (2003)
*Sources*: Morgan Stanley, *Risk Magazine* (January 2004), authors' analysis.

In the same way as for the credit derivatives market, it behoves us to be cautious with the figures recorded in this segment, since they vary greatly according to the size of the underlying market concerned: in ascending order, public transactions only, rated transactions, all transactions (public or bilateral, rated or not). They may also fluctuate depending on the reference used: some market analyses only mention risk tranches placed with investors, while others take the total notional amount of the portfolio subject of the CDO transaction as a reference.

Figure 5.5 nevertheless shows the explosion of this market and its different phases, as described in the previous chapter.

In terms of underlying assets, leveraged loans, structured finance transactions (ABSs and CDOs) and CDSs are the three main categories used in synthetic CDO arbitrage transactions according to Morgan Stanley, as shown in Figure 5.6.

The credit derivative and CDO markets have grown massively since their emergence in 1995–1997. Let us now examine the main players in these markets.

## 5.2   MAIN PLAYERS

In earlier chapters we presented the potential uses of credit derivatives for the main players in the capital markets: financial intermediaries and institutional investors, banks and corporates.[10] What are the relative market shares of these various categories, and what specific position do they hold in the credit derivatives and structured credit products market?

---

[10] Section 2.3.

**Table 5.5**   Main protection buyers

|                  | 1998/1999 | 2001/2002 | 2003/2004 |
|------------------|-----------|-----------|-----------|
| Banks            | 63%       | 52%       | 51%       |
| Securities houses| 18%       | 21%       | 16%       |
| Hedge funds      | 3%        | 12%       | 16%       |
| Other*           | 16%       | 15%       | 17%       |

*Note*: * Corporates, insurance companies, etc.
*Source*: BBA. Reproduced by permission of BBA.

**Table 5.6**   Main protection sellers

|                       | 1998/1999 | 2001/2002 | 2003/2004 |
|-----------------------|-----------|-----------|-----------|
| Banks                 | 47%       | 39%       | 38%       |
| Insurance companies*  | 23%       | 33%       | 20%       |
| Securities houses     | 16%       | 16%       | 16%       |
| Hedge funds           | 5%        | 5%        | 15%       |
| Other                 | 9%        | 7%        | 11%       |

*Note*: * Including financial guarantors.
*Source*: BBA. Reproduced by permission of BBA.

The BBA figures give us an overall view of the market, segmented into protection buyers and sellers. This is shown in Tables 5.5 and 5.6, with the addition of figures from the Fitch survey, enabling us to make a more detailed analysis of the role of the various player categories.

The Fitch reports complete these data by giving the net positions for the main categories of player: banks, insurance and reinsurance, and financial guarantors. In all, according to the figures compiled by the rating agency, at end 2003 banks (the leading banks worldwide and brokerage houses) reportedly transferred credit risk in the amount of around $260 bn to other players in the credit derivatives and structured credit products market, while financial guarantors and insurance companies subscribed to some $462 bn credit risk in synthetic form (i.e. excluding an additional $83 bn in cash CDOs). The strategy of the various players will now be examined in more detail.

### 5.2.1   Banks

The BBA survey clearly shows that credit institutions remain and are likely to remain the dominant players in the market, even though their market share is gradually falling and the insurance and reinsurance companies are gaining ground. These figures are corroborated by those of the Fitch rating agency. The latter are shown in Figure 5.7 for the banking segment.[11]

This result should be interpreted according to the type of bank considered:

- The large world-ranking banks and the main brokerage houses appear to be net protection buyers structurally.
- Regional banks, especially those in Europe and Asia, appear to be above all risk-takers (to diversify their portfolios). Fifty per cent of the banking institutions surveyed in these two

[11] All bank types: leading world-ranking banks, brokerage houses, regional banks.

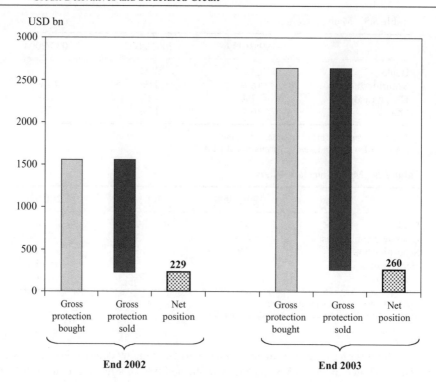

**Figure 5.7**    Banks' position in the global credit derivatives market
*Source*: Fitch Ratings (2002 and 2003). Reproduced by permission of Fitch Ratings.

regions appear to be net protection sellers at end 2003 (versus 67% at end 2002), especially the German Landesbanken (to the tune of an estimated $29 bn at end 2003), the Asian and Benelux-based banks.

Figure 5.8 shows the relative numbers of European and Asian banks depending on their position in the credit derivatives market at end 2002.

In terms of distribution per product, CDSs represent 80% of European banks' business as against 66% for North American ones, reflecting their positions as market leaders and providers of liquidity, a role taken on by their front-office trading functions, not least at the big investment banks. This domination of the investment banks was recently criticized by PIMCO, one of the main fixed income asset managers in the world (a subsidiary of Allianz Group), which accused certain credit institutions of placing large protection buying orders on certain firms, using proprietary information obtained through banking contacts.

The investment banks are seen as pioneers in the credit derivatives market. Originally, the main activity for most of them was to educate the final users (customers), since the credit derivatives market was above all supply-driven. As shown earlier, credit derivatives were originally designed and used by the main Wall Street banks to manage their counterparty risks in the OTC derivatives markets. They were then quite naturally offered to commercial banks managing their credit portfolios, and then to institutional investors and other speculative funds so that they could take positions on assets or improve the risk/reward profile of their portfolio.

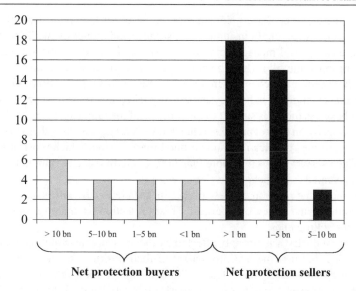

**Figure 5.8**   Analysis of the position of European and Asian banks in the global credit derivatives market (end 2002)
*Source*: Fitch Ratings (2003). Reproduced by permission of Fitch Ratings.

The education of the final users progressed steadily with the many publications and conferences on the subject of credit derivatives, and the constitution of study groups like that of the British Bankers' Association, grouping 70 banks, or the ISDA group.

Banks (in the wider sense, commercial and investment banks) should continue to occupy a dominant position in the market, via both their trading activities and their traditional role as lenders. In both the United States and Europe, banks as a whole have the greatest exposure to credit risk. The credit portfolio managers of these institutions are therefore the main protection buyers in the CDS market but have traditionally been much more timid in selling protection. However, with the huge increase in credit spreads in 2001 and 2002, a minority took this opportunity to unlock their hedges, the market value of which had risen considerably, and cash in on them. This was the first glimmer of active credit risk management. Moreover, the more sophisticated of them noted that this evolution in the market offered attractive opportunities to improve yield and diversify their portfolios via straight protection selling.

### 5.2.2   Insurance, Reinsurance Companies and Financial Guarantors

Insurers in the wider sense (life and nonlife insurance companies, reinsurance companies, monoline insurers or financial guarantors) are the second most active category of players in the credit derivatives and structured credit products market. These are traditionally risk-takers, and therefore protection sellers, mainly via structured products (portfolios of risks offer diversification benefits akin to the mutualization of risks principle, which is at the heart of the insurance business), and more infrequently via individual CDSs. Thus, the Fitch surveys show that for these institutions, portfolio products represent the vast majority of their exposure (more than 90% in 2003 and 2002).

The reason these players have gained a growing share of the credit derivatives market is that insurance companies (credit insurance, reinsurance and monoline) with specialized skills in credit risk analysis and management have massively entered the market, and traditional insurance companies (multiline) have begun using them to diversify their portfolios. The latter have chosen both senior tranches and more risky ones in CDO transactions. On the contrary, monoline insurance companies have systematically taken positions in super senior tranches, because their business model is subject to the scrutiny of the rating agencies (their competitive edge depends directly on their capacity to retain an AAA rating, enabling them to enhance bond issues, not least in the American municipal bond market, from which most of these players come). The Fitch survey shows that more than 90% of credit risk exposure in this group is for underlying risks rated A or above.

Figure 5.9 shows the position of these players in the credit derivatives market. They invest both in the synthetic and cash CDO markets. Their protection buying positions are negligible compared to the selling ones.

The insurance industry was strongly affected by the unfavorable evolution of credit spreads in 2001 and 2002, because the mark-to-market of their positions became extremely volatile and also because they actually made losses. Some insurance companies were thus obliged to pull in their horns or even actually leave the market (Chubb, Pacific Life, Winterthur, Aegon).

Reinsurers were confronted with credit events that virtually wiped out their investments in certain equity or mezzanine CDO tranches. Significant losses were thus recorded by Centre Re, SCOR or Swiss Re, causing them to withdraw from the market. The latter company adopted a different strategy, choosing active management of its portfolio with no further investment, and taking a strategic positioning in direct competition with the investment banks via its subsidiary Swiss Re New Markets.

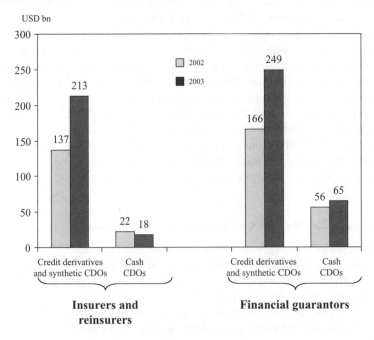

**Figure 5.9**   Net position of insurers in the global credit derivatives market (protection selling)
*Source*: Fitch Ratings (2004 and 2003). Reproduced by permission of Fitch Ratings.

As regards the monoline insurance companies, only time will tell if the more volatile credit spreads of the credit derivatives market will still make it tempting, or whether they will be constrained to refocus on their traditional bond enhancement and securitization markets.

### 5.2.3   Hedge Funds and Traditional Asset Managers

The significant market share gained by asset managers and hedge funds in recent years, not least in protection buying, is worthy of note. The BBA survey shows that almost 30% of responses anticipated that they would occupy second place in the protection buying category in 2006. According to the 2004 Fitch Ratings survey, hedge funds comprised a sizeable percentage of the most active counterparties' trading volume (between 20% and 30%).

#### 5.2.3.1   Hedge Funds

The growing share of hedge funds in the credit markets can be explained by several factors:

• Improved market liquidity, together with greater price transparency.
• Overall deterioration of corporate creditworthiness in 2001–2002, giving new opportunities for arbitrage.
• Growing importance of alternative management strategies and consequent flow of funds towards these new investment vehicles.

The particular characteristic of these players is that they are active in every segment of the credit market: bonds, CDSs, convertible bonds, bank loans, CDOs and portfolio products, structured correlation products, index products, options on spreads and CDS, etc.

These players' credit risk portfolios are relatively large, as shown in Figure 5.10.

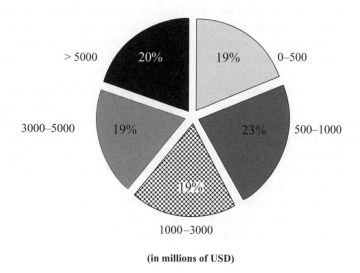

(in millions of USD)

**Figure 5.10**   Hedge funds' credit portfolios
*Sources*: Mercer Oliver Wyman, Patel (2004a), authors' analysis.

This figure is drawn from a Mercer Oliver Wyman survey of 80 hedge funds in the United States and Europe.

In the hedge fund market segment, several groups can be distinguished according to their investment strategies and their use of credit derivatives:

- 'Equity' funds dealing with credit risk.
  - Convertible bond arbitrage funds, the goal of which is to arbitrage the implied market volatility of equity unbundled from convertible bonds and its historical volatility. (They seek to cover the credit risk of the bonds they are holding and are therefore structurally net protection buyers.)
  - Capital structure arbitrage funds. These usually take long positions in shares and short positions in credit risk on the same underlying firm, and occasionally the reverse.
- Fixed income relative value funds, which are gaining ground in the credit market, with multiple strategies:
  - Term structure arbitrage of an issuer's credit curve.
  - Arbitrage between bond and derivatives markets.
  - Recovery rate arbitrage between senior and subordinated debt on the same issuer.
  - Pair trading on the future evolution of credit spreads between two issuers and/or different classes of asset.
- Finally, a new category of hedge fund has recently entered the market: this is that of investment vehicles specially designed for the credit markets, especially the structured product compartment. Players such as Blue Mountain ($750 m under management), Panton Alternative Partners, or CQS Management fall into this category.[12]

Convertible bond arbitrage funds, historically the most active in the credit market, had a relatively peaceful period between 2002 and 2004 compared to 2001, for two main reasons. First, the amount of new convertible issues fell by half in 2002, a trend confirmed in 2003–2004. Of these new issues, only half were rated investment grade, thus having a limited impact on the CDS market. Second, the specific nature of the old convertible bonds, which are now behaving like classic bonds, due to the virtually nil value of the embedded call option following the crash in equity markets, has removed a large part of these investors' traditional field of operations.

Capital structure arbitrage funds should continue to be active traders in the credit derivatives market. This is due more especially to fundamental trends in the capital markets, characterized by increased asset volatility and deteriorating issuer creditworthiness, conducive to the implementation of such strategies. The higher a firm's leverage is, the more suited the various hypotheses of the equity–credit arbitrage model are. For many firms, the debt/market value ratio has risen significantly since 1999, and the increased volatility of the stock markets has only multiplied the arbitrage possibilities.

Finally, the new funds dedicated to the credit markets have grown massively since early 2003. As pointed out by Eric Odberg, in charge of credit derivatives sales at Goldman Sachs New York, 'Hedging activity by banks has been limited this year. It's hedge funds that are

---

[12] See Patel (2004b).

largely driving growth'.[13] These are major players in some products, such as:

- Index products (81% of US hedge funds as against 61% in Europe use them).
- Credit spread options and CDSs, the average monthly volumes of which doubled between 2003 and early 2004.
- Investments in the equity tranches of CDOs.

### 5.2.3.2   Traditional Asset Managers

In Europe, the coming years should see increased participation of traditional asset managers in two main sectors:

- Active credit management funds, in strong progress since the arrival of the euro, should make more and more use of the CDS market in managing their positions. This trend should be facilitated by the easing of the regulations, which enable UCITs to participate in this market. In France, for instance, a decree[14] made on 10 December 2002 authorised UCITs to conclude credit derivatives contracts in certain conditions (to do with their management systems, in particular) and within certain limits. Similar provisions are expected in other markets in the Eurozone (e.g. Germany in the first half of 2005).
- The leading asset managers should also benefit from the rapid growth in the European managed CDOs market. These managers are more and more in demand from investment banks wishing to conclude transactions that are then distributed to institutional investors. AXA Investment Managers (AXA IM) is one of the pioneers of this development strategy in the managed CDO sector. In early 2004, in association with JP Morgan, AXA IM launched the biggest ever managed CDO transaction (Overture) worth $5 bn, which was heavily over-subscribed. Most of the big fund managers have also been solicited by investment banks (Invesco, Pimco, DWS, IXIS AM, Fortis IM, etc.), not to mention the appearance of many specialized boutiques (Duke Street, C-Bass, Zeiss, Faxtor, Unika, etc.), positioned as specialized collateral managers on certain asset classes such as leveraged loans, high-yield bonds or asset-backed securities.

### 5.2.4   Corporates

As we saw in Chapter 2, corporates, like banks, could, in theory, become heavy users of credit derivatives, as they have done for interest and exchange rate products. Thus, during the energy crisis in California, Enron was a major user of CDS to hedge the counterparty risks arising from its physical and energy derivatives transactions. The Siemens Group, via its subsidiary Siemens Financial Services (SFS), is also a well-known player in 'vanilla' credit derivative products. SFS manages the Siemens Group credit risk portfolio on receivables or advances on equipment. It is thus a pioneer amongst corporates with a strategy directly copied from that of banks, using such notions as RAROC.

Overall, however, corporates still remain on the margins of the credit derivatives market, even though their participation should increase, not least for regular issuers in the bond markets. That is because it is in the credit derivatives market that credit spread is traded, a key variable

---

[13] Quoted by Patel (2004b).
[14] Decree 2001-1439 amending decree 89-624 on OPCVM (UCITs).

on which corporate funding strategies are based. CFOs and treasurers are therefore obliged to be, at the very least, attentive observers of this market, and are even led to play an active role in order to optimize their funding conditions, as we saw earlier. Moreover, this market offers new opportunities to corporates (via the implementation of hedging or investment strategies), even if they do not appear to be urgent and need specific analysis beforehand.

There is no doubt that the extension of the credit derivatives market to the ultimate clientele of corporates is a major challenge to its growth and sustainability. Today, this segment represents the 'new frontier' for investment banks systematically seeking new markets and new applications for their products.

Looking beyond the corporate final client, another question to be asked is whether the retail market in credit derivatives has any role to play, especially in the structured products segment. The retail market is a major source of income and recurrent profit for investment banks (not least structured equity products), and is a sizeable outlet for the distribution of cash bonds in some countries (Switzerland, Benelux and Italy,[15] among others).

It must be admitted that hitherto, credit derivatives and structured credit products have not really found a market in the retail segment (except for a few private banking transactions, which resemble small institutional transactions). Asset manager Robeco's efforts to place managed CDOs and the recent announcement by UBS of its launch of a product designed for its retail clientele, UBS Credit Portfolio CDO,[16] are perhaps signs that a new market segment is opening up for these products.

## 5.3   AT THE HEART OF THE MARKET: THE INVESTMENT BANKS

The various surveys of the credit derivatives market show clearly that banking institutions are the main players in the credit derivatives and structured credit products market. One particular category of players at the heart of this segment is worth examining closely: investment banks. These are subsidiaries of the large commercial/universal banks (JP Morgan, Deutsche Bank, Citigroup, CSFB, UBS, BNP Paribas, SG CIB, ABN Amro, etc.) or brokerage houses (Goldman Sachs, Morgan Stanley, Merrill Lynch, Lehman Brothers, Bear Stearns, etc.). According to the Fitch surveys, of the 25 main counterparties in the credit derivatives market, most are investment banks (the only exceptions being insurance company AIG, through its AIG Financial Products subsidiary in 2002 and 2003, and Ambac in 2003).

Table 5.7 gives the ranking of the leading 15 investment banks active in the credit derivatives and structured credit products market. We shall detail below the relative positions of these institutions in the credit derivatives and structured credit products markets respectively, and describe their functions.

### 5.3.1   Position of the Investment Banks in the Credit Derivatives Market

The main players in the credit derivatives market have traditionally been the American merchant banks. Precursors were Bankers Trust (bought out by Deutsche Bank in 1997) and Credit Suisse Financial Products (CSFP, the former CSFB subsidiary in the derivatives markets).

---

[15] Until the Cirio and Parmalat scandals in 2003–2004, which led to the virtual closing of the Italian retail market in bond distribution.
[16] This is comprised of floating-rate notes (FRNs), the coupons of which are indexed to the performance of a pool of underlying credits composed of 100 well-known names in the retail market, equally weighted (see Ferry and Haddow-Allen, 2004).

**Table 5.7** Top 15 counterparties in the global credit derivatives market

| 2003 | 2002 |
|---|---|
| 1. JP Morgan | JP Morgan |
| 2. Deutsche Bank | Merrill Lynch |
| 3. Goldman Sachs | Deutsche Bank |
| 4. Morgan Stanley | Morgan Stanley |
| 5. Merrill Lynch | Credit Suisse First Boston |
| 6. Credit Suisse First Boston | Goldman Sachs |
| 7. UBS | UBS |
| 8. Lehman Brothers | Citigroup |
| 9. Citigroup | Lehman Brothers |
| 10. Bear Stearns | Commerzbank |
| 11. Commerzbank | Toronto Dominion |
| 12. BNP Paribas | Bank of America |
| 13. Bank of America | Bear Stearns |
| 14. Dresdner | BNP Paribas |
| 15. ABN Amro | Société Générale |

*Source*: Fitch Ratings (2003 and 2004). Reproduced by permission of Fitch Ratings.

Today, there are three main categories of player in the market:

1. The leading American banks with large lender networks and the necessary technical expertise in derivatives. These were the most active in the market as of 1995–1996: JP Morgan, Citibank, Bank of America, etc.
2. The main US brokerage houses, which are now on an equal footing with the above: Merrill Lynch, Morgan Stanley, Goldman Sachs, Bear Stearns and Lehman Brothers.
3. The European 'universal' banks, that managed to widen the breach into the markets in 1997–1998 and developed their activities from London outwards: Deutsche Bank, CSFB, BNP Paribas, UBS, Commerzbank, Société Générale and Barclays Capital.

Second-ranking players include the Japanese banks which entered the market a little later, mostly by luring teams away from their competitors in London. Only Nomura International and Mizuho were able to maintain an acceptable market share.

In their 2004 capital raising and risk management poll of investment bank customers,[17] Euromoney magazine provides a ranking of the main houses in the credit derivatives market. This is drawn up on the basis of voting by the clients of the large financial institutions. The results, per type of product, are set forth in Table 5.8.

JP Morgan is the bank most regularly acknowledged as leader in the 'vanilla' credit derivatives market. Also in the leading group are Deutsche Bank, Goldman Sachs and Morgan Stanley.

These results are confirmed by the annual *Risk* magazine 'Global Derivatives Awards' for 2004 and 2003, where JP Morgan and Deutsche Bank sit prominently atop the other houses. The latter also provides ranking indications for brokers, the role of which is to inform the market-makers on prices and put them in contact to enable them to conclude transactions. The main brokerage houses receiving awards in the *Risk* magazine 2004 and 2003 surveys are GFI, Credit Trade, Creditex, Cantor Fitzgerald and Icap.

---

[17] 373 respondents including treasurers and financial officers at corporates, financial institutions, supranational organizations and sovereign/state agencies.

**Table 5.8**   Results from *Euromoney* magazine 2004 risk management poll

| Credit derivatives overall advice | | | Default swaps pricing | | | Exotic/structured | | |
|---|---|---|---|---|---|---|---|---|
| 2004 | 2003 | | 2004 | 2003 | | 2004 | 2003 | |
| 1 | 1 | JP Morgan | 1 | 1 | JP Morgan | 1 | 2= | JP Morgan |
| 2 | 2 | Deutsche Bank | 2 | 3 | Deutsche Bank | 2 | 4 | Goldman Sachs |
| 3 | 8 | Morgan Stanley | 3 | 10= | Morgan Stanley | 3 | 12= | Citigroup |
| 4 | 4 | Citigroup | 4 | 10= | Barclays | 4 | — | HSBC |
| 5 | 20= | Lehman Brothers | 5 | 6 | Goldman Sachs | 5= | 5= | Merrill Lynch |
| 6 | 6= | Goldman Sachs | 6 | 5 | Citigroup | 5= | 1 | Deutsche Bank |
| 7 | 5 | HSBC | 7 | 7= | BNP Paribas | 7 | 7= | BNP Paribas |
| 8 | 3 | UBS | 8 | 4 | HSBC | 8= | 7= | CSFB |
| 9 | 10= | Barclays | 9 | 2 | UBS | 8= | 2= | UBS |
| 10= | 14= | BNP Paribas | 10 | 14= | Lehman Brothers | 10= | — | Bank of America |
| 10= | — | Bear Stearns | | | | 10= | — | ING Group |

*Source*: *Euromoney* (2004). Reproduced by permission of Euromoney.

### 5.3.2   Positions of the Investment Banks in the CDO Market

The same institutions also figure prominently in the structured credit market. Historically, the large commercial banks were at an advantage since they built up their expertise in synthetic securitization from their own balance sheet. This was the case for JP Morgan, who became the acknowledged leader of this market, with its BISTRO transactions as of 1997. The main European banks followed a similar route (Deutsche Bank, Société Générale, UBS, BNP Paribas, etc.) before capitalizing on their experience and offering structuring services to third parties.

Conversely, the brokerage houses adopted a different strategy, since they did not have the captive test bench of their parent company's balance sheet. They therefore used above all their capacity to originate and place investments, and capitalized on their high-quality relationships with financial institutions to win CDO arrangement mandates. This was the case for players such as Lehman Brothers, Goldman Sachs, Morgan Stanley or again Bear Stearns. Furthermore, these American investment banks relied on their track record in the securitization and CBO market to sell their expertise to the European financial institutions.

The 2004 *Euromoney* magazine ranking for portfolio credit derivatives is provided in Table 5.9.

According to the *Risk* magazine annual awards, in synthetic CDOs, as in credit derivatives, the same houses have also dominated the market until 2004 (JP Morgan, Deutsche Bank, Goldman Sachs, Morgan Stanley). Two new players have appeared in 2004 as leading the pack in all CDO product categories: Barclays Capital and Dresdner Kleinwort Wasserstein, thus showing that barriers to entry in the CDO business are diminishing.

*Creditflux* magazine also provides annual league tables on CDO arrangers by types of product. The 2004 ranking of arrangers is reproduced in Figure 5.11 for all bespoke trades (excluding asset-referenced deals).

Unsurprisingly, most of the same names appear in this ranking. On that basis, one must acknowledge that the credit derivatives and structured credit products market is really in the hands of 10–20 major houses. This situation has led banking regulators to consider tightening their oversight of these activities for fear of over-concentration and huge counterparty risks. We shall come back to this in Chapter 7 (Section 7.2).

**Table 5.9** Results from *Euromoney* magazine 2004 risk management poll

| Portfolio | | |
|---|---|---|
| 2004 | 2003 | |
| 1 | 2 | JP Morgan |
| 2 | 12= | BNP Paribas |
| 3 | 4 | Goldman Sachs |
| 4 | — | HSBC |
| 5= | 5= | Citigroup |
| 5= | 1 | Deutsche Bank |
| 7 | 7= | UBS |
| 8 | 12= | ABN Amro |
| 9 | — | CSFB |
| 10= | 7= | Morgan Stanley |
| 10= | 12= | Barclays |

*Source*: *Euromoney* (2004). Reproduced by permission of Euromoney.

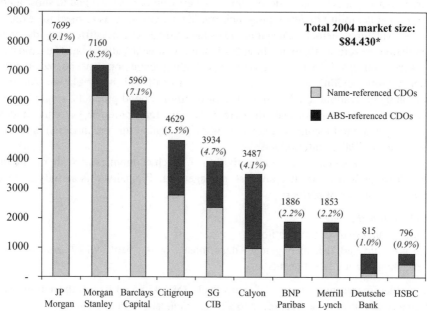

Total risk distributed
$ million
(*market share %*)

**Figure 5.11** Leading portfolio credit swap counterparties
*Sources*: *Creditflux*, authors' analysis.

### 5.3.3  Functions and Organization of Investment Banks

Investment banks fulfill two major roles in the credit derivatives and structured credit products markets:

- That of market-maker/intermediary and provider of liquidity for first-generation products, especially CDSs.
- That of 'structurers' of tailor-made products and arrangers of transactions for asset-side (creation of on-demand investment products) or liability-side clients (risk hedging, regulatory arbitrage and restructuring solutions for banking institutions, institutional clients and possibly corporates).

Thus, most players in the market are organized into two functions (not counting sales/distribution/marketing, which are sometimes dedicated to credit derivatives and structured credit products in the big brokerage houses):

- A trading function.
- A structuring/financial engineering function (often including quantitative research and modeling expertise).

These are completed by the coverage activity (marketing and sales), which generally is not dedicated to credit derivatives.

*5.3.3.1  Functions and Organization of the Trading Department*

In a credit market in continuous development, investment banks have had to show innovative capacities and flexibility in developing their trading activities, so as to meet the expectations of an ever-widening clientele. The latter views the credit asset class differently, depending on the regulations governing them, the finality of their investments, and so on. Thus, most leading banks very soon opted for the creation of two trading teams, one specialized in structured products ('exotic' credit), where the first parameter dealt with is correlation, and the other concentrating on 'vanilla' credit, composed of traditional bond products, single-name CDSs and index products (extending even to govies in certain organizations). As for the models used in the equity and fixed income markets, the principle behind this organization is to stimulate flows on the 'vanilla' credit products.

The key success factor in the flow activity is to reach economies of scale on the basis of volume, transactional recurrence and risk management. Typically, this activity is done with three main categories of partner:

1. Bank customers.
2. Market counterparties (competitors).
3. The portfolio and risk management departments of the bank, which conclude hedging transactions through its intermediary.

These partners represent an average of respectively 45%, 45% and 10% of the notional amounts dealt by a typical flow desk, according to a recent Standard & Poor's survey.[18]

Like its main competitors, SG CIB has, for instance, organized its teams on the flow – exotic model, even going so far as to segment its 'vanilla' trading activities according to sectors as early as end 2001. In 2003, the creation of a trading activity in index products completed this

---

[18] See Azarchs (2003).

'flow' section. The strategy of integrated trading of these products paid off, since the years 2002 and 2003 saw the convergence of bond spreads and derivatives, and the emergence of 'basis' arbitrage strategies between bond spreads and CDSs. The leading investment bank in the credit derivatives market in 2002, Goldman Sachs, took an even more innovative route: it set up trading indicators that associated equity and credit spread volatilities and maximized synergy amongst its equity and credit research teams.

As regards 'exotic' trading activity, the growth of credit correlation books required an organization that would allow dynamic management of positions. The gamma positions of these books are rarely neutral and require frequent readjustment, depending on spread variations. These books then generate quite considerable protection buying or selling flows in the 'vanilla' CDSs market. Moreover, the necessity to control second-degree risk better and the profits generated by these activities led to the creation of new hedging techniques, thus bolstering the development of the market.

### 5.3.3.2  Functions and Organization of the Structuring Department

In this department, there are multi-skilled teams, their activities being a blend of financial engineering and securitization, legal framing, financial modeling and trading. The role of these teams is constantly to create new products, for only innovation can guarantee success in this market. New products are designed either on the basis of a 'push' marketing strategy (products designed by the investment bank that will then be marketed systematically to the clientele by the sales force) or on the basis of a 'pull' approach (to meet a specific customer's precise need). Moreover, on complex products like CDOs, structurers usually have a marketing and sales role, helping the non-specialist sales force to win the customer base over to the special features and applications of these new products. These teams are usually the prime movers in developing and popularizing the new instruments: options on CDSs, fixed recovery CDSs, constant maturity default swaps (CMDSs), which ultimately may become flow products.

### 5.3.3.3  Coverage Functions and Organization

The third part of the equation is the sales teams, or 'coverage' as it is known in the banking world. Most investment banks have a general-purpose coverage organized into flow product sellers (including bonds and CDSs) and specialists in structured products and on-demand solutions (including CDOs). Moreover, in Europe, these teams are usually organized on the basis of the languages used (France–French-speaking Belgium and Switzerland; Spain, Italy, Portugal, Germany–Switzerland–Austria; Benelux, Scandinavia, United Kingdom and Ireland, etc.).

In the early days of the market, investment banks used product managers and/or sales teams especially for credit derivatives and structured products, due to their innovative nature and the particularities of the final customers. With the development of the market and the 'evangelization' of the customer base, the tasks were returned to the general-purpose coverage teams. Some client segments continue to be covered by specialists, not least hedge funds (the leading banks in this segment have set up prime brokerage teams covering the entire product range), or again reinsurance/monoline insurance companies, specialized in the credit market, which have built up privileged relationships with the structuring teams in the investment banks and are rarely directly covered by the sales teams.

Finally, one last characteristic of the investment banks' coverage strategies is increasingly to ally fixed income sales teams with the senior bankers in charge of commercial relationships with financial institutions. Success in these combinations gives an edge in obtaining origination mandates for balance sheet CDOs or portfolio restructuring transactions, usually extremely profitable activities for intermediaries. Some American banks, leaders in this field, even create 'transversal platforms' on product lines (corporate banking, advisory, equity derivatives, fixed income, etc.), to give better service to certain specific customer segments such as insurance companies, which share common problems (equity capital optimization, rating, asset/liability management, investment portfolio diversification, etc.).

The market in credit derivatives and structured products has undergone colossal growth since its beginnings in the 1990s. Today, two product compartments stand out as leaders:

1. CDSs, which are above all traded by leading investment banks, second-ranking banks and hedge funds.
2. CDOs, the engineering and structuring of which remain the prerogative of the investment banks, even though the leading asset managers are increasingly present in this market, and which are placed with a huge customer base: insurance/reinsurance/financial guarantors, banks, investment and pension funds, and perhaps a future retail market too.

For both these products, the investment banks are at the heart of the market and form its cornerstone. Indeed, it is probably the most profit-making activity they have had since 2000–2001 and the reversals in the stock market and mergers and acquisitions. This cycle has not yet reached an end, as evinced by the ever-increasing numbers of users taking an interest in these products and their multitude of applications. In Chapter 7, we shall return to the many implications of development in the credit derivatives market for the capital markets in the wider sense.

# 6
# Pricing Models for Credit Derivatives

The development of derivative markets in the last decades has been closely linked to the development of mathematical models for pricing and hedging derivative instruments. Not surprisingly, the growth in credit derivatives has generated a considerable literature on the modeling, pricing and hedging of these products. Conversely, much of the innovation in the credit derivatives market would not have been possible without the existence of quantitative approaches to credit risk. As a result of the availability of quantitative pricing models, the credit derivatives market has become increasingly sophisticated, issuing complex multi-name and hybrid credit derivatives, such as those described in Chapters 3 and 4.

The approach of market operators to the pricing of credit-sensitive products is to avoid using model-based pricing criteria whenever possible. The pricing of cash credit products – bank loans in particular – is based on market demand and supply and, in this respect, is more like the cash equity market than the options market. With the steady increase of liquidity in the CDS market, these products have become mainstream 'vanilla' instruments, with market prices driven by supply and demand. However, for more complex over-the-counter credit derivatives and for correlation products such as first-to-default swaps or CDO tranches, pricing cannot be done in a model-free way and quantitative modeling is thus unavoidable.

Quantitative models of credit risk have been developed to respond to two types of question:

- The first type of question is to quantify the risk of a portfolio of credit exposures. Here, the objective is to predict the probability of future credit events – rating transitions, defaults and movements in credit spreads – and to quantify the dependence between such credit events for different obligors. A major obstacle here is that, defaults being rare events, there is scarce historical data available to estimate and calibrate such models. If one succeeds in doing so, the model provides a solution to simulate risk scenarios for future credit events and compute the distribution of profit and loss for a portfolio of credit exposures. This distribution can then be used to compute measures of risk for the portfolio, such as Value at Risk (VaR) or expected shortfall.
- The second type of question deals with the pricing and hedging of credit derivatives. The question here is of a different nature from the preceding one. Even if a good econometric model for predicting default probabilities has been built (which is quite a difficult task in itself!), it is not straightforward to price a credit derivative in line with the market, since the econometric estimates do not take into account the default risk premium implicit in market credit spreads. In fact, the latter are hugely volatile and the default probabilities they imply have typically been well above historical default rates (such as those computed by rating agencies for instance).[1] Therefore, the approach to pricing and hedging credit derivatives is typically to specify an arbitrage-free pricing model, calibrate the parameters of the model to a set of liquid market instruments such as CDSs (or asset swaps) and use these parameters

---

[1] Thus enabling an arbitrage between market-implied and 'historical' rating-implied default probabilities, which has fuelled the growth in synthetic arbitrage CDOs.

to price other instruments. The default probabilities computed from such market-implied parameters should then be interpreted as risk-neutral probabilities of default and can be very different from those observed historically.

This relative value approach has been further strengthened by the fact that it is not feasible to synthesize credit derivatives through dynamic trading in and hedging of basic underlying contracts such as corporate bonds. As a consequence, rather than seeking to attribute values to credit derivatives on an 'absolute scale', pricing models currently in use in the market are primarily used to price credit derivatives in such a way that relative arbitrage does not arise among the prices of various instruments incorporating the same underlying credit risks. In this respect, one of the interesting consequences of the development in credit derivatives has been to push the market towards a more systematic and coherent pricing of credit risk.

This chapter is an overview of the main approaches used in the pricing and hedging of credit derivatives. We have chosen to emphasize the methodology and the main assumptions in the pricing models and to present the intuition behind their results, referring the reader to the References for the mathematical details of the models discussed.

Structural models, discussed in Section 6.1, represent defaults as endogenous events described as the first instant when a state variable (the 'firm value') falls below a certain barrier. Reduced-form models, discussed in Section 6.2, represent defaults as exogenous events, the probability of which is implied from observed credit spreads. In both cases, one needs to complement these approaches with a model for default correlation in order to price basket products such as first-to-default swaps and CDOs: this methodology is discussed in Section 6.3. Section 6.4 compares advantages and drawbacks of the various modeling approaches and raises some difficulties inherent to the design and use of credit risk models.

# 6.1   STRUCTURAL MODELS

In their seminal 1973 article 'The pricing of options and corporate liabilities,' Black and Scholes not only proposed a method for pricing and hedging options on stocks but also put forth the idea that the debt of a firm can be viewed as an option on the value of its assets. This idea, subsequently developed by Merton (1974) and others, led to a modeling approach which represents default as an endogenous event defined in terms of the capital structure of the firm, hence the name of structural models given to this approach in the literature.

## 6.1.1   The Black–Scholes Option Pricing Model

We briefly review below the Black–Scholes (1973) option pricing model, which is the cornerstone of arbitrage pricing of derivatives. Consider an asset $V_t$ whose return is composed of a deterministic trend and a random component, given by a Brownian motion with volatility coefficient $\sigma$:

$$\frac{dV_t}{V_t} = \mu \, dt \, + \, \sigma \, dW_t$$

A call option on $V_t$ with maturity $T$ and strike price $K$ is a contract that gives the holder the right, but not the obligation, to buy a unit of the underlying asset $S$ at date $T$, at the fixed price $K$. The terminal payoff at $T$ of such a contract is therefore $\max(V_T - K, 0)$.

An important idea proposed by Black and Scholes is that this terminal gain can also be realized by trading in the underlying asset, if one maintains a position $\varphi_t$ in the latter given by:

$$\varphi_t = \Delta(t, V_t) = N(d_1(V_t, K)) \quad \text{with} \quad R(t, T) = \frac{1}{T-t}\left[\int_0^T r(t)\,dt\right]$$

$$N(u) = \int_{-\infty}^{u} \frac{\exp(-z^2/2)}{\sqrt{2\pi}}\,dz \quad \text{and} \quad d_1(V_t, K) = \frac{\log(V_t/K) + (R(t, T) + \sigma^2/2)(T-t)}{\sigma\sqrt{T-t}}$$

and a position in cash $\psi_t$, such that the portfolio is self-financing. The resulting trading strategy, called 'delta hedging' strategy, enables the unpredictable fluctuations in the value of the option to be matched by the fluctuations in the position in the underlying asset. The value of this portfolio will then match that of the option, regardless of the scenario which occurs in the market. This strategy effectively 'replicates' the call option by trading in the underlying asset. In mathematical terms, one obtains equality between the two random payoffs with probability 1:

$$\max(V_T - K, 0) = \int_0^T \varphi_t\,dV_t + \int_0^T \psi_t\,dB(t, T) + C(T, K)$$

where $C(T, K)$ denotes the initial capital required for setting up such a hedging portfolio. The Black–Scholes approach also allows us to compute the cost of such a hedging strategy. It is given by the expectation of the terminal payoff of the option, computed by replacing $V_t$ by an auxiliary process $X_t$ called the 'risk-neutral process':

$$C(T, K) = \exp\left[-\int_0^T r(t)\,dt\right] E[\max(X_T - K, 0)] \quad \text{with}$$

$$\frac{dX_t}{X_t} = r(t)\,dt + \sigma\,dW_t \quad X_0 = V_0$$

Since the hedging portfolio replicates the terminal value of the option, the absence of arbitrage opportunities imposes that the value of the option be equal to the cost of the hedging strategy: the value of the call option is therefore given by $C(T, K)$ above. This formula expresses the 'risk-neutral pricing principle': the option value is equal to the discounted risk-neutral expectation of its terminal payoff.

In the case of a call option, the value $C(T, K)$ can be computed explicitly:

$$C(T, K) = V_0 N(d_1(V_0, K)) - K \exp\left[-\int_0^T r(t)\,dt\right] N(d_2(V_0, K))$$

$$d_1(V, K) = \frac{\log(V/K) + (R(t, T) + \sigma^2/2)(T-t)}{\sigma\sqrt{T-t}}$$

$$d_2(V, K) = \frac{\log(V/K) + (R(t, T) - \sigma^2/2)(T-t)}{\sigma\sqrt{T-t}}$$

This valuation approach is not limited to call options and can be applied to put options, barrier options, Asian options, etc. Pricing by replication is made possible by the fact that the

Black–Scholes model is an example of a complete market: any option can be synthesized by a dynamic hedging strategy using the underlying asset. The value of such an option is then determined uniquely through the absence of arbitrage, as being equal to the cost of its hedge. Let us emphasize the fact that the possibility of hedging is linked to the fact that in these models the risk represented by the derivative payoff is 'spanned' by instruments traded in the market.

As we shall see below, the assumption of market completeness is not always realistic in default risk models. But the risk-neutral pricing principle holds in a more general context. In models where one cannot replicate all payoffs by trading in the underlying, the assumption of a linear pricing rule and absence of arbitrage still leads to a risk-neutral pricing rule. In that case, it is not uniquely determined and must be extracted from prices by postulating a form for the risk-neutral dynamics and calibrating it to prices of liquid market instruments.

### 6.1.2   Merton's Structural Model of Default Risk (1976)

#### 6.1.2.1   Model Overview

Merton's model is the prototype of structural models of default risk and can be viewed as a transposition of the Black–Scholes methodology to capital structure arbitrage. Consider a firm whose capital structure is composed of two components: an equity component and a debt component, the debt being represented for simplification as a single zero-coupon bond with maturity $T$. Denote by $V(t)$ the total value of the assets of the firm: $V(t)$ is then equal to the sum of the equity and debt components: $V(t) = D(t) + S(t)$.

The evolution of $V(t)$ is, as in the Black–Scholes model, the exponential of a Brownian motion:

$$V_t = V_0 \exp\left[(\mu - \sigma^2/2)t + \sigma W_t\right]$$

$$\frac{dV_t}{V_t} = \mu \, dt + \sigma \, dW_t$$

The firm's debtholders cannot impose default before the maturity $T$. It can only occur at maturity if the firm has insufficient assets to refund the debt. At date $T$, if the value of the firm's assets is more than the nominal value of the debt, the latter is repaid to debtholders and there is no default. Otherwise, debtholders receive the available assets (the value of which is less than the nominal of the debt). Thus, the payoff at maturity to the debtholders is given by:

$$D_T = \min(V_T, L) = L - \max(L - V_T, 0)$$

The expression of this payoff shows it to be equivalent to the payoff of a riskless bond with nominal $L$ combined with a short position in a put option written on $V(t)$ with strike price $L$. Similarly, stockholders will receive at maturity $T$, either the total assets minus the debt repayment or zero in case of default. The terminal payoff to shareholders is thus equivalent to the payoff of a call option on $V(t)$ with strike price $L$:

$$S(T) = \max(V(T) - L, 0)$$

Shares in the company are thus viewed as call options on the assets of the firm. Valuing these options using the Black–Scholes approach, we obtain the following expression for the value of the risky debt:

$$D(t, T) = V_t N(-d_1(V_t, L)) + L B(t, T) N(d_2(V_t, L))$$

Similarly, the value $S(t)$ of the firm's equity can be computed using the Black–Scholes formula for a call option:

$$S_t = V_t N(d_1(V_t, L)) - L \, \exp\left[-\int_t^T r(u) \, du\right] N(d_2(V_t, L))$$

As we noted above, the Black–Scholes model is an example of a complete market: any derivative written on $V(t)$ can be hedged by a dynamic portfolio involving the underlying and cash. Similarly, in the Merton model, the default exposure of the debtholders may be hedged by holding a position in the assets of the firm $V(t)$ and in cash (for instance Treasury bonds or, more typically, a position paying Libor). In practice, $V(t)$ is not a liquid traded asset so maintaining a dynamic position in $V(t)$ may not be possible. However, the completeness of the model implies that the default risk of the bond can be hedged with other combinations of two non-redundant instruments. Where the equity of the firm is traded on the market, one can use the stock and cash. This viewpoint enables us to use structural models to hunt for relative value arbitrage between stocks and corporate bonds.

### 6.1.2.2    Term Structure of Credit Spreads

The value $D(t)$ of the risky debt can be translated into an expression for the credit spread $s(t, T)$ relative to the benchmark default-free rate $r(t)$:

$$s(t, T) = -\frac{\log\left(\frac{1}{l(t)} \times N(-d_1(V_t, L)) + N(d_2(V_t, L))\right)}{T - t}$$

where

$$l(t) = \frac{L \, B(t, T)}{V_t}$$

is the nominal leverage ratio, defined as the ratio of the nominal value of the debt, discounted at the risk-free rate, to the total assets of the firm. In particular, it is possible to verify, using properties of the function $N(\cdot)$ that, when we approach maturity, the credit spread goes either to 0 (if the leverage ratio is less than unity $l(t) < 1$) or to infinity if the capital structure is leveraged ($l(t) > 1$). This property, which is common to all variants of Merton's model where $V(t)$ follows a diffusion process, results from the fact that in such models, default is modeled as a predictable event. Since $V(t)$ is a continuous process, if it is below the default threshold $L$ just before the maturity, then it is highly likely that it will remain below the threshold at repayment date, hence default is quasi-certain, leading to a large credit spread. On the other hand, if $V(t) > L$ just before maturity, i.e. it is at a finite distance from the default threshold, then default is highly improbable and the credit spread is very small and tends towards zero as we reach maturity. Empirical observations contradict this extreme behavior: short-term credit spreads are neither zero nor very large; they can assume arbitrary values depending on the issuer. These short-term credit spreads reflect the fact that market participants anticipate an unpredictable jump-to-default as possible. In fact, as we shall see below, if $V(t)$ is not continuous and undergoes unpredictable jumps, the short-term credit spreads can be set arbitrarily.

### 6.1.2.3    Value of Equity Options

In the Merton model, since equity is modeled as a call option on the firm's assets $V(t)$, the equity value $S(t)$ does not follow a lognormal process:

$$dS_t = N(d_1(V_t, L)) \, dV_t + m(t) \, dt = \sigma \, \Delta(t, V_t) \, V_t dW_t + a \, dt \qquad \text{(SM)}$$

where $\Delta(t, V_t)$ is the (Black–Scholes) delta representing the sensitivity of the equity value to $V(t)$. In particular the instantaneous volatility of the equity is given by the following relationship:

$$\Delta(t, V_t)\, \sigma \frac{V_t}{S_t}$$

which is a randomly fluctuating quantity. Therefore, if one looks at values of equity options (for example calls on $S(t)$), the Merton model will price them at values which, expressed in terms of Black–Scholes implied volatilities, will lead to an implied volatility smile or skew. In fact, call options on $S(t)$ can be viewed as a compound option (option on an option) on $V(t)$, for which closed-form pricing formulas are available (Geske, 1977). Although, as pointed out by Hull *et al.* (2005), the resulting implied volatilities do not give realistic fits to observed implied volatility skews or smiles. It is interesting that this simple model already gives the possibility of pricing in a single framework both credit-sensitive products written on the debt of the firm and options written on the equity of the firm.

### 6.1.2.4    Calibration of Model Parameters

In structural models, the credit spread depends on parameters that are not directly observable in the markets, such as the volatility $\sigma$ of the firm's assets and the default threshold $L$. How can these parameters be estimated in practice? The idea is to express the model parameters in terms of quantities, which are either directly observable or which can be estimated from observable data.

One idea is to use information from equity prices to estimate parameters and use them to compute credit spreads. As noted above, the instantaneous volatility of the equity value is given by:

$$\sigma_S = \Delta(t, V_t)\, \sigma \frac{V_t}{S_t}$$

Since the equity value has a random 'volatility,' using the standard deviation of equity returns is not a consistent approach. If equity options are quoted on the market, one can substitute the implied volatility obtained from equity options as a proxy for $\sigma_S$.

Since we have three unknown quantities $V(t)$, $L$ and $\sigma$, one can use for instance the equity price $S(t)$ plus the prices of two equity options. As equity options generally exhibit an implied volatility skew, $\sigma_S$ will depend on the choice of the strike of the options (since the skews implied by this model do not correspond to those observed in equity options as established by Hull *et al.* (2005)).

The procedure above allows us to compute CDS spreads from equity prices and their volatility. This approach is less interesting if CDS contracts are liquid. One can then proceed differently, by calibrating the model to the term structure of credit spreads and then using it to price an equity default swap for instance.

### 6.1.3    Limitations and Extensions of the Merton Model (1976)

The Merton model is the prototype of credit risk models based on the value of the firm. Its main advantage is its simplicity but it also has several empirical and theoretical shortcomings, which have generated various extensions, which we shall now discuss briefly.

### 6.1.3.1  Default Prior to Maturity

One of the drawbacks of the Merton model is that default can only occur at the maturity of the debt. In practice, corporate default may occur at any date and the timing of default is of primary importance for bondholders. Black and Cox (1976) thus proposed a generalization of the Merton model in which default happens when the process $V(t)$ representing the assets of the firm hits a (possibly time-dependent) barrier $H(t)$ representing safety covenants for the firm. The default time is therefore modeled as a first exit time of the process $V(t)$ from the region of nondefault. When $V(t)$ is the exponential of a Brownian motion, distribution of first exit times from constant or exponentially varying barriers may be computed in close form, allowing us to compute the probability of default. As in the Merton model, the value of the corporate bond $D(t, T)$ may be represented as the sum of a riskless zero-coupon bond plus a put option on $V(t)$, but now the option is a down-and-out barrier option.

Since barrier options can be priced explicitly in a Black–Scholes model, one can use formulas analogous to (but more complicated than) the Merton model for the value $D(t, T)$ of the corporate debt and for the term structure of credit spreads. However, the extra complexity of the pricing formulas makes the calibration of the parameters model difficult. For instance, the value of a barrier option is not monotonous with respect to volatility, so the calibration procedure described above for the Merton model will yield multiple solutions. Also, pricing more complex payoffs can become quite heavy. For example, an equity call in this model is priced as a call on a knock-out barrier option, so even equity call options require computationally intensive pricing procedures.

An interesting feature of default barrier models is that one can use the flexibility of choosing a time-dependent barrier $H(t)$ in order to obtain an improved fit with the observed term structure of credit spreads. This effectively means abandoning the capital structure interpretation of the default barrier as the 'level of debt' and using it as a parameter to reconstruct risk-neutral default probabilities from credit spreads. An interesting extension of the Black and Cox model with time-dependent parameters, which retains its tractable features, has been proposed by Brigo and Tarenghi (2005).

### 6.1.3.2  Behavior of Short-Term Credit Spreads

Many empirical studies show that structural models such as the Merton model generate short-term credit spreads which are unrealistic (Jones et al., 1984). In order to obtain realistic short-term spreads, one is often forced to choose unrealistically high values for the volatility of the firm's assets. This problem is not specific to Merton's model: any model where the default is a predictable event has the property that the credit spreads diverge (to infinity) prior to default. Two strategies have been proposed to solve this problem:

1. Instead of modeling the value $V(t)$ by a continuous process, use a process with unpredictable jumps, such as a Poisson process or more generally, any process with unpredictable jump times. In this case, one can instantaneously jump across the default threshold without necessarily being close to it, which leads to a nonzero probability of default even for short maturities. This is the approach of reduced-form models described in the next section and, more generally, of 'hybrid' models where $V(t)$ may have both a diffusion and a jump component.
2. Model the default threshold as a random variable whose value is revealed only after default. In this case, even if $V(t)$ is a continuous process, default becomes an unpredictable event.

### 6.1.3.3  Random Default Barriers

A simplifying hypothesis in the Merton model is the assumption that the default threshold $L$ has a known value: in the original formulation it is equal to the nominal value of the firm's debt. In reality the debt of a firm may be composed of a series of bonds issued with different maturities, bank loans and various IOUs, which makes it difficult to determine the 'default threshold' $L$. In fact, the default threshold is only known *a posteriori*: after default has occurred, we deduce that the level $L$ has been hit by $V(t)$. A more natural idea is therefore to view the default threshold as a random variable. This is the approach used by CreditGrades (Finger, 2002). As in the Merton model, we assume that the firm's assets follow a Black–Scholes model:

$$dV_t = \sigma V_t dW_t$$

but where the default threshold is represented as a random variable $L$ independent from $V_t$:

$$L = B \exp(\lambda Z - \lambda^2/2) \quad \text{where} \quad Z \sim N(0, 1)$$

The default time is then defined as the first instant when $V(t)$ reaches the level $L$. Using a Gaussian approximation, the survival probability between 0 and $t$ can be approximated by:

$$P(t) = N\left(\frac{A(t)}{2} + \frac{\log(d)}{A(t)}\right) d N\left(\frac{A(t)}{2} - \frac{\log(d)}{A(t)}\right)$$

$$d = \frac{V_0 \exp(\lambda^2)}{B}, \quad A(t)^2 = \sigma^2 t + \lambda^2$$

Since both $V_0$ and $\sigma$ are not observable, some approximation is needed to express them in terms of observable quantities in order to calibrate the model. Finger proposed to choose $V_0 = S_0 + B$ where $S_0$ is the initial value of the equity and $B$ the expectation value for the barrier. For the initial equity volatility, they note that if $V_0$ is well above the barrier level then:

$$\sigma_S = \Delta(0, V_0)\, \sigma \frac{V_0}{S_0} \cong \sigma \frac{S_0 + B}{S_0}$$

This approximation corresponds to a 'displaced lognormal' model for the equity dynamics, which is a commonly used model for the implied volatility skew in the equity options market. Using these two approximations the survival probability can now be expressed in terms of observable quantities:

$$P(t) = N\left(-\frac{A(t)}{2} + \frac{\log(d)}{A(t)}\right) - d N\left(-\frac{A(t)}{2} - \frac{\log(d)}{A(t)}\right)$$

$$d = \frac{(S_0 + B) \exp(\lambda^2)}{B}, \quad A(t)^2 = \left(\frac{S_0 \sigma_S}{S_0 + B}\right)^2 t + \lambda^2$$

From the survival probability one can then obtain an expression for the spread of a CDS. The five-year CDS spread computed in this manner is called the 'CreditGrade' of the issuer. The impact of the uncertainty $\lambda$ on the default threshold is to generate plausible credit spreads for short maturities, whereas in the Merton or Black and Cox models such spreads are either zero or infinity.

### 6.1.4   Pricing and Hedging Credit Derivatives in Structural Models

Let us now examine the implications of structural models for the pricing and hedging of credit derivatives. In the structural models discussed above, any exposure to the debt or equity of a firm subject to default risk is modeled as a contingent claim on the value of the firm $V(t)$. The value of such a position is then computed using the viewpoint of option pricing theory and, by analogy with equity options, one can compute the sensitivities ('Greeks') of this position with respect to the underlying (delta, gamma) and its volatility (vega). The exposure of a debtholder is therefore represented as a long position in an option on $V(t)$, i.e. a long position on the volatility of the firm's assets.

Note that, in principle, any complex credit derivative can be priced in a structural model since any credit-sensitive payoff can be expressed as an option on the value of the firm $V(t)$ and the problem becomes equivalent to pricing a complex option in the Black–Scholes model. However, even for common derivative structures, the pricing model can quickly become quite complex.

Consider the example of an option with strike $K$ on a corporate bond. In the Merton or Black and Cox model, its terminal payoff is given by:

$$(D(T_1, T_2) - K)^+ = (LB(T_1, T_2) - P_T(T_2, L) - K)^+ = (K + LB(T_1, T_2) - P(T, L))^+$$

where $P_T(T_2, L)$ denotes the value at $T$ of a put option on $V(t)$ with maturity $T_2$ and strike price $L$, i.e. a call option written on a put option on $V(t)$. In the Black–Cox model, the put option is a down-and-out barrier option, so even simple European calls on bonds are actually path-dependent options on $V(t)$, and require numerical methods to be priced.

In a structural model, we can hedge the risk of such an exposure by trading in equity, cash and option-type products such as convertible bonds. The idea of hedging is the same as in the Black–Scholes model: maintaining a portfolio which is locally neutral, i.e. with zero sensitivity with respect to the risk factors, by dynamically adjusting one's position in equity or other credit-sensitive instruments.

Since structural models provide a link between values of equity and credit-related instruments, they can also be used in principle to detect opportunities for relative value arbitrage between equity and credit. Given a level of equity volatility, a structural model will predict a certain level for the credit spread of the firm's debt. If the debt trades in the market with spreads either substantially above or below this rate, the model suggests an arbitrage strategy. This type of equity–credit arbitrage has become popular in recent years, especially strategies involving convertible bonds.

The central idea in structural models is that default risk is represented through the volatility of a single state variable $V(t)$, enabling us to use analogies with equity derivative pricing tools. But the same state variable governs equity risk, so credit risk and equity risk are perfectly correlated in this approach. An advantage of this assumption, as we noted above, is to allow the pricing in the same framework of equity options and credit derivatives. Such models can in principle be calibrated jointly to hybrid products involving both credit and equity exposures. But this assumption seems paradoxical since one of the main purposes of introducing credit derivatives is due to the impossibility of hedging credit exposures with equity-based products. On the contrary the reduced-form approaches, which we discuss now, allow us to unbundle credit risk from equity risk and thus model them separately.

## 6.2    REDUCED-FORM MODELS

While structural models for credit risk present some attractive features, the main one being their familiarity for quants who are used to the Black–Scholes approach to option pricing, they have several important drawbacks:

- Structural models reduce credit risk to a form of 'market risk', when represented by the volatility of the firm's asset value. This implies a strong link between the equity and debt instruments of a given firm. Although such a link is qualitatively present, the quantitative relations implied by structural models are often empirically too restrictive.
- The main risk factor, the 'value of the firm' is not directly observable. This complicates the use of the model and the estimation of its parameters. In many cases, one uses stock prices as proxy, very often leading to very crude approximations.
- It is difficult to integrate extra factors of risk – such as randomness in interest rates – while maintaining a reasonable level of complexity.
- Structural models often imply that default events are predictable.[2] In practice, even though the knowledge of the firm's capital structure is definitely useful for predicting default, such analyses are often done *a posteriori* inasfar as knowledge of the capital structure is not updated on a regular basis (typically, once or twice a year when accounting information is publicly disclosed) and such information can rarely be used to predict default. Finally, there are numerous examples such as Enron or Parmalat in which, as a result of accounting fraud for instance, default happens as a surprise to market observers. These examples point to the necessity of allowing for unpredictable defaults.

In addition to these conceptual drawbacks, one should reckon the practical difficulties encountered when calibrating such models. In practice, it can be quite difficult to reproduce observed term structures of credit spreads using Merton (1975) and Black–Cox (1976) models.

Reduced-form models, also called intensity-based models, were introduced to resolve these shortcomings: they model the default as an exogenous event whose rate of occurrence, the hazard rate, becomes the parameter of the model. By doing so, they enable easy computation of default probabilities and an easy calibration to observed spread curves.

The approach underlying these models is quite different from that of structural models: instead of starting from a hypothetical process representing the 'value of the firm', and trying to explain the observed credit spreads, one takes the observed credit spreads as inputs and tries to build a model of default probabilities at different horizons compatible with these. As we shall see below, reduced-form models lead to explicit formulas for the value of risky debt and relate in a simple manner default probabilities with credit spreads, thus allowing us to calibrate model parameters to the observed term structure of credit spreads.

### 6.2.1    Hazard Rate and Credit Spreads

Let $\tau$ denote the random time of default of a firm having issued debt: this is a random variable, for which we are interested in modeling the probability distribution. The main variable in

---

[2] While this is true for the Merton and Black–Cox models, the predictability of default does not hold any more in models with random default barriers (CreditGrades) or models where the 'value of the firm' follows a process with jumps.

reduced-form models is the risk-neutral rate of default per unit time, also called the hazard rate, defined as the probability per unit time of default occurring, given the knowledge that the firm has not yet defaulted. If $\tau > t$, then the probability that default occurs during the time interval $[t, t + \Delta t]$ is given by:

$$\lambda(t)\Delta t + o(\Delta t)$$

where $o(\Delta t)$ denotes a term negligible with respect to $\Delta t$. Typically, if time is measured in annual units, $\lambda$ is a small number: default rates $\lambda(t)$ are between 0.1% and, say, 3%.

The probability of survival, i.e. the absence of default between $t$ and $t + \Delta t$, is therefore:

$$1 - [\lambda(t)\Delta t + o(\Delta t)]$$

Assume now that, conditionally on no default before $t$, the event of default during $[t, t + \Delta t]$ is independent of the past. Dividing $[0, t]$ into $n$ periods of length $\Delta t$, we obtain that the probability of no default between 0 and $t$ is as follows:

$$\prod_{k=1}^{n}(1 - \lambda(t_k)\Delta t) \quad \text{with} \quad t_k = k\Delta t$$

Taking logarithms and using the fact that $\log(1 + x) = x + o(x)$ for $x$ close to zero, we obtain:

$$\log \prod_{k=1}^{n}(1 - \lambda(t_k)\Delta t) = \sum_{k=1}^{n}\log(1 - \lambda(t_k)\Delta t) = -\sum_{k=1}^{n}\lambda(t_k)\Delta t + o(\Delta t) \rightarrow$$

$$-\int_{0}^{t}\lambda(s)ds \quad \text{as} \quad \Delta t \rightarrow 0$$

So, as $\Delta t \rightarrow 0$, the expression for the probability of survival up to $t$ becomes:

$$\prod_{k=1}^{n}(1 - \lambda(t_k)\Delta t) \quad \rightarrow \quad P(\tau > t) = \exp\left[-\int_{0}^{t}\lambda(s)\,ds\right]$$

Conditioning on information that default has not occurred before $t$, we obtain that the probability of survival up to $T$ is:

$$P(\tau > T \mid \tau > t) = \exp\left[-\int_{t}^{T}\lambda(s)\,ds\right]$$

Let us now introduce the benchmark discount rate $r(t)$ relative to which credit spreads will be computed: typically this will be Libor or the risk-free Treasury rate. The value of a default-free zero-coupon bond is given by:

$$B(t, T) = \exp\left[-\int_{t}^{T}r(s)\,ds\right]$$

Denote by $D(t, T)$ the value at time $t$ of a corporate bond with nominal \$1 and maturity $T$. Denoting by $R$ the recovery rate at default, the corporate bond will pay \$1 at maturity ($T$) in the absence of default between 0 and $T$, and 0 otherwise (adjusted for $R$). The value of this bond is given by the discounted risk-neutral expectation of its terminal payoff:

$$D(t, T) = \exp\left[-\int_t^T r(s)\,ds\right] E[1(\tau > T) + R\,1(\tau \le T)\,|\,\tau > t]$$

$$= \exp\left[-\int_t^T r(s)\,ds\right] E[1(\tau > T) + R\,(1 - 1(\tau > T))\,|\,\tau > t]$$

$$= \exp\left[-\int_t^T r(s)\,ds\right] [(1 - R)\,E[\,1(\tau > T)\,|\,\tau > t] + R]$$

$$= (1 - R)\exp\left[-\int_t^T (r(s) + \lambda(s))\,ds\right] + R\,\exp\left[-\int_t^T r(s)\,ds\right]$$

Comparing this expression with the value of a default-free bond, we observe that the principal effect of default risk is to modify the discount factor by adding a spread to the short rate: this spread is none other than the hazard rate $\lambda(t)$. This is one of the principal results of reduced-form models. The hazard rate can be identified from the term structure of credit spreads, a quantity that is observable in the market. Please note, however, that the above relation requires knowledge of the recovery rate, which is typically quite uncertain. In the case of zero recovery:

$$D(t, T) = \exp\left[-\int_t^T (r(s) + \lambda(s))\,ds\right] = \exp\left[-\int_t^T r(s)\,ds + (T - t)\,s(t, T)\right]$$

so the term structure $s(t, T)$ of credit spreads is simply given by:

$$s(t, T) = \frac{1}{T - t}\int_t^T \lambda(u)\,du$$

The hazard rate $\lambda(t)$ can thus be chosen to reproduce an arbitrary term structure of credit spreads. This is an important advantage of reduced-form models when compared to structural models, where the form of the credit spread term structure is imposed. In particular, it is possible to obtain arbitrary credit spreads for short maturities, which was not possible in the Merton or Black–Cox models.

As noted above, retrieving hazard rates from credit spreads requires knowledge of the recovery rates. Since these are unknown in practice, the market standard is to use data collected by rating agencies for estimates of the average recovery rate by seniority and instrument type. However, these statistics are not available for all issuers. [3] Furthermore, the picture is somewhat complicated by recent observations (Altman et al., 2002), that there is a significant negative correlation between default and recovery rates. One way to incorporate this effect is to assume

---

[3] See Section 1.2.2.

that recovery rates are stochastic, but the main issue then becomes how to jointly calibrate the recovery rate and the hazard rate to a set of given credit spreads.

### 6.2.2  Pricing and Hedging of Credit Derivatives in Reduced-Form Models

To illustrate how the above concepts can be used to price credit derivatives, let us apply them to the pricing of CDSs. As discussed in Section 1.2.3.1, the breakeven spread in a CDS should be the spread at which the present values of premium payments and the probability-weighted payoff of the protection legs are equal. Assume for simplicity that the hazard rate $\lambda$ and the discount rate $r$ are constant. The premium leg pays continuously a spread $S$ and its present value is given by:

$$S \int_0^T dt \, \exp[-t \, (r + \lambda)] = \frac{S(1 - \exp[-T \, (r + \lambda)])}{r + \lambda}$$

The protection leg pays $(1 - R)$ in case of default: this occurs with probability $\lambda(t)dt$ during $[t, t + dt]$. So the discounted value of the protection leg is:

$$(1 - R) \int_0^T \lambda \, dt \, \exp[-t \, (r + \lambda)] = \frac{\lambda \left[1 - \exp\left(-T(r + \lambda)\right)\right]}{r + \lambda}(1 - R)$$

Equalizing the two expressions yields the following expression for the fair value of the CDS spread:

$$\boxed{S = \lambda \, (1 - R)}$$

This relation states that the credit spread compensates the investor for the risk of default per unit time. Note that in this simple case where the term structure of interest rates is flat, the interest rate does not appear in the relation between the CDS spread and the default parameters: this corresponds to the idea that a position in CDS is a pure 'credit exposure' and, at least at first order, does not incorporate interest rate risk. When the term structure is not flat, the above computations can be carried out similarly but the interest rate dependency does not simplify: the CDS spread is then exposed to movements in the yield curve.

The main idea of the above-mentioned relation between hazard rates and CDS spreads is that once the CDS spreads are known, it is possible to deduce the hazard rate using the relation above and price any credit derivative. Note that this hazard rate is a risk-neutral rate of default, implied by market-quoted CDS spreads. In principle, and also in practice, it can be quite different from historically estimated default rates or those implied by transition rates of credit ratings. In the language of arbitrage pricing theory, the hazard rate represents the risk-neutral probabilities of default while historical studies estimate 'objective' default probabilities. Once the (risk-neutral) hazard rate has been calibrated to spreads on credit-sensitive bonds or CDSs, it can be used to value a credit-sensitive payoff $H$, by taking the discounted risk-neutral expectation of $H$:

$$V_t(H) = \exp\left[-\int_t^T r(s) \, ds\right] E[H|F_t]$$

Denoting by $H_0$ the payoff in case of default and $H_1$ the payoff in case of survival, we obtain:

$$V_t(H) = \exp\left[-\int_t^T r(s)\mathrm{d}s\right]\left(1 - \exp\left[-\int_t^T \lambda(s)\mathrm{d}s\right]\right) E[H_0 \mid F_t]$$

$$+ \exp\left[-\int_t^T (r(s) + \lambda(s))\,\mathrm{d}s\right] E[H_1 \mid F_t]$$

This pricing approach guarantees the absence of arbitrage opportunities between, on the one hand, the instruments priced in this manner and, on the other hand, liquid instruments to which the models are calibrated (CDSs, corporate bonds, etc.). However, it cannot give us an indication of the 'fair value' of a credit spread in absolute terms. Also, while it is still possible to compute 'sensitivities' of the model price of a credit derivative with respect to, for instance, CDS spreads on the underlying credits, there is no element in the model that allows us to interpret such sensitivities as hedge ratios (see the discussion on delta hedging in Chapter 4). In fact, as opposed to structural models, which typically lead to complete markets, hedging in reduced-form models cannot be done by simple delta hedging. Delta hedging will only neutralize a derivative with respect to small movements in an underlying spread but not to losses incurred in case of jump-to-default (which is actually the main concern!) or unknown recovery rates. These need to be measured independently, typically through stress-test scenarios. Arrangers are then led to calculate reserves on their initial profit and loss, which are released over time, in order to account for these risks.

### 6.2.3  Accounting for the Volatility of Credit Spreads

We have observed that, in models where the hazard rate $\lambda(t)$ is deterministic, credit spreads are proportional to hazard rates up to a correction involving discount factors. Therefore when the hazard rate is chosen to be a deterministic function of time, credit spreads will end up having zero volatility: in particular, credit spread options should be priced at intrinsic value. In practice, credit spread options trade at a premium in the market and credit spreads are volatile. In order to incorporate this feature in pricing models, it is therefore necessary to model the default rate itself as a (positive) random process $\gamma(t)$, the *default intensity*. The default intensity plays, in random intensity models, a role similar to the short-term interest rate in interest rate models. As a consequence, most random intensity models build heavily on analogies with short rate models in interest rate theory and the same types of process are often used. An example often used is the Cox–Ingersoll–Ross model:

$$\mathrm{d}\gamma(t) = -a\,(b - \gamma(t))\,\mathrm{d}t + c\sqrt{\gamma(t)}\,\mathrm{d}W_t$$

This approach yields a positive hazard rate with a mean-reverting behavior in the long run.

Contrary to the deterministic hazard rate model where the hazard rate $\lambda(t)$ could be read off from the credit spread term structure (see above), in random intensity models the relation between the (observed) credit spreads and the (unobserved) default intensity is more involved: specifying the parameters for the evolution of the default intensity requires calibration to the credit spreads.

For more details on random intensity models, see Schönbucher (2002) or Jeanblanc and Rutkowski (2000).

### 6.2.4   Accounting for Interest Rate Risk

Interest rate fluctuations are important factors in explaining the variation of credit spreads. In an empirical study, Longstaff and Schwartz (1995) showed that the explanatory power of changes in interest rates in accounting for changes in credit spreads is higher than that of equity returns. It is therefore natural to model the joint fluctuations of interest rates and credit spreads. While this can be quite challenging in structural models, in the reduced-form approach one can easily build joint models for the evolution of interest rates and default intensities (which are, in that case, modeled as being random). A terminal payoff $H$ sensitive to interest rate and default risk can then be valued as:

$$V_t(H) = E\left[\exp\left[-\int_t^T r(s)\,ds\right] H \mid F_t\right]$$

The expressions involved in this computation are of the same type as the ones encountered in short rate models. An example is the case where the default intensity and the short-term interest rate are both modeled by square-root (Cox–Ingersoll–Ross) processes:

$$d\gamma(t) = -a_1 (b_1 - \gamma(t))\,dt + c_1\sqrt{\gamma(t)}\,dW_t^1, \quad dr(t) = -a_2 (b_2 - r(t))\,dt + c_2\sqrt{r(t)}\,dW_t^2$$

where a correlation is introduced between the Brownian motions $W^1$ and $W^2$ (Schönbucher, 2002).

Note however that computations can become quite heavy in such models and the choice of specific forms for the stochastic processes is mainly driven by the wish to obtain some analytical tractability rather than based on any economic or econometric rationale.

## 6.3   PRICING MODELS FOR MULTI-NAME CREDIT DERIVATIVES

The models presented above deal with the credit risk attached to a single obligor. As discussed in Chapter 4, among the most active products in the credit derivatives market today are multi-name credit derivatives, such as CDOs, which involve exposures to a basket of correlated credit risks. The pricing and hedging of such products require, in addition to models for single-name credit spreads, the specification of a model for the dependence between the defaults of different names. This dependence is often denoted by the generic term 'default correlation', which is somewhat misleading. As noted above, default risk can be represented by different choices of variables (time of default, indicator of default, default intensity, etc.) and each choice will lead to a different way of defining 'default correlation'. Furthermore, as we shall see below, what we are really talking about is the dependence structure of default variables rather than the correlation coefficients. Since all these variables typically have a distribution quite different from a normal distribution, these two notions turn out to be quite dissimilar.

Given the wide range of possible pricing models for single-name credit derivatives, one can easily imagine that the range is even wider for multi-name derivatives. Surprisingly, however, a market consensus has emerged in recent years, especially in the CDO market, on the use of what has now become a standard model: the Gaussian copula model. The main advantage of this model is its simplicity. It has become a standard means of quoting values of CDO tranches in terms of 'implied correlations' (a concept we shall explain below). In this respect, it plays a similar role to the Black–Scholes model in the equity option markets. However, this model has severe shortcomings and for this reason many market participants use alternative models for risk management, while still using the Gaussian copula model for pricing and quoting purposes.

Obviously, multi-asset models should be consistent with the models used for single-name credit risk. Both the structural and the reduced-form approaches can in principle be extended to the multi-asset case. In this respect, structural models have a better tractability in the case of large portfolios of credit risks and have gained favor among practitioners.

### 6.3.1 Correlation, Dependence and Copulas

The need for multivariate modeling in finance is, of course, not specific to credit risk models. Multivariate Gaussian models have been used since Markowitz (1959) for portfolio optimization and asset allocation. In a multivariate Gaussian model, the properties of each variable are specified by its mean and variance, while the dependence properties are completely specified via a matrix of correlation coefficients. By separating the marginal distributions of assets and their dependence structure in this way, the Gaussian model enables the parameters (mean and variance) of the marginal distribution of individual assets to be specified or estimated separately from the parameters describing their correlations. In this case, knowing the correlation matrix is sufficient to define the joint distribution completely: the expectation of any function of the variables can then be computed or simulated from the knowledge of the means, variances and the correlation matrix. Multivariate versions of the Black–Scholes model can be introduced along these lines since, in the Black–Scholes model, the log prices are Gaussian variables.

Unfortunately, many variables of interest in credit risk modeling, such as default times or default indicators, are not Gaussian. In fact, they are often positive variables (such as default times) or discrete variables (default indicators). The situation is then less simple. For instance, if we take $n$ random variables $U_i$ that are uniformly distributed on $[0,1]$, knowledge of pairwise correlation coefficients is not sufficient to deduce the joint distribution. Even a simple quantity such as $P(U_1 + \cdots + U_n > x)$ requires knowledge of the joint distribution function of $(U_1, \ldots, U_n)$, and not only of the correlation coefficients. This is due to the fact that there are infinitely many ways to 'couple' uniform random variables – i.e. define a dependence structure among them – in order to build a multivariate model, while preserving their marginal distributions. Any probability distribution

$$C : [0, 1]^n \rightarrow [0, 1]$$
$$(u_1, \ldots, u_n) \rightarrow P(U_1 \leq u_1, \ldots, U_n \leq u_n)$$

such that the corresponding marginal distributions are uniform on $[0,1]$, represents such a possible choice. A function with these properties is called a *copula* function: it 'couples' $n$ uniformly distributed random variables to generate a joint distribution whose dependence structure is encoded in the choice of $C$.

This phenomenon is not specific to uniform distribution. In fact, any random variable $X$ with distribution function $F$ can be transformed into a random variable $U$ with uniform distribution via the transformation $U = F(X)$. Therefore, the joint distribution of a set of random variables $(X_1, \ldots, X_n)$ with arbitrary marginal distributions $(F_1, \ldots, F_n)$ can be specified by transforming them to uniformly distributed random variables via $U_i = F(X_i)$ and then choosing a copula function for $(U_1, \ldots, U_n)$:

$$F(x_1, \ldots, x_n) = P(X_1 \leq x_1, \ldots, X_n \leq x_n) = C(u_1, \ldots, u_n) = C(F_1(x_1), \ldots, F_n(x_n))$$

A key observation is that in the above representation we have decomposed the joint distribution $F$ into two ingredients: the marginal distributions $(F_1, \ldots, F_n)$ and the dependence structure, specified through the copula function $C$. For non-Gaussian random variables, the role of the correlation coefficients is thus played by the copula function. Conversely, any multivariate distribution can be decomposed into its marginal distributions and a copula function. For example, the copula function for a multivariate Gaussian distribution $\Phi_\Sigma$ is given by:

$$C_{\text{Gauss}}(u_1, \ldots, u_n) = \Phi_\Sigma \left[ \Phi_1^{-1}(u_1), \ldots, \Phi_n^{-1}(u_n) \right]$$

where the $\Phi_i$ are univariate Gaussian distributions, representing the marginal distribution. This copula function, called the Gaussian copula, is entirely specified by a correlation matrix but, contrary to the multivariate Gaussian model, allows us to 'couple' marginal distributions, which are not necessarily Gaussian. Other examples of copulas used in credit modeling are the Student $t$, Clayton and Marshall–Olkin copulas. The main difference between these copula functions and the Gaussian copulas is that they allow for more dependence among large occurrences of the variables (i.e. 'tail dependence').

For modeling dependence among defaults of different firms, one can apply the above ideas to the default times $\tau_1, \ldots, \tau_n$. The marginal distributions of the default times can be modeled using one of the structural or reduced-form models presented above, and calibrated to credit spreads curves. The choice of a copula then gives a model for the default dependence, consistent with the individual default probabilities. However, it remains to estimate the copula function from empirical data. To do this using historical data on joint defaults is difficult since these are extremely rare events. Moreover, pricing applications require knowledge of the copula function for the risk-neutral distribution of default times. Except for standardized baskets such as CDX or iTraxx, for which such parameters can be implied from market prices, risk-neutral copulas are difficult, if not impossible, to infer from observations. A common practice is to use historically estimated parameters, but the justification for this approach is not clear: it implies that there is no risk premium associated to 'default correlation', which does not seem easy to justify.

### 6.3.2   The Gaussian Copula Model

While any choice of copula function is in principle possible for describing the dependence among default times, in general such models are tedious to simulate and the specification of the structure and parameters of copula functions is neither straightforward, nor intuitive. Among all copula models, a variant based on the Gaussian copula, proposed by Li (2002), has gained popularity in the market and become the market quoting convention for CDO tranches.

#### 6.3.2.1   Overview of the Model

Consider a portfolio of obligors issued by $N$ different credit-risky entities whose default times are denoted $\tau_1, \ldots, \tau_n$. We assume that we can observe the credit spreads and thus extract their distributions $(F_1, \ldots, F_n)$. To introduce dependence between defaults, we now use a Gaussian copula, defined by $n$ auxiliary variables, which form a Gaussian vector with correlation matrix $\Sigma$:

$$F_i(T_i) = \Phi(X_i) \quad \text{with} \quad X = (X_1, \ldots, X_n) \sim N(0, \Sigma)$$

To specify the correlation matrix $\Sigma$, Li makes the assumption that the multivariate distribution of default times and the multivariate distribution of asset returns share the same dependence structure, characterized by the correlation matrix of equity returns. This assumption can be justified if one refers to the multi-asset structural models discussed above, but note that the distribution of default times here need not be obtained from a structural model.

A case frequently used in practice is the one where correlations are equal, i.e. $\Sigma$ is given by:

$$\Sigma = \begin{pmatrix} 1 & .. & .. & \rho \\ .. & 1 & .. & .. \\ .. & .. & 1 & \rho \\ \rho & .. & \rho & 1 \end{pmatrix}$$

The correlation parameter $\rho$ then represents an average measure of the correlation of equity returns. Such a structure is in fact equivalent to a one-factor model for $(X_1, \ldots, X_n)$:

$$X_i = aX + \sqrt{1 - a^2}\, \varepsilon_i, \quad a^2 = \rho,\ X, \varepsilon_i \text{ i.i.d. } N(0, 1)$$

Let us now consider a time horizon $t$, representing for instance the payment date for a CDO tranche. To simulate the defaults having occurred in the portfolio at date $t$, we need to know the probability of default before $t$, given by $F_i(t)$, of each obligor and the dependence structure. Define now, for each obligor, a threshold $\theta_i$ such that the default probability equals the probability that $X_i$ does not exceed the threshold: $F_i(t) = \Phi(\theta_i)$. Threshold values $\theta_i$ can then be calibrated directly to default probabilities at maturity $t$, simulating the Gaussian vector $(X_1, \ldots, X_n)$ and then comparing $X_i$ to the threshold $\theta_i$ in each scenario to determine whether the obligor $i$ has defaulted or not.

When the correlation parameter $\rho$ is changed, the individual default probabilities, hence the expected losses, do not change. For a CDO, this leaves the total expected loss unaffected. However, changing the correlation parameter can have a strong impact on the shape of the distribution of losses. As a result, the expected loss for individual tranches will be affected by correlation. Figure 6.1 displays the distribution of losses in a homogeneous portfolio for two different values of $\rho$. At low correlation, there is very little likelihood that the mezzanine or

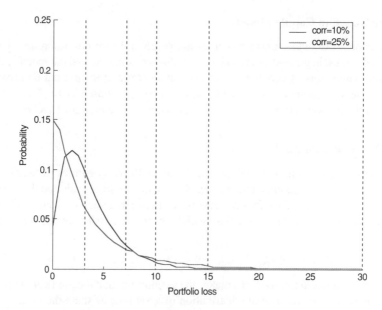

**Figure 6.1**   Distribution of losses for iTraxx NA IG
*Note:* Index $= 70$; recovery rate $= 40\%$; expected loss $= 3.4\%$.

senior tranche will be affected by defaults, so their expected loss is small. This is why senior tranches can be attributed high ratings even if the underlying portfolio is not investment grade. The higher the default correlation, the more likely it is that senior tranches will be affected by default.

### 6.3.2.2  Implied Correlations and Base Correlation

In the Gaussian copula model, the fundamental driver of tranche price is the correlation parameter: it plays the same role as the volatility in a Black–Scholes model. Following the line of reasoning presented above, one can see that the spread on a junior tranche will decrease when $\rho$ increases, while the spread on the senior tranche will increase with $\rho$. Using this monotone dependence, one can invert the market spread for a given senior or mezzanine tranche with respect to $\rho$ and compute the 'implied correlation', which yields the same value for the tranche in the Gaussian copula model.

However, this is not always possible for a mezzanine tranche. Figure 6.2 is an example of dependence for the spread on a 3%–7% tranche, which displays a nonmonotone dependence on $\rho$.

This can be understood using the fact that the payoff of a mezzanine tranche with attachment points can be seen as the difference between the payoffs of two call options on the total loss $L$ of the portfolio:

$$L_{A,B} = (L - A)1_{L\in[A,B]} + (B - A)1_{L\in[B,N]} = (L - A)^+ - (L - B)^+$$

Each call option has a value, which is increasing with $\rho$, but not necessarily their difference. However, if we consider not only the tranche values, but the sum of all tranches up to a given attachment point $B$, then this super-tranche is a call option on $L$ with strike $B$ and monotone

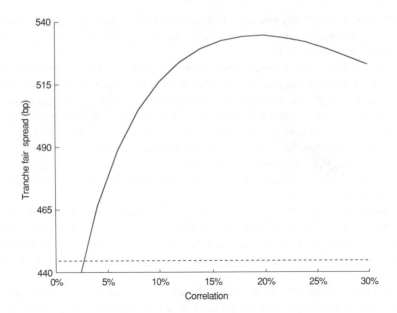

**Figure 6.2**   Mezzanine tranche value sensitivity to correlation in a Gaussian copula model

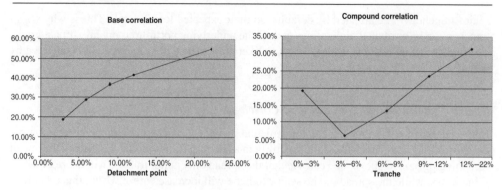

**Figure 6.3**   Base vs. compound correlation for iTraxx (March 2004)

dependence in $\rho$. Thus, inverting its market value to obtain $\rho$ yields a single value of $\rho$, called the base correlation for the attachment point $B$. Base correlation is used as a quoting convention for CDO tranches since 2003.

It is now possible to observe tradable tranche spreads for different levels of seniority. If we attempt to imply the market correlation using a single-parameter Gaussian copula model fitted to observed market tranche spreads, we can identify a skew in the average correlation as a function of the width and attachment point of the tranche as shown in Figure 6.3. This skew, present both in base and compound correlations, illustrates that the dependence structure as specified by the model is inconsistent with the market pricing of CDO tranches.

### 6.3.2.3   Limitations and Extensions of the Gaussian Copula Model

Appreciated for its simplicity and computational tractability, the Gaussian copula model has some serious drawbacks, which should discourage market practitioners from using it as a realistic risk management tool.

Empirical studies of asset returns and returns of credit-sensitive instruments show that, while assuming the same dependence structure (copula) for equity returns and credit returns is reasonable, this dependence structure is not well described by a Gaussian copula (Mashal et al., 2003) but requires more dependence in the tails. Thus, models built with Gaussian copulas will generally underestimate default correlations, and thus undervalue junior tranches and overvalue senior tranches of multi-name credit products. Copulas with tail dependence, such as Student copulas, can produce more realistic joint-default scenarios and valuations.

Nevertheless, this model has become a standard tool in the CDO markets and has been extended in various ways.

As noted above, the simple one-factor correlation structure is quite restrictive and in contradiction with the implied correlation skews. Multifactor extensions (Laurent and Gregory, 2004) inherit the tractability properties of the Li model and can be used to generate more flexible correlation matrices and lead to correlation skews, though not exactly of the type observed in the market.

A second type of extension is to introduce dynamics. The Gaussian copula model, and more generally 'copula models', are one-period models: they do not specify any dynamics for credit spreads. In the next two sub-sections, we will see examples of dynamic models that have been proposed to model default correlations across time.

### 6.3.3   Multi-Asset Structural Models

'Default barrier' models discussed in Section 6.1 allow for a straightforward generalization to the multivariate case and enable dynamics to be introduced, which are absent in the copula approaches outlined above.

Each firm $i = 1, \ldots, N$ is represented by a state variable $V_t^i$ representing the 'value of the firm', modeled as before using a geometric Brownian motion. The default time of firm $i$ is represented as the first time $V_t^i$ reaches the default barrier $H_i(t)$, the value of this barrier (possibly time-dependent) being chosen to calibrate the credit spread curve of issuer $i$. Correlation between default times can then be obtained by introducing a correlation between the processes $V_t^i$:

$$\frac{dV_t^i}{V_t^i} = \mu \, dt \, + \, \sigma_i \, dW_t^i \, \mathrm{cov}\left(W_t^i, W_t^j\right) = \rho_{ij} t$$

$$\tau_i = \inf \left\{ t \geq 0, \; V_t^i \leq H_i(t) \right\}$$

Hull and White (2001) use piecewise linear default thresholds to replicate, given marginal default probabilities. As for the specification of the correlation coefficients, it can easily be shown following the reasoning presented in Section 6.1 that, in this model, equity returns inherit the same correlation structure so, at least in principle, the default correlation coefficients can be retrieved from the equity returns correlations.

Such models share the same analytical tractability as single-asset structural models and the toolbox of computational tools and approximations used for the multivariate Black–Scholes model can be used in this context. One important difference with multi-asset equity models is that, joint defaults being much less frequent than individual default events, a straightforward Monte Carlo simulation of this model can be quite slow and requires variance reduction techniques such as importance sampling (Glasserman and Li, 2003). Hull *et al.* (2005) explore a one-factor version of this model where the correlation matrix $\rho_{ij} = a_i a_j$ has rank one. This model can be viewed as a dynamic version of the Gaussian copula model discussed above and allows fast computation by exploiting conditional independence of the state variables $V_t^i$ given the (single) factor.

Naturally these models inherit the shortcomings of single-asset structural models, such as the difficulties in fitting short-term credit spreads and the predictability of default events. Also, the dependence structure implied by such multivariate structural models is necessarily a Gaussian copula, so the problems encountered with the Gaussian copula model, such as the absence of dependence in the tails, will also be encountered here. Nevertheless, they have become popular with practitioners because of their simplicity and ease of implementation.

### 6.3.4   Dependent Defaults in Reduced-Form Models

Dependence among defaults can also be introduced in reduced-form models, by introducing correlation in the (random) default intensities describing each entity. In this approach, the credit risk of each entity is modeled by specifying a hazard rate $\lambda_i(t)$, modeled as a random process.

The idea is to specify a factor model for the joint evolution of the processes $\lambda_i(t)$. The simplest specification is a one-factor model given by:

$$\lambda_i(t) = \lambda_0(t) + y_i(t)$$

where $\lambda_0(t)$ represents a common factor, generating dependence among defaults and $y_i(t)$ the idiosyncratic component of the hazard rate. Given the relation in Section 6.2 between hazard rates and CDS spreads, this approach can be interpreted as modeling default correlations via correlations among CDS spreads.

More general multifactor models have been considered, where $\lambda_i(t)$ is specified as a linear combination of several common driving factors plus an idiosyncratic component. Such specifications turn out to be difficult to calibrate to market data. In general, the model does not enable marginal default probabilities to be separated from the dependence structure ('copula'), so one cannot proceed by calibrating the model first to single-name CDS spread curves, and then calibrating dependence parameters: all model parameters must be calibrated in a single step. Also, this specification has been criticized as not being able to generate sufficient dependence among defaults. In particular, even high correlation levels between hazard rates do not result in 'clustered defaults', while driving the correlation parameters close to 1 in the Gaussian copula models gives this effect (for a discussion of this point, see Das *et al.* 2005).

## 6.4   DISCUSSION

### 6.4.1   Comparing Structural and Reduced-Form Modeling Approaches

The main differences between both families of model are summarized below:

- Structural models price credit risk relative to the equity, while reduced-form models use other, more liquid credit-sensitive instruments, such as CDSs. In particular, reduced-form models have nothing to say about the relative value of credit instruments with respect to equity products.
- As a result, while structural models can be used for relative value arbitrage between equity and credit and for pricing hybrid products, this is not the case for reduced-form models.
- On the other hand, structural models often give poor fits to observed credit spreads and the calibration procedure is not straightforward, whereas reduced-form models can easily be calibrated to any credit spread curve using the relation of the hazard rate with the credit spreads, which is directly observable in the market.
- Structural models represent the default time as the first time when a continuous process $V(t)$ ('firm value') reaches a barrier: default is therefore a predictable event, the probability of which increases as $V(t)$ approaches the barrier. In reduced-form models, the default time is an exogenous and unpredictable random time whose (conditional) probability distribution is modeled by the hazard rate. It is the unpredictable feature of default in these models, even shortly before it occurs, which leads to nonzero credit spreads, even for short maturities.
- Structural models allow straightforward generalization to the multi-asset case, the dependence between defaults being modeled via the correlation between values of the different firms assets. Generalizing reduced-form models to multiple names is less intuitive and

requires the specification of default correlation at a more abstract level, by introducing copulas, dependence between random default barriers or between random intensities.

- Reduced-form models enable randomness in interest rates to be incorporated and products with joint exposure to interest rates and credit risk to be modeled. By contrast, incorporating random interest rates in structural models is difficult and leads to intractable models.

### 6.4.2   Complex Models, Sparse Data Sets

The models discussed above are among the simplest ones that have been proposed in the literature. During the last decade, numerous theoretical contributions on credit risk modeling have been proposed, including various generalizations of the above models: structural models with stochastic or state-dependent volatility, structural models where the value of the firm undergoes jumps, reduced-form models incorporating rating transitions and stochastic hazard rates correlated with interest rates, etc. While these models can provide useful insights into the nature of credit risk, their complexity contrasts strongly with the sparseness of empirical data sets, which, in principle, should be used to calibrate the model parameters.

While this is already true for single-name credit models, the situation is even worse for multi-asset models where, aside from standardized baskets such as iTraxx, there are few, if any, prices available, which give any indication about default correlation parameters. This is an important obstacle in using complex models. Where a feasible and stable procedure is not available for calibrating the parameters of a pricing model, it cannot be used in applications. Unfortunately, this point has not been considered sufficiently in the theoretical literature on credit risk modeling, leading to a plethora of models, which are impossible to use in practice.

Facing such shortcomings in market data, many users have attempted to complete them using information obtained from econometric models estimated from historical data. In structural models, using historical data on equity returns or option-based indicators of equity volatility makes perfect sense since the model links these quantities to credit spreads. Also, in such models default correlations are in principle linked to correlations in equity returns, which are again observable.

The issue of the lack of data is more subtle in the case of reduced-form models. First, note that the hazard rates in reduced-form models represent risk-neutral (or market-implied) default probabilities: even where one has a good econometric model for historical default rates or rating transitions, it is not obvious how they can be used to improve estimates of risk-neutral hazard rates. Indeed, due to the risk premium required for default risk, we expect risk-neutral hazard rates to be systematically higher. Finally, one should note that credit spreads are not only determined by default risk but also by liquidity cycles in the market: such liquidity fluctuations have led in recent years to huge fluctuations in the order of magnitude of credit spreads.

In both classes of model, emphasis has been on default probabilities but little work has been done on recovery rates, which are even more uncertain than default probabilities. Some authors have argued that modeling recovery rates as stochastic processes and allowing for negative correlation between recovery and default rates is essential for a proper valuation of credit derivatives (Frye, 2003).

Given the lack of data, the importance of making plausible modeling assumptions becomes even more crucial: rather than a way of explaining a set of observations, the model becomes a tool for extrapolating beyond existing observations. Unfortunately, pricing models tend to be chosen more for their ease of implementation or 'analytical tractability' rather than the economic meaningfulness of their assumptions. The impact of the various modeling assumptions used in the pricing of credit derivatives is not negligible, leading to huge model risks for arrangers on these sophisticated products, such as CDOs (Cont, 2006). This topic of model risk needs to be studied more closely and given proper attention by financial institutions' top management.

To conclude, let us emphasize that the lack of data is not only an 'empirical' issue, which should be left to the end-user of the pricing model or to the econometrician to deal with. In order for models to be applicable, the nature of available data has to be taken into account from the outset, in the very formulation of these models. Only pricing models whose results are expressed in terms of observable variables can be calibrated and used in practice.

### 6.4.3  Stand-alone Pricing Versus Marginal Pricing

Notwithstanding their methodological differences, structural models and intensity-based models share an important feature when it comes to pricing credit derivatives: just as in the Black–Scholes model, their approach to pricing is a stand-alone approach insofar as they seek to attribute a value to a derivative instrument regardless of the context in which it is being used, the only reference to the market being the calibration of the parameters to a set of market prices (for example CDS spreads). While this stand-alone pricing might be relevant for standardized products such as CDSs, it is less obvious to justify for bespoke structured products. As noted in previous chapters, one of the main drivers behind the growth in credit derivatives is their usage as credit portfolio hedging or diversification tools for investors and banks. From the point of view of these users, stand-alone pricing of a credit derivative does not give the correct notion of value: instead, the value of a credit derivative should be determined by its marginal impact on the risk/return profile of their initial credit portfolio. The value of the additional exposure gained by selling a CDS or subscribing a CDO mezzanine tranche, for instance, will then depend on the investor's portfolio composition and risk aversion.

In this context, the value of a credit derivative can be seen as the price at which the investor will be indifferent towards the transaction, given her portfolio and her risk aversion. This approach of viewing a derivative transaction as a 'risk transfer' is in fact rather classical in insurance and deserves to be explored further in the context of pricing structured credit products (see for example Barrieu and El Karoui, 2003).

The pricing and hedging of credit derivatives is far from being a fully explored topic: many challenges remain, especially regarding a better understanding of default correlation modeling, the management of the risk of correlation products and the design of models that are both rich enough and amenable to calibration with available data.

# 7
# The Impact of the Development in
## Credit Derivatives

Because banks occupy a central position in the credit derivatives markets, they are at the heart of any changes. We have observed many times in earlier chapters that banks could gain much from increased use of credit derivatives. Quite apart from these advantages for the banks, the impact of the growing use of credit derivatives by banks and other players in the capital markets must also be examined. They profoundly affect banks' strategies, business models and environment.

The purpose of this chapter is to examine the fundamental changes currently taking place in the financial markets and analyze them objectively. The essential questions about credit derivatives can be divided into three main groups:

1. The new role of banking institutions in a market-driven credit industry: do banks continue to act in their traditional role as lenders, or are they gradually moving towards a business model that could be described as a 'risk transformation factory'?
2. The central, but delicate issue of regulations for the capital markets, which are now globalized and deregulated: more especially, is the exponential growth in credit derivatives indicative of a major financial crisis in the making, in the sense that they are like a virus contaminating the entire economic system with credit risk? Are credit derivatives and other financial derivatives really the 'weapons of mass destruction' of the financial world so vilified by some market observers, like the American investor Warren Buffett?
3. The actual *raison d'être* of derivatives, especially credit derivatives: do they constitute a ground-breaking revolution in the financial markets, or are they merely at the heart of an ongoing innovative process focusing constantly on optimized risk management?

Even though the formulation of these questions already hints at the authors' opinion on these problems, the purpose of this chapter is to make as objective as possible an analysis, using as many factual examples as possible.

The chapter is therefore organized into three sections. The first discusses the effect that the development of credit derivatives has had on banking institutions. Already in November 1996, the *Economist* wrote: 'The growth of credit derivatives could change the very nature of banking itself. If credit risk can be divorced easily from loans, the link between a bank and its borrowers will change: the possibility of default will no longer tie the two so closely together. Inevitably, that will be another nail in the coffin of old-fashioned relationship banking.' The transformation of bank management methods and the arrival of credit risk management at the banks' portfolio level are recent, but already fairly well-established, phenomena for the most sophisticated institutions. Indeed, such skills are a prerequisite for banks wishing to use complex products like credit derivatives for risk management.

In this chapter, we first wish to describe the evolution of banking institutions towards economic, pro-active management of their credit portfolios, and the effect of these changes on their strategy, organization and culture.

Second, we examine the symbiotic relationships between credit derivatives and financial regulations. The capital adequacy standards governing banking activities are particularly strict. It is no exaggeration to say that the emergence of an active market in credit derivatives was the catalyst for reform of the Basel I Accords and for the advances proposed in the new Basel II framework.

In addition to these far-reaching changes, the possible threat to the stability of a globalized, deregulated financial system posed by credit derivatives must be examined. We shall return to the ongoing debate, in both the general public and among the world supervisory authorities (Joint Forum for Financial Stability, Basel Committee), on the potential danger posed by these new instruments.

We conclude this chapter by examining the creation and emergence of credit derivatives in the light of over 30 years of the far-reaching, ongoing, innovation that so characterizes the financial industry. In this sense, they should not be viewed as a 'financial revolution' breaking with the historic practices of the financial industry, but rather as a major evolution developing from the efforts of risk managers to arrive at ever-more finely tuned levels of analysis that will enable high-performance management strategies to be implemented.

## 7.1    THE IMPACT OF THE GROWTH IN CREDIT DERIVATIVES ON BANKING INSTITUTIONS

Over the past 20 years, banks' traditional role as intermediaries has been profoundly changed, due to the developments in the financial markets (globalization, deregulation, sophistication) that have led to increasingly fierce competition between financial institutions.

Thus, several phenomena illustrating these changes can be observed:

- Financial disintermediation.
- The all-powerful creed of 'shareholder value', leading banking institutions to continually optimize their use of capital, truly the economic 'sinews of war'.
- Competition in the credit markets and the use of bank loans as a 'loss leader', thus leading to the question of whether the corporate lending business is intrinsically profitable.

We shall return first to these underlying trends in the capital markets. We shall then move on to trends in the area of bank portfolio management and credit risk pricing. Finally, we shall take a look at 'twenty-first century banking'. This will emerge as a new model, the strategy, organization and culture of which have been fundamentally changed by the predomination of the capital markets.

### 7.1.1    Far-Reaching Changes in the Capital Markets

As already underlined, the banking institutions' traditional credit business is their riskiest activity, as illustrated by the many disasters caused by underperforming loan portfolios, among others.[1] The wave of bankruptcies in the early 2000s, epitomized by the Enron and WorldCom bankruptcies, was a timely reminder of the cyclical vulnerability of the banking system. Thus, this characteristic requires banks to manage their credit risk more actively. Furthermore, the current climate in the capital markets characterized by disintermediation, the all-powerful creed of shareholder value and fierce competition in credit incites banks to act more dynamically.

---

[1] See Chapter 1 for the characteristics of credit risk.

### 7.1.1.1  Financial Disintermediation

In ordinary economic terms, the *raison d'être* of banking institutions is to collect funds from economic agents that are structurally savers (i.e. lenders), such as households, and redistribute this liquidity in the form of loans to agents that are structurally borrowers, such as firms. The banks are remunerated for this intermediation service in the form of a margin (intermediation margin) corresponding to the difference between the interest rate at which the financial institutions remunerate cash deposits and that at which they lend those same sums.

The phenomenon of financial disintermediation, particularly acute in the United States, results in reduced margins for banks, thus deteriorating the profitability of the classic lending business. Thus, many of the funds traditionally collected by banks moved towards vehicles offering more attractive placements such as UCITs (mutual funds in the United States and unit trusts in the United Kingdom), life insurance, or even hedge funds for wealthier households, etc. Secondly, firms with good creditworthiness had access to much cheaper funding sources by raising finance directly from investors in the capital markets and thus short-circuiting the traditional bank intermediary. This practice was made possible notably by the development of new financial products such as commercial paper issues, medium-term notes, eurobonds and note issuance facilities among others.

This financial disintermediation thus resulted in increased competition for the remaining borrowers, and deteriorating quality of banks' loan portfolios, since the well-rated corporates found finance directly with investors in the financial markets.

### 7.1.1.2  The All-Powerful Creed of Shareholder Value

The development of shareholders' power and corporate governance rules in the United States promoted the creed of shareholder value, obliging corporate management to take only the decisions likely to increase corporate market value. Although this did not apply specifically to banks, it nevertheless affected them. Among others, the goal of maximized shareholder value in banks led to waves of restructuring and concentrations, via massive merger and acquisition operations. These strategic alliances were dictated by the banks' desire to reach critical mass in the various businesses, which were busily going global.

This urge was all the greater in the United States, where the banking market was strictly compartmentalized by restrictive regulations, in terms both of businesses and geography. The wave of deregulation in the 1990s led to national concentrations, with the emergence of retail banking giants such as Citigroup, Bank of America or JP Morgan (the result of a merger between JP Morgan and Chase Manhattan, later joined by Bank One). However, it also allowed 'one-stop shop' combinations, the archetype of which was Citigroup (before the divestiture of the insurance company Travelers), which offered under the same umbrella retail banking, insurance, investment banking (Schroder, Salomon Brothers, Smith Barney), asset management, etc. Other groups also adopted this 'financial conglomerate' strategy (Morgan Stanley-Dean Witter, JP Morgan-Chase, etc.).

In wholesale banking, most of the independent boutiques virtually disappeared between 1997 and 2000. They were bought up by the American commercial banks with ambitions in merchant banking, or by European players seeking to beef up their presence in the United States (NationsBank-Montgomery Securities, Bankers Trust-Alex Brown, Bank of America-Robertson, Stephens, ING-Furman Selz, Société Générale-Cowen & Co., UBS-PaineWebber, etc.). Conversely, the big merchant banks began to encroach onto the stamping ground of the commercial banks by underwriting and syndicating loans.

In Europe, the pattern of concentration was slightly different, remaining within the borders of the various member states in a common market that did not yet enable synergies to be developed in retail banking because of the heterogeneous national regulations. One characteristic example of this is the French experience with the acquisition of Crédit Lyonnais by Crédit Agricole and of IXIS by Groupe Caisse d'Epargne, BNP's takeover of Paribas, and that of CIC by Crédit Mutuel. In wholesale banking, on the other hand, the main players have long since become European, or even global (Deutsche Bank, UBS, Credit Suisse, BNP Paribas, etc.), since their business is by definition international.

In the financial industry today, 'bigger is better'. The new banking giants manage colossal credit portfolios, and their control methods are changing and rapidly becoming more sophisticated.

### 7.1.1.3  Competition in the Credit Markets and the Use of Bank Loans as a Loss Leader

One last fundamental trend in the credit markets is the fierce competition between the main banks.[2] In an aggressively competitive environment, borrowers have insisted that bank syndicates cut their size, because they wish to deal directly only with a small group of core relationship bankers. This enables them, first, to cut the administrative costs of borrowing, and second, to gain powerful leverage in negotiations with banks when they are refinancing their existing credit facilities. Thus, when Fiat and Electricité de France launched the takeover for Montedison via their joint vehicle Italenergia at the end of 2001, they agreed to negotiate only with a restricted syndicate of five banks (Capitalia, Deutsche Bank, IntesaBCI, San Paolo IMI and SG) for total bank funding of €6 bn!

Thus, banks have had to agree to take more and more exposure to certain borrowers onto their balance sheets. The downside is that they have been obliged to reduce their customer base drastically, and focus on the accounts offering them a satisfactory overall rate of return.

Furthermore, in a market where the credit offer is structurally greater than demand, the banks have had to reduce their prices to promote relationship banking, and hope that these cuts in income will be offset by cross-selling of other products to those same borrowers (the concept of 'one-stop shopping'). Thus for these banks, credit has become a vital loss leader that allows them to attract fees.[3] The following two examples illustrate this strategy. The first is a commercial bank (HSBC) seeking to strengthen its positions as an investment bank, and the other is a merchant bank (Morgan Stanley) wishing to defend its market share.

- In February 2002, the UK giant HSBC announced it was going to place its balance sheet assets at the service of its investment bank.[4] Noting that the most resistant economic models in periods of high tension were those of diversified financial groups such as JP Morgan or Citigroup, with power in both retail and wholesale banking, HSBC decided to increase the investment bank share of its income and offer its corporate customers a complete range of products and services.

---

[2] In this sub-section and later in the chapter, we shall cover the patterns in commercial credit business, i.e. corporate lending.
[3] See Silverman and Pretzlik (2001): 'US banks say lending is vital for attracting fees'.
[4] See l'Agefi (2002).

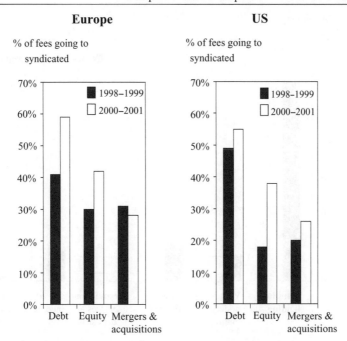

**Figure 7.1**  Investment banking cross-sell from syndicated loans
*Sources*: Oliver, Wyman & Co., Morgan Stanley (2002). Reproduced by permission of Mercer Oliver Wyman.

- Conversely, the American merchant bank Morgan Stanley revealed in August 2001 that it wished to increase its corporate lending capacity, to 'confront the increasing competition from the large banking groups that manage to win lucrative investment bank contracts. Morgan Stanley thus injected $2 billion into its Utah subsidiary to increase its corporate lending capacity, even though it had a negative effect on the bank's overall return on equity'.[5] Other brokerage houses such as Goldman Sachs were also obliged to change their strategy in this field to defend themselves against the competition.

This strategy of using bank credit as a loss leader to attract lucrative investment banking contracts paid off, if the survey by Oliver, Wyman & Co. and Morgan Stanley is to be believed. Figure 7.1 shows their analysis.

However, there is a downside to this strategy: if bank credit is used as a loss leader, its pricing is no longer subject to economic reasoning.[6] The consequence of this is that plain vanilla lending activities are not profitable for banks.

Thus, in the same survey, Oliver, Wyman & Co. and Morgan Stanley assessed the economic profitability of the various business lines in European banks in 2000 and 2001. This analysis shows that the economic return[7] of lending activities is negative (−$1200 bn at European level), and that it is the only activity with negative economic returns. It is true that it attracts

---

[5] *La Tribune* (2001).
[6] See Silverman (2002) on this: 'The pains and gains of relationship banking'.
[7] This can be defined as the operating profit from the activity less expected losses less the cost of capital.

USD billion

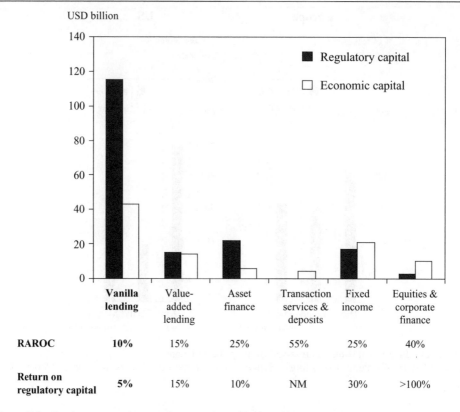

| | Vanilla lending | Value-added lending | Asset finance | Transaction services & deposits | Fixed income | Equities & corporate finance |
|---|---|---|---|---|---|---|
| **RAROC** | **10%** | 15% | 25% | 55% | 25% | 40% |
| **Return on regulatory capital** | **5%** | 15% | 10% | NM | 30% | >100% |

**Figure 7.2**    Product economics: regulatory and economic capital usage (2000–2001)
*Sources*: Oliver, Wyman & Co., Morgan Stanley (2002). Reproduced by permission of Mercer Oliver Wyman.

the greatest capital usage for banking institutions, in terms both of regulatory and economic capital. The results of this analysis are presented in Figure 7.2.

These results also show that there is a considerable discrepancy between the returns on the various activities, depending on whether they are measured in relation to the institution's economic capital (RAROC[8]) or regulatory capital. We shall return to this later.

Faced with these fundamental trends of disintermediation, maximized shareholder value, growing competition in the credit markets and low intrinsic profitability of lending activities, banking institutions were forced to act. In this new climate, they are now evaluating their competitiveness not only in terms of balance-sheet size or amount of loans outstanding, but also in terms of return on economic capital and level of stockmarket capitalization. These requirements have led them to rethink and adapt the management of their credit portfolios.

### 7.1.2   An Economic Approach to Credit Risk Management

We shall now present a brief overview of banking institutions' activities using an economic approach to credit risk management. We shall cover the principles of portfolio management and

---

[8] Risk-adjusted return on capital.

economic credit pricing and the main tools available to banking institutions for implementing these active management strategies. We shall conclude with a concrete example.

### 7.1.2.1 Portfolio Management and Economic Pricing of Credits

As shown earlier, because the banks' priority strategic goal is to generate value for shareholders, they have been led to set up active management strategies for their credit portfolios. The main principles of this are presented below.

#### Principles of portfolio management

If banks are to comply with portfolio management principles, they must master the following techniques for their credit portfolio as a whole:

- Calculating the default probabilities on the various credits in the portfolio (and the volatility of these default rates).
- Determining the loss suffered in the event of default, for each credit.
- Correctly assessing the impact of portfolio diversification, not least by means of a correlation analysis of the credits in it.
- Obtaining a measurement of the economic capital needed to support the bank activities. This level is also determined on the basis of the overall risk profile that the management of the institution wish to adopt.
- Ultimately, building up an efficient credit portfolio in the meaning of Markowitz, that is, maximizing return for a given risk level, or minimizing the latter for a given return. This means allocation of the institution's capital for the most profitable activities, on the basis of their actual capital usage, thus adjusted for risk.

This often proves to be a complicated practice, because of the lack of relevant information, as underlined in Chapter 6. It requires the portfolio manager to be constantly vigilant to ensure increased efficiency, and adapt each loan (investment) to the institution's portfolio composition. The latter condition has led banks to set up sophisticated systems for measuring economic capital and pricing credit risk.

#### Determining economic capital

As a general rule, banks use three measurements of capital:

1. Accounting capital corresponds to the physical capital held by a bank; it includes share-holders' equity, long-term subordinated debt and their hybrid forms. Although accounting definitions differ depending on the system, the introduction of the International Financial Reporting Standards (IFRS) in 2005 should lead to a degree of convergence here.
2. Regulatory capital corresponds to the minimum amount of capital with which the banking activities supervisory authorities allow a bank to exercise.
3. Finally, the economic capital can be defined as the target amount of capital a banking institution must hold to back its transactions, depending on a required level of solvency. This is calculated by aggregating all the risks borne by a bank.

In order to determine the economic capital, banks use models based on assessment of probability density function (PDF) of the credit losses. This function enables assessment of the probability that the losses on the risk portfolio will exceed a threshold $X$ (solvency threshold, expressed as a fractile). Synthetically, it can be said that a portfolio is all the riskier as the distribution 'tail' is 'fat' (or, in other words, the portfolio assets are strongly correlated), and in this case, the amount of economic capital required by the financial institution will be all the greater.

The main parameters enabling distribution of credit losses to be determined are the definition of the credit loss itself, the choice of a timescale and modeling of the correlation between the assets analyzed.[9]

### The concept of loss

Two approaches to loss are used:

- binary models of default/nondefault;
- models based on the evolution (discrete or continuous) of the creditworthiness of each credit – a gain (or loss) can stem from a change in creditworthiness, even if the default does not occur in the period under examination.

In the binary model, only default entails loss. This approach is justified by the fact that the banks are not obliged to mark their loans to market in their banking book. The only variables, therefore, are default probability and the recovery rate. Moreover, this modeling approach provides considerable leeway for implementation and calibration.

### Choice of a time scale

Contrary to VaR analysis of market risk in which the term is a few days, the framework timescale used in credit risk is usually a year. This is based on the assumption that the timescale required for a bank to get rid of its bad debts or change its balance-sheet composition is at least a year. For market risks, the delay required to settle or liquidate positions is theoretically a mere few days. This analysis timescale can also be explained by the infrequency of the events used in the modeling of a credit portfolio, especially rating and default changes.

The choice of a year is not based on any strictly established rule. It can be justified in some cases where the approach is by transitions or multi-states, on condition the assets are effectively negotiable or could be hedged at reasonable cost over the period. However, the choice of a year is more arbitrary for a binary model based on defaults. First of all, it must take account of the total time of risk exposure during which a default could occur, and that might vary considerably from one asset to another. Secondly, the major criticism of this choice is that credit risk accumulates with time and is, further, correlated over time.

### Solvency threshold

Finally, the solvency threshold must be defined, since it enables economic capital to be deduced from loss distribution. Unlike modeling, which requires unavoidable technical components, the choice of confidence interval is more strategic than technical for a bank. For the model to become a tool for allocating capital, the portfolio manager must determine the desirable degree of risk aversion, that is, the confidence interval tolerated in the distribution, or again, the quantile of this maximum tolerable risk beyond which current income and capital do not cover the maximum risk.

---

[9] We shall not return to this here because it was explained amply in Section 6.3.

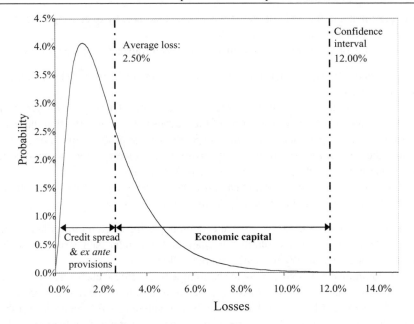

**Figure 7.3**   Economic capital definition

This problem is linked to the bank's goal of financial soundness in relation to the risk of bankruptcy. In most cases it can be likened to a risk class determined by the rating agencies (for example, 99.97% for an AA rating at Standard & Poor's).

Figure 7.3 presents a PDF type. The important variables mentioned in this part are shown (average loss, fractile and economic capital).

## Towards economic credit pricing

Over the past two decades, the criteria used for measuring bank performances have changed considerably. The years 1970–1980 saw the reign of balance-sheet size and the race for market shares. These imperatives were adhered to, to the detriment of banking activities' profitability. The latter appeared in the 1980s: the banks then wished to evaluate the profitability of each of their businesses, not least by implementing systems of cost allocation. In credit activities, bank performance was measured (and this is still the case today for many of them) by the return on regulatory capital, the deforming effects of which have already been shown. In the 1990s, measures for risk-adjusted return on capital were introduced.[10]

Today, RAROC-type methods of measuring trading performances are widespread, and are a logical development from the measurements of economic capital presented earlier. The general principle of a RAROC system is to set aside an amount of economic capital deemed sufficient to hedge the risks arising from the positions taken by the bank for each transaction, such risk being assessed *a priori*. For credit transactions, this amounts to unbundling the regulatory

---

[10] This summary gives a very general view of the banks' position. Some of them developed measurements of return on economic capital right from the early 1980s.

capital requirements at the level of each transaction/customer, by over-weighting the riskiest transactions and counterparties, and vice versa.

The stages of economic capital determination for each transaction are as follows:

- Analyzing each activity/product and unbundling the risks into primary risks (currency, credit, interest rate, etc.).
- Quantifying the amount of risk in each primary risk category. This is generally determined by means of a Monte Carlo-type simulation of the various parameters affecting the transaction risk, each simulated parameter following a specific law of probabilities. For credit risk, it is mainly the default rate volatility that needs to be modeled and then translated into loss volatility around the average anticipated loss, as seen earlier.
- Calculating the amount of economic capital to be set aside against the transaction, corresponding to the unexpected amount of potential losses on the portfolio.

Application of RAROC methods to arrive at economic pricing of credit nevertheless supposes that the credit risk, especially its volatility, is quantified. As underlined earlier, these data may be delicate to obtain, especially for bank loan portfolios.

The most common practices today are to use a single measuring scale for risk within the bank, enabling the various credits (obligors and proposed transactions) to be ranked from 1 to 10, for instance. Credits ranked 1 are considered to be the equivalent of AAA securities for the rating agencies, while those ranked 10 are on the verge of being written off by the bank. The credit analysts re-evaluate each transaction/counterparty periodically, and confirm or reject the internal rating. Using these classifications, it is possible to calculate the historical averages and variations in default rates, and the associated loss amounts (by establishing correspondences with the historical data provided by the rating agencies). Once the losses have been anticipated and their distribution of probabilities calculated, credit pricing becomes a rational exercise and so the bank can decide whether to reduce or increase its exposure to the borrower concerned.

The economic rate of return of a credit transaction can then be evaluated *ex ante* as the quotient of the net banking income (NBI) less expected losses[11] (EL) over the amount of economic capital (EC):

$$RAROC = \frac{NBI - EL}{EC}$$

Ranking credit transactions according to the RAROC criterion gives the risk manager a reference tool that is radically different from the traditional measurement of return on regulatory capital (quotient of the net banking income over the amount of regulatory capital). RAROC is therefore a decision-making tool for deciding to lend money in the light of the bank's target return on capital and the composition of its portfolio. Ultimately, banks able to determine and build efficient credit portfolios would be capable of gaining a substantial comparative edge over their competitors; in theory, they would no longer need to charge their customers for the costs arising from the risks on a loan that they can diversify.

The corollary of implementing economic credit risk management and pricing methods is that loans can be the object of *ex ante* provisions. Hitherto, banks have used *ex post* provisioning of their corporate loan activities, i.e. a method consisting of making provisions for the amount

---

[11] This is usually calculated as the product of default probability, the bank's exposure and the loss in the event of default. It is not a risk since it is anticipated, but it represents simply the 'economic cost' of granting credit.

of potential losses on a given counterparty where that counterparty's default materialized. By opposition, *ex ante* provisioning of bank debts means that the provision is calculated as soon as the loan is granted.

Inasfar as the banks have developed an internal information system (ratings, historical data) enabling them to calculate the average loss on each new loan *ex ante*, they are capable of constituting provisions corresponding to these future anticipated risk predictions.

Pre-provisioning of bank debts enables the gains and losses on a bank's credit activities to be spread out over time, thus reducing their volatility (traditionally high due to excessive provisioning during recessions). The advantage of this is that shareholders and counterparties of the bank have a clearer picture of its performance, and this should result in higher market capitalization.

Because they act as a catalyst in developing a more sophisticated approach to credit risk, particularly by enabling statistical models for quantifying it, credit derivatives have become the banks' preferred instrument for economic management of their credit portfolios. In parallel to these products, other techniques are used by banks. These will be discussed in the next sub-section.

### 7.1.2.2   *Main Tools Available to Banks for Active Management of their Credit Portfolios*

Active management of a bank's portfolio requires proper trading tools. Since the early 1990s, two corollary phenomena have been at work:

- The growing liquidity of credit instruments: thus, bond issues which, since the introduction of the European single currency, have now reached a minimum critical mass enabling active negotiation, or again, the large syndicated bank loans, which increasingly include transfer clauses.
- The appearance of products enabling credit to become more liquid: credit derivatives of course, and securitizations and synthetic securitizations.

In other words, credit is now actively traded in the market. As a BIS working group recently wrote in a report, 'Recent developments seem to represent something of a step change. Increasingly, banks work on the basis that loans will not be held on the balance sheet until maturity. Rather, they are beginning to think about credit exposures as a tradable commodity, whether singly or packaged together.'[12]

Three main techniques have gradually been perfected by the banks to manage their credit portfolios and make them more liquid. They are trading of bank loans in the secondary market, securitization of bank loans, and credit derivatives. We shall develop the first of these, since the other two have been discussed amply elsewhere in this book.[13]

### Secondary loan trading

Since the early 1990s, the secondary loan market has become one of the banks' preferred vehicles for managing their credit portfolios.

---

[12] BIS Working Paper (2003).
[13] See Chapter 4.

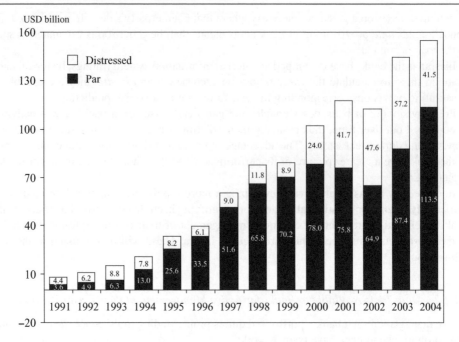

**Figure 7.4**   Growth of the US secondary loan trading market
*Sources*: The Loan Pricing Corporation/GoldSheets. Reproduced by permission of the Loan Pricing Corporation.

*Emergence of the market*

The secondary loan market appeared in the United States in 1991, with four market-makers managing this activity with $1.5 bn of capital. During the 1980s, transactions on bank loans had taken place, but they were not the subject of an active market with market-makers. They were mostly conducted by banks wishing to get rid of already provisioned loans which, in their view, were unlikely to return to par value. The counterparties at the time were speculative 'vulture funds', which bought these debts at 20 or 25 cents on the dollar and gambled on improved creditworthiness in the medium term to attain a yield that would be equivalent to what they could have earned on an equity position. The 1990s were characterized by the fact that all types of credit were traded, not just distressed assets.

Figure 7.4 shows the evolution of this market in loan volumes traded in the United States, observing the distinction between distressed debt (which, by definition, trades at under 80% of par) and par or near-par debt that trades at between 80% and 100% of par value.

**1996–2001, the turning point**

With $155 bn traded in the United States in 2004, the market reached critical mass, after a decade of growth. The first trend to be confirmed was the spread of this market to other continents. In Europe, the market reached $30 bn worth of transactions in 2001, double the 1997 level, according to the Loan Market Association. Over 200 loans are currently listed on the London Stock Exchange. In Asia, no figures are available as yet. However, the crisis of late 1997 clearly contributed to the surge in this activity, especially through the 'portfolio clean-outs' undertaken by the large Japanese banks. One of the difficulties peculiar to the Far Eastern markets is that the legal documentation of bank credits often includes clauses giving borrowers the right to refuse to allow loans to be transferred to other creditors. As was the case for credit derivatives, one of the major obstacles to development of the secondary bank loan market was the time needed to draw up complicated legal documents allowing such loan transfers.

This was corrected by forming professional associations to draw up standard contracts. Thus, in late 1995, the main market-makers in the United States grouped together to form the Loan Syndication and Trading Association (LSTA), in charge of homogenizing the documentation for trading bank loans. This association has over a hundred members today. In Europe, the Loan Market Association formed in mid-December 1996 for the same purpose, as expressed in its memorandum of association: 'The LMA is looking to simplify and standardize the sale of performing loan assets through setting up standard settlement and operational procedures, codes of practice, a loan valuation mechanism, documentation and the education of both borrowers and lenders.' By the end of 2004, the LMA counted over 200 members (54 full members, the big banks active in the credit markets, and associated and courtesy members including other banks, fund managers, insurance companies, legal firms, etc.). The impressive growth in mergers and acquisitions at the end of the 1990s helped to establish the secondary loan market firmly in the capital market world. These transactions obliged a small number of banks to set up very large credit lines for a few large borrowers, with an attendant risk of over-concentration and the need for active management. The UK bank Barclays, at the height of the market in 2000, thus had €20 bn exposure in the telecom sector, concentrated on three borrowers (Vodafone, France Telecom–Orange and British Telecom).[14]

### Market prospects

For the observers of the secondary bank loan market, the development of 'jumbo loans'[15] was truly the turning point towards a mature, active market, and convergence between the various credit markets (catalyzed by the development of credit derivatives). There are several reasons for optimism about the secondary loan market.

- By offering an additional means for banks to manage their exposure to credit risk dynamically, it meets a basic need.
- It also contributes to more transparent bank loan pricing in the primary market, as practiced in the bond markets.
- Many investment funds are allocating an increasing amount of their portfolios to syndicated loans, and are placing great emphasis on the liquidity of the assets they acquire, so that they can close out their positions.
- Borrowers are now much more aware of the needs of their lead lending banks and no longer object to the changes of document needed for developing the secondary market (transfer clauses).
- The number of market-makers is increasing, thus improving liquidity. Many banks have set up loan trading departments aimed at the secondary market, to complete their primary activity.

---

[14] See *The Economist* (2000): 'The Bigger They Are'.

[15] France Telecom, for instance, borrowed €30 bn in July 2000 (Barclays, BNP Paribas, Citibank, CSFB, Morgan Stanley and SG were the arrangers). Jumbo loans were also arranged in other sectors, mostly for mergers and acquisitions (acquisition of Seagram by Pernod Ricard, buy-back of BOC by Air Liquide, takeover of Blue Circle by Lafarge, Italenergia, merger of SEITA with Tabacalera, etc.).

Loan trading in the secondary market has increasingly become a useful tool with which banks can manage their credit risk. The major drawback compared to credit derivatives is the absence of confidentiality for transactions. Borrowers know that where a bank no longer holds their risk on its balance sheet, it must inform them under most statutory regulations. That is a point in common with cash securitization transactions (as opposed to synthetic ones).

### Securitization of bank debts

A second technique used by banks to actively manage their loan portfolios is securitization. We shall not go back over this, since it was described in detail in Chapter 4.

### Credit derivatives

As instruments for managing credit risk, credit derivatives have undoubted advantages for banks opting for economic portfolio management policies:

- They are a relatively simple, flexible and economic method of trading credit risk, and thus enable credit portfolios to be adjusted dynamically.
- They avoid the constraints inherent to the underlying credit markets: poor liquidity, risk of having to show a loss if an asset is sold, etc.
- The banks may now take credit positions without having to fund them, since credit derivatives are off-balance-sheet instruments.
- Credit derivatives enable short positions to be taken on credits, a strategy that is often impossible in the underlying markets where no repo possibilities exist.
- Finally, they enable leverage positions that cannot be replicated in the cash markets.

However, the crucial advantage of credit derivatives is the confidential nature of their transactions. Traditional banking activity must juggle credit risk-taking with ongoing commercial relationships. To increase exposure to a counterparty, a bank must lend it more money; and once this decision has been taken, its detachment from the debtor takes place gradually, at the rhythm of repayment installments. Credit derivatives thus offer a confidential (highly prized by banks) way of discreetly jettisoning certain loans without harming the commercial relationship with their best borrowers, who are by definition those to whom they are over-exposed.[16]

This confidential aspect is particularly important in the case of commercial relationships with European borrowers, who fear the total lack of intermediaries in the credit market. Thus, loan trading in the secondary market is less developed in Europe than in the United States.

Credit derivatives upset the traditional applecart of 'risk–commercial relationships'. This is where they will play an increasingly active role in dynamic management of credit risk by banks.

### 7.1.2.3  Examples of Using Credit Derivatives to Optimize the Return on a Customer Relationship.

One of the big problems in portfolio management by a commercial bank is to determine the economic return on a banking relationship.

---

[16] Moreover, credit derivatives could contribute to improved commercial relationships because the decision circuits can be made more efficient. If banks have an *a posteriori* means of hedging over-exposure to a precise risk by using the credit derivatives market, then they have full leeway to offer more credit to their best customers without having to undertake complex financial analyses and convene traditional credit committees, which substantially slow the decision process. This is the strategy used by Deutsche Bank, for instance, with its Loan Exposure Management Group.

## Marginal economic capital

While the ultimate goal of the models for assessing the credit risk on a portfolio is the appropriation of economic capital as a whole, it also enables decisions to be made for individual transactions. Thus the notion of marginal economic capital enables evaluation of the economic return on any new transaction envisaged by the financial institution. To do this, the impact of a new transaction on the bank's portfolio must be measured. The marginal economic capital of a credit, here, is defined as the difference between the amount of economic capital needed before and after inclusion of the credit in the portfolio, over the nominal size of the credit in question.

An analysis in terms of marginal economic capital must intuitively show the effects of concentration (a new credit granted to an entity to which the bank is already heavily exposed should require more capital) and diversification. If the RAROC definition presented earlier is used, the economic return on a new credit transaction can be written:

$$\text{transaction RAROC} = \frac{\text{transaction margin} - \text{provisions}}{\text{marginal economic capital}}$$

To illustrate this notion of marginal economic capital, we shall give an example. First of all, the reference portfolio must be defined, on the basis of which we will be able to make a few numerical applications. The reference portfolio is described in Table 7.1.

After simulation over one year, with an assumed average recovery rate of 50%, this portfolio presents the following characteristics:

- expected loss: 0.610%
- fractile at 99.90%: 6.929%
- economic capital: 6.319%

Let us now measure the impact of including several groups of assets in this reference portfolio. The simulation principle selected was to add 100 new assets to the initial reference portfolio. These new assets were either similar in size to those initially defined (for instance, 1 million euros for entities rated B) – scenario 1; or larger – scenario 2, to reveal concentration patterns. See Table 7.2.

The results for A, Baa and Ba ratings can be explained by the choice of correlation rate assumptions. The concentration effect is lower than the diversification effect because the

**Table 7.1**  Description of the reference portfolio

| Rating | Number of loans in the portfolio | Unitary size (€m) | Portfolio contribution | Correlation rate[a] |
|---|---|---|---|---|
| Aaa | 20 | 20 | 6.46% | 2.30% |
| Aa | 30 | 15 | 7.26% | 2.30% |
| A | 75 | 10 | 12.11% | 4.10% |
| Baa | 325 | 5 | 26.23% | 6.00% |
| Ba | 760 | 3 | 36.80% | 6.50% |
| B | 650 | 1 | 10.49% | 6.70% |
| Caa | 40 | 1 | 0.65% | 7.60% |
| **Total** | **1900** | | **100.00%** | |

[a] Simple correlation assumptions: constant correlation rates between assets of the same rating category, nil correlation rates between the various rating categories.

**Table 7.2** Computations of marginal economic capital

| | Addition of 100 assets rated A | | Addition of 100 assets rated Baa | | Addition of 100 assets rated Ba | | Addition of 100 assets rated B | |
|---|---|---|---|---|---|---|---|---|
| | Scenario 1 | Scenario 2 | Scenario 1 | Scenario 2 | Scenario 1 | Scenario 2 | Scenario 1 | Scenario 2 |
| Unitary size (€M) | 10 | 40 | 5 | 20 | 3 | 12 | 1 | 4 |
| Total size (€M) | 1000 | 4000 | 500 | 2000 | 300 | 1200 | 100 | 400 |
| Expected loss | 0.56% | 0.47% | 0.59% | 0.54% | 0.62% | 0.62% | 0.65% | 0.71% |
| 99.9% fractile | 6.29% | 5.03% | 6.65% | 6.03% | 7.14% | 7.59% | 7.14% | 7.75% |
| Economic capital (€M) | 20.91 | 73.56 | 15.24 | 59.11 | 32.30 | 123.69 | 16.79 | 73.20 |
| **Marginal economic capital** | **2.09%** | **1.84%** | **3.05%** | **2.96%** | **10.77%** | **10.31%** | **16.79%** | **18.30%** |

**Table 7.3**   RAROC and regulatory ROE compared

| Rating | Spread | ROE | RAROC | Theoretical measures | |
|--------|--------|-----|-------|-----------------------|--|
|        |        |     |       | Expected loss | Economic capital |
| Aa | 0.15% | 1.88% | 14.50% | 0.01% | 1.00% |
| A | 0.30% | 3.75% | 13.25% | 0.04% | 2.00% |
| Baa | 0.50% | 6.25% | 13.33% | 0.10% | 3.00% |
| Ba | 2.00% | 25.00% | 14.50% | 0.55% | 10.00% |
| B | 4.50% | 56.25% | 13.75% | 2.30% | 16.00% |

correlation assumption is relatively low for these ratings; for instance, going from €10 m to €40 m for each of the 100 entities rated A introduced in the initial reference portfolio reduces the marginal capital from 2.09% to 1.84%.

On the other hand, for entities rated B (for which the correlation rate selected is relatively high), a concentration effect can be observed: the increased capital allocation (from an average €1 m to €4 m) has a positive impact on the marginal capital (which rises from 16.79% to 18.3%). For entities rated Ba, the two effects more or less cancel each other out.

## RAROC and profitability measurement

It is interesting to note that the marginal regulatory capital (in the framework of the Basel I Accords) is constant for all asset classes. Each exposure is weighted 100%[17] (assuming assets of the corporate credit type), independently of its rating or its marginal contribution to the overall portfolio.

As indicated earlier, one of the purposes of developing credit risk models is to provide a consistent measurement of the profitability of banking institutions' activity. The fact that regulatory return on equity[18] has become one of the most commonly used indicators of bank performance has led to substantial misapprehensions.

First of all, this measurement of ROE does not reflect the real risk (because the return on the transaction is not adjusted by the average risk borne on it by the bank), and secondly, the capital is fixed at the regulatory 8%.

It is true that at aggregated level, there is nothing to refute the overall figure of 8%. However, the fact that it is the same for all banks is an obvious problem. We have seen that economic capital should be determined depending on the target rating chosen by the bank management. For a given portfolio, the amount of capital should therefore be different for an institution like Société Générale (rated Aa3/AA) or for Lehman Brothers (rated A3/A−), since the target fractiles are not the same.

Table 7.3 presents the regulatory (ROE) and economic (RAROC) returns for various ratings, based on simulations presented earlier on economic capital and average market spreads.

It can immediately be observed from the table that the move to 'economic' mode eliminates the distortions due to the uniform calculation of ROE under the Basel I rules. These distortions had harmful consequences for some commercial banks, which thus committed themselves to rating classes offering the highest ROEs (leveraged loans, high-yield bonds, project finance)

---

[17] Which means that the regulatory capital to be set aside will be 100% × 8% × nominal amount of the exposure.

[18] Expressed as the annual profitability of an individual transaction divided by the amount of regulatory capital to be set aside by the financial institution.

or offloaded creditworthy assets (with low ROE), via securitization transactions. However, to some extent, this pattern was regulated by the rating agencies that lowered the ratings of these banks, and therefore the conditions at which they could get funding in the markets deteriorated.

## Application of credit derivatives to optimization of customer ROE

The operation of a commercial bank is relatively simple. While its primary function is lending, most of its income comes from side business. Thus, if a bank opens a line of credit for a customer, it hopes in exchange to have more lucrative business with that customer on the side.

Let us take the example of Société Générale and France Telecom SA (rated Baa2/BBB+ by the rating agencies). Let us suppose that Société Générale lends €100 m to France Telecom, at a spread of 35 basis points. Let us suppose that the economic capital for this type of credit is 3% (in line with the foregoing estimations). The RAROC on the individual credit transaction is mediocre: 8.33%, that is [(0.35% − 0.1%)/3%], but Société Générale also hopes to gain from its relationship with France Telecom additional business, thus providing it with higher returns (interest rate or currency derivatives, advisory, asset management, etc.).

Let us assume that these side activities enable the bank to generate an additional margin of 50 basis points. The RAROC of the overall relationship with France Telecom is then 25%, that is [(0.35% + 0.5% − 0.1%)/3%].

The purchase of a CDS on France Telecom could allow the Société Générale portfolio manager to free up the capital set aside for the loan. Even if the cost of this hedge is higher than the loan spread (55 basis points for France Telecom's BBB-type risk), it will still be profitable overall, as shown in Table 7.4 (only half of the loan is hedged in this example).

This optimization can be taken a step further, by analyzing the effect of a portfolio diversification transaction conducted at the same time as a hedge transaction.

Credit derivatives also enable the portfolio manager to introduce new risks into the bank's portfolio. Let us go back to our example and suppose that Société Générale has substantial exposure to France Telecom SA. Initially, lending money to France Telecom is the same as including a BBB-rated asset in the portfolio. It is weighted $100 (i.e. 20 times the average weighting of BBB-rated assets in the typical portfolio). If the marginal economic capital needed for this entity is calculated, it comes to 5.5%. Secondly, let us suppose that the Société Générale portfolio manager has the opportunity to hedge this asset completely and replace it by 20 BBB-rated

**Table 7.4**  Economic benefits of an individual hedging transaction using a CDS

|  | Before hedging | After hedging |
| --- | --- | --- |
| Net loan margin (*including CDS cost*) | 0.350% | 0.075% |
| Expected loss for a BBB borrower | 0.100% | 0.050% |
| Economic capital | 3.000% | 1.500% |
| **RAROC** | **8.333%** | **1.667%** |
| Additional income | 0.500% | 0.500% |
| **Global RAROC** | **25.000%** | **35.000%** |
| CDS cost |  | 0.550% |

assets each with a weighting of \$5. The marginal economic capital for these 20 assets is 3.1%.

This example highlights the diversification effect perfectly. The cost of the transaction is low or nil (the extra cost of hedging the France Telecom loan can be offset by the spread of the 20 new assets brought into the portfolio), the expected loss has not changed, but the marginal economic capital has been reduced.

This portfolio management transaction can also be imagined via a one-for-one trade. Société Générale could, for instance, buy a CDS from SCH (a Spanish bank) to hedge part of its exposure on France Telecom SA, and in exchange, sell a CDS on Repsol (a Spanish oil company to which SCH is heavily exposed) to SCH. This transaction is an arbitrage of the utility functions of Société Générale and SCH.

In fact, although the banks' portfolio management departments have understood the need for portfolio hedging which is their core business, they are still reluctant to diversify, the corollary of which is to take new credit risk into the bank's risk portfolio. One example of this is the Portfolio Management department of JP Morgan, a pioneer in this field and probably one of the most active banks in this market), which bought protection on its portfolio at the end of 2003, in the form of credit derivatives in a total notional amount of \$37 349 bn (of which \$2.2 bn in the form of CDOs), but sold protection in diversification for only \$67 m![19]

Is it likely that there will be radical changes in the traditional business of banking with the emergence of a new approach to balance sheet-driven management and risk pricing, and the increasing availability of new management tools and techniques? We shall attempt to answer this question in the next section.

### 7.1.3   Overview of the Banks of the Twenty-First Century: the Effect of Credit Derivatives on Banks' Strategy, Organization and Culture

We think that the rapid development of the new credit risk management techniques, credit derivatives, loan trading in the secondary market, securitization and the far-reaching trends affecting the competitive environment of the banks are likely to put an end to their traditional role of funding intermediation.

This analysis supposes that financial institutions are capable of adapting to the new conditions in the credit markets, and that this change is effected on three fronts: banking strategy, organization and culture. We shall sketch the profile of the banking institutions that will be in competition in tomorrow's credit markets, although to a large extent this is already the case for many of the leading players in the credit markets (JP Morgan, Deutsche Bank, Barclays Capital, UBS, etc.).

#### 7.1.3.1   Strategy

The traditional paradigm in the credit markets[20] is thus: the banks are in relation with borrowers and lend them cash in the form of loans. Traditionally, as mentioned before, these assets, lacking liquidity, had to be kept on the banks' balance sheets, thus requiring substantial capital to be put aside, and were underpriced. This was because for most banks, credit was strategically

---

[19] *Source*: JP Morgan, annual report 2003.
[20] The analysis that follows is mainly focused on the wholesale credit business, as opposed to the loans to retail customers or SMEs.

treated as a loss leader, as demonstrated earlier, and the return on this commercial relationship came from other services and transactions (relationship banking).

However, the new competitive environment in which the banks work, and the new credit risk management techniques highlighted the fact that the banks, which are at the source of this risk because they cultivate the commercial relationship, were not the ideal institutions for holding risk.

Thus, in 1998, JP Morgan announced that it was studying the possibility of selling its entire loan portfolio and no longer keeping any exposure to the credit risk arising from its syndicated loans business, in a bid to improve its ROE, despite the fact that it was well known for the quality of its relationships with large corporations. In 1997, 50% of its capital was allocated to the bank loan portfolio – some $6 bn. Because the rating agencies had indicated that the deteriorated creditworthiness of this portfolio could lead to its rating being cut, it transferred exposures and bought massive amounts of protection. Thus, between 1997 and 1999, the amount of capital set against loans was halved, not least because of transactions like the BISTRO[21] program or the use of CDSs for the larger concentrations. At the end of this program in 1999, JP Morgan was able to buy back shares in the amount of $3 bn, with the agreement of the rating agencies.

This active management strategy is, of course, implemented chiefly for loan portfolios. However, it also applies to exposures to counterparty risk on derivatives. Here, several models can be identified, depending on how sophisticated the institution is:

- The banks' historic model did not allow the counterparty risk inherent in derivatives trans-actions to be unbundled. The risk was then managed using the traditional credit limits set by risk management departments for each counterparty, or by reserve mechanisms.
- The leading banks in this field wished to move away from this static model and systematically price the counterparty risk inherent in their derivatives transactions. In these models, it was systematically calculated for every new transaction. It was then traded differently depending on how sophisticated the institution was:
  - The simplest model was to enter a provision in the trader's profit and loss account, which was marked-to-market and enabled possible losses due to counterparty default to be hedged.
  - A more sophisticated model transferred the amount of this provision into a special reserve, either at the level of the division in question (decentralized model) or at the level of the bank (centralized model, whatever the underlying asset traded). An active management function for this reserve was then created, with its own profitability targets and means of action.

To return to the example of JP Morgan in late 2003, 40% of the protection bought in no-tional amount (i.e. $14.89 bn out of $37.35) were hedges for exposure to counterparty risk on derivatives contracts.

By using this strategy, the commercial banks are thus denying their traditional role as lenders-investors, and are becoming 'risk intermediaries', closer to the role of merchant banks in the bond markets, for example. For these banks, a transaction no longer necessarily implies that they retain the risk in their books. This new strategic option has several major consequences:

- First, it results in progressive polarization of credit business into three key functions: orig-inating, structuring and transformation of risk, and its distribution to investors.

---

[21] See Chapter 4.

- Second, it prefigures the necessary specialization of institutions that cannot compete on all three fronts.
- Finally, it will lead to financial institutions considering credit as a single financial product.

Today, the credit markets have three arms:

- Origination. Unlike the traditional environment of the credit markets, sourcing of credit risk requires neither balance sheet size, nor commercial relationships, since the exposures can be 'acquired' by the intermediary on a liquid secondary market, or in the form of structured securities (CBOs/CLOs), or in the synthetic form of a credit derivative. This has far-reaching implications, not least for all the banks with a developed network for underwriting of credit risk. Thus, as shown by the Fitch Ratings survey on the credit derivatives market in 2003, most regional banks in Europe (especially the German Landesbanken) and Asia are net protection sellers.
- Risk structuring and transformation. This key skill is needed by most of the big banks inasfar as the added value in the credit business lies increasingly in the technical capacity to alter the payout and risk profile of assets so as to provide an optimum response to investors' demands by creating bespoke products.
- Distribution. Bespoke structured credit products are easier to place than one-size-fits-all bonds. For other exposures, resulting from imperfect supply–demand adequation, the banks will need to use the range of credit risk management tools that we have described above.

On the new credit markets, the winning strategy is to have an adequate range of competencies and play a pro-active role throughout the credit value chain, from origination to structuring and then distribution.

The institutions the most likely to succeed in this new environment are those that acknowledge that the added value in the credit business is gradually moving from underwriting to distribution: it is, so to speak, the 'just in time' revolution in credit, to take an expression from the automobile industry. The investor orders his finished product, the financial institution 'underwrites' the raw material – the credit risk – either itself or by buying it in the secondary market in a more or less structured form, alters the risk/return characteristics (this stage can be subcontracted to specialized entities such as risk managers), and distributes the finished product to its customer.[22] The customer is optimally satisfied, and a minimum amount of balance sheet, and therefore of capital, has been used.

This has vast implications for banking institutions: very few (except the bulge-bracket) can compete and generate value on all credit businesses. The traditional commercial banks, with strong regional presence and little activity in the financial markets, will concentrate on originating risk while maintaining close relationship banking with borrowers, and provide credit facilities and manage their balance sheets dynamically, using the range of techniques presented earlier. The large 'universal' banks should gradually move away from origination and concentrate on structuring and distributing credit products. Some merchant banks, without a significant sales force, will specialize in market making for these instruments and will act as risk managers, serving as counterparties to the institutions structuring the finished credit products. Finally, the final holders of the credit risk will be the institutional investors, hedge funds, insurance companies specialized in this type of risk, and ultimately retail investors.

---

[22] The sale of credit products is becoming more and more like that of equity products: the credit investors buy 'stories' backed by high-quality internal research, just as equity investors do.

The second key success factor in the new credit markets is to acknowledge that credit, of whatever form (loan, bond) is a market instrument. JP Morgan was the first bank, in 1998, to group all its credit business into a single front-office, including arrangement and syndication of bank loans.[23] This strategy has been copied since then by almost all the big investment banks, with Goldman Sachs going a step further in 2004 and integrating its equity and credit businesses.

The banks have, of course, found it difficult to take account of these new demands in their organization, insofar as historically, commercial and merchant banking have always been separate.

### 7.1.3.2   Organization

The banks in the new credit markets are now facing three organizational problems.

The first is to set up a system of comprehensive reporting that enables them to identify and manage all the credit risks they run at any time in all bank activities,[24] similar to that practiced for market risks. The information relating to these risks must be transmitted to a central credit risk management unit that is responsible for the institution's portfolio of exposures, which aggregates the individual counterparty risks in each portfolio for each debtor and uses internal models (similar to those described earlier) to optimize the return on capital of the institution. It is this unit that then transfers to the various product lines (credit derivatives, trading of loans and bonds in the secondary and primary markets, securitization, etc.) the job of hedging certain exposures or diversifying the bank's overall portfolio. The challenge is therefore to build effective links between the various units trading credit (especially between commercial and merchant banks) and not consider them as autonomous.

The new theoretical model of bank organization was aptly described by Oliver, Wyman & Co. and Morgan Stanley in their study. See Figure 7.5. It is also this centralized department for credit risk management that enables banks to set up a system for pricing credit lines per individual obligor, which applies to each activity, in relation to the composition of the bank's portfolio. The bank can then manage its overall return on capital with a given customer, fixing the priority of each transaction opportunity depending on its anticipated return and usage of capital (reflecting the risk of the transaction). It is the latter measurement that also enables the bank to set limits to its economic commitments, and they are no longer arbitrarily determined by volumes of outstanding loans.

The second question is the place of credit derivatives in the financial institutions' organization: should it be an independent business, or integrated into the banks' derivatives departments? Should it be linked to primary activities and syndication?

It seems to us that the trap to avoid at all costs is that each product line trading credit in the bank has its own system for trading credit derivatives and manages its credit portfolio individually, because this type of organization would not enable the risk/return profile to be optimized at the level of the institution.

There should be a single credit derivative product line in the institution, but it must be able to manage all internal requests for hedging and diversification. Therefore links must be built with those departments likely to need such services, in association with the independent risk management functions of the bank.

---

[23] See Hylson-Smith (1998).

[24] This system obviously includes the activities in the bond markets and bank loans, as well as all the activities in OTC derivatives (swaps, interest rate, currency, equity and commodity option buying, etc.) for which counterparty risk is borne by the bank.

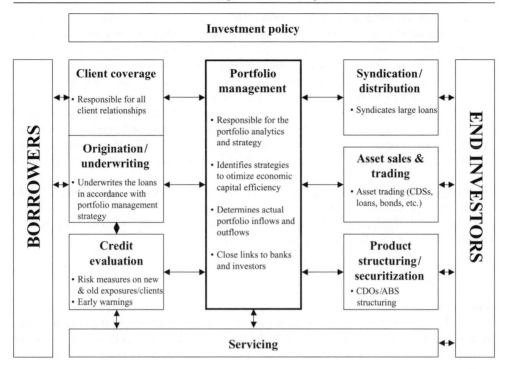

**Figure 7.5**   Banks' organizational model: the role of portfolio management
*Sources:* Oliver, Wyman & Co., Morgan Stanley (2002). Reproduced by permission of Mercer Oliver Wyman.

Furthermore, the organization the institution chooses will depend on its strategic goals in the credit derivatives market. If its goal is to use these instruments not just as tools for managing internal risk, but also as investment and hedging products to offer their customers, then it seems legitimate to us that these activities be in close association with the departments that deal in underlying assets in the institution, that is, those trading bonds and loans in the secondary market, thus enabling a better overview of flows and identification of arbitrage opportunities among the various credit markets. It is this model that has been set up by most of the large players in the market.

Whatever the organization chosen, it is important to note that it should not jeopardize the 'Chinese walls' systems designed to guarantee that no one department of a bank can 'insider trade' on the information from another. This is the concern closest to the heart of the regulatory authorities and its purpose is to ensure market transparency and promote trust between the players as to the fairness of the information available to them. This is a recurrent problem in the financial institutions, which must centralize risk management while at the same time ensuring that no confidential information escapes from behind these Chinese walls. It is particularly evident in the relationship between a bank's capital market activities and its investment banking activities.

Here, too, we see the current debate on side business and loss leader products raising its head again, since they imply that a bank is ready to undertake unprofitable transactions to promote other, more lucrative ones with the same customers. Although this behavior can be analyzed and justified on commercial grounds, as evinced above, the press have in the past few months highlighted a number of excesses, accusing some banks of dumping. As far as credit derivatives are concerned, we must insure that market traders do not have access to non-public information (for instance, where a bank's advisory teams have received instructions to restructure a firm's debt, or where its underwriters are working at setting up a sizeable credit line that could have an impact on the firm's rating) and use it to take positions in the market.[25]

Finally, the last comment on organization concerns the banks' policy for remunerating their traders. In the RAROC world, the remuneration systems should depend not just on the growth of income or profits generated by the individual trader or his department, but should reflect the return on the activity more exactly (level of risk borne, and corresponding capital usage).

This type of initiative on the part of bank managements could change an institution's 'credit culture'. It supposes first of all that front-offices are recognized as important in the organization of a single center for trading the institution's credit risk, and secondly, that a decision-making system based on the RAROC of each credit transaction is set up.

### 7.1.3.3   Culture

With the arrival of credit derivatives, the banks found themselves confronted with an even more radical phenomenon that for most of them put the last nail in the coffin of their credit culture by moving credit risk management, hitherto the specialty of the commercial banks, over to the portfolio managers and the technicians of the front-offices structuring and trading these new instruments.

This gradual transformation resulted in enhancement of the transactional and quantitative aspects of the banking business, to the detriment of its traditional qualitative, relational and commercial role. As Rod Ballek, in charge of managing Citibank's loan portfolio, pointed out: 'Relationship management was the legacy of 183 years of business at Citibank.'[26]

It was the gradual integration of credit trading and active management of exposures arising from the classic loan business into banks' functions that, little by little, put an end to two centuries of tradition.

For the moment, credit derivatives have not yet rendered traditional banking business obsolete. It can be expected that there will initially be increased complementarity between the various functions in banking, to optimize credit and balance sheet risk management.

Most bankers still define their jobs as relationship banking, in which the purpose is to create a climate of trust with the customer and understand and meet his needs as well as possible. Furthermore, given the gradual changes in mentality and practice happening before our eyes, it should not be forgotten that good sense and intuition are still sometimes the banker's greatest assets, not least in a market notorious for its inefficiency. As Moody's Investor Service analysts point out: 'First and foremost, we believe that credit risk models and the reliance on credit derivatives can be very effective risk management tools but that they will not replace sound human judgment. Prudent lending practices and the banker's own experience and intuition will continue to be very important ingredients. Banking in general and lending money in particular will remain very much a people's business rather than a model-driven decision.'[27]

---

[25] This remark in fact applies to most market activities, in particular in the equity markets, and not just credit derivatives.
[26] Quoted by Edwards (1995).
[27] Theodore and Madelain (1997).

Credit derivatives are at the heart of the current changes in banking business. Financial institutions are increasingly obliged to adopt a pro-active credit risk management policy, pressured by a fierce competitive climate. To do this, they are equipped with new techniques: trading of bank loans in the secondary markets, securitization and, of course, credit derivatives. The latter have shown themselves to be the most effective and profitable of the above for the banks, inasfar as, among others, they enable transactions and underlying names to remain confidential.

The growing use of these new management techniques has led banks to redefine their role in the financial markets in general, and the credit markets in particular. Their traditional role as intermediaries and risk holders is no longer sufficient; now they must define a new strategic position somewhere along the credit value chain.

The development of the credit derivatives market and its further implications for the capital markets will be presented in the next section.

## 7.2  CREDIT DERIVATIVES AND FINANCIAL REGULATIONS

This section is more particularly concerned with the impact of credit derivative development on the regulation of banking activities and the capital markets. We shall therefore first look at the new capital adequacy standards for banking institutions (Basel II). Credit derivatives were one of the major innovations in the last decade leading the supervisory authorities to review the initial, now obsolete, framework of the Basel I Accords.[28] Paradoxically, these new rules, to be implemented by 2007, should have major implications for the credit derivative and structured credit market, especially as regards the type of risk transfer transactions used by the banks.

We shall then look at the media debate on the role of credit derivatives in financial instability and their risk for users. Are they really weapons of mass destruction, as Warren Buffett would have us believe? Or are they, on the contrary, an innovation enabling better distribution of credit risk, thus contributing to avoidance of a major financial crisis?

The third part of this section will present a more contrasted reality: like all innovations, credit derivatives reveal new risks that will need better management and control.

### 7.2.1  Credit Derivatives and the New Basel II Regulations

The emergence of an active market in credit derivatives and structured credit in 1996–1997 was one of the main causes of a revision of the regulatory framework of banking activities provided by the Basel I Accords in 1988. There were two main reasons, in fact:

1. By leading the various market traders to consider the real economic value of credit risk and forcing them to price credit risk rationally, credit derivatives revealed the distortions and inconsistencies of the Basel I Accords.
2. As seen earlier, they were the preferred instruments chosen by the banks to conduct regulatory arbitrage strategies, especially via synthetic securitization transactions.

Regulatory arbitrage can be defined as a process by which a financial institution seeks to reduce its regulatory capital requirements without reducing the level of risk on its activities (or the reverse). All securitization transactions on banks' high-quality underlying credit portfolios (in

---

[28] See Chapter 1 for the Basel I regulations and their limits.

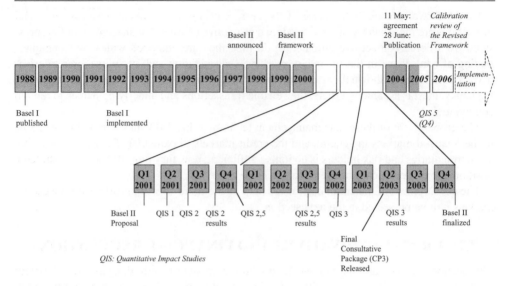

**Figure 7.6**  Basel II implementation timeline
*Sources:* Mercer, Oliver & Wyman, *Les Echos*, authors' analysis.

which the sponsor retained the first loss risk) were considered by the supervisory authorities to be part of this widespread movement towards regulatory arbitrage, and were deplored by the consultancy documents preparing for the reform of the Basel I Accord on capital adequacy: 'Securitization activities are usually motivated mostly by regulatory arbitrage needs',[29] or again: 'In the absence of new regulations, the Basel I Accords remain vulnerable to regulatory arbitrage'.[30]

Later in this section we shall present the framework and principles of the new Basel II Accords, the new rules governing measurement of capital adequacy for credit risk and the implications of these changes for the credit derivatives market, particularly for CDOs.

### 7.2.1.1  Context and Principles of the Basel II Accords on Capital Adequacy

On 11 May 2004, the Basel Committee officially announced it had reached a consensus on the pending issues that had blocked completion of the new agreement on the future prudential rules. The final document was published on 28 June 2004 and should enter into force as of 2006, it being understood that the big international banks should have another year to comply with all the details.

### Five years of revision

The press release of 11 May 2004 set the seal on a revision process that had begun in 1998–1999 with the announcement that the regulations were to be revised and the publication of the first consultation document. Figure 7.6 shows the main stages in this process.

---

[29] Basel Committee, document for consultation, 1999.
[30] Basel Committee, working document on securitization, 2002.

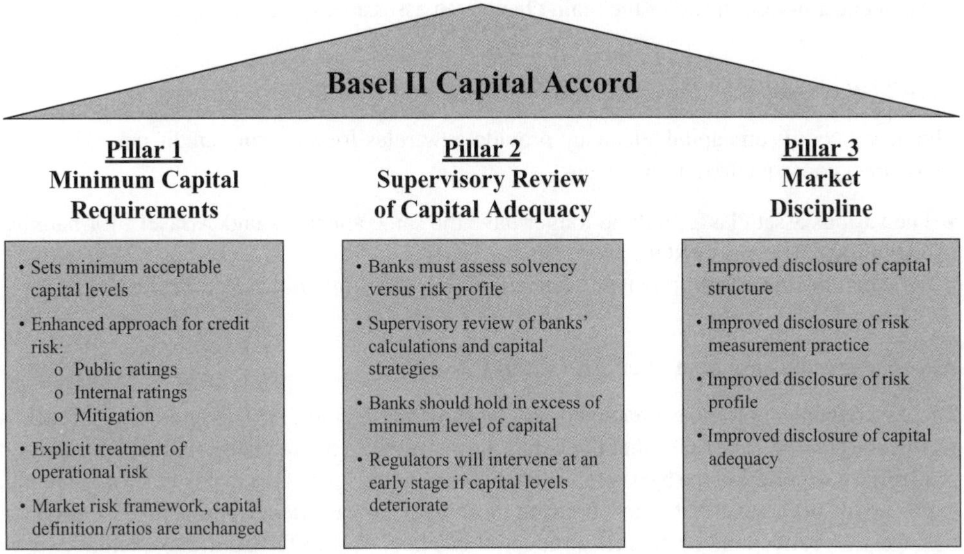

**Figure 7.7**    Framework of the Basel II Accord
*Sources*: Mercer, Oliver & Wyman. Reproduced by permission of Mercer Oliver Wyman.

### The scope of the new agreement

This new Accord on capital adequacy does not apply to all banking institutions equally. Thus, while all EU banks, asset managers and insurance companies should be subject to it[31] because the rules will be transposed into the European Capital Adequacy Directive, American banks will not be obliged to comply. Only US banks with total balance sheet in excess of $250 bn or with over $10 bn worth of international assets will be obliged to comply with Basel II. The large banks are therefore clearly at an advantage compared to their competitors, supposing that the new standards effectively enable capital requirements to be optimized. Some 10 of them should be bound by the Accords, including the 'majors' (JP Morgan, Citigroup, Bank of America, Wachovia, Wells Fargo and Washington Mutual), while 10 others are likely to opt voluntarily to comply.

### The main lines of Basel II

The principles governing Basel II do not differ fundamentally from those of Basel I, even though the new agreement is much more complete, covering three complementary 'pillars' and taking account of credit risk as well as market and operational risk.

Figure 7.7 presents the overall framework of the new Basel II Accords.

Pillar I, which is what concerns us here, shows that most of the new measures concern measurement of credit risk, to which we shall return later, and explicit taking account of operational risk in calculating the total of risks weighted by the McDonough ratio.[32] The methods for calculating this ratio and its new target (8%), the definition of capital (numerator) and of assessing market risk do not change.

---

[31] Inasfar as it is provided that the new standards will concern all financial institutions receiving deposits.

[32] The former Cooke ratio is now called the McDonough ratio after the Chairman of the Basel Committee at the time.

The next sub-section shows the main changes in assessment of credit risk.

### 7.2.1.2   Presentation of the New Rules for Assessing Credit Risk

The new Accords on capital adequacy provide new rules for assessing credit risk. They will have direct consequences in two ways:

- The various asset classes will no longer have the same appeal as under Basel I for banking institutions, in terms of ROE.
- Financial institutions will be led to adapt their business mix to these new rules.

**Approaches to assessment of credit risk in Basel II**

The new document provides three methods, as shown in Figure 7.8. The standard approach is identical to that of Basel I, in that the banks are required to divide their credit exposures into prudential categories on the basis of the apparent characteristics of the exposures (for example, exposure to corporate credit or to a housing mortgage). However, the approach sets forth fixed risk weights corresponding to each prudential category that differ from those laid down by Basel I.

Table 7.5 shows the weightings proposed by Basel II, using Standard & Poor's rating scale. For banks, the Committee offers two options. In the first, the banks' weightings are one category under sovereign risk with a ceiling at 100% (except where the weighting is over 100%). In the second, it proposes individual assessment of each bank, independently of its country of origin.

For the more sophisticated approaches (simple and complex), based on internal ratings, the Basel II Accord consecrates the banks' internal risk management systems by letting them determine the key parameters for assessing credit risk. However, they cannot determine all the data needed to calculate capital requirements themselves. That is why the risk weighting and,

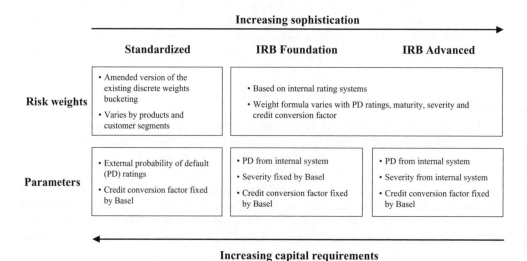

**Figure 7.8**   The three approaches to credit risk under Pillar 1
*Sources*: Mercer, Oliver & Wyman. Reproduced by permission of Mercer Oliver Wyman.

**Table 7.5**   New risk weightings in the Basel II standardized approach

|                    | AAA to AA− | A+ to A− | BBB+ to BBB− | BB+ to B− | < B− | Non rated |
|--------------------|------------|----------|--------------|-----------|-------|-----------|
| Sovereign          | 0%         | 20%      | 50%          | 100%      | 150%  | 100%      |
| Banks – Option 1   | 20%        | 50%      | 100%         | 100%      | 150%  | 100%      |
| Banks – Option 2   | 20%        | 50%      | 50%          | 100%      | 150%  | 50%       |
| Corporates         | 20%        | 50%      | 100%         | 100%      | 150%  | 100%      |
| Securitized assets | 20%        | 50%      | 50%          | 150%      | 1200% | 1200%     |

of course, the capital requirements are obtained by combining the quantitative data supplied by the banks and the formulae laid down by the Committee.

The Basel II framework is clearly an improvement as regards credit risk measurement by the tutelary authorities. However, some remarks about its implementation are needed:

• Under the rating agencies' criteria, a rating expresses the equivalent default risk, whatever the nature of the issuer; yet this does not appear when the weightings applied to sovereign borrowers are compared to those of banks or corporates of the same rating.
• The threshold effect – less considerable for banks than for corporates – not least between AA− and A+ (20% to 100%) strongly favors the rating agencies' judgment, which is sometimes based on the consensus of analysts rather than on purely quantitative data.

The changes will have considerable impact on banks.

### Effect of the new Basel II rules on measurement of risk-weighted assets

In the framework of the Basel I Accords, capital adequacy requirements based on risk-weighted assets were relatively uniform, whatever the asset class. With the new rules, certain types of activity will be penalized and other lines of business will be more attractive for banks.

Among the lines of business that will be granted lighter capital charges are:

• Credit to large corporates.
• Mortgage loans.
• Retail loans.
• Leasing.

However, other lines of business should be penalized more, such as project finance, loans to small and medium-sized enterprises or sovereign loans.

Figure 7.9 gives results based on a simulation by Mercer, Oliver & Wyman for various asset classes depending on the method considered.

Finally, these new rules should also have an impact on the various categories of financial institution.

### Impact of the new Basel II rules on the various types of financial institution

One of the main purposes of the Basel I Accords was to introduce a level playing field between banks, to avoid unfair competition in a context of rapid globalization. It cannot be said for certain that the new Basel II Accords will achieve this goal. This is because there clearly

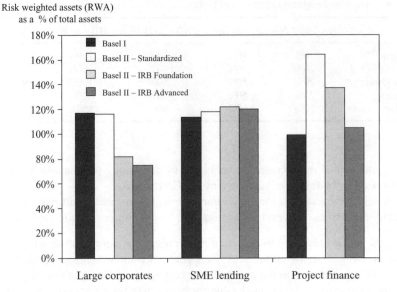

Risk weighted assets (RWA)
as a % of total assets

**Figure 7.9**   Average expected risk-weighted assets per product type
*Sources*: Mercer, Oliver & Wyman. Reproduced by permission of Mercer Oliver Wyman.

appears to be a premium on sophistication, and the large banks, with resources and skills for investment and development of highly performing risk measurement systems, will be favored and can opt for methods based on internal rating. This characteristic of the Basel II Accords was thus recently criticized by the American banking regulatory bodies such as the FDIC and the OCC.[33]

However, alongside that general remark, it is likely that the adoption of these new rules will lead to substantial changes for the capital markets, such as:

- The impossibility for European bank–insurance groups to benefit from the difference between the banking regulations and the insurance regulations on current capital adequacy standards applying to credit risk.
- The expected deterioration in ROE for asset management activities in Europe, which for the moment demand little in terms of capital adequacy for the banking groups.
- The reduction in capital adequacy requirements for financial institutions specialized in mortgage loans and consumer credit, which could become preferred acquisition targets for the large financial conglomerates.
- The question of Basel II Accords implementation for banks in emerging economies (since their assets are by definition riskier than those of the Basel Committee member countries, they could be unjustly penalized in terms of capital adequacy requirements). Already, several large emerging economies have decided not to comply with the suggested implementation calendar (including China).

---

[33] See Barré and Madelaine (2004).

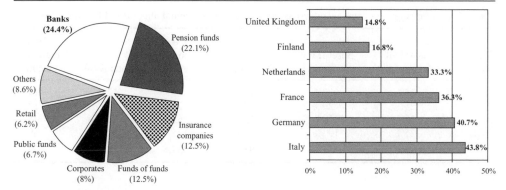

**Figure 7.10**   Role of banks in venture capital in Europe
*Sources*: European Venture Capital Association, *Les Echos*.

Even if their entry into force is likely to bring substantial benefits for European banking institutions,[34] there has been criticism of their forthcoming implementation. Chief among these is that the new standards may strengthen the pro-cyclical nature of credit, by requiring less capital in periods of 'economic abundance' and more capital when the assets on banks' balance sheets deteriorate.

The second criticism concerns the treatment of small and medium-sized enterprises. The banks have traditionally funded this sector, the breathing heart of the economy and employment. This is particularly true of Germany, where the Mittelstand enterprises are very dependent on bank loans. However, by introducing stricter capital adequacy requirements for this category of borrowers, the Basel II Accords could potentially dry up this source of finance. Already, many German banks, especially the three large commercial banks (Deutsche Bank, Dresdner Bank and Commerzbank), have been subjected to a barrage of criticism at their reluctance to fund the national economy.

Another field of activity potentially affected by the implementation of Basel II is venture capital. In Europe, it is the banks that are the main source of funding for this activity, through their private equity business. Figure 7.10 shows their importance in this funding.

Finally, the new rules will be applied subject to a certain degree of interpretation by the national supervisory authorities. Here again, the reform is not necessarily conducive to the creation of uniform rules of competition for all banks.

Apart from these implications, the new regulatory framework of the Basel II Accords should bring substantial changes for banks in the way they use credit derivatives and CDOs to manage their capital.

### 7.2.1.3   Effect on the Credit Derivatives and CDO markets

In the working documents leading up to the new prudential regulations (Basel II), the Basel Committee clearly identified the regulatory problems associated with synthetic securitizations. The concern of the regulatory authorities is now clearly to limit regulatory arbitrages by encouraging real transfer of risk.

---

[34] See Pinson (2004).

**Table 7.6**    Computation of risk-weighted assets and regulatory capital under Basel II rules

| Rating class | As a % of total portfolio | Basel II risk weighting | RWA drawn (€m) | RWA undrawn (€m) | Total RWA | Total regulatory capital |
|---|---|---|---|---|---|---|
| AAA | 25% | 20% | 100 | 25 | 125 | 14 |
| AA | 25% | 20% | 100 | 25 | 125 | 14 |
| A | 25% | 50% | 250 | 62.5 | 312.5 | 35 |
| BBB | 25% | 100% | 500 | 125 | 625 | 69 |
| | **100%** | | **950** | **237.5** | **1187.5** | **132** |

Thus, the new risk weighting system should contribute to reducing the capital needed against investment grade exposures (from 8% today to 2–3%), which will change the scene for regulatory arbitrage transactions using credit derivatives. As a result, most synthetic CDO transactions carried out by banks on investment grade portfolios will no longer be worthwhile under Basel II.

## Example

To illustrate this, let us return to the fictitious example from Section 4.2.3, which is a synthetic balance sheet-driven CDO transaction, in fact, serving as a regulatory arbitrage transaction.

To calculate the new capital adequacy requirement on the reference portfolio in question, we have assumed the following distribution per rating (by definition, these are investment grade ratings):

- AAA: 25%
- AA: 25%
- A: 25%
- BBB: 25%

More simply, we shall assume that the two-thirds drawing rate is uniformly spread over the various ratings. Finally, we suppose that the seller bank is complying with the standardized method under Basel II.

Thus, it is possible to determine the new capital requirements applying to the reference portfolio, as shown in Table 7.6.

The amount of initial regulatory capital tied up by the portfolio is thus only €132 m, as against €278 m under the Basel I rules. With the new rules, the risk-weighted assets and regulatory capital savings for the bank under Basel II are now respectively only.[35]:

- €377.5 m in risk-weighted assets (1187.5 − 810);
- €42 m in regulatory capital (132 − 90).

If the same approach is taken in judging whether it is worthwhile for the sponsor bank to undertake the transaction, then the capital savings are multiplied by the target ROE for the bank (say, 15% before tax), which theoretically corresponds to the minimum rate of return that will be generated by the capital freed up by the transaction:

$$€42m \times 15\% = €6.3m$$

---

[35] Provided the super senior swap counterparty is rated AAA or AA.

In this example, the cost of the transaction (€8.1 m per year) is higher than the target amount shown above, and so the sponsor bank has no interest in undertaking it.

This simplified example shows that the new Basel II Accords do manage to discourage regulatory arbitrage transactions effectively. This new situation is likely to have significant repercussions on the synthetic securitization market.

### Effects of Basel II on the balance sheet-driven CDO market

The framework of Basel II should bring significant changes to the synthetic balance sheet-driven CDO business. Already, the volume and format of synthetic balance sheet-driven CDOs have changed markedly over the past few years, anticipating the new challenges.

Thus, in its report for the second half of 2001 on the CDO market, Moody's underlined the significant slowing in business:

- First, most of the banks likely to benefit from this type of transaction had already traded a significant part of their balance sheets.
- Second, many banks no longer wished to use this type of transaction because Basel II was imminent.

When examined, the transactions carried out before the report were ineffective overall, viewed in the light of the new regulatory framework, essentially because of the marginal share of subordinated risk transferred to the investors. To illustrate this, we can analyze the synthetic balance sheet-driven CDO transactions used by French banks, taking account of the latest Basel II working documents.

We used the internal ratings based (IRB) approach to determine the amount of capital required for each reference portfolio ($K_{IRB}$) under Basel II. The following hypotheses were used for each rating, and are presented in Table 7.7.

As under Basel I, the banks were obliged to deduct from their capital all the subordinated tranches they kept. Thus, a synthetic CDO transaction was only worthwhile if the amount of these tranches was substantially smaller than the capital required against the reference portfolio (denoted $K_{IRB}$), under the Basel II regulations.

To simulate the capital adequacy requirements of Basel II for the reference portfolios in the following example, we have made a number of assumptions as to the percentage of entities not publicly rated. The rating agencies introduce a bias because they rate conservatively the

**Table 7.7**  Capital requirements for each rating category

| Rating | $K_{IRB}$ |
|--------|-----------|
| A+     | 0.4%      |
| A      | 0.6%      |
| A−     | 1.3%      |
| BBB+   | 2.2%      |
| BBB    | 3.3%      |
| BBB−   | 5.8%      |
| BB+    | 9.2%      |
| BB     | 13.2%     |
| BB−    | 18.9%     |

**Table 7.8**     Synthetic CDO-driven regulatory arbitrage opportunities under Basel II

| Transaction | Sponsor bank | Average rating | % of public ratings (estimate) | Adjusted average ratings | Equity tranche retained | Indicative $K_{IRB}$ |
|---|---|---|---|---|---|---|
| Igloo | Natexis | Baa1 | 50% | A3/Baa1 | 1.70% | 1.70% |
| OLAN I | BNP Paribas | A3 | 80% | A3 | 1.71% | 1.30% |
| OLAN II | BNP Paribas | Baa1 | 50% | A3/Baa1 | 1.90% | 1.70% |
| Euro Liberté | BNP Paribas | Baa3/Ba1 | 0% | Baa3 | 4.30% | 5.80% |
| Sirius | Crédit Lyonnais | Baa2 | 20% | Baa1 | 2.25% | 2.20% |
| CHLOE I | CAI | Baa1 | 50% | A3/Baa1 | 2.00% | 1.70% |
| CHLOE II | CAI | Baa1 | 85% | Baa1 | 2.50% | 2.20% |

entities only internally rated by the sponsor banks. We have attempted to correct this bias to determine the average rating as it would be calculated if only taking account of the IRB (in the Basel II IRB method). See Table 7.8.

As can be observed, in most of the transactions under review, the equity tranche kept by the bank is near or superior to the capital amount that would be required under Basel II regulations. In practice, this means that the capital savings would be very small, or even nil, for the sponsor banks and therefore, there would be no opportunity for regulatory arbitrage.

The only transaction that might be worthwhile would be the BNP Paribas Euro Liberté CDO, the reference portfolio of which comprises middle-market loans, provided that the sponsor bank managed to sell the BB-rated mezzanine tranches that are generally difficult to place with investors.

## Expected changes in the balance sheet-driven CDO market

In the framework of Basel II, it is therefore clear that synthetic balance sheet-driven CDOs offer relatively little interest, as arranged hitherto. Possible solutions for the banks could therefore be:

• Either to turn to assets attracting greater capital requirements (such as leveraged loans, non-investment grade corporates or SMEs, etc.).
• Or to transfer the subordinated (first loss) risk on transactions structured on investment grade underlying assets.

The main obstacles to such strategies are the cost of transferring these risky assets, associated with the lack of transparency inherent in their type. They are rarely officially rated exposures or else they have a complex risk profile, such as project finance loans, which is less well rated by the agencies and attracts less interest from investors. However, several significant transactions have been conducted in these areas.

In 2002, a bespoke synthetic CDO was arranged by Bank of America for Centre Solutions (a subsidiary of Zurich Financial Services), with Springfield Investment Management as managers. The reference portfolio contained only leveraged loans underwritten by Bank of America, the subordinated risk of which was transferred to Centre Solutions via a credit derivative. Similarly, in Europe, a growing number of CDOs have concerned leveraged loans, for purposes of balance sheet management and arbitrage (UniCredito with Harbourmaster CLO 1 and Allied Irish Bank with Tara Hill).

The main difficulty with first loss risk distribution in investment grade portfolios is that banks generally wish to retain active management of the reference credit portfolio, so that they can replace the loans that have been repaid by new exposures. This flexibility does, however, entail a risk of moral hazard. The bank could be tempted to include credit exposures on which the market anticipations are not favorable, to the detriment of the investors. This risk frightens off the great majority of investors and creates *de facto* an additional risk premium compared to a transaction on a static portfolio. To reduce this premium, banks must behave as transparently as possible, revealing the reference portfolio (but some institutions still refuse to do so under bank secrecy rules), and/or offering investors the right of veto to regulate the management of the underlying portfolio.

Some banks were obliged to adopt an alternative strategy. Thus, Société Générale developed transactions avoiding this risk of moral hazard, in partnership with third parties (insurance or reinsurance companies) charged with managing the underlying portfolio. The main benefits of these transactions are:

- A high degree of transparency.
- Resolution of the problems inherent to legal documentation (not least the definition of the credit event restructuring and the cash settlement method enabling investors to buy back defaulting loans to benefit from any possible improvement in price).

The result of these arrangements was that the sponsor bank and investors were more equally treated. The advances were made possible by the private, bilateral nature of the transactions and the investors' level of sophistication. Similar transactions were then offered to a larger number of investors, with the right of veto on the underlying portfolio management being entrusted with a principal investor (the buyer of the first loss tranche), together with the interests of the senior counterparties. Société Générale and Axa Investment Managers thus successfully arranged two transactions of this type (Grande Armée in 2001 and Champs-Elysées in December 2001). Axa IM subscribed the first loss tranches and was charged with the initial selection of the portfolio and management of the loan substitutions. The senior tranches were then distributed to a more traditional clientele, which could thus benefit from the presence and expertise of a well-known asset manager for the selection and management of the reference portfolio. Société Générale was thus able to transfer a substantial amount of the economic capital in the portfolio without significantly adding to the cost of this risk transfer.

Finally, the lower diversity in the European bond (and CDS) market, compared to the American market, could also be a factor of growth in synthetic balance sheet-driven CDOs. Bank loan portfolios offer significant diversity, since many European corporates have no access to the financial markets, or have not wished to seek funding there. With balance sheet-driven transactions, the investors gain access to a new credit risk universe. According to the British Bankers' Association, the volume of corporate lending to large European corporates is four times that in the corporate bond market.

Credit derivatives have forced the Basel Committee to re-evaluate the capital adequacy rules for banking institutions and thus have had a considerable impact on the capital markets. However, in the medium term, they drive another nail into the coffin of the synthetic balance sheet-driven securitization market, at least in its traditional form.

It is, indeed, this question of risk transfer that has been at the heart of the heated debate on credit derivatives since 2002. This is dealt with in the next section.

## 7.2.2    Credit Derivatives and the Instability of the Financial System

Since the wave of bankruptcies in 2001–2002, many publications, press articles and interventions by the supervisory authorities have raised the issue of credit derivatives and their role in the instability of the financial system.

There are three main series of questions that have been asked about this:

- The first, as of 2001, arose from the work of the banking system and insurance supervisory authorities, especially in the United Kingdom and France. It was followed by a report published in January 2003 by the Committee on the Global Financial System: 'Credit risk transfer'.
- The second wave came in early 2003 after the Berkshire Hathaway insurance company's annual report for 2002 was published. In this report, the company's CEO, American millionaire Warren Buffett, published a stringent criticism of derivatives, especially credit derivatives, that he qualified as 'financial weapons of mass destruction'.
- Finally, the third wave of questions came after Fitch Ratings published the first version of its survey of the credit derivatives market in March 2003, further completed in September 2003, entitled 'Global credit derivatives: a qualified success'.

The main observations and criticisms expressed in the foregoing publications will be reviewed briefly here. Later, we will be able to present a more rounded picture.

### 7.2.2.1    The Supervisory Authorities' Studies

In June 2001, the Bank of England published a document on the subject of the credit derivatives market and financial instability.[36] Most of the paper is devoted to description of the products, changes in the market and associated risks (legal documentation, counterparty risk, etc.). It also adopts a benevolent view of these developments, showing satisfaction that 'development of these markets has clear potential benefits for financial stability, as they allow the origination and funding of credit to be separated from the efficient final allocation of the credit risk'.

In France, the Banking Commission and the Insurance Control Commission also examined this subject.[37] Acknowledging that market players were not particularly affected by the events of the second half of 2001, the regulators insisted that financial institutions integrate the risk inherent to credit derivatives into their normal risk management. This 'first line of defense' was to be further backed up by 'the tutelary authorities who should set prudential requirements specifically for this activity'. The analysis ended by underlining the importance of international co-operation on supervising these markets and common or concerted monitoring by the banking and insurance supervisory bodies.

Another, more interesting comment was made in the publication by the Committee on the Global Financial System in January 2003. It started off by pointing out that instruments for transferring credit risk are not an innovation, since they have traditionally been present in the form of guarantees and letters of credit or credit insurance. The current development of the market is characterized first by the proliferation of instruments available to market players,

---

[36] 'The Credit Derivatives Market: its development and possible implications for financial stability', Financial Stability Review, June 2001.

[37] 'Les dérivés de crédit, nouvelle source d'instabilité financière?' (Are credit derivatives a new source of financial instability?) Revue de Stabilité Financière, Commission Bancaire & Commission de Contrôle des Assurances, November 2002.

and second by the emergence of portfolio products, which no longer limit the transfer of risk associated with a single issuer.

After describing the players in the market, the Committee then raised incentive issues inherent to the transfer of credit risk and the structural implications the development of credit derivatives would have.

## Incentive issues

It was clear to the Committee that there was a discrepancy between protection buyers' and sellers' incentives. This leads to three questions:

• Discrepancy in information – it is conceivable that, inasfar as he has commercial relationships with the reference borrower, a protection buyer has inside information on the financial health of the borrower that the seller does not have, thus inciting the buyer to subscribe to a protection.
• The relationships between the agent and the principal – where the protection buyer maintains his relationship with the reference borrower, the latter can be tempted to act as an agent of the protection seller.
• Finally, the issue of incomplete contracts – this arises where a transaction transferring credit risk does not necessarily provide for all possible eventualities.

These subjects have been amply discussed in financial theory. However, it should be noted that the first two issues only arise if the risk transfer transaction entails an ongoing relationship between the protection buyer and the reference borrower.

The Committee asked further questions on the relationships between the protection buyer and the borrower and between the former and its shareholders and creditors.

## Structural implications

The Committee highlighted two structural implications in the development of the market in credit risk transfer:

• The central role now played by the rating agencies, no longer required merely to assess the default probability of an issuer via a rating, but to pronounce on the future performance of structured products like CDOs.
• The issue of reallocating credit risk within and outside of the banking system, not least to insurance companies.

## The Committee's recommendations

At this stage, the Committee's recommendations are cautious: its chief remarks are directed at improving the transparency of financial institutions and supervising the rating agencies.

In conclusion, it would appear that the supervisory authorities are finding it difficult to decide about credit derivatives and financial instability. The various publications are relatively cautious and they acknowledge the overall resilience of the market and players to the credit shocks that occurred in 2001–2002 among others. Their difficulty in drawing conclusions at this time is due mostly to the absence of detailed information and the speed with which the credit risk transfer markets are changing. A further survey was commissioned by the Basel

Joint Forum, the conclusions of which were published in September 2004. For the moment it appears that the transfer of synthetic risk will not jeopardize overall financial stability.[38]

However, other observers have been less circumspect than the supervisory authorities and have roundly condemned the development of credit derivatives.

### 7.2.2.2   Criticism from Market Practitioners

In the 2002 annual report of his company Berkshire Hathaway, the American millionaire investor Warren Buffett launched an attack on credit derivatives that he described as 'time bombs'. Among his chief complaints, unsurprisingly, were:

- The absence of regulations and supervision of market players.
- The risk of valuing positions in mark-to-model, likely to lead to considerable financial reporting inaccuracies.
- The concentration of counterparty risks into a few large brokerage houses that would come to dominate the derivatives markets.
- The amount of leverage.
- Etc.

Although this tirade was not leveled directly at credit derivatives, they were nevertheless concerned, all the more so as the press reveled in their contrast with the views of Alan Greenspan, the Chairman of the Fed, who at the time this annual report came out was boasting the merits of credit derivatives, the use of which had, according to him, greatly contributed to averting a major financial crisis. One of the reasons for which Warren Buffett had criticized derivatives was that he had found himself in a delicate position after Berkshire Hathaway bought up the reinsurance company General Re. This had a subsidiary that was particularly active in the financial and derivatives markets, General Re Securities. After vainly attempting to sell it, the Berkshire Hathaway board decided to put it into liquidation, but they were confronted with the difficulty of valuing the 14 384 derivatives positions in its portfolio and settling the contracts.

Shortly after Warren Buffett's broadside, another emblematic figure in the US capital markets criticized credit derivatives. Bill Gross, the star bond manager at PIMCO criticized the bank intermediaries in the credit derivatives market for using the inside information they collected in their capacity as borrowers and thus swindling the investors. This echoes one of the concerns of the Committee on Global Financial Stability. This criticism was well received because it recalled the excesses of the investment banks during the Internet bubble (not least the links between equity research and equity capital markets departments).

These are two starkly extreme views, thoroughly well aired as we shall see later. They were, however, repeated by the Fitch Ratings report on the credit derivatives market that was published in March 2003.

### 7.2.2.3   The Fitch Ratings Report

The publication of the first Fitch Ratings report on the global credit derivatives market was something of a bombshell. Even though its conclusions do not enable us to glean much information on the real influence of credit derivatives on financial instability, its interpretation by

---

[38] See Jeffrey (2004).

the economic press was that it was clearly an alert. Over the succeeding three weeks, the two main French economic newspapers headlined, for instance:

- 'Credit derivatives, a time bomb?' (*La Tribune*, 17 March 2003).
- 'Banks rapped on knuckles with credit derivatives' (*Les Echos*, 24 March 2003).
- 'Uncontrolled boom in credit derivatives' (*La Tribune*, 31 March 2003).

However, on closer examination, it appears that the report's conclusions were repeated without discernment. Naturally, we are not denying the relative absence of transparency in this market, as in all emerging markets, nor the absence of data on hedge funds, which did not wish to take part in the survey. However, it should be noted that it is not just credit derivatives for which the reporting is defective. The new Basel II Accords have recommended (in Pillar 3) greater transparency of information on financial institutions' activity in both risk management and derivatives in general.

One other target of negative criticism was Fitch's overall figures for transfer of credit risk between the banking sector, structural protection buyers, and insurance and other financial guarantors. According to Fitch, some $100 bn of exposure were transferred from the banking system to these protection sellers, a figure re-evaluated at $229 bn in the updated version of September 2003. However, this aggregate figure covers fundamentally different realities, as we shall see later, and it is impossible to draw a definite conclusion from it.

In the following section we shall try to present a more contrasted situation. Taken all in all, the influence of the credit derivatives market is still negligible compared to the financial system as a whole.

### 7.2.3   A More Rounded Picture

If we look at the various questions posed on the credit derivatives market closely, we will see that the real key lies in the nature of the risks transferred. Most of the criticisms leveled at credit derivatives concern the implicit link between the bank intermediaries' activities in the financial market and their traditional role as lenders (in other words, between their trading books and their banking books).

However, as demonstrated below, it is difficult to believe that there is massive transfer of credit risk from banking balance sheets to the portfolios of the insurance companies. Furthermore, it is not at all certain that credit derivatives contributed to averting a substantial crisis in 2001–2002. The banks' resistance was due more to their high level of capitalization and their better assessment of risk than to their use of miracle instruments. Finally, the debate should be focused on the real risks that can arise from development of the credit derivatives market.

#### 7.2.3.1   The Truth of Risk Transfers via the Credit Derivatives Market

The Fitch Ratings market analysis says nothing about a fundamental aspect of the market in credit risk transfer – its origin, that is, whether it is really transferred from the banks' balance sheets or whether in fact it is sourced in the financial markets.

The survey published in December 2003 by Standard & Poor's (S&P) gives a few precious, concrete indications on the true composition of risk transfer. This survey reports that 'of the $3 trillion total notional amount of credit derivatives outstanding, only about $100 billion represents a transfer of credit risk from banks' lending and trading activities to other market participants. The remainder represents the dealing books of the fifteen dealing banks that

**Table 7.9**    JP Morgan's credit derivatives positions (year end 2003)

| USD million | Portfolio management | | Dealer/clients | | Total |
| --- | --- | --- | --- | --- | --- |
| | Protection bought | Protection sold | Protection bought | Protection sold | |
| **2003** | **37 349** | **67** | **264 389** | **275 888** | **577 693** |
| | *6%* | *0%* | *46%* | *48%* | *100%* |

dominate the business and, to a much lesser extent, investments in credit risks by banks and insurance companies'.[39]

There are several comments to be made on this. First, the figure is half that finally estimated by Fitch ($100 bn as against 229). Secondly, the volume of trading is clearly highlighted. Most of the dealing in the credit derivatives market is by banks today:

- As market-makers in credit.
- And as structurers of bespoke products for investors.

It should be noted, for instance, that the structuring of a single tranche CDO for an investor requires the bank intermediary wishing to hedge its long position to sell protection in a notional amount of some five to seven times (on average) the notional amount bought via the CDO. Even if not all deltas are traded in this market, this activity contributed greatly to the growth in amounts traded. In this sense, the commercial banks are like the investment banks. Their use of credit derivatives for hedging their own risks is marginal. Most of the risks underlying the structured products created by these intermediaries are sourced in the financial markets, in the form of either bonds or CDSs.

Overall, the S&P analysis is corroborated by the figures published by JP Morgan, the main dealer in credit derivatives worldwide, at the end of 2003. Table 7.9 shows the bank's positions in notional amounts. JP Morgan's market-making and customer-driven business represent 94% of its notional amounts.

Thirdly, the estimated amount of risk transfers is relatively low compared to the aggregate amounts of the bank loan and bond portfolios held by the banking system, which are valued at $29 000 bn and $5500 bn respectively by S&P.

If we now take the place of the structural risk-takers (investors, insurers, reinsurers and financial guarantors), what do we see? First, given the figures set forth above, it seems difficult to hold the banks responsible for any losses suffered by the risk-takers. Most of the products they underwrite are not sourced from bank balance sheets, for which the intermediaries might possibly have benefited from information asymmetry, but in fact from capital markets. Second, the average creditworthiness underwritten by these participants remains very high. As S&P notes, 'another aspect of the credit derivatives business that has limited the amount of risk transferred away from the banking system is that the risk that can be protected with CDSs is largely investment grade'.[40] Furthermore, as seen above, in all the balance sheet-driven securitizations structured by the banks, the latter have kept the first loss tranche in their books, thus reducing the number of actual transfers of risk.

---

[39] Azarchs (2003).
[40] Azarchs (2003).

Number of
failures

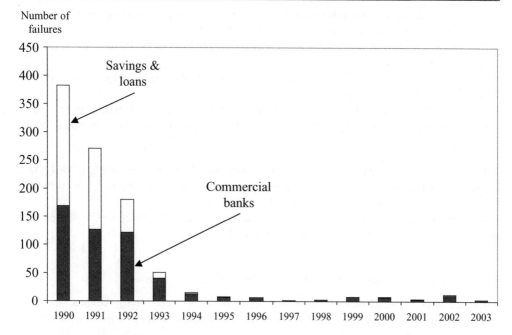

**Figure 7.11**   US credit institutions failures (1990–2003)
*Source*: Office of the Comptroller of the Currency.

This analysis is corroborated by the Fitch figures, which show clearly that 96% of the risks subscribed by the insurers (not including financial guarantors) are investment grade. For financial guarantors, 95% of the risk is rated A or over, which is not surprising since their economic model is highly dependent on their capacity to keep their AAA/Aaa rating.

This analysis shows that credit risk transfer away from the banking system is a relative phenomenon. The conclusion pre-empts a good many of the criticisms made of credit derivatives. On the other hand, did these instruments really play a role in averting a significant banking crisis in 2001–2002?

### 7.2.3.2   An Economic Crisis without a Banking Crisis

The US Federal Reserve and its Chairman, Alan Greenspan, have frequently praised the role of credit derivatives in recent years, in averting tension for the banks, such as occurred in earlier credit cycles.[41] It is true that the default cycle of 2001–2003 saw not a single big default of a credit institution. Figure 7.11 presents the default statistics for US credit institutions over 1990–2003.

Contrary to the previous wave of defaults (1990–1991), American banks have shown strong resistance to the vagaries of the economic climate. However, it would be exaggerated to attribute this to credit derivatives, not least because in this case they do not deal in them.

More generally speaking, the Standard & Poor's study concludes that 'the credit derivatives markets have not helped banks escape the ills of credit cycles'.[42] On the other hand, several factors contributed to strengthening banking institutions' resilience:

---

[41] See for instance Horwood (2004).
[42] Azarchs (2003).

- Effective implementation of the Basel I regulations as of 1992, leading banking institutions to accumulate much higher average levels of capitalization.
- The intrinsic profitability of banks, especially the retail banks in the United States, the UK, Australia, France and Spain.
- The end of a cycle of strong economic growth (1995–2000), which enabled financial institutions to build up their capital.
- Advances in management of concentration risks and diversification of credit portfolios (corporate loans having gradually fallen as a percentage of bank balance sheets compared to the 1980s).

It is therefore as exaggerated to say that banks succeeded in coming through the 2001–2002 economic crisis thanks to credit derivatives as to blame these instruments for uncontrolled spread of credit risk throughout the financial system.

Nevertheless, there are a number of real risks associated with the development of the credit derivatives market that need to be closely monitored.

### 7.2.3.3  Real Risks Associated with Development of Credit Derivatives

There are three major challenges to the development of the credit derivatives market in the next few years, it being understood that advances have already been made in these areas.

**Controlling counterparty risk**

The credit derivatives market is extremely concentrated. According to Standard & Poor's, 83% of the notional amounts of credit derivatives traded are held in the books of 17 banks. Moreover, it is common to see exposures of nearly $5 bn notional amount with a single counterparty.[43] Although these institutions are relatively well rated by the rating agencies (with ratings of A or higher), the default of one could cause a chain reaction (see the LTCM syndrome). This systemic risk is all the greater where there is a simultaneous default of a major intermediary in the market and a frequently traded reference entity.

This almost happened in 2001, with the bankruptcy of Enron, which was also a major player in the CDS market. The way the market players sorted out the settlement of the contracts shows how strong these instruments are. In fact, as long as most of the business in credit derivatives consists of trading in the financial markets, they are not treated differently from other derivatives and therefore benefit from the credit risk management methods in use on these markets (ISDA Master Agreement, netting and collateralization).[44]

**More active regulation**

It seems essential, parallel to the development of this market, to step up the presence of the regulatory authorities in specific areas, even though this is required in other areas than credit

---

[43] This does not correspond to counterparty risk since that is equal to the cost of replacing the contracts (its mark-to-market).

[44] Paradoxically, in France, banks are the most exposed to counterparty risk when hedging banking book exposures, since the French Commission Bancaire requires exclusion of the credit derivative from the ISDA Master Agreement.

derivatives too:

- A regulatory basis is needed that is common to banks and insurance companies, to avoid regulatory arbitrage between two sectors and serious discrepancies in assessment of credit risk (this is progressing well in Europe, via the Directive transposing the Basel II regulations).
- The rating agencies must be supervised, since they will be led to play a central role in future credit markets (in this respect, the new Basel II rules allow large-scale outsourcing of capital adequacy standards assessment to private agencies under no particular constraints). The arrival of new competition in the field could be welcome news.
- Finally, the sempiternal issue of regulating hedge funds, which since the LTCM debacle shows that they are a far greater danger to financial stability than any new instrument, including credit derivatives.

### The imperative for increased transparency

One last field in which the dealers in the credit derivatives market must make an effort is in reporting transparency. It is in all their interests to communicate on good practice in this area, thus evangelizing the financial community. The Basel II regulations will ensure this with the third pillar of the Accords.

This section has enabled us to examine the implications for the regulations of the financial system of development in credit derivatives.

The first field in which they made a major impact was in the regulations on banking activities. The Basel II Accords have, accordingly, sought to align the capital adequacy requirements with economic reality, especially in the field of credit risk, as the previous rules were completely obsolete. One of the chief consequences of this evolution is that regulatory arbitrage transactions have become much less attractive, after having driven growth in synthetic CDO transactions in 1999–2000.

We also examined the influence of credit derivatives on the stability of the global financial system. It must be said that our analysis has revealed that, for the time being at least, they are a far cry from the decried weapons of mass destruction, and nor indeed were they the saviors of the banking institutions in the debacle of 2001–2002, given the relatively modest volume of transactions in these products.

That being said, these products still have enormous potential and have been the major innovation of the past decade in finance. The last section of this chapter will place the emergence of credit derivatives in the historical context of evolution in the capital markets and risk management.

## 7.3  CREDIT DERIVATIVES: A FINANCIAL REVOLUTION?

Credit derivatives are at the heart of the major changes transforming the capital markets. We have seen how their increasing use by financial institutions is likely to bring gradual change to their role on the financial markets. We have also shown to what extent these new instruments have led to far-reaching renewal of the regulatory framework applying to credit and other financial institutions (Basel II) or again, exactly what their contribution to financial instability is.

In this last section, we wish to broaden the scope of our analysis and describe what the implications are for the capital markets as a whole. First of all, we shall go back to 'particle finance theory', which, as in nuclear physics, provides a template for analysis of development in the financial markets through risk management and unbundling risk into elementary components. Secondly, we shall see that this approach has direct consequences for the capital markets, whether in credit risk pricing, optimal allocation of risk, or completion and integration of the markets. Finally, we shall conclude on the nature of credit derivatives: although they are not, as such, a financial revolution, they are unquestionably the chief innovation of the last ten years, and prefigure others.

### 7.3.1   Introduction to Particle Finance Theory

By singularizing the credit risk of each borrower, credit derivatives are the missing piece in the particle finance theory that lurks beneath the development of the derivatives markets and is at the heart of risk management.

In a now-famous article, 'Financial markets in 2020', Charles S. Sanford, the former CEO of Bankers Trust, the pioneer of the derivatives markets, defined what he called particle finance theory. By drawing a parallel between the evolution of physics and biology on the one hand and finance on the other, Sanford premised that derivatives are in the process of revolutionizing the finance world by turning finance into the science of risk management – any type of risk that could be run by a firm in the course of its business.

In this scheme of things, today's banks will become tomorrow's risk managers, required to extract the elementary risks from economic activities, describe them in terms of probability of its occurrence, and repackage them into bespoke financial instruments enabling them to be transferred to counterparties more capable of dealing with them than the initial risk bearers. It should be noted, for instance, that with the emergence of portfolio management functions in commercial banks and the new strategic and organizational bank models,[45] this vision is fast being attained.

Until now, we have been in the 'Newtonian' era of classic finance, in which 'we tend to look at financial instruments – like shares, bonds and loans – in static highly aggregated terms'[46]. But, as in physics, which has begun to study the infinitely small by breaking up bodies into atoms, molecules and other particles; as in biology, which has moved from studying human anatomy to studying that of cells and genes, finance, especially with the development of derivatives and the constant technological improvements, 'will substantially reduce the amount of unwanted risk borne by individuals, institutions and the system as a whole. [We] will find better ways to quantify, price and manage today's familiar risks. [We] will also uncover, quantify, price and manage risks that exist today but are hidden from view. The net benefits will be great – even granting that new and unforeseen risks could be created by this environment'.[47]

The emergence of credit derivatives is a typical example of the practical application of particle finance theory. They are, moreover, the most important building blocks missing in this theory, and already benefit from the attributes of risk analysis for equity, interest rates, currency and commodities among others, even though they could still be unbundled into elementary components. Thus, in the 1980s, Shearson Lehman proposed to create a new type of instrument, unbundled stock units (USUs),[48] the purpose of which was to unbundle equity risk into basic components and separate value into the voting right and the right to

---

[45] See Section 7.1.
[46] Sanford (1993).
[47] Sanford (1993).
[48] See Brealey and Myers (1991).

economic cash flows (dividends and capital gains).[49] This innovation, probably in advance for its time, remained a dead letter. However, it was passed down to financial invention posterity since it was precisely the precursor of the particle finance that characterizes modern financial markets.

The basic contribution of credit derivatives in this vision can be measured. They are the preferred means for dissociating default risk from the borrower. More sophisticated variations,[50] such as default-and-out spread options, or CDS–CMDS combinations, even enable the default risk to be unbundled from the risk of spread variation.

Implementation of this theory has many consequences for the capital markets.

### 7.3.2   Implications of 'Particle Finance Theory' for the Capital Markets

The development of the credit derivative market has far-reaching implications for the structure and evolution of the capital markets. There are three sorts of consequence:

1. They contribute to rational and homogeneous pricing of credit risk, whatever the underlying support of this risk.
2. They promote the integration of the credit markets, and in addition, contribute to unify up-to-now fragmented capital markets.
3. They work in favor of an optimum allocation of credit risks at global economy level.

We shall go over these three consequences in detail.

#### 7.3.2.1   Rational and Homogeneous Pricing of Credit Risk

By imposing itself as a liquid market, trading an ever-increasing number of underlying risks (even of corporates not issuing on the bond markets), the market in credit derivatives has gradually become a reference place for the pricing of credit risk, as discussed in this book. Thus, they enable the banks to ascertain the 'true' cost of credit, whereas before this was largely a tributary of cyclical volatility (and the abundance or rarity of funds) and banking relationships.

In this capacity, they enable a little 'rationality' to be introduced into the equation of credit risk pricing. Thus, according to Stuart Lewis, European head of Loan Exposure Management at Deutsche Bank, 'we are gradually bringing the methods for calculating ROE on loans to our customers towards market prices. Credit derivatives prices are a major part of this model because they are what we pay to manage our credit portfolios actively'.[51] Thus, bank portfolio managers are capable of determining the 'subsidy' they will grant their customers by checking the difference between the price of credit in the derivatives markets and the conditions to which the particular loan will be subject. It is this 'subsidy' that they must later offset with ancillary income, where the strategic choice of 'loss leader' credit has been made.

The development of credit derivatives has not led necessarily to overall improvement on credit spreads in the loan market, even though at the height of the recent crisis in 2001–2002, some attempts at repricing were observed; but at least, the banks now know what they cost them and are able to implement a rational approach, in order to make relationship banking

---

[49] The latter two parameters could even be unbundled, or rights created on dividend volatility, etc.
[50] See Chapter 2.
[51] Quoted by Chassany (October 2003).

profitable. As noted by Meredith Coffrey, an analyst at Loan Pricing Corporation: 'Pricing is becoming more economic. But it's not becoming absolutely economic.'[52]

A second significant example in this field is the debate that raged in the financial community in summer 2001, on pricing of undrawn loan commitments. Goldman Sachs, the merchant bank, accused its chief competitors hailing from commercial banking (particularly JP Morgan) of dumping on loan commitments to generate more profitable side products such as bond issues or advisory services in mergers and acquisitions. This criticism was justified, as we have seen, in a strategic environment where credit is often used as a loss leader. What was new, however, was that Goldman Sachs asked the US Financial Accounting Standards Board (FASB) if these products could receive accounting treatment as derivatives.[53]

The reasoning was as follows: banks grant credit lines on the implicit assumption that they will not be used. One of the commonest scenarios in which borrowers are led to draw on their credit lines is when they are in difficulty (such as Xerox in 2002 for instance). Thus, these products could be seen as a combination of a CDS and a spread option in which the bank is selling the option. Also in this case, the role of the credit derivatives market is crucial in arriving at rational pricing of these instruments.

Goldman Sachs's request to treat these products like derivatives echoes the wider debate on whether to lay down IAS standards on mark-to-market treatment of all financial instruments on banking institutions' balance sheets, including loans. In this field, the undeniable benefits resulting from transparency and real prices might be annihilated by the increased volatility in earnings. However, it seems to us that in the long run, this will be unavoidable and risk management methods will be perfected accordingly.

Let us imagine that ultimately, there will be a completely liquid and efficient credit derivatives market: the default risk of risky borrowers is priced and traded in the market. Any credit instrument (bank loan, letter of credit, bond, etc.) can be unbundled into elementary components that can be priced in the market. If we take the example of a fixed rate bond:

risky bond = Treasury bond of equivalent duration + interest rate swap + CDS

With an equation like this, and supposing the market prices each elementary risk efficiently, there will be a single price for risky credit and any deviation from that theoretical price will give rise to arbitrage opportunities that should bring the asset back to its fair value.

Similarly, it is now possible to give an exact valuation of a swap or other vulnerable derivative (i.e. subject to default risk for one or other of the counterparties). The derivatives market-makers' bid–ask range should reflect the potential counterparty's credit risk, as well as the capital requirements needed for the transaction and the net cost (or gain) attached to collateral posting to reduce this counterparty risk.

Pricing of a bid on a rate swap could be expressed thus:[54]

> price of rate swap without credit risk
> + administrative costs
> + counterparty default probability × value of a call swaption
> − (market-maker default probability × value of a put swaption)
> + (marginal economic capital × RAROC)

---

[52] Quoted by Silverman (2002).
[53] See Dunbar (2001).
[54] See Shimko (1998).

+ (marginal collateral paid × [RAROC − risk-adjusted yield on collateral])

− (marginal collateral received × risk-adjusted yield on collateral invested)

In this field, as seen in Chapter 3, hybrid products also enable the creation of useful building blocks.

This homogeneous pricing of credit risk, independently of the nature of the underlying assets, enabled by a liquid and efficient credit derivatives market which values the default probability for each debtor, is the driving force of credit market integration.

### 7.3.2.2  Growing Integration of the Credit and Financial Markets

We maintain that, by completing the derivatives market in virtually all aspects of financial risk, credit derivatives are capable of fostering growing integration of, on the one hand, credit markets, and on the other hand, the various capital markets.

One of the main effects of development in the credit derivatives markets is that it has contributed to homogeneous assessment of credit risk, whatever the underlying instrument type. In this respect, credit derivatives are the cornerstone of tomorrow's credit markets, because they are instruments by which rational assessment of credit risk seems possible, whatever the nature of the underlying financial asset containing this risk. Thus, as Charles Smithson explains: 'If a particular credit is traded in more than one debt market, an arbitrage is possible. Before the advent of credit derivatives, nothing guaranteed that two credit markets – e.g. the bond market and the syndicated loan market – had the same implied future default probabilities. If they are not the same, a credit derivative transaction can be used to arbitrage the two markets.'[55]

From the moment credit risk is assessed and priced homogeneously for all types of instrument, then the various credit markets will be forced to integrate under the pressure of the arbitrages between the various products, once all these instruments have been adjusted according to their legal and financial characteristics (prepaid options, expected recovery rate in the event of default, maturity and rate characteristics). This is true especially of the bank loan and bond markets.

Asarnow and Ginzburg (1995) think that historically, arbitrage opportunities persisted in these markets for several reasons:

- Investor bases were not the same.
- Liquidity in the secondary loan market remained low.
- There is no mechanism for taking a short position on a bank loan.

However, as seen earlier, these conditions are less and less prevalent:

- Increased liquidity in the secondary loan market has tended to blur the differences between bank loans and bonds.
- There is less and less segmentation between investors in each market with the arrival of many investment funds in the bank loan markets.
- Finally, credit derivatives enable short positions to be taken on bank debt.

Thus, progressive unification of the credit market is now a possibility.

By favoring a homogeneous approach to a borrower's credit spread and by allowing inter-market arbitrages, credit derivatives are a means of integrating the markets.

---

[55] Smithson and Holappa (1995).

By putting the finishing touch to the range of derivatives, credit derivatives will not only integrate but also unite the various capital markets. It is in this that they illustrate the theory of particle finance.

Credit derivatives already allow corporates to arbitrage their capital structure. Investors use them to benefit from pricing anomalies in the equity and debt of a single firm. Thus, in November 2003, the premium on Ford's five-year CDS increased by 80 basis points because a downgrade from Standard & Poor's was anticipated, while the equity volatility remained the same. Arbitragists therefore seized the opportunity to buy put options largely out-of-the-money (i.e. with a very low strike price), at attractive premiums because of the low underlying volatility, while at the same time selling protection at high spread levels. Similarly, it could be argued that EDSs allow equity–credit arbitrages that contribute to the convergence of these markets. These two markets are increasingly correlated because of volatility spreading from the equity markets to the credit markets.[56]

To some extent, positions on credit derivatives can be hedged dynamically by using the equity markets for corporate risks or the currency markets for emerging sovereign risk. These instruments also contribute to credit risk assessment that is more and more like that used for market risk.[57] Credit derivatives therefore build the missing link between existing capital markets by promoting unity.

### 7.3.2.3  Optimum Allocation of Credit Risk

By offering financial intermediaries the possibility to transfer the credit risk hitherto bundled into debt instruments, credit derivatives will contribute to optimum allocation of credit risk at the level of the entire economy.

As Charles Smithson notes: 'The market for credit risk is arguably the largest in the world. Yet, size notwithstanding, it is highly fragmented by product as well as by geographic boundaries; the result is that credit risk is sub-optimally held across financial institutions and investors. The great potential of credit derivatives is their ability to link these diverse market segments and promote the efficiency of origination and holding of credit exposure.'[58] As seen earlier, financial institutions will gradually adapt their strategy depending on their comparative advantage along the credit value chain: origination, structuring and distribution; this adaptation will contribute to better allocation of credit risk.

Thus, it is possible to draw a parallel between the development of the credit derivatives market and their role in the credit markets, and collateralized mortgage obligations (CMOs)[59] for the mortgage loan markets in the United States. These instruments enable the cash flows generated by the underlying mortgage loan portfolio to be redirected, to mitigate the risk of prepayment inherent in these assets.[60] They are typically structured in several classes (A, B, C and Z), for example. The last tranche, which is not paid if the first three have not been paid back

---

[56] See Prandi (2003).

[57] This correspondence is needed. In the OTC derivatives markets, an extreme scenario with violent price movements would transform market risk into counterparty risk (credit exposures).

[58] Smithson *et al.* (1996).

[59] CMOs can be defined as structured bonds, backed by a portfolio of mortgage loans. See Fabozzi (1993).

[60] Mortgage holders in the United States have a prepayment option with the financial institution from which they have borrowed. This prepayment risk is analyzed either as a 'contraction' risk (refinancing existing facilities) if the mortgage rates fall, or an 'extension' risk if they rise. For these reasons, it has little appeal for traditional bond investors.

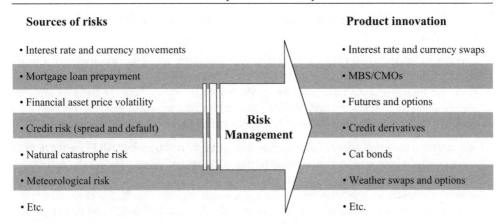

**Figure 7.12**   Financial market risks and product innovation

by the cash flows generated by the underlying asset, protects the buyers from the extension risk. It attracts mostly long-term bond investors, seeking to reduce the risks of reinvesting coupons and principal that are inherent in classic bond products.

Like credit derivatives, CMOs enable the transfer, but not the elimination, of the various forms of prepayment risk to investors with a comparative advantage in managing this type of risk. In this respect, they enable risks to be allocated more efficiently in the economy.[61]

Credit derivatives play a similar role in the credit markets (mainly bonds and bank loans for the moment), thus contributing to the breaking up of the traditional credit cycle characterized by a single institution that originates, structures and holds or distributes the risk. Each phase of this cycle should be carried out by a different financial intermediary, with a comparative edge in executing the phase.

The credit markets are not alone in benefiting from the fact that credit derivatives enable greater overall efficiency in allocating credit risk. The *raison d'être* of credit derivatives and risk management is to apply these techniques for unbundling and transferring risk to the economy as a whole, and even to society itself. In this sense, credit derivatives can be seen to participate in an ongoing innovative process and are precursors of other innovations.

### 7.3.3   An Innovation that Heralds Others

The creation and development of credit derivatives has enabled the ever-more pressing need for financial intermediaries to manage their credit risks to be met. They are part of a pattern of innovation that has characterized the capital markets over the past 30 years.

Figure 7.12 shows the main sources of risk in the capital markets and the product innovations that have addressed it in chronological order of their development.

---

[61] Mortgage loan originators (commercial banks, savings banks, credit unions, etc.) find short-term finance by issuing securities in the money or CD markets. Having 20 or 30-year instruments on the asset side of the balance sheet which, on top of that, include prepayment risks, would cause considerable asset–liability matching risks.

It can thus be seen that credit derivatives (CDSs)[62] are indeed a new product class, characterized in that:

- Contrary to variation and volatility risks, CDSs enable coverage of the occurrence of a single discrete event (default or credit event).
- Thus, the total risk associated with the credit derivative is not very far from its notional amount (subject to recovery rate) unlike other derivatives in which the risk, measured by mark-to-market, usually only represents a minor percentage of the notional amount.

This innovation has other applications, such as in alternative risk transfer (ART), on the boundary between the insurance and capital markets; this is the case of catastrophe bonds (cat bonds). These structured products have a payoff, which depends on the occurrence or non-occurrence of a natural disaster in a precise region during a given period. Should the event occur, the settlement amount is determined using an index of the damage suffered by the industry or by calculating the losses actually suffered by the protection buyer. There are clear similarities with CDSs.

Today, derivatives technology is developed by the intermediaries for an ever-widening range of risk:

- Inflation.
- Macroeconomic indicators,[63] such as employment, retail sales, industrial output, GDP growth, etc. (market sponsored by Goldman Sachs and Deutsche Bank).
- Weather risk: development of a market in swaps and options on average temperature or rainfall, for instance.
- Carbon dioxide emission certificates.
- Broadband capacities; etc.

It is even possible to imagine that the risk management techniques by means of derivatives could be extended to society at large, including private individuals. This is the idea defended by Robert Shiller, an economics professor at Yale University, since 1993. In a recent work, *The New Financial Order: Risk in the 21st Century*, Shiller (2003) makes several suggestions for creating 'macro securities' that would enable private individuals to hedge the main risks they are confronted with during their lives (variations in the price of their homes, for example, or the risk of losing their jobs). Technological advances should enable a mass of indices to be created and the information on them to be distributed, as well as organization of how to balance supply and demand.

Beyond these proposals, which may seem like economy-fiction to some of our readers, the challenge for today's capital markets is to maintain liquidity. It regularly decreases due to the herd-like behavior of capital market players and the relative reluctance of the intermediaries to commit capital to back their trading activities.[64] This lack of liquidity has a direct effect on asset volatility, thus penalizing the intermediaries because more capital is required in the VaR models, thus entailing a vicious circle. Perhaps derivatives could come to the rescue of market players and manage the liquidity risk?

In the new credit markets described here, credit derivatives will be playing a special role. As they are used by dealers, credit risk will be priced rationally and homogeneously for the various

---

[62] Credit spread derivatives can be classified in the category of options and futures since they enable positions to be taken on the volatility of a 'continuous' underlying asset, i.e. credit spread.
[63] See Cass (2002).
[64] See Persaud (2000).

financial instruments involving credit risk. Therefore, the various credit markets will gradually integrate and the arbitrage opportunities still offered today will disappear. Ultimately, there should be a stronger, closer tie between the various capital markets, and above all, the equity, interest rate and credit markets. The emergence of credit derivatives corresponds precisely to the development of particle finance theory, the purpose of which is the identification, management and optimum allocation of the risks inherent to economic activity between investors.

Derivatives are not just new financial instruments, they are a method of unbundling, analyzing and managing economic risks.

This last chapter has enabled us to draw a full picture of the implications for the capital markets of development in credit derivatives. The first fundamental trend is more active management of credit risk and banks' portfolios of obligations, whatever the nature of the underlying exposure. This strategic imperative was a clear necessity and resulted in unprecedented growth in the 'velocity' of credit products, that is, their tradability. These changes had major effects on the commercial and investment banks' economic models and forced them to revise their strategic position in the credit markets.

A second field strongly affected by the emergence of credit derivatives is the regulation of financial activities. Although these instruments contributed largely to the revision of the Basel I Accords, observers concentrated, wrongly, on the threat they might pose to the stability of the global financial system. We have endeavored to demonstrate that at this stage, they have played only a marginal role in this area. We should not, however, lose sight of the real risks and challenges that arise from development of this market.

Finally, credit derivatives seem to be the most important financial innovation in the past ten years and are clearly part of a far-reaching process of development in the financial and derivatives markets, described by 'particle finance theory'.

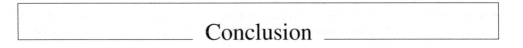

# Conclusion

In 1998, we concluded the first edition of this work by highlighting the most crucial challenge faced by the credit derivatives market at the time: the creation of liquidity. How much ground has been covered over the past seven years!

Several factors have contributed to the increase in liquidity on the CDS market, and they have ensured that CDSs have become mainstream capital market instruments. These factors include:

- Standardization of legal contracts.
- Clarification of the regulations (for banks).
- Advances in information technology, risk management processes and trading infrastructures.
- Emergence of market standards for structuring, modeling and pricing.

The unprecedented default wave of 2001–2002 also challenged the resilience of the credit derivatives market and proved its solidity. This 'baptism of fire' gave credit derivatives a central role in the capital markets, which will no doubt grow in the years to come. Their strong growth has in turn broadened the range of applications and number of users, and further fuelled product innovation.

It is very likely that the credit derivatives market will grow in an already-established pattern, like that followed by interest rate, currency and equity derivatives: pioneered by banks, often for their own needs, these other forms of derivatives were then offered to a sophisticated customer base of institutional investors, before being extended to the 'mass market segments' of corporates, retail and private banking investors. Eventually, credit derivatives seem to have the potential to become the biggest over-the-counter derivatives market, due to the omnipresence of credit risk in the financial and commercial markets and their ever-widening range of applications.

Arguably the most important consequence of credit derivative growth, apart from the improvements in risk management methods and tools, is its impact on the banking business. It seems clear today that banks no longer lend money the way they used to. Credit derivatives have obliged banks to overhaul their former decision-making processes, pricing and risk management methods. Moreover, the supervisory authorities have been led to revise the capital adequacy rules with the forthcoming implementation of Basel II in 2007.

At the end of the day, the sustainability of credit derivatives, as a new product class, will depend on their added value for financial intermediaries (investment banks and brokers) and final users (commercial banks, institutional investors and, to a lesser extent, corporates). Let us summarize the main advantages of credit derivatives.

- **Credit risk hedging.** Credit derivatives enable credit risk to be unbundled and transferred to a third party, independently from the other 'risk components' (e.g. rate, currency) of a financial asset.
- **Efficient management of credit portfolios**, as evidenced by modern financial theory. Credit derivatives enhance liquidity in the underlying credit markets, enable short position-taking and portfolio adjustments at lower transaction costs.
- **Tailor-made synthetic debt generation.** Intermediaries are now in a position to offer investors customized credit products in terms of underlying risk, leverage, format (cash or off-balance sheet), maturity, coupon, currency, etc.
- **Separation of lending decisions from traditional commercial relationship management.** Banks may now take on credit risk without nurturing a direct commercial lending relationship with borrowers.
- **Funding arbitrage.** By using credit derivatives, banks and investors may allocate the funding cost of a credit investment to the party with the most competitive position in the market, independently of the credit risk exposure.
- **Implied default rate and credit spread curve arbitrage.** With the increased liquidity of the CDS market and the rise in credit indices, capital market players can implement the same arbitrage strategies as those used in the interest rate market, for instance.
- **Homogeneous and rational pricing of credit.** Credit pricing has too often been distorted by the constraints of the cash market (e.g. lack of liquidity of a bond issue) and the commercial considerations of banks (offering cut-price loans to secure ancillary business with borrowers). Credit derivatives provide transparent pricing of the credit risk attached to an obligor.
- **Fostering an economic vision of capital requirements.** Credit derivatives act as a catalyst for the development of quantitative and risk-adjusted measurements of return on capital and the implementation of related strategies.
- **Optimal allocation of credit risk** among banks, institutional investors and other capital market players on a macroeconomy scale is now possible by using the risk transference properties of credit derivatives.

In conclusion, we believe that credit derivatives represent a new building block in 'particle finance theory'. According to the latter, derivatives are not merely financial instruments, but provide a method for systematically analyzing and unbundling contracts and assets into 'primary units of risk', enabling optimal management. As explained by Sanford: 'Long before 2020, credit risks will be disaggregated into discrete attributes that will be readily traded, unbundled and rebundled. Intermediaries will manage a large book of diversified long and short positions in credit attributes. They will make markets in credit risk attributes and in bundles of attributes customized to suit the particular needs of their clients. Such tailored products will permit each business to price and manage credit risk arising from its activities in a way that is best for that business. Perhaps even residual credit risks left after this process will be covered by a third-party insurance policy. As the discipline of particle finance evolves, the primary job of financial institutions will be to help clients put theory to practical use.'[1]

The economy and society on the whole should benefit from the development of this new class of derivative products. By allowing the identification and analysis of risks, as well as allowing

---

[1] Sanford (1993).

economic agents to transfer them to adequate and willing counterparties, credit derivatives should enable a global reallocation of credit risk on the scale of the global economy. This trend should result in diminished capital requirements across the board, since those institutions unfit to warehouse credit risk will be able to offload it and reallocate capital to more profitable business lines.

This risk optimization process is the fundamental *raison d'être* of risk management, the fields of application of which are not limited to finance, even though capital markets are at the forefront of this movement. Financial contracts (swaps and structured notes) already trade on underlying natural catastrophe and weather risks, for instance, offering insurance companies alternative risk transfer opportunities compared to traditional reinsurance methods.

In the light of these changes, credit derivatives clearly emerge as the major breakthrough of the past two decades in the financial markets. They are part of the fundamental process of innovation that drives the capital and derivatives markets and that has been successfully described by 'particle finance theory'.

# References

*Agefi (L')*. 2002. HSBC souhaite que sa taille bilantielle profite à sa banque d'investissement, 19 February.

*Agefi (L')*. 2003. Les défauts européens de 2002 dans les annales, 14 May.

Altman, E.I. 1989. Measuring corporate bond mortality and performance. *The Journal of Finance*, Sept, pp. 909–922.

Altman, E.I. and Kishore, V.M. 1996. Almost everything you wanted to know about recoveries on defaulted bonds. *Financial Analysts Journal*, Nov/Dec, pp. 57–64.

Altman, E.I., Brady, B., Resti, A. and Sironi, A. 2002. The link between default and recovery rates: implications for credit risk models and procyclicality. Working Paper, New York University, April.

Asarnow, E. and Ginzburg, A. 1995. Relative-value investing comparing loans and bonds. The Corporate Loan Investor, Citicorp, 15 June, pp. 10–18.

Azarchs, T. 2003. Demystifying banks' use of credit derivatives. RatingsDirect, Standard & Poor's, 8 December.

Bank of International Settlements. 2002. 72nd Annual Report, Basel, July.

Bank of International Settlements. 2003. 73rd Annual Report, Basel, July.

Barré, N. and Madelaine, N. 2004. Bâle II pose des problèmes de concurrence aux Etats-Unis. *Les Échos*, 26 May, p. 34.

Barrieu, P. and El Karoui, N. 2003. Optimal design of derivatives in illiquid markets. *Quantitative Finance*, **2**(3), 181–188.

Batchelor, C. 2004. CDS market liquidity 'can be sporadic'. *Financial Times*, 8 June, p. 29.

Batterman, J. and Merritt, R. 2005. Credit default swap (CDS) options: what they are, who is using them, and why. FitchRatings, 18 March.

Bessis, J. 1995. *Gestion des risques & gestion actif-passif des banques*. Dalloz.

Black, F. and Cox, J. 1976. Valuing corporate securities: some effects of bond indenture provisions. *The Journal of Finance*, pp. 351–367.

Black, F. and Scholes, M. 1973. The pricing of options and corporate liabilities. *The Journal of Political Economy*, June, pp. 637–654.

de Bodard, E., Philouze, D. and Fons, J.S. 1994. Défaillances sur les marchés de long terme et taux de défaillance 1970–1993. Global Credit Research, Moody's Investors Service, April.

Brealey, R. and Myers, S. 1991. *Principles of Corporate Finance*, 4th edn. McGraw Hill, chapters 17 and 18.

Brigo, D. and Tarenghi, M. 2005. Credit Default Swap Calibration and Counterparty Risk Valuation with a Scenario-based First Passage Model. Banca IMI.

Carty, L., Keenan, S. and Shotgrin, I. 1998. Historical default rates of corporate bond issues. Global Credit Research, Moody's Investors Service, February.

Cass, D. 2002. Goldman and Deutsche to launch economic data options. *Risk*, August.

Chassany, A.-S. 2002. Les banques font face à une montée des risques sans précédent. *La Tribune*, 9 October, p. 19.

Chassany, A.-S. 2003. Les dérivés de crédit poussent les banques à rentabiliser leurs prêts. *La Tribune*, 13 October, p. 18.

Chavagneux, C. 2002. Les banques et la croissance. *Alternatives Économiques*, No. 206, September.

Committee on the Global Financial System (CGFS). 2003. Credit risk transfer. Bank for International Settlements, January.

Cont, R. 2006. Model uncertainty and its impact on the pricing of derivative instruments. *Mathematical Finance*, in press.

Das, S.R., Duffie, D., Kapadia, N. and Saita, L. 2005. Common failings: how corporate defaults are correlated. Working Paper, University of Massachusetts, February.

Dunbar, N. 2001. The battle over loan accounting. *Risk Magazine*, Jun, 26–28.

van Duyn, A. 1995. Credit risk for sale. Any buyers? *Euromoney*, April, pp. 41–43.

Edwards, B. 1995. Let's shuffle those loans. *Euromoney*, August, pp. 22–26.

Fabozzi, F. 1993. *Bond Markets Analysis and Strategies*, 2nd edn. Prentice Hall.

Ferry, J. and Haddow-Allen, F. 2004. Boom time for structured products? *Risk*, February, pp. S7–S9.

Finger, C. (ed.). 2002. *CreditGrades Technical Document*. RiskMetrics Group.

Finnerty, J.D. 1993. An overview of corporate securities innovation. *The New Corporate Finance: Where Theory Meets Practice*, ed. D.H. Chew, Jr. McGraw Hill, pp. 212–228.

Fitch Ratings. 2003. Global Credit Derivatives: A Qualified Success. Fitch, March & September.

Fitch Ratings. 2004. Global Credit Derivatives Survey: Single-Name CDS Fuel Growth. Fitch, 7 September.

Fouquet, C. 2001. Faillites: les chances de survie dépendent de la taille. *Les Échos*, 13 December, p. 6.

Freeman, A. 1993. A comedy of errors. *The Economist*, International Banking Survey, 10 April.

Frye, J. 2003. A false sense of security. *Risk*, August, pp. 95–99.

Geske, R.L. 1977. The valuation of corporate liabilities as compound options. *Journal of Financial Quantitative Analysis* **12**: 541–552.

Glasserman, P. and Li, J. 2003. Importance sampling for portfolio credit risk. Working Paper, Columbia University.

Goldstein, M. and Turner, P. 1996. Banking crises in emerging economies: origins and policy options. Working Paper No. 46, Bank of International Settlements, October.

Guyot, E. 1998. Peregrine lets a risky deal slip through. *The Wall Street Journal Europe*, 21 January, pp. 11 & 16.

Horwood, C. 2004. The credit derivatives divide. *Risk*, February.

Houweling, P., Mentink, A. and Vorst, T. 2002. Is liquidity reflected in bond yields? Evidence from the Euro corporate bond market. Working Paper, Erasmus University Rotterdam, April.

Hull, J. and White, A. 2001. Valuing credit default swaps II: modeling default correlations. *Journal of Derivatives*, **8**(3), 12–22.

Hull, J., Predescu, M. and White, A. 2005. The valuation of correlation-dependent credit derivatives using a structural model. Working Paper, University of Toronto.

Hull, J., Nelken, I. and White, A. 2005. Merton's model, credit risk and volatility skew. *Journal of Credit Risk* **2**(1).

Hylson-Smith, S. 1998. Treading on the thin ice of credit. International Financing Review of the Year 1997, pp. 54–60.

International Swaps and Derivatives Association (ISDA). 1998. Credit risk and regulatory capital, March.

International Swaps and Derivatives Association (ISDA). 2003. Credit Derivatives Definitions.

Iskandar, S. 1998. Asian crisis boosts credit derivatives. *Financial Times*, 12 January, p. 27.

Jeanblanc, M. and Rutkowski, M. 2000. Modelling default risk: an overview. In *Mathematical Finance: Theory and Practice*, eds R. Cont and J. Yong. Higher Education Press, pp. 171–269.

Jeffery, C. 2004. Regulators put credit risk transfer into the spotlight. *Risk*, April, p. 8.

Jones, E.P., Mason, S.P. and Rosenfeld, E. 1984. Contingent claims analysis of corporate capital structures: an empirical investigation. *The Journal of Finance*, July, pp. 611–627.

Lachèvre, C. 2002. Les agences de notation inquiètes des risques susceptibles d'affecter le marché du crédit. *Les Échos*, 20 February, p. 25.

Larrain, G., Reisen, H. and von Maltzan, J. 1997. Emerging market risk and sovereign credit ratings. Technical Papers No. 124, OECD Development Centre, April.

Laurent, J.P. and Gregory, J. 2004. In the core of correlation. *Risk Magazine*, October, pp. 87–91.

Li, D.X. 2002. On default correlation: a copula function approach. *The Journal of Fixed Income* **9**: 43–54.

Longstaff, F.A. and Schwartz, E.S. 1995. A simple approach to valuing risky fixed and floating rate debt. *The Journal of Finance*, July, pp. 789–819.

Lubochinsky, C. 2002. Quel crédit accorder aux spreads de crédit?, *Revue de Stabilité Financière*, November, pp. 85–102.

Manda, A. and Gutscher, C. 1998. BIS gives investment-bank bonds a boost. *The Wall Street Journal Europe*, 17–18 April, p. 28.

Markowitz, H.M. 1959. *Portfolio Selection: Efficient Diversification of Investments*. John Wiley & Sons.

Mashal, R., Naldi, M. and Zeevi, A. 2003. Extreme events and multi-name credit derivatives. In *Credit Derivatives, The Definitive Guide*. Risk, London.

Mercer, O.M. 2003. The New Rules of the Game, Implications of the New Basel Capital Accord for the European Banking Industries, London, June.

Merritt, R.W., Linnelle, I. and Grossman, R. 2004. Self-referenced CLNs raise questions and concerns. Fitch Ratings, 13 January.

Merton, R. 1974. On the pricing of corporate debt: the risk structure of interest rates. *Journal of Finance*, **29**, 449–470.

Nisbet, P.A. 1995. Managing credit exposure with credit derivatives. *The Corporate Loan Investor*, Citicorp, 25 February, pp. 9–12.

Parsley, M. 1996. Credit derivatives get cracking. *Euromoney*, March, pp. 28–34.

Patel, N. 2004a. New type of CDS gets off the ground. *Risk*, April, p. 12.

Patel, N. 2004b. Cruising into credit. *Risk*, April, pp. 33–38.

Persaud, A. 2000. The puzzling decline in financial market liquidity. *Risk*, June.

Pinson, G. 2004. Les banques européennes empocheront les bénéfices de l'accord de Bâle II. *La Tribune*, 2 June, p. 22.

Prandi, M. 2003. La problématique de la dette fait converger les marchés d'actions et d'obligations. *Les Échos*, 28 February, p. 22.

Raulot, N. 2003a. Les produits structurés compriment les primes de risque. *La Tribune*, 28 May, p. 22.

Raulot, N. 2003b. Les agences de notation ont mangé leur pain blanc. *La Tribune*, 1 October, p. 58b.

Remolona, E.M., Bassett, W. and Geoum, I.S. 1996. Risk management by structured derivative product companies. Federal Reserve Bank of New York, Economic Policy Review, April, pp. 17–34.

Sanford, C.S. 1993. Financial markets in 2020. Bankers Trust New York Corporation, New York.

Schönbucher, P. 2002. *Credit Derivatives Pricing*. John Wiley & Sons.

Shiller, R. 2003. *The New Financial Order: Risk in the 21st Century*. Princeton University Press.

Shimko, D. 1998. When credit is due. *Risk*, March, p. 35.

Silverman, G. 2002. The pains and gains of relationship banking. *Financial Times*.

Silverman, G. and Pretzlik, C. 2001. US banks say lending vital for attracting fees. *Financial Times*, 6 December, p. 24.

Smithson, C. and Holappa, H. 1995. Credit derivatives, what are these youthful instruments and why are they used? *Risk*, December, pp. 37–38.

Smithson, C., Holappa, H. and Rai, S. 1996. Credit derivatives (2), a look at the market, its evolution and current size. *Risk*, June, pp. 47–48.

de Teran, N. 2004. Banks use swaps to beat tight spreads. *Financial News*, March.

Theodore, S.S. and Madelain, M. 1997. Modern credit-risk management and the use of credit derivatives: European banks' brave new world (and its limits). Global Credit Research, Moody's Investors Service, March.

Thind, S. 2003. Staying away in droves. *Risk*, July, pp. S2–S3.

*Tribune (la)*. 2001. Morgan Stanley veut augmenter sa capacité de prêt aux entreprises. 17 August.

Wakeman, L.M. 1990. The real function of bond rating agencies. In *The Modern Theory of Corporate Finance*, 2nd edn, ed. C.W. Smith, Jr. McGraw-Hill, pp. 410–415.

Wolf, M. 2001. The age of financial instability. *Financial Times*, 13 June.

# Further Reading

Bank of International Settlements. 2001. Basel Committee on Banking Supervision, The New Basel Capital Accord, Basel, January.

Bank of International Settlements. 2001. 71st Annual Report, Basel, July.

Bank of International Settlements. 2001. The Global OTC Derivatives Market at End-June 2001, Basel, 20 December.

Bank of International Settlements. 2003. OTC Derivatives Market Activity in the First Half of 2003, Basel, 12 November.

Bank of International Settlements. 2004. OTC Derivatives Market Activity in the Second Half of 2003, Basel, 14 May.

Bank of International Settlements. 2005. Monetary and Economic Department, International Banking and Financial Market Developments, Basel, June.

Baudu, L.J. 2003. Pourquoi Buffett les déteste. *La Tribune*, 31 March, p. 2.

Bielecki, T. and Rutkowski, M. 2002. *Credit Risk: Modeling, Valuation and Hedging.* Springer Finance.

Braouezec, Y. 2003. Les options réelles. *Economica*.

Bream, R. and Wiggins, J. 2002. Step-up bond deal fashion may return. *Financial Times*, 24 January, p. 22.

Bream, R. and Wiggins, J. 2002. Financial insurers step into spotlight. *Financial Times*, 15 August, p. 19.

British Bankers' Association. BBA credit derivatives reports (1996, 1999–2000, 2001–2002, 2003–2004).

Brody, K. 2003. CDO market looks to a broader asset base. *Risk*, May, pp. S10–S11.

Brown, M. (with research by D. Skalinder). 2004. Lead banks sit pretty atop volatile market (Capital raising and risk management poll). *Euromoney*, October, pp. 42–54.

Buehler, K.S., D'Silva, V. and Pritsch, G. 2004. The business case for Basel II. *The McKinsey Quarterly*, No. 1. McKinsey & Co.

Buffett, W. 2002. Berkshire Hathaway Annual Report.

Cass, D. 2001. Credit market convergence: an ever-changing landscape. *Risk*, August.

Centre for the Study of Financial Innovation (CSFI). 2002. Banana Skins 2002: A CSFI Survey of the Risks Facing Banks.

Centre for the Study of Financial Innovation (CSFI). 2003. Banana Skins 2003: A CSFI Survey of the Risks Facing Banks.

Chassany, A.-S. 2003. Une révolution dans la gestion des risques. *La Tribune*, 31 March, p. 2.

Chassany, A.-S. 2004. Les banques ont du mal à mesurer leurs risques opérationnels. *La Tribune*, 27 April, p. 19.

Cheng, V. 2002. Risk transfer and the implications of Basel II. *Global Finance*. Fox-Pitt, Kelton, 11 July.

Chocron, V. 2002. La Commission Bancaire alerte sur les risques de crédit. *La Tribune*, 3 July, p. 23.

Commission Bancaire. 1997. Instruments dérivés de crédit, premières orientations en matière de traitement prudentiel. Documents de discussion & d'étude no. 1, June.

Commission Bancaire. 1998. Bulletin de la Commission Bancaire no. 18, April, pp. 8–14.

Commission Bancaire. 2003. Introduction au Rapport 2002 de la Commission Bancaire, July.

Commission Bancaire (Secrétariat Général de la). 2004. Modalités de calcul du ratio international de solvabilité au 01/01/2004, Annexe 15, Banque de France.

Counis, A. 2002. Le Comité de Bâle parvient à un accord sur les futures règles prudentielles. *Les Échos*, 3 July, p. 20.

Counis, A. 2004. La Commission Bancaire attire l'attention sur les dangers des dérivés de crédit. *Les Échos*, 13 May, p. 41.

Counis, A. 2004. Les banques européennes s'inquiètent d'éventuels ajustements outré-Atlantique. *Les Échos*, 26 May, p. 34.

Davidson, C. 2004. Cutting capital. *Risk*, April, pp. 70–71.

Davies, M. and Pugachevsky, D. 2004. Pricing and hedging credit default swaps on indices. Bear Stearns, February.

Desjardins, C. 2003. Les banques se font tirer l'oreille sur les dérivés de crédit. *Les Échos*, 24 March, p. 28.

Desjardins, C. 2003. Les titrisations 'CDO' portées par ces instruments financiers. *Les Échos*, 24 March, p. 28.

DNA Training and Consulting, Newsletter Issue No. 21, August–December 2003.

*The Economist*. 2000. Danger signs, 10 June, pp. 103–104.

*The Economist*. 2000. The bigger they are, 28 October, pp. 91–97.

*The Economist*. 2002. The only way is up, maybe, 27 July, p. 58.

*The Economist*. 2002. Free the New York three, 18 May, p. 13.

*The Economist*. 2002. The firms that can't stop falling, 7 September, p. 65.

European Central Bank. 2004. Credit risk transfer by EU banks: activities, risks and risk management, May.

Evans, J. 2002. Credit risk and its management raise a paradox. *Euromoney*, March, pp. 52–54.

FitchRatings. 2003. Synthetic Index – Benchmarking Portfolio Performance. Fitch, June.

Fons, J. 2001. Regulatory Change and Basel. Moody's Investors Service, 10 May.

Fons, J., Cantor, R. and Mahoney, C. 2002. Understanding Moody's Corporate Bond Ratings and Rating Process. Moody's Investors Service, May.

International Financing Review. 2002. Deutsche and Goldman offer joint economics products, 4 May, p. 132.

Jaeck, C., Spitz, T. and Taïeb, J.-É. 2000. Modèles de risque de credit et allocation de capital. Ecole Nationale de la Statistique & de l'Administration Économique.

JP Morgan Chase. Annual reports 2003, 2002 and 2001.

Lachèvre, C. 2004. Les premières options de crédit viennent d'être lancées. *Les Échos*, 26 May, p. 28.

Lando, D. 2000. Some elements of rating-based credit risk modeling. In *Advanced Fixed Income Valuation Tools*. John Wiley & Sons, pp. 193–215.

Monnoyeur, P. 2004. Les dérivés d'actions et de crédit convergent, facilitant la mise en place de stratégies à fort effet de levier. *L'Agefi*, 19 February, p. 5.

Nevstad, H. 2004. Credit spread warrants. Introducing credit spread options to corporate bond investors. Dresdner Kleinwort Wasserstein, 25 May.

Oliver, Wyman & Co. and Morgan Stanley. 2002. The Future of European Corporate & Institutional Banking: The Need to Differentiate, March.

Plender, J. 2002. The limits of ingenuity. *Financial Times*, 17 May, p. 19.

Polyn, G. 2002. Shiller backs private hedging product. *Risk*, February, p. 8.

Prato, O. 2002. Les dérivés de crédit, nouvelle source d'instabilité financière? Secrétariat Général de la Commission Bancaire, Revue de Stabilité Financière, November, pp. 69–84.

Raulot, N. 2003. L'essor incontrôlé des dérivés de crédit. *La Tribune*, 31 March, p. 2.

Raulot, N. 2003. Seuls 10% des dérivés sont issus de la Bourse. *La Tribune*, 31 March, p. 3.

Reuters. 2002. UBS Warburg hedged 30% of 2001 lending. *Financial Times*, 15 March, p. 23.

*Risk Magazine*. 2003. Credit derivatives. Global derivatives awards 2003, September.

*Risk Magazine*. 2004. Credit derivatives. Global derivatives awards 2004, September.

*Risk Magazine*. 2004. Credit derivatives house of the year: Morgan Stanley. Risk awards 2004, January, p. 18.

*Risk Magazine*. 2005. Credit derivatives house of the year: Deutsche Bank. Risk awards 2005, January, p. 27.

Rule, D. 2001. The credit derivatives market: its development and possible implications for financial stability. Bank of England, Financial Stability Review, June.

Segond, V. 2003. Les dérivés de crédit, bombe à retardement? *La Tribune*, 17 March, p. 63b.

Shiller, R. 2003. Risk management for the masses. *The Economist*, 22 March, pp. 74–75.

de Solleu, G. 2004. Le nouveau ratio remporte un satisfecit. *Les Échos*, 2 June, p. 22.

de Solleu, G. 2004. Le Trésor tente de convaincre Bruxelles contre Bâle II. *Les Échos*, 4 June, p. 20.

Wessel, D. 2002. New futures could help folks insure against economic risk. *The Wall Street Journal*, 5 September.

Winters, B. 2002. JP Morgan's global derivatives leadership. JP Morgan, 11 March.

Wolcott, R. 2004. Credit derivatives indexes look set for merger. *Risk*, March, p. 13.

Wolcott, R. 2004. Two of a kind. *Risk*, March, pp. 24–26.

Wolcott, R. 2004. CFOs come out in private. *Risk*, April, pp. 65–66.

Wolcott, R. 2004. Collateral managers go creative. *Risk*, April, pp. 68–69.

Wolcott, R. 2005. The case for constant maturity default swaps. *Risk*, March, pp. 42–43.

# Index

A.M. Best & Co., 15
Abbey National, 129
ABN Amro, 96, 115, 168–74
active-regulation needs, real risks, 240–1
actively-managed arbitrage-driven synthetic
    CDOs, concepts, 128–33
actively-managed portfolios, banks, 205–41, 249
AIG Financial Products, 64–5
Air Canada, 159
Alstom, 26
Altman, Edward I., 19
American Municipal Bond Association Corp
    (AMBAC), 30
American options, 56
applications
    CDSs, 66–79, 103, 125, 152, 155–63, 165–7,
        172–4, 216–18, 248–9, 251
    CLNs, 49–50, 78, 92–4, 115–25, 156–60
    CMDS, 52, 243
    credit derivatives, 49–50, 52, 54, 66–79,
        102–3, 149–74, 198–249, 251–3
    EDSs, 54, 78–9, 147, 246
    iTraxx indices, 102–3, 139–40
    private individuals, 248–9
arbitrage, 14, 66–70, 102–7, 119–24, 147, 152,
    159, 166–7, 172–4, 223–4, 229–32, 241,
    245–9, 252–3
    balance sheet-driven CDOs, 119–24, 128,
        147, 230–3
    credit curve arbitrage, 69–70, 252
    recovery rate arbitrage, 70
    regulatory arbitrage, 14, 119–24, 152, 172–4,
        223–4, 229–32, 241
    relative value arbitrage, 68, 102–3, 166–7,
        175–6
arbitrage CBOs/CLOs, concepts, 107–14, 125
arbitrage-driven synthetic CDOs
    actively-managed structures, 128–33
    characteristics, 126–7
    concepts, 124–47, 159

examples, 128–33
first structures, 124–8
historical background, 124, 126
on-demand structures, 133–47
overview, 143–7
reversal of the market, 127–8
structures, 124–33
arbitrage-free pricing models, concepts, 175–6
Argentina, 43, 159
Aria CDO, 141
Armstrong World Industries, 38
Asarnow, E., 245
Asian banks, 162
Asian crisis (1997), 19, 150–2
Asian options, 177–8
asset categories, banks, 12–14, 120–4
asset managers, 2, 152, 165–8, 201–2, 228–9
    *see also* institutional investors
asset swaps
    *see also* credit spreads
    CDSs, 45–9
    concepts, 21–4, 32–3, 45–9, 57–60, 69–70,
        154–60, 175–6
    definition, 21
    trends, 21–2
asset switch swaps
    *see also* total (rate of) return swaps
    concepts, 63
asset-backed commercial paper (ABCPs), 112
asset-backed securities (ABSs)
    *see also* collateralized debt obligations
    concepts, 105–14, 141–2, 158–60, 171
asset/liability management, 2
asymmetrical profitability profile, credit risk,
    7–8
AT&T, 128, 159
Australia, 155, 240
Austria, 173
Axa Investment Managers, 129–33, 141, 144,
    167, 233

BAFIN, 92
balance sheet-driven CDOs
    concepts, 114–24, 128, 147, 230–3
    expected changes, 232–3
    overview, 119
    regulatory arbitrage, 119–24, 152, 172–4,
        229–33, 241
    trends, 114–15, 232–3
Bank of America, 29, 119, 127, 159, 201–2, 232
Bank of England, 12, 234–5
Bank for International Settlements (BIS), 8, 10,
        11–12, 23–4, 149–50, 153–7
bank loans see loans
Bankers Trust, 31, 155, 168–74, 201–2, 242
banking books, regulatory standards, 1, 11–14,
        23–4, 30, 42, 44, 72–3, 152
bankruptcies, 2, 4–8, 19, 26, 36, 39–43, 120,
        128, 150–1, 200, 207, 234–5, 239–40
    statistics, 4–8
    Z-scores, 19
banks, 1–14, 19–20, 23–4, 30, 44, 66, 70–3, 79,
        111–12, 118–47, 150–74, 198–249
    actively-managed portfolios, 205–41, 249
    asset categories, 12–14, 120–4
    balance sheet-driven CLOs, 114–24, 128, 147,
        230–3
    Basel I regulations, 11–14, 23–4, 30, 118–24,
        200, 215–17, 223 41, 249
    Basel II regulations, 14, 120–4, 154, 200,
        223–41, 251
    capital adequacy regulations, 1, 11–14, 23–4,
        30, 44, 72–3, 114–24, 152–4, 200, 205–6,
        215–17, 223–41, 249, 251
    commercial banks, 152, 168, 201–23, 238–41,
        251–3
    competitors, 200–4, 218, 244
    'credit crunch', 6, 150
    credit derivative applications, 66, 70–4, 79,
        160–74, 198, 199, 212–49
    credit ratings, 6, 13, 207, 225–41
    crises, 2, 4–7, 11–12, 19–20, 150, 199–204,
        238–41
    critique, 223, 234–41, 244–9
    cultural issues, 199, 217, 222–3
    developments, 1, 151–74, 199–249, 251–3
    economic capital, 204–17
    financial disintermediation, 200–1
    financial instability, 223, 234–41
    insurance issues, 12, 27
    inter-bank recovery swaps, 136
    investment banks, 31, 81, 124, 128–9, 162–3,
        167–74, 201–2, 238–41, 251–3
    market share, 161–8, 202–3, 207
    merchant banks, 29, 151, 154, 168–9, 201–4,
        218–19
    off-balance-sheet activities, 12–14, 31

    'one-stop shopping' concepts, 202–3
    organizational issues, 199, 217, 220–3
    price cuts, 202–3
    RAROC, 204, 207–9, 213–17, 222, 244–5
    regulatory standards, 1, 11–14, 23–4, 30, 42,
        44, 72–3, 114–24, 152–4, 200, 204, 215–17,
        223–41, 249, 251–3
    relationship banking, 199–200, 202–3, 212–17,
        219–20, 243–4
    reporting systems, 220–2
    returns, 13–14, 123–4, 204–23, 226–32, 240–1,
        244–9
    risk, 1–3, 10–14, 120–4, 150–74, 199–249
    'risk intermediaries', 218–41
    roles, 1, 200–49
    runs, 12
    secondary markets, 26–7, 209–12, 219
    securitization of bank loans, 114–24, 209, 212,
        238–9
    shareholder value, 200–2
    strategic issues, 199, 217–23
    sub-participation uses, 26–7
    systemic risk, 11–12, 150
    trends, 162–3, 199–249
    types, 161–3, 168–74, 201–2
    venture capital, 229
    vulnerabilities, 200–4
    world-ranking banks, 161–3
Barclays, 211
Barclays Capital, 170
barrier options
    concepts, 60, 177, 182
    default-and-out barrier options, 60, 243
base correlation, concepts, 138–9, 193–5
Basel I regulations
    amendments, 13–14, 223–41, 249
    concepts, 11–14, 23–4, 30, 118–24, 200,
        215–17, 223–41, 249
    critique, 13–14, 23–4, 30, 200, 223–41, 249
Basel II regulations
    CDOs, 229–41
    concepts, 14, 120–4, 154, 200, 223–41, 251
    critique, 223–41
    implementation date, 14, 223–5, 251
    McDonough ratio, 225
    pillars, 225–41
    principles, 224–41
    scope, 225
Basel Joint Forum, 236
basis, 42, 44–9, 54–5, 66–70, 151
    definition, 69
    trading, 69–70
basket credit default swaps, concepts, 81–90, 133,
        155–60
BBVA, 145
BCI, 119

Bear Stearns, 168–74
behavioral risk, 126, 248–9
Belgium, 173
Berkshire Hathaway, 234, 236
bid–offer spreads, recovery rates, 136–40
bilateral markets, 151
binary options, 60
BIS *see* Bank for International Settlements
BISTRO program, 116–19, 218
Black, F., 176–93
Black–Scholes options pricing model, 176–93
Bloomberg, 144
BNP Paribas, 29, 119, 141–2, 168–74, 202, 232
bonds, 4, 8–33, 38–55, 56–60, 67–70, 94–5, 105–24, 154–5, 165–7, 188–90, 201, 233
  *see also* funded instruments; rating agencies
  CBOs, 105–14
  CDSs, 45–9, 67–70
  convertible bonds, 41, 48, 125–8, 152, 165–7
  coupon sizes, 24
  forwards, 56
  put options, 30, 177–83
  types, 9, 18, 20–4, 30, 201
booms, 149, 151
borrower risk *see* issuer risk
British Bankers' Association (BBA), 149–59, 161–3, 165–6
Brownian motion, 176–83, 189, 195
Buffet, Warren, 223, 234, 236

call options, 57–60, 177–83
  *see also* options
Cantor Fitzgerald, 169–74
Capital Adequacy Directive (CAD), EU, 13–14
capital adequacy regulations, 1, 11–14, 23–4, 30, 44, 72–3, 114–24, 152–4, 200, 205–6, 215–17, 223–41, 249, 251
  Basel I regulations, 11–14, 23–4, 30, 118–24, 200, 215–17, 223–41, 249
  Basel II regulations, 14, 120–4, 154, 200, 223–41, 251
  CAD, 13–14, 225–6
  concepts, 1, 11–14, 23–4, 30, 44, 114, 200, 205–6, 215–17, 223–41, 249, 251
capital markets
  *see also* institutional investors
  Basel II regulations, 228–41
  changes, 1, 200–4, 228–49, 251–3
  concepts, 8–11, 66–70, 79, 160, 174, 199–249, 251–3
  credit derivative applications, 66–70, 79, 160, 199–249
  credit risk, 8–11, 251–3
  credit spreads, 11, 19–24
  definition, 8

integration trends, 147, 152, 245–9
  particle finance theory, 242–9, 252–3
capital structure arbitrage
  concepts, 102–3, 166–7
  credit indices, 102–3
capital-guaranteed/protected products, hybrid instruments, 90–4
capped/floored total return swaps, concepts, 63
cash credit indices, concepts, 94–5
cash instruments, 4, 8–11, 22, 45–9, 67–8, 155
  *see also* funded . . .
cash settlements, CDSs, 41, 82–90
cash-flow CDOs, concepts, 107–14, 117–24
cash-flow diversion rules, CDOs, 111–12
Casino Guichard Perrachon SA, 60
cat bonds, 247–8, 253
CDO-squared products (CDO 2), 141–3
CDS-based credit indices, 95–6
CDX, 139, 141, 191
Center for the Study of Financial Innovation (CSFI), poll, 1–2
Centre Re, 164
cheapest-to-deliver option, CDSs/asset-swaps spreads, 46
Cheyne Capital, 129, 132, 141
Chicago Board of Trade, 8
Chicago Mercantile Exchange, 8
China, 228
'Chinese walls', 221
CIC, 202
Cirio, 153–4
Citi Big, 94–5
Citibank, 1, 29, 33, 95, 119
Citigroup, 96, 168–74, 201–3
classes, credit derivatives, 32
clearing houses, 27–9
Coffrey, Meredith, 244
collateral, 4, 15, 16–18, 25–9, 64–5, 81, 85–6, 89–90, 103–47, 155–60, 167, 174, 189–98, 217, 229–41, 246–7
  *see also* netting . . .
collateralized bond obligations (CBOs)
  arbitrage CBOs/CLOs, 107–14, 125
  CLOs contrasts, 112–13
  concepts, 105–14, 125, 160
  overview, 113–14
  underperformance, 113–14
collateralized debt obligations (CDOs)
  *see also* asset-backed securities; structured products
  actively-managed arbitrage-driven synthetic CDOs, 128–33
  arbitrage-driven synthetic CDOs, 124–47, 159
  balance sheet-driven CDOs, 114–24, 128, 147, 230–3
  Basel II regulations, 229–41

collateralized debt obligations (CDOs)
  (*Continued*)
  cash-flow CDOs, 107–14, 117–24
  cash-flow diversion rules, 111–12
  CDO-squared products, 141–3
  concepts, 15, 81, 85–6, 89–90, 103–47,
    155–60, 167, 174, 189–98, 217, 229–41
  critique, 147, 155–60, 174, 229–41
  default risk, 110–11
  first arbitrage-driven synthetic CDOs, 124–8
  I/C (interest cover) tests, 111–12
  IRR, 112
  loan contrasts, 111–12
  O/C (over-collateralization) tests, 111–12
  on-demand CDOs, 133–47
  portfolio management, 110–14
  pricing models, 189–98
  ramp-up period, 112–13
  rating agencies, 15, 107–14, 116–28, 131–3
  reinvestment risks, 112–13, 126–7
  structure, 109–14, 115
  types, 105–47
collateralized loan obligations (CLOs), 105,
    107–14, 117–24, 156–60
  arbitrage CBOs/CLOs, 107–14
  CBOs contrasts, 112–14
  concepts, 105, 107–14, 117–24, 156–60
  overview, 113–14
  synthetic CLOs, 115–24
collateralized mortgage obligations (CMOs),
    246–7
commercial banks, 152, 168, 201–23, 238–41,
    251–3
commercial mortgage-backed securities (CMBS),
    106–7
commercial paper, 201
commercial risk, hedging, 74–9
Committee on the Global Financial System,
    234–41
commodities, 11, 90, 150
competitors, banks, 200–4, 218, 244
complete markets, pricing concepts, 178–83
complex financial instruments, 1–2
conclusions, credit derivatives, 251–3
conditions to payment, CDSs, 40–55
confidentiality benefits, credit derivatives, 212–13
Conseco, 5, 43
consortiums, project finance sponsors, 75–6
constant maturity default swaps (CMDSs)
  *see also* credit default swaps
  advantages, 53, 78–9, 243
  applications, 52, 173, 243
  concepts, 49, 51–3, 78–9, 173, 243
  critique, 53, 78–9, 243
  mechanism, 52–3
  premiums, 52

constant maturity swaps (CMSs), concepts, 51–3
construction rules, credit indices, 98–101
'contingent' approaches, 94
convertible bonds, 41, 48, 125–8, 152, 165–7
convertible debt, 9, 41, 125–8, 152, 165–7
convexity, 135–40
Cooke ratio, 225
copula model, 133, 137–8, 140, 189–98
corporate bonds, 4, 8–11, 14–24
corporate governance, 201–2
corporates
  credit derivative applications, 66, 73–9, 152,
    157–8, 160, 167–8, 245–9, 251
  funding strategies, 74, 77–9, 167–8, 201
  hedging applications, 74–9, 167–8
  investment strategies, 74, 77–9, 167–8
  key accounts, 76
correlation
  base correlation, 138–9, 193–5
  concepts, 135–40, 154, 189–98
  default risk, 84–90, 135–47, 189–98
  risk, 135–40, 154
correlation products
  *see also* second-generation credit derivatives
  concepts, 81, 84–90, 103, 105–47, 154, 165–7
  risk management, 137–40, 154
counterparty risk
  *see also* unfunded instruments
  CLNs, 49–50
  collateral, 27–9
  concepts, 3–4, 8–11, 27–33, 49–50, 125–8,
    140, 162–3, 208–9, 218–19, 236–41
  management methods, 27–9, 240–1
  OTC markets, 9–11, 27–9, 31
  real risks, 240–1
coupon sizes
  capital-guaranteed/protected products, 91–4
  credit spreads, 24
covenants, concepts, 25–7, 33
coverage functions, investment banks, 173–4
Cox, J., 181–2
Cox–Ingersoll-Ross model, 188–9
CQS Management, 166
Crédit Agricole, 202
credit card loans, 114
credit conversion factor (CCF), Basel I
    regulations, 12, 226–7
'credit crunch', systemic risk, 6, 150
credit curve arbitrage, 69–70, 252
credit default swaps (CDSs)
  advantages, 36, 45–7, 76–9, 95, 103, 155–60,
    174, 218, 248–9, 251
  applications, 66–79, 103, 125, 152, 155–63,
    165–7, 172–4, 216–17, 218, 248–9, 251
  Armstrong World Industries, 38
  asset-swap spreads, 45–9

basket credit default swaps, 81–90, 133, 155–60
bonds, 45–9, 67–70
CDS-based credit indices, 95–6
characteristics, 35–55
concepts, 35–55, 66–79, 81–90, 95, 118, 122, 125–47, 149–50, 152, 155–63, 165–7, 172–4, 180–98, 216–18, 233, 248–9, 251
conditions to payment, 40–55
credit events, 36–7, 39–55, 82–90, 96–103
critique, 36, 45–55, 76–9, 103, 155–60, 174, 233, 248–9, 251
deliverable obligations, 41–55
fixed/floating legs, 36–7
funded variants, 49
historical background, 39, 95
ISDA Definitions, 37–45, 82, 240
legal documents, 37–55, 82, 150–2, 251
obligations category, 38–55
off-balance-sheet activities, 47
options, 58–60, 165–7
parties, 36–7
premiums, 36–55, 83–90, 118, 127–8, 136, 140–7, 180–98
Railtrack case, 41, 43
reference entities, 36–55, 82–90, 118–47
reference obligations, 38–55, 82–90
restructuring events, 39–40, 42–6
settlement methods, 36, 40–55, 61, 82–90
standard mechanism, 36–7, 251
'successor' considerations, 38
tailor-made products, 47, 66–70, 172–4, 238
trends, 35, 95, 149–50, 155–63, 165–7, 174
variants, 49–55
credit derivatives
see also credit default swaps; individual products
advantages, 29–33, 47, 76–9, 212, 236–41, 242–9, 251–3
applications, 49–50, 52, 54, 66–79, 102–3, 149–74, 198–249, 251–3
banks, 66, 70–3, 79, 160–74, 198, 199, 212–49
birth, 31–2, 154, 162–3
capital market players, 66–70, 79, 160, 199–249
characteristics, 31–3, 35–55
classes, 32
concepts, 1–3, 8–11, 24–33, 35–79, 147–74, 199–249, 251–3
conclusions, 251–3
confidentiality benefits, 212–13
corporates, 66, 73–9, 152, 157–8, 160, 167–8, 245–9, 251
critique, 29–33, 36, 45–55, 76–9, 83–4, 88–90, 92–4, 103, 107–8, 147, 155–60, 174, 199–249, 251–3

dangers, 223, 234–41
definition, 29
derivatives' contrasts, 31–2
development, 1, 8–9, 24–5, 29–33, 39, 95, 150–74, 199–249, 251–3
emergence, 1–3, 8–11, 24, 29–33
financial instability, 223, 234–41
financial revolution, 241–9
first-generation credit derivatives, 78–9, 82, 150–74
historical background, 1, 8–9, 24–5, 29–33, 39, 95, 150–74
industrialization processes, 152
institutional investors, 66–70, 144, 152–74, 227–41, 251–3
insurance/reinsurance companies, 152, 161, 163–5, 233, 237, 241, 253
integration trends, 147, 152, 245–9
investment banks, 31, 81, 124, 128–9, 162–3, 167–74, 201–2, 238–41, 251–3
investors, 32, 36–79, 82–103, 124–47, 152–74, 198, 199–249, 251–3
ISDA Definitions, 37–45, 82, 240
issuers, 32, 36–79, 82–103, 161–8, 182
liquidity issues, 2–3, 9, 23–4, 151–2, 172–4, 200–4, 209–23, 248–9, 251–3
major players, 66–79, 144, 152, 160–74, 234–41, 251–3
maturity, 32, 36–79, 83–103, 134–47, 156–60, 181, 186–9
multi-name credit derivatives, 189–98
nature, 31–3
new class of products, 32, 236–49, 251–3
OTC markets, 9–11, 31–3, 149–50, 175–98, 251–3
particle finance theory, 241–9, 252–3
precursors, 30
pricing, 8, 175–98, 243–9
private individuals, 248–9
real risks, 240–1, 249
reduced-form pricing models, 183–90, 195–9
regulatory standards, 1, 11–14, 23–4, 30, 42, 44, 72–3, 114–24, 150–4, 200, 204–6, 215–17, 223–41, 249, 251–3
second-generation credit derivatives, 49, 81–103, 152–74, 189
securitizations, 115–24
statistics, 9–11, 149–74, 199–249
structural pricing models, 176–84
supervisory authorities' studies, 234–41, 251
synthetic CLOs, 115–24
types, 35–79
unbundling, 32–3, 198, 218, 223–41, 242–9, 252–3
underlying assets, 32–3, 35–79, 157–60, 175–98, 249

credit derivatives (*Continued*)
  users, 66–79, 144, 152, 160–74, 198, 234–41,
    251–3
  yields, 31, 66–70, 82–3, 92
credit event derivatives
  concepts, 35–55, 60
  definition, 35
Credit Event Notices, CDSs, 40
credit events, 36–7, 39–55, 60, 82–90, 96–103,
    120–4, 159, 175–98, 233
  CDSs, 36–7, 39–55, 82–90, 96–103
  famous events, 43, 159
  path dependency, 143
  standard events, 46, 120–4, 150–2
credit indices
  *see also* second-generation credit derivatives
  capital structure arbitrage, 102–3
  cash credit indices, 94–5
  CDS-based credit indices, 95–6
  concepts, 81, 94–103, 139–40, 156–60, 165–7,
    190–8
  construction rules, 98–101
  iTraxx indices, 96–103, 139–40, 191–2
  mechanisms, 96–8
  premiums, 96–103
  term structure trades, 102–3
  users, 103, 139–40, 156–60, 165–7
Crédit Lyonnais, 202
credit markets
  *see also* markets
  arms, 219–20
  integration trends, 147, 152, 245–9
  liquidity issues, 2–3, 9, 23–4, 151–2, 172–4,
    200–4, 209–23, 248–9, 251–3
Crédit Mutuel, 202
credit ratings
  *see also* rating agencies
  ABSs, 107–8
  banks, 6, 13, 207, 225–41
  concepts, 3–20, 25–7, 29, 48–9, 84–90,
    94–103, 107–8, 116–28, 131–3, 141–7,
    157–60, 207–9, 213–17, 225–41
  credit-risk assessments, 11–20, 25–7, 48–9,
    94–103, 107–8, 116–28, 131–3, 141–7,
    157–60, 207–9, 213–17, 225–41
  critique, 19–20, 235–41
  downgradings, 3, 6, 16–18, 25–6, 28–9
  fundamental analysis, 15–20
  grades, 15–20, 25–7, 87–90, 94–103, 107–8,
    116–28, 131–3, 141–7, 157–60, 207–9,
    213–17, 225–41
  OTC derivatives markets, 29
  statistics, 6, 15, 19–20
credit risk
  *see also* creditworthiness . . . ; default . . . ;
    risk

assessments, 9–27, 48–9, 84–90, 94–103,
    107–8, 116–28, 131–3, 141–7, 152–74,
    175–98, 207–9, 213–17, 225–49
  asymmetrical profitability profile, 7–8
  Basel II regulations, 14, 120–4, 154, 200,
    223–41, 251
  capital markets, 8–11, 251–3
  characteristics, 4–8
  concepts, 1–33, 35–79, 93–4, 116–47, 150–74,
    175–98, 212–49, 251–3
  credit spreads, 11, 19–24, 181
  definition, 1–4
  derivatives markets, 9–10, 27–33
  formula, 4
  hedges, 30–3, 66–70, 74–9, 94, 102–3, 114,
    125–8, 133–6, 146–7, 151–2, 160–8,
    172–83, 201, 238–41, 252–3
  idiosyncratic component, 4, 19, 26
  importance, 8–11
  incentive issues, 235–41
  indirect exposure, 75–9
  macro management, 26–7, 70–1, 102–3
  management methods, 1–2, 24–33, 66, 120–6,
    135–47, 200–23, 225–41, 242–9, 252–3
  measurement, 11–24
  Merton's structural model of default risk,
    178–86
  micro management, 25–7, 71–3
  modelling, 1, 175–98, 251–3
  OTC markets, 9–11, 27–9
  quantitative models, 175–6, 208
  rating agencies, 11, 13, 14–20, 25–6, 48–9,
    84–90, 94–103, 107–8, 116–28, 131–3,
    141–7, 157–60, 207–9, 225–41
  recovery rates, 4, 16–18, 19–24, 83–102,
    135–47, 166–7, 185–9
  reduced–form models, 183–90, 195–9
  regulatory standards, 11–14, 23–4, 30, 72–3,
    114–24, 152, 200, 215–17, 223–41, 249,
    251–3
  specific risk, 4, 7–8
  structural models, 176–84, 195–9
  systemic risk, 4–8, 97–8, 150
  term structures, 13–14, 166–7
  transfers, 32–3, 198, 218, 223–41, 242–9,
    252–3
  trigger events, 25–6, 28–9, 35–55, 60, 82–90,
    96–103, 120–4, 159, 175–98, 233
  types, 3–4, 246–9
  unbundling, 32–3, 198, 218, 223–41, 242–9,
    252–3
credit risk management, 1–2, 24–33, 66–73,
    120–6, 135–47, 200–23, 225–41, 242–9,
    252–3
  concepts, 1–2, 24–33, 240–1, 242–9, 252–3
  derivatives markets, 27–9

macro management, 26–7, 70–1, 102–3
micro management, 25–7, 71–3
particle finance theory, 242–9, 252–3
traditional methods, 24–9
trigger events, 25–6, 28–9, 35–55, 82–90, 96–103
credit spread caps, concepts, 60
credit spread derivatives
  concepts, 36, 55–60
  definition, 35, 55
  types, 55–60
credit spread forwards
  concepts, 55–60
  mechanism, 56
credit spread options
  concepts, 55–60, 167
  mechanism, 57–8
credit spread warrants (CSWs), 60
credit spreads
  see also asset swaps
  concepts, 11, 19–24, 35, 54–60, 135–47, 154–60, 164–5, 181–2, 184–7, 243–4
  coupon sizes, 24
  credit-risk assessments, 11, 19–24, 181
  definition, 20
  determinants, 23–4
  discount rates, 24
  first approach, 20–1
  hazard rates, 184–90, 195–9
  nature, 22–4
  pricing models, 181–2, 184–7
  regulatory standards, 23–4
  risk, 11, 19–24, 135–47, 181, 184–7
Credit Suisse First Boston (CSFB), 29, 41, 115–16, 126, 168–74, 202
Credit Trade, 169–74
credit value chain, concepts, 246–7
credit–linked notes (CLNs)
  see also credit default swaps
  advantages, 51, 78
  applications, 49–50, 78, 92–4, 115–25, 128, 156–60
  basket of credits, 82–90, 155–60
  concepts, 49–51, 78, 82–90, 92–4, 115–25, 128, 156–60
  critique, 51, 78, 92, 156–60
  mechanism, 50–1
Creditex, 169–74
Creditflux magazine, 159, 170–1
CreditGrade, issuers, 182
creditworthiness risk
  see also credit risk
  basis level, 48–9
  concepts, 3–4, 14–20, 25–7, 30, 48–9, 53, 83–90, 201, 210–11

crises, 2, 4–7, 11–12, 19–20, 150, 199–204, 238–41
critique
  credit derivatives, 29–33, 36, 45–55, 76–9, 83–4, 88–90, 92–4, 103, 107–8, 147, 155–60, 174, 199–249
  markets, 223, 234–41
cultural issues
  banks, 199, 217, 222–3
  derivatives, 248–9
currency derivatives, 10–11, 150, 247
  see also exchange rates
  OTC markets, 10–11, 150
  statistics, 10–11, 150
customers
  optimized returns, 212–17, 220, 252–3
  relationship banking, 199–200, 202–3, 212–17, 219–20, 243–4
  returns, 212–17, 243–4

dangers, credit derivatives, 223, 234–41
de Bodard, Eric, 26
debt
  CDOs, 15, 81, 85–6, 89–90, 103–47, 155–60, 167, 174, 189–98, 217, 229–41
  developing countries, 2
  equity contrasts, 9
  high-yield debt, 2, 22–3, 95, 109–14, 141–2, 160, 167, 215–17
  'mezzanine' debt, 109–14, 125–8, 133–40, 147, 160, 164–5, 193–4
  outstanding debt, 2
  recovery rates, 4, 16–18, 19–24, 83–102, 135–47, 166–7, 185–9
  senior debt, 4, 9, 16–18, 25–7, 109–28, 134–47
  types, 9, 16–18, 134–47
debt restructuring, 39–40, 42–6, 172–4, 233
debtors
  concepts, 3–4, 16–20
  exposure, 4, 8–14, 27–9, 75, 249
  types, 4, 9
Deckungstock, 92
default risk
  see also credit risk
  CDOs, 110–11
  concepts, 3–4, 16–24, 30, 32, 70–3, 84–90, 110–11, 135–47, 175–98, 226–41, 243–9, 252–3
  correlations, 84–90, 135–47, 189–98
  Merton's structural model of default risk, 178–86
  modelling, 1, 175–98, 251–3
  options, 30, 243
  risk-neutral probabilities, 176–89
default statistics, outstanding debt, 2, 4–8, 16–17
default swaptions, concepts, 58–60

default thresholds, random default barriers, 182, 195
default-and-out options, 60, 243
deliverable obligations, CDSs, 41–55
delta-hedging strategies, 94, 133–41, 177–83, 188, 238
dependent defaults, reduced-form models, 195–6
deregulation, 1, 200–2
Derivative Product Companies (DPCs), 29
derivatives
  concepts, 1, 8–11, 24–33, 245–9
  credit derivatives' contrasts, 31–2
  credit risk, 9–10, 24–33
  cultural issues, 248–9
  developments, 1, 8–9, 29–33, 199–249, 251–3
  historical background, 1, 8–9, 24–5, 29–33, 39, 95, 150–74
  types, 9, 30, 246–9
Deutsche Bank, 29, 33, 96, 119, 126–30, 141, 154–5, 168–74, 202, 229, 243
Deutsche Börse–Eurex, 8
developmental impacts, credit derivatives, 1, 8–9, 24–5, 29–33, 39, 95, 150–74, 199–249, 251–3
Dexia, 128, 144
digital options *see* binary options
disclosure requirements, Basel II regulations, 225–41
discount rates, credit spreads, 24
distribution arm, credit markets, 219–20
diversification, 2, 26, 66–70, 102–3, 106–24, 161–5, 190, 198, 205–23, 233, 240–1
domestic sovereign debt, 9
double leverage, CDO-squared structures, 143
Dow Chemical, 87–9
Dow Jones, 94, 96
Dresdner Kleinwort Wasserstein (DKW), 60, 170, 229
Drexel Burnham Lambert, 109
DRI McGraw-Hill, 19
Duchess I CDO, 114
DWS, 167
dynamic hedging, concepts, 178–83

economic capital, 204–17, 244–9, 252–3
  banks, 204–17
  definition, 205, 207
  determination, 205–9
  marginal economic capital, 213–17, 244–9
economic climate, 2, 4–8, 11–12, 97–8, 150, 223, 234–41, 248–9, 252–3
  booms, 149, 151
  crises, 2, 4–7, 11–12, 19–20, 150, 199–204, 238–41
  deterioration, 2, 239–41
  financial instability, 223, 234–41

prospects, 252–3
  systemic risk, 4–8, 11–12, 97–8, 150
  threats, 223, 234–41
economic credit, pricing, 207–9, 244
economic rate of return
  banking relationships, 212–17
  concepts, 208–9, 252–3
economic warfare, optimized capital management, 1
*Economist* magazine, 199
Electrolux, 146
emerging markets, 2, 43–5, 141, 151–2, 228–9
  Basel II regulations, 228–9
  CDSs, 43–5, 141
  debt crises, 2
Enron, 5, 19–20, 43, 126–8, 150–1, 159, 167–8, 184, 200, 240
equities, 8–14, 42, 49, 53–5, 78–9, 81, 90–4, 137–40, 147, 150, 166–7, 176–83, 204
  debt contrasts, 9
  IPOs, 9
  options, 4, 9, 30–1, 55–60, 138, 149, 165–7, 176–83
  share buybacks, 9
equity default swaps (EDSs), 42, 49, 53–5, 78–9, 147, 246
  *see also* credit default swaps
  advantages, 54–5
  applications, 54, 78–9, 147
  concepts, 49, 53–5, 78–9
  critique, 54–5, 78–9
  mechanism, 54
equity derivatives
  concepts, 8–11, 53–5, 81, 90–4, 137–40, 150, 166–7
  historical background, 8–9
  OTC markets, 10–11, 150
  statistics, 10–11, 150
equity risk, 9
'equity' tranche, 109–28, 134–40
escrow funds, 28–9
Euribor, 22, 47, 56, 68–70, 72–3, 112, 131
euro, 15, 152, 154–5
euro-medium term notes (EMTNs), 51
eurobonds, 146, 154–5, 201
*Euromoney* magazine, 169–71
Euronext, 8
European options, 56
European Union (EU), 13–14, 15, 44–5, 95, 99–101, 139–40, 144–5, 150–5, 162, 168–74, 201–4, 210–11, 225–33
  banking developments, 200–4, 210–11, 225–33
  Basel II requirements, 225–33
  Capital Adequacy Directive (CAD), 13–14, 225–6

UCIT Directives, 145, 167
US contrasts, 154–5, 200–4, 225
Eurostoxx, 94
exchange rate risk, 29–30, 114, 126, 135–40
exchange rates, 2, 29–30, 114, 126, 135–40, 150
  *see also* currency . . .
exotic options, 58
  *see also* options
exposure, 4, 8–14, 27–9, 75–9, 249
  debtors, 4, 8–14, 27–9, 75, 249
  hedging, 75

Federal Deposit Insurance Corporation (FDIC), 12, 228
Federal Reserve, 12, 120, 236, 239
Fiat, 202
finance theory, particle finance theory, 241–9, 252–3
Financial Accounting Standards Board (FASB), 244
financial disintermediation, 200–1
financial guarantors, 163–5, 174, 237
financial instability, 223, 234–41
financial instruments
  risk spectrum, 8–10
  types, 4, 9
financial intermediaries, 160–8, 172–4, 218–49, 251–3
  *see also* investment banks
financial markets *see* capital markets
financial practices, developments, 1
financial ratios, 26
financial revolution, credit derivatives, 241–9
financial risk, 8–11, 74–9
Financial Services Authority (FSA), 154–5
financial systems
  deregulation, 1, 200–2
  globalization, 6, 200
  instability, 223, 234–41
  liberalization, 6, 200–2
  threats, 223, 234–41
first arbitrage-driven synthetic CDOs, concepts, 124–8
first-generation credit derivatives, 78–9, 82, 150–74
  *see also* credit default swaps; credit spread . . . ; synthetic replication . . .
first-to-default credit swaps
  *see also* second-generation credit derivatives
  advantages, 88–90
  concepts, 82–90, 133, 136–40, 175–6
  critique, 83–4, 88–90
  examples, 87–9
  heterogeneity/homogeneity considerations, 86–90
  *i* to *j*-to-default products, 89–90

premiums, 83–90, 175–6
structure, 82
variants, 82–90
Fitch Ratings, 14–16, 60, 145–6, 150–3, 157–8, 161–5, 168–74, 234, 236–8
fixed payout total return swaps, concepts, 63
fixed payouts, CDSs, 42
fixed-rate credit-linked notes, 92–4
fixed-rate instruments, 21–4, 36–7, 57–60, 92–4
  asset swaps, 21–4, 57–60
  CDSs, 36–7
floating rate rating-sensitive notes, 30
floating-rate instruments
  asset swaps, 21–4, 57–60
  CDSs, 36–7
Ford Motors, 145–6, 246
Fortis Investments, 141, 145, 167
forward rate agreements (FRAs), 31–2, 56
forwards
  bonds, 56
  credit spread forwards, 55–60
France, 2, 89, 120, 133, 167, 173, 202, 216–17, 233–7, 240
France Telecom, 211, 216–17
FTSE, 94
fundamental analysis
  credit ratings, 15–20
  historical perspective, 19–20
funded instruments
  *see also* issuer risk
  CDS variants, 49
  concepts, 4, 8–11, 25–7, 49
funding risks, concepts, 2–3
funding strategies, corporates, 74, 77–9, 167–8, 201
futures, 9

gamma, 135–40, 183
Gaussian model, 182, 189–98
General Motors, 146–7
General Re Securities, 236
Genuity, 128
geographical-zone market structures, 154–5, 173–4
Germany, 167, 173
GFI, 169–74
Ginzberg, A., 245
Glacier Finance CDO, 115–16
globalization, 6, 200
Goldman Sachs, 52, 166–74, 220, 244
Goldman Sachs/Loan Pricing Corporation Leveraged Loan Index, 95
'The Greeks', 183
Greenspan, Alan, 236, 239
Gross, Bill, 236
guarantees, 4, 27, 64–5, 163–5, 174

hazard rates, reduced-form models, 184–90,
    195–9
hedge funds, 152, 160–8, 172–4, 201, 241
    *see also* institutional investors
hedges, 30–3, 66–70, 74–9, 94, 102–3, 114,
    125–8, 133–6, 146–7, 151–2, 160–8,
    172–83, 201, 238–41, 252–3
    Black-Scholes options pricing model, 176–93
    delta-hedging strategies, 94, 133–41, 177–83,
        188, 238
herd instincts, 248–9
high-yield debt, 2, 22–3, 95, 109–14, 141–2, 160,
    167, 215–17
highly leveraged transactions (HLTs), 88
homogenous reference baskets, first-to-default
    credit swaps, 86–90
homogenous/rational credit-risk pricing, particle
    finance theory, 243–9, 252–3
Hong Kong, 155
hostile takeovers, 2, 30, 202
    *see also* mergers . . .
HSBC, 202–3
Hull, J., 195
hybrid products, 9, 12–14, 53–5, 81, 90–4, 152,
    175–6
    *see also* second–generation credit derivatives
    advantages, 92–4
    capital-guaranteed/protected products, 90–4
    concepts, 81, 90–4, 152, 175–6
    critique, 92–4
    examples, 93–4
    multiple investment strategies, 90–4
    types, 90–4, 175–6
    yields, 92
hybrid risks, concepts, 137

*i* to *j*-to-default products, first-to-default credit
    swaps, 89–90
iBoxx Cash Index, 95
iBoxx indices, 96, 102, 139–40
Icap, 169–74
idiosyncratic component, credit risk, 4, 19, 26
iGamma, 135–40
implied correlations, 189, 193–8
in-the-money options, 31, 57, 58
incentive issues, credit risk transfers, 235–41
index options, 60
indices, credit indices, 81, 94–103, 139–40,
    156–60, 165–7, 190–8
indirect exposure, credit risk, 75–9
Industrial Bank of Japan, 115
industrialization processes, credit derivatives, 152
inflation, 90, 248
information and communication technologies,
    developments, 1, 248–9, 251–3
initial margins, 27, 28–9

initial public offerings (IPOs), declining
    trends, 9
innovations, 55, 101–3, 114, 139–41, 175, 201,
    223, 241–9, 251–3
    cash-flow CDOs, 114
    credit indices, 101–3, 139–40, 190–8
    EDSs, 55
    financial revolution, 241–9
    iTraxx indices, 101–3, 139–40, 191–2
    single-tranche synthetic CDOs, 140–1
inside information, 235–41
institutional investors
    *see also* capital markets
    Basel II regulations, 227–41
    CDOs, 144
    credit derivative applications, 66–70, 144,
        152–74, 227–41, 251–3
    types, 152
insurance policies, 12, 27
insurance/reinsurance companies, 152, 161,
    163–5, 233, 237, 241, 253
    *see also* institutional investors
integration trends, credit derivatives, 147, 152,
    245–9
intensity-based models *see* reduced-form models
inter-bank recovery swaps, concepts, 136
interest rate derivatives, 8–11, 21–4, 31–2, 51–3,
    81, 90–4, 149–50, 247
    historical background, 8–11
    OTC markets, 10–11, 149–50
    statistics, 10–11, 149–50
interest rate risk, 9, 21–4, 29–30, 112–14, 126–7,
    137, 188–9
interest rate swaps, concepts, 21–4, 31–2, 51–3,
    92–4, 149, 247
interest rate swaptions, 92–4
interest rates, 2, 8–11, 21–4, 29–30, 31–2, 51–3,
    81, 90–4, 112–14, 126–7, 137, 149–50,
    188–9, 247
internal rate of return (IRR), CDOs, 112
internal ratings based approach (IRB), Basel II
    regulations, 226–41
internal risk management systems, Basel II
    regulations, 225–41
International Accounting Standards (IASs), 244
International Financial Reporting Standards
    (IFRS), 205
International Financing Review, 101, 159
International Index Company (ICC), 96–8
International Swaps and Derivatives Association
    (ISDA), 27, 37–45, 82, 150, 240
    Definitions, 37–45, 82, 240
    historical background, 42–3
internationalization, 1, 6, 200
Internet bubble (2000–2001), 9
Invesco, 167

investment banks, 31, 81, 124, 128–9, 162–3,
     167–74, 201–2, 238–41, 251–3
     *see also* banks
     CDO market, 170–4
     concepts, 162–3, 167–74, 201–2, 238–41,
          251–3
     coverage functions, 173–4
     credit derivatives, 31, 81, 124, 128–9, 162–3,
          167–74, 201–2, 238–41, 251–3
     functions, 172–4, 201–2, 238–41, 251–3
     rankings, 168–9
     structuring functions, 173–4, 238
     trading functions, 172–4, 238
investment strategies, corporates, 74, 77–9,
     167–8
investment-grade category, credit ratings, 15–20,
     87–9, 141–7, 160, 232–3
investors, credit derivatives, 32, 36–79, 82–103,
     124–47, 152–74, 198, 199–249, 251–3
Ireland, 173
issuer risk
     *see also* funded instruments
     concepts, 3–4, 9, 25–7
     credit risk management, 25–7
issuers
     credit derivatives, 32, 36–79, 82–103, 161–8,
          182
     CreditGrade, 182
Italy, 89, 173
iTraxx indices, 96–103, 139–40, 191–2
     *see also* credit indices
IXIS Asset Management, 133, 141, 167,
     202

Japan, 115, 155, 169, 211
Jazz CDO I, 129–32
JECI index, 95–6
JP Morgan, 10–11, 28, 29, 53–4, 63, 95–6,
     116–19, 126, 129, 133, 141, 144, 150,
     168–74, 201–3, 218, 220, 238, 244
JP Morgan's BISTRO, 116–19
'jump-to-default' risk, 94, 136–40, 188–90
junior subordinated bonds, 18
     *see also* bonds
junk bonds, 2, 95, 109

KBC, 119
key accounts, corporates, 76
KMV, 20, 86
Korea, 151

legal documents
     CDSs, 37–55, 82, 150–2, 251
     ISDA Definitions, 37–45, 82
legal risks, concepts, 2–3, 42, 44–5, 251
Lehman Brothers, 126, 168–74

Lehman Brothers Credit Index, 95
Lehman Brothers European Cash Index, 95
Lehman Brothers High Yield Loan Index, 95
Lehman, Shearson, 242–3
letters of credit, 27
leveraged buyouts (LBOs), 30, 88
Lewis, Stuart, 243
Li, D.X., 191, 194
liberalization, financial systems, 6, 200–2
Libor, 22, 30, 61–5, 93–4, 112
life insurance, 201
Liffe, 8
liquidity issues
     challenges, 251–3
     credit markets, 2–3, 9, 23–4, 151–2, 172–4,
          200–4, 209–23, 248–9, 251–3
     risk, 2–3, 151–2, 172–4, 248–9
LMA *see* Loan Market Association
Loan Market Association (LMA), 210–11
Loan Pricing Corporation, 95, 244
Loan Syndication and Trading Association
     (LSTA), 211
loans, 4, 8–11, 25–7, 32–3, 38–55, 111–12, 159,
     165–7, 175, 200–23, 244–9
     *see also* funded instruments
     CDOs, 111–12
     credit risk management, 25–7
     loss leaders, 200–4, 217–18, 243–4, 252–3
     pricing, 25–7
     secondary markets, 26–7, 209–12, 219
     terms and conditions, 25–7
London
     *see also* United Kingdom
     market advantages, 154–5
     Stock Exchange, 210–11
loss concepts, economic capital, 206–9
loss leaders, bank loans, 200–4, 217–18, 243–4,
     252–3
LTCM, 240–1
Lucent, 75

McDonough ratio, 225
macro management, credit risk, 26–7, 70–1,
     102–3
management methods, credit risk, 1–2, 24–33, 66,
     120–6, 135–47, 200–23
Marconi, 128, 159
margin calls, 26, 27–9
marginal economic capital, 213–17, 244–9
marginal pricing, stand-alone pricing, 198
mark-to-market dependencies, credit-risk
     assessments, 10–11, 27–9, 92–4, 151, 164–5,
          236
market makers
     concepts, 103, 172–4, 210, 238
     credit indices, 103

market risk
   *see also* exchange rate . . . ; interest rate . . .
   concepts, 2–3, 7–8, 14, 24–5, 29–30, 32–3,
      184, 225–41, 246–8
   profitability profile, 7–8
   VaR, 24–6
market risk management, 29–30
market shares, main players, 161–8, 202–3, 207
markets
   banks, 66, 70–3, 79, 160–74, 199–249
   bilateral markets, 151
   booms, 149, 151
   capital markets, 8–11, 19–24, 66–70, 79, 160,
      174, 199–249, 251–3
   complete markets, 178–83
   credit derivatives, 1, 8–11, 24–5, 29–33, 35, 39,
      95, 114–15, 147, 149–74, 234–49, 251–3
   credit risk transfers, 32–3, 198, 218, 223–41,
      242–9, 252–3
   critique, 223, 234–41
   development, 151–74, 199–249, 251–3
   financial instability, 223, 234–41
   geographical-zone structures, 154–5, 173–4
   historical background, 1, 8–9, 24–5, 29–33, 39,
      95, 150–74
   industrialization processes, 152
   inside information, 235–41
   institutional investors, 66–70, 144, 152–74
   insurance/reinsurance companies, 152, 161,
      163–5, 233, 237, 241, 253
   integration trends, 147, 152, 245–9
   investment banks, 31, 81, 124, 128–9, 162–3,
      167–74, 201–2, 238–41, 251–3
   London, 154–5
   major players, 66–79, 144, 152, 160–74,
      234–41, 251–3
   major structural changes, 152
   organized markets, 1, 8–10, 27–9, 32
   OTC, 1, 8–11, 27–31, 149–50
   overview, 150–60
   particle finance theory, 242–9, 252–3
   product-type structures, 155–6
   secondary markets, 26–7, 67–8, 209–12,
      219
   statistics, 9–11, 149–74, 199–249
   structural issues, 152, 154–60
   syndication, 25–7, 209–23
   threats to growth, 153–4
   transparency concerns, 235–41
   trends, 30, 35, 95, 114–15, 147, 149–74,
      199–249
Markowitz, H.M., 190
maturity, credit derivatives, 32, 36–79, 83–103,
    134–47, 156–60, 181, 186–9
Mazataud, Paul, 15
mean, multivariate models, 190–1

medium-term notes, 201
Mellon Bank, 31
Mercer, Oliver Wyman and Company, 2, 165–6,
    203–4, 220–1, 224, 227–8
merchant banks, 29, 151, 154, 168–9, 201–4,
    218–19
mergers and acquisitions, 2, 9, 15, 30, 37–8, 174,
    201–3
Merrill Lynch, 87–9, 95, 168–74
Merton, R., 176, 178–86
'mezzanine' debt, 109–14, 125–8, 133–40, 147,
    160, 164–5, 193–4
micro management, credit risk, 25–7, 71–3
Mirant, 159
modelling
   concepts, 175–98, 244–9, 251–3
   copula model, 189–98
   Cox-Ingersoll-Ross model, 188–9
   model risks, 198
   Monte Carlo simulation, 195, 208
   multi-asset structural pricing models, 195,
      197–8
   multi-name credit derivatives, 189–98
   pricing, 175–98, 244–9, 251–3
   reduced-form models, 183–90, 195–9
   risk, 1, 175–98, 244–9
   structural models, 176–84, 195–9
modified modified restructuring (Mod Mod R),
    concepts, 44–5
modified restructuring (Mod R), concepts, 44–5
monoline insurance companies, 164
Monte Carlo simulation, 195, 208
Moody's Investors Service, 3–6, 13–20, 26, 85,
    94–5, 113, 116–17, 131–3, 159
moral hazard, 233
Morgan Guaranty Trust (MGT), 116–18
Morgan Stanley, 95–6, 126–7, 144, 168–74,
    201–3, 220
mortgage-backed securities (MBS), 52, 247
mortgages, 52, 114–15, 246–7
multi-asset structural pricing models, 195, 197–8
multi-name credit derivatives, 103–47, 189–98
   *see also* collateralized . . .
   pricing models, 189–98
multiline insurance companies, 164
multinational companies, reference entities,
    36–55
multiple investment strategies, hybrid products,
    90–4
mutual funds, 201
   *see also* unit trusts

Nationally Recognized Statistical Ratings
    Organizations (NRSRO), 15
nature, credit derivatives, 31–3
NatWest, 114–15

negative gamma, 135–40
net banking income (NBI), 208–9
Netherlands, 132, 145
netting and collateral agreements, OTC markets, 27–9, 240
new class of products, credit derivatives, 32, 236–49, 251–3
nGamma, 136–40
Nikkei-linked bonds, 31
Nokia, 67, 75, 95, 152
Nomura, 41, 169
Norway, banking crises, 2
Notice of Publicly Available Information, CDSs, 40

obligations category, CDSs, 38–55
Odberg, Eric, 166–7
OECD, 23–4, 72–3, 121
off-balance-sheet activities
  banks, 12–14, 31
  CDSs/cash comparisons, 47
Office of the Comptroller of the Currency (OCC), 12, 228
Oliver Wyman and Company, 2, 165–6, 203–4, 220–1, 224, 227–8
on-demand CDOs
  see also single-tranche synthetic CDOs
  concepts, 133–47, 172–4
  latest developments, 140–3
  overview, 143–7
  risk management, 135–40
  users, 144–7, 172–4
'one-stop shopping' concepts, banks, 202–3
operating risks, concepts, 2–3, 225–41
optimized capital management, 1, 125–8, 220, 246–7, 252–3
options, 4, 9, 30–1, 55–60, 138, 149, 165–7, 176–83
  barrier options, 60, 177, 182
  Black-Scholes options pricing model, 176–93
  call options, 57–60, 177–83
  CDSs, 58–60, 165–7
  credit spread options, 55–60, 167
  default risk, 30, 243
  default-and-out options, 60, 243
  payer options, 58–60
  put options, 30, 54–5, 57–60, 177–83, 246
  receiver options, 58–60
  types, 56–8, 165–7, 176–7
organizational issues, banks, 199, 217, 220–3
organized markets, 1, 8–10, 27–9, 32
  see also markets
origination arm, credit markets, 219–20
out-of-the-money options, 54–5, 246
outstanding debt, default statistics, 2, 4–8, 16–17

over-the-counter markets (OTC), 1, 8–11, 27–9, 31, 149–50, 175–98, 251–3
  concepts, 9–11, 30, 31–3, 149–50, 175–6, 251–3
  counterparty risk, 9–11, 27–9, 31
  credit derivatives, 9–11, 31–3, 149–50, 251–3
  credit ratings, 29
  credit-risk assessments, 9–11, 27–9, 152–74, 175–98
  exponential growth, 30, 149–50
  netting and collateral agreements, 27–9, 240
  statistics, 10–11, 149–74
Overture CDO, 133, 141

'P&L in the event of default', 136–40
Pacific Gas & Electric, 5, 43, 159
Panton Alternative Partners, 166
Parmalat, 97–8, 153–4, 159, 184
particle finance theory, concepts, 241–9, 252–3
path dependency, credit events, 143
payer options, concepts, 58–60
pension funds, 152, 174
  see also institutional investors
Peregrine Securities, 7
physical settlements, CDSs, 40–2, 61, 82–90
pillars, Basel II regulations, 225–41
PIMCO, 162–3, 167, 236
Poisson processes, 181
portfolios
  banks, 198, 205–41, 249
  diversification, 2, 26, 66–70, 102–3, 106–28, 161–5, 190, 198, 205–23, 233, 240–1
Portugal, 173
position limits, 27–9
premiums, 36–79, 83–103, 118–47, 180–98, 245–9
  see also pricing
  CDSs, 36–55, 83–90, 118, 127–8, 136, 140–7, 180–98
  CMDSs, 52
  credit indices, 96–103
  first-to-default credit swaps, 83–90, 175–6
  risk, 20–4, 32
price discovery procedure, CDSs, 42
pricing
  see also premiums
  arbitrage-free pricing models, 175–6
  banks, 202–3
  Black-Scholes options pricing model, 176–93
  concepts, 8, 175–98, 243–9, 251–3
  copula model, 189–98
  credit derivatives, 8, 175–98, 243–9
  economic credit, 207–9, 244
  homogenous/rational credit–risk pricing, 243–9, 252–3
  loans, 25–7

pricing (*Continued*)
  marginal/stand–alone pricing, 198
  Merton's structural model of default risk,
    178–86
  models, 175–98, 244–9, 251–3
  multi-asset structural pricing models, 195,
    197–8
  multi-name credit derivatives, 189–98
  reduced-form models, 183–90, 195–9
  relative-value approach, 176
  replication approaches, 177–83
  risk-neutral pricing principle, 176–89
  structural models, 176–84, 195–9
private individuals, credit derivatives,
    248–9
private investors, bond issues, 9, 23
private issuers, 9
product-type market structures, 155–6
profitability profiles, risk, 7–8, 215–17
put options, 30, 54–5, 57–60, 177–83, 246
  *see also* options

quantitative models, credit risk, 175–6,
    208
quasi-sovereign debt, 9

Rabobank, 119, 145
Railtrack, 41, 43, 128, 159
ramp-up period, CDOs, 112–13
random default barriers, default thresholds, 182,
    195
rating agencies
  *see also* credit ratings
  CDOs, 15, 107–14, 116–24
  concepts, 11–20, 25–6, 48–9, 84–90, 94–103,
    107–8, 141–7, 157–60, 207–9, 213–17,
    225–41
  credit-risk assessments, 11–20, 25–6, 48–9,
    84–90, 94–103, 107–8, 116–28, 131–3,
    141–7, 157–60, 207–9, 213–17, 225–41
  critique, 19–20, 235–41
  fundamental analysis, 15–20
  grades, 15–20, 25–7, 48–9, 87–90, 94–103,
    107–8, 116–28, 131–3, 141–7, 157–60,
    207–9, 213–17, 225–41
  historical background, 14–15
  major players, 14–15
  OTC derivatives markets, 29
  roles, 14–15, 26
  statistics, 15, 19–20
  supervision needs, 241
  symbol systems, 15–20
  transition matrices, 16–19, 175
re-couponing practices, 28–9
real risks, credit derivatives, 240–1, 249
receiver options, concepts, 58–60

recovery rates
  arbitrage concepts, 70
  characteristics, 16
  concepts, 4, 16–18, 19–24, 70, 83–102,
    135–47, 166–7, 185–9
  historical volatility, 16, 18
  seniority of debt, 16–18
reduced-form models
  credit risk, 183–90, 195–9
  dependent defaults, 195–6
reference entities, 36–79, 82–90, 118–47,
    157–60, 213–17, 230–41
  CDSs, 36–55, 82–90, 118–47
  market structures, 157–60
reference obligations, CDSs, 38–55, 82–90
regulatory arbitrage, 14, 119–24, 152, 172–4,
    223–4, 229–32, 241
regulatory ROE, 215–17, 226–8
regulatory standards, 1, 11–14, 23–4, 30, 42, 44,
    72–3, 114–24, 150–4, 200, 204–6, 215–17,
    223–41, 249, 251–3
  active-regulation needs, 240–1
  balance sheet-driven CDOs, 119–24, 152,
    230–3
  Basel I regulations, 11–14, 23–4, 30, 118–24,
    200, 215–17, 223–41, 249
  Basel II regulations, 14, 120–4, 154, 200,
    223–41, 251
  CAD, 13–14, 225–6
  credit derivatives, 14, 30, 72–3, 114–24, 150–4,
    200, 215–17, 223–41, 249, 251–3
  credit spreads, 23–4
  credit-risk assessments, 11–14, 23–4, 30, 72–3,
    114–24, 152, 200, 215–17, 223–41
  deregulation, 1, 200–2
  FSA, 154–5
  synthetic CLOs, 120–4
reinsurance companies, 152, 161, 163–5, 233,
    253
reinvestment risks, CDOs, 112–13, 126–7
relationship banking, 199–200, 202–3, 212–17,
    219–20, 243–4
relative value arbitrage, concepts, 68, 102–3,
    166–7, 175–6
replication approaches, pricing, 177–83
Repon 15 CDOs, 127–8
Repon 17 CDOs, 141
reporting systems, banks, 220–2
repurchase agreements (repos), 46–7
residential mortgage-backed securities (RMBS),
    106
restructuring events
  CDSs, 39–40, 42–6
  concepts, 39–40, 42–6, 172–4, 233
  modified versions, 43–5
retail clientele, 144–5, 168, 174, 251

return on equity (ROE), 88, 123–4, 215–17,
    226–8, 243–4
returns, 9–14, 19–24, 88, 112, 123–4, 138–9,
    167–8, 204–23, 226–8, 243–9, 252–3
    *see also* yields
    banking relationships, 212–17
    banks, 13–14, 123–4, 204–23, 226–32, 240–1,
        244–9
    credit spreads, 11, 19–24
    customers, 212–17, 243–4
    economic rate of return, 208–9, 212–17, 252–3
    IRR, 112
    RAROC, 13–14, 167–8, 204, 207–9, 213–17,
        222, 244–5
    risk, 13–14, 20–4, 162–3, 167–8, 204, 207–9,
        213–17, 222, 244–9
Reuters, 87–9
reverse TROR swaps, concepts, 62
Rho, 137–8
risk, 1–33, 35–79, 112–14, 120–4, 135–47,
    150–98, 199–249, 251–3
    *see also* credit risk; market risk
    aversion, 198
    banks, 1–3, 10–14, 120–4, 150–74, 199–249
    Basel II regulations, 14, 120–4, 154, 200,
        223–41
    concepts, 1–33, 112–14, 135–47, 198, 204,
        207–8, 223–41, 246–9, 251–3
    credit spreads, 11, 19–24, 135–47, 181, 184–7
    'jump-to-default' risk, 94, 136–40, 188–90
    Merton's structural model of default risk,
        178–86
    modelling, 1, 175–98, 244–9
    premiums, 20–4, 32
    profitability profiles, 7–8, 215–17
    quantitative models, 175–6, 208
    real risks of credit derivatives, 240–1, 249
    regulatory standards, 11–14, 23–4, 30, 72–3,
        114–24, 152, 200, 215–17, 223–41, 249
    returns, 13–14, 20–4, 162–3, 167–8, 204,
        207–9, 213–17, 222, 244–9
    spectrum, 9
    structural models, 176–84, 195–9
    transfers, 32–3, 198, 218, 223–41, 242–9,
        252–3
    types, 2, 3–9, 29–30, 112–14, 135–47, 224–6,
        246–8
Risk Awards, 101
'risk intermediaries', banks, 218–41
*Risk* magazine, 169–71
risk management, 1–2, 24–33, 66, 120–6, 135–47,
    200–23, 225–49, 252–3
    *see also* credit risk . . . ; market risk . . .
    Basel II regulations, 225–41, 251
    correlations, 84–90, 135–47, 154, 189–98
    economic approach, 204–23, 252–3

on-demand CDOs, 135–40
    particle finance theory, 242–9, 252–3
risk-adjusted return on capital (RAROC), 13–14,
    167–8, 204, 207–9, 213–17, 222, 244–5
risk-free rates, 20–4
risk-neutral pricing principle, 176–89
risk-weighted assets (RWAs), concepts, 12–14,
    120–4, 225–41
risky bonds, equation, 244–5
Robeco, 129, 132–3
ROE *see* return on equity
ROSE Funding I, 115
Royal Bank of Scotland, 114
runs on banks, 12
Russian debt, 42–3

S&P 500, 94
Sakura Bank, 115
Salomon Brothers, 201
Sanford, Charles S., 242, 252
Sanwa Bank, 115
savings and loans banks, US, 2, 239–40
SBC, 87–9
scandals, 2, 5, 19–20, 43, 126–8, 131, 150–1,
    153–4, 159, 167–8, 184, 200, 240
Scandinavia, 173
SCH, 217
Scholes, M., 176–83
Schroder, 201
Scor, 128, 144, 164–5
second-generation credit derivatives, 49, 81–103,
    105–47, 152–74, 189
    *see also* basket credit default swaps;
        collateralized debt obligations; credit
        indices; hybrid products
    concepts, 49, 81–103, 152–74, 189
    types, 81, 155–60, 189
secondary markets
    cash positions, 67–8
    loans, 26–7, 209–12, 219
    markets, 26–7, 67–8, 209–12, 219
secured bonds, 18
    *see also* bonds
Securities and Exchange Commission (SEC), 15
securitizations
    *see also* collateralized debt obligations;
        structured products
    advantages, 108
    bank loans, 114–24, 209, 212, 238–9
    concepts, 47, 79, 103–47, 209–10, 212, 223–41
    credit derivatives, 115–24
    critique, 107–8, 223–41
    mechanism, 107–8, 114–24
    rating agencies, 15, 116–24
    trends, 47, 114–15, 141–2, 209–10
'self-managed' CDOs, concepts, 140–1

senior debt, 4, 9, 16–18, 25–7, 109–28,
134–47
seniority of debt, 4, 9, 16–18, 25–7, 109–28,
134–47
settlement methods
CDSs, 36, 40–55, 61, 82–90
concepts, 40–55, 61, 82–90
types, 40–2, 61, 82
SG, 96, 168–74
share buybacks, 9
shareholder value, 200–2
shares see equities
Shiller, Robert, 248
short positions, 46, 48, 102–3, 146
Siemens Financial Services (SFS), 167–8
Singapore, 155
single-tranche synthetic CDOs
see also on–demand CDOs
concepts, 133–47
overview, 143–7
users, 144–7
skews, correlation, 138–9
smiles, correlation, 138–40
Smith Barney, 201
Solent Capital, 141
Solutia, 128, 159
solvency threshold, economic capital, 206–7
sovereign debt, 9, 20–4, 151–4, 158–60
sovereign eurobonds, 9
sovereign risk, 75–9, 93–4, 151–4
Spain, 145, 173, 217, 240
special purpose vehicles (SPVs), 64–5, 107–32
specific risk, concepts, 4, 7–8
speculative-grade category, credit ratings, 15–20,
162–3
sponsors, project finance transactions, 75–6
spread-adjusted notes, 30
spread-protected debt securities, 30
stand-alone pricing, marginal pricing, 198
Standard & Poor's (S&P), 5–6, 13, 14–17, 94–5,
128, 159, 207, 226–7, 237–40, 246
state-dependent volatility, 197
Steady State, 7
step-up coupons, 25–6
step-up range accrual CLNs, 83–4
stochastic volatility, 197
straddles, 59–60
strategic issues, banks, 199, 217–23
structural models, pricing, 176–84, 195–9
structured investment vehicles (SIVs), 112
structured products, 2, 15, 23–4, 31, 55, 103–47,
149–74, 251–3
see also securitizations
types, 15, 103–47, 149–50
structuring functions, investment banks, 173–4,
238

Student copulas, 191–5
sub-participation uses, banks, 26–7
subordinated debt, 9, 12–14, 16–18, 121–4,
126–8, 134–5
'successor' considerations, CDSs, 38
Suez, 54–5, 87–9
Sumitomo Bank, 115
supervisory authorities' studies
see also regulatory standards
credit derivatives, 234–41, 251
swaps, 4, 9, 21–4, 28–9, 31–3, 35–55, 61–6,
81–103, 136, 151–2, 251–3
see also credit default swaps; individual
products
concepts, 4, 9, 21–4, 31–3, 81, 251–3
inter-bank recovery swaps, 136
re-couponing practices, 28–9
types, 21–4, 31–2, 35–55, 61–6, 81, 136
swaptions, concepts, 58–60, 92–4
Sweden, banking crises, 2
Swiss Bank Corporation, 115–16
Swiss Re, 164–5
Switzerland, 173
symbol systems, rating agencies, 15–20
syndication, concepts, 25–7, 209–23
synthetic CLOs
concepts, 115–24
JP Morgan's BISTRO, 116–19
key elements, 118–19
regulatory analysis, 120–4
synthetic replication products
see also total (rate of) return swaps
concepts, 35, 49–51, 61–6, 115–24
definition, 35, 61
examples, 63–5
mechanism, 61
systemic risk
banks, 11–12, 150
concepts, 4–8, 11–12, 97–8, 150
'credit crunch', 6, 150

T-bonds, 64–5, 116–19
tailor-made products, 47, 66–70, 172–4, 238,
252–3
tailored investment strategies, credit derivative
applications, 47, 66–70, 252–3
takeovers see mergers and acquisitions
Tanemura, Ron, 33
Teleglobe, 128
term structure trades, credit indices, 102–3
term structures, credit risk, 13–14, 166–7
terms and conditions, loans, 25–7
tier I/II capital, Basel I regulations, 12–14,
120–4
time scales, economic capital, 206–7
Tokyo-Mitsubishi, 115

total (rate of) return swaps
  *see also* synthetic replication products
  cash flow structure, 61–5, 67
  concepts, 31, 61–6, 156–60
  mechanism, 61
  variants, 62–3
TRAC-X indices, 96–7, 139–40
TRACERS index, 95–6
trade receivables
  balance sheet CLOs, 114
  CDSs, 39
trading books, regulatory standards, 13–14
trading functions, investment banks,
    172–4, 238
transaction RAROC, 213–17
transaction structure, synthetic securitization,
    121–4
transition matrices, rating agencies,
    16–19, 175
transparency concerns, markets, 235–41
trigger events, 25–6, 28–9, 35–55, 60, 82–90,
    96–103, 120–4, 159, 175–98, 233
TROR swaps *see* total (rate of) return swaps
Turkey, 93–4
types, credit derivatives, 35–79

UBS, 29, 115–16, 154–5, 168–74, 201–2
UCITs, 145, 167, 201
unbundled stock units (USUs), 242–3
unbundling
  credit risk, 32–3, 198, 218, 223–41, 242–9,
    252–3
  particle finance theory, 242–9, 252–3
underlying assets, credit derivatives, 32–3, 35–79,
    157–60, 175–98, 249
underwriting, 221
unfunded instruments
  *see also* counterparty risk; credit default swaps
  concepts, 4, 9–11, 27–33
unit trusts, 201
  *see also* mutual funds
United Kingdom (UK), 2, 12, 114, 153–5, 173,
    201–2, 210–11, 234–5, 240
  *see also* London
  Bank of England, 12, 234–5
  banking crises, 2
  market advantages, 154–5
United States (US), 2, 4–8, 12, 14–15, 31, 44–5,
    109, 120, 139, 150–4, 162, 168–74, 201–4,
    210–11, 225, 228, 239–40, 246–7

banking crises, 239–41
banking developments, 200–4, 210–11, 225,
    228
bankruptcies, 4–8
Basel II regulations, 225, 228
CMOs, 246–7
European contrasts, 154–5, 200–4, 225
savings and loans banks, 2, 239–40
universal banks, 168–74, 219–20
  *see also* banks
unsecured bonds, 18
  *see also* bonds

Value at Risk (VaR), 1, 24–5, 175, 206
'value of the firm', 184
variance, multivariate models, 190–1
vega, 183
vendor financing, hedging, 75–9
venture capital, 229
Vodafone, 87–9, 211
volatility
  Black-Scholes options pricing model, 176–83
  concepts, 176–83, 188–9, 197
'vulture funds', 210–11

Wal-Mart, 63–5
Wall Street, 31, 82, 150, 154, 162
weather derivatives, 247, 253
Wendt, Gary, 43
White, A., 195
whole business securitization (WBS), 106–7
wholesale banks, 201–2
world-ranking banks, 161–3
WorldCom, 5, 43, 126, 128, 131, 159, 200
Wriston, Walter, 1

Xerox, 159, 244

yields
  *see also* returns
  credit derivatives, 31, 66–70, 82–3, 92
  enhancement strategies, 68–70
  high-yield debt, 2, 22–3, 95, 109–14, 141–2,
    160, 167, 215–17
  hybrid products, 92

Z-scores, 19
Zurich Financial Services, 232

*Index compiled by Terry Halliday*